Judaism DECODED

THE ORIGINS AND EVOLUTION OF JEWISH TRADITION

JLI
JEWISH LEARNING INSTITUTE

Course Editor
Rabbi Mordechai Dinerman

Curriculum Development
Rabbi Eli Raksin
Rabbi Naftali Silberberg
Mrs. Chava Shapiro

Judaism Decoded
is a revised and updated version of the JLI course
From Sinai to Cyberspace
authored by
Rabbi Berel Bell
edited and produced by
Chana Silberstein, PhD

Printed in the United States of America

The Rohr Jewish Learning Institute
822 Eastern Parkway, Brooklyn, NY 11213

(888) YOUR-JLI/718-221-6900
www.myJLI.com

THE ROHR JEWISH LEARNING INSTITUTE
gratefully acknowledges
the pioneering and ongoing support of

George and Pamela Rohr

Since its inception,
the Rohr JLI has been
a beneficiary of the vision, generosity,
care, and concern
of the Rohr family.

In the merit of
the tens of thousands of hours of Torah study
by JLI students worldwide,
may they be blessed with health,
Yiddishe nachas *from all their loved ones,*
and extraordinary success
in all their endeavors.

The Rohr Jewish Learning Institute acknowledges the generous support of the following individuals and foundations:

PRINCIPAL BENEFACTOR

GEORGE ROHR
New York, NY

ADVISORY BOARD OF GOVERNORS

YAAKOV AND KAREN COHEN
Potomac, MD

YITZCHOK AND JULIE GNIWISCH
Montreal, QC

BARBARA HINES
Aspen, CO

DANIEL B. MARKSON
S. Antonio, TX

DANIEL AND ROSIE MATTIO
Seattle, WA

DAVID MINTZ
Tenafly, NJ

DR. STEPHEN F. SERBIN
Columbia, SC

LEONARD A. WIEN, JR.
Miami Beach, FL

PARTNERING FOUNDATIONS

WILLIAM DAVIDSON FOUNDATION

MEROMIM FOUNDATION

KOHELET FOUNDATION

CRAIN-MALING FOUNDATION

WORLD ZIONIST ORGANIZATION

AVI CHAI FOUNDATION

OLAMI—WOLFSON FOUNDATION

RUDERMAN FAMILY FOUNDATION

ESTATE OF ELLIOT JAMES BELKIN

KOSINS FAMILY FOUNDATION

PILLARS OF JEWISH LITERACY

KEVIN BERMEISTER
Sydney, Australia

PABLO AND SARA BRIMAN
Mexico City, Mexico

ZALMAN AND MIMI FELLIG
Miami Beach, FL

YOSEF GOROWITZ
Redondo Beach, CA

DR. VERA KOCH GROSZMANN
S. Paulo, Brazil

HERSCHEL LAZAROFF
Monsey, NY

JENNY LJUNGBERG
New York, NY

DAVID MAGERMAN
Gladwyne, PA

DR. MICHAEL MALING
Deerfield, IL

YITZCHAK MIRILASHVILI
Herzliya, Israel

BEN NASH
New Jersey

YAIR SHAMIR
Savyon, Israel

LARRY SIFEN
Virginia Beach, VA

SPONSORS

MARK AND REBECCA BOLINSKY
Long Beach, NY

DANIEL AND ETA COTLAR
Houston, TX

GORDON DIAMOND
Vancouver, BC

AMIR AND DAFNA ELYASHAR
Ramat Aviv, Israel

SHMUEL AND SHARONE GOODMAN
Chicago, IL

JOE AND SHIRA LIPSEY
Aspen, CO

ELLEN MARKS
S. Diego, CA

RACHELLE NEDOW
El Paso, TX

PETER AND HAZEL PFLAUM
Newport Beach, CA

FRANK (A"H) AND FRUMETH POLASKY
Saginaw, MI

MOSHE AND YAFFA POPACK
Fisher Island, FL

HERCHEL AND JULIE PORTMAN
Denver, CO

EYAL AND AVIVA POSTELNIK
Marietta, GA

DR. ZE'EV RAV-NOY
Los Angeles, CA

CLIVE AND ZOE ROCK
Irvine, CA

ZVI RYZMAN
Los Angeles, CA

ALAN ZEKELMAN
Bloomfield Hills, MI

MYRNA ZISMAN
Cedarhurst, NY

DEDICATED TO

Mr. David Mintz

ר' דוד יצחק שי' בן שרה דבורה

FOUNDING MEMBER OF JLI'S EXECUTIVE ADVISORY BOARD
With deep appreciation for his leadership and partnership
in bringing Torah study to all corners of the world.

Inspired by an enduring
and special relationship with the Lubavitcher Rebbe,
whose many blessings and sage advice continue
to guide his personal and communal activities,
he serves as a shining example
to his family, community, and Klal Yisrael.

May he and his family enjoy
health, happiness, nachas, success, and abundance
in all their endeavors, as they go from strength to strength
in their service of G-d and the Jewish people.

Rabbi Moshe Kotlarsky, Chairman
Rabbi Efraim Mintz, Executive Director
THE ROHR JEWISH LEARNING INSTITUTE

ENDORSEMENTS

Anyone with an interest in legal reasoning should engage with the Talmud, which records some of the oldest and most subtle interpretations of fundamental law. *Judaism Decoded* offers a fine introduction to Talmudic methods.

Jeremy Rabkin, PhD
Professor of Law, George Mason University
Member, Board of Directors, United States Institute of Peace
Arlington, VA

This course provides participants with a fascinating introduction to the basic principles that underlie the traditional Jewish concept of oral law, the complement to the written Torah that spells out Jewish law and tradition and allows Judaism to deal with the new circumstances it confronts in each generation. Participants will come to understand the interpretive mechanisms which allow the Torah to provide eternal guidance of the Jewish people.

Lawrence H. Schiffman, PhD
Judge Abraham Lieberman Professor of Hebrew and Judaic Studies
Director of the Global Institute for Advanced Research in Jewish Studies
New York University
New York, NY

JLI's course *Judaism Decoded* is an extraordinarily sophisticated examination of Talmudic methodology. It is perfectly organized, and will enrich both those with little familiarity with the Talmud, as well as the many who study it daily but do not know how it came to be. The course is not afraid of tackling the toughest questions about the nature and legitimacy of rabbinic law, combining high academic rigor with fundamental rooting in Jewish tradition.
This is adult education at the highest level—an essential program of study for anyone interested in understanding the Jewish law as a living system. I have enjoyed past JLI courses, but this one I just can't wait to take.

Eugene Kontorovich, PhD
Professor of Law, Northwestern University School of Law
Chicago, IL

It's only non-Jewish religions and cultures that called Jews the "People of the Book." For Jews the "Bible" is part of a much larger whole, comprising both the Oral and Written Torahs. The Talmud, the monument of the Oral Torah, is the treasure house of the Jewish people, comprising thousands of years of Jewish wisdom, the secrets to understanding the Bible, and every facet of life. This superb course will enable each participant to enter into its fascinating world, sharpen his or her mind, understand the foundations of Jewish law, and its application to critical contemporary issues.

Susan Handelman, PhD
Director of Graduate Studies, Department of English, Bar Ilan University
Tel Aviv, Israel

Judaism Decoded by the Rohr Jewish Learning Institute provides an important foundation for understanding and clarifying both the history of the Jewish intellectual tradition and the customs of the Jewish heritage. In my judgment, this introductory course effectively leads students through the critical questions of our faith and scaffolds textual sources to develop complex insights into depth of the Jewish oral tradition. I am sure JLI's *Judaism Decoded* will make a meaningful contribution to their wealth of courses.

Alan H. Kadish, MD
President and Chief Executive Officer,
Touro College and University
New York, NY

The Rohr Jewish Learning Institute has been in the forefront of the Jewish world in developing innovative teaching materials that help Jews discover the richness, depth and beauty of the Torah. All of their work is of the highest quality. This is no "Talmud for Dummies." JLI does not shy away from exploring the complexities and ambiguities of our classical texts and the student who is willing to work and grapple with the fascinating questions being addressed will emerge joyously amazed at how eternally relevant G-d's Torah is. To JLI, I offer my thanks; to the students, I offer my congratulations. You are embarking on the greatest of all journeys—the quest for truth through the study of Torah.

Rabbi Yitzchak A. Breitowitz
Rabbi, Kehillat Ohr Somayach
Jerusalem, Israel
Formerly, Associate Professor,
University of Maryland School of Law

TABLE OF CONTENTS

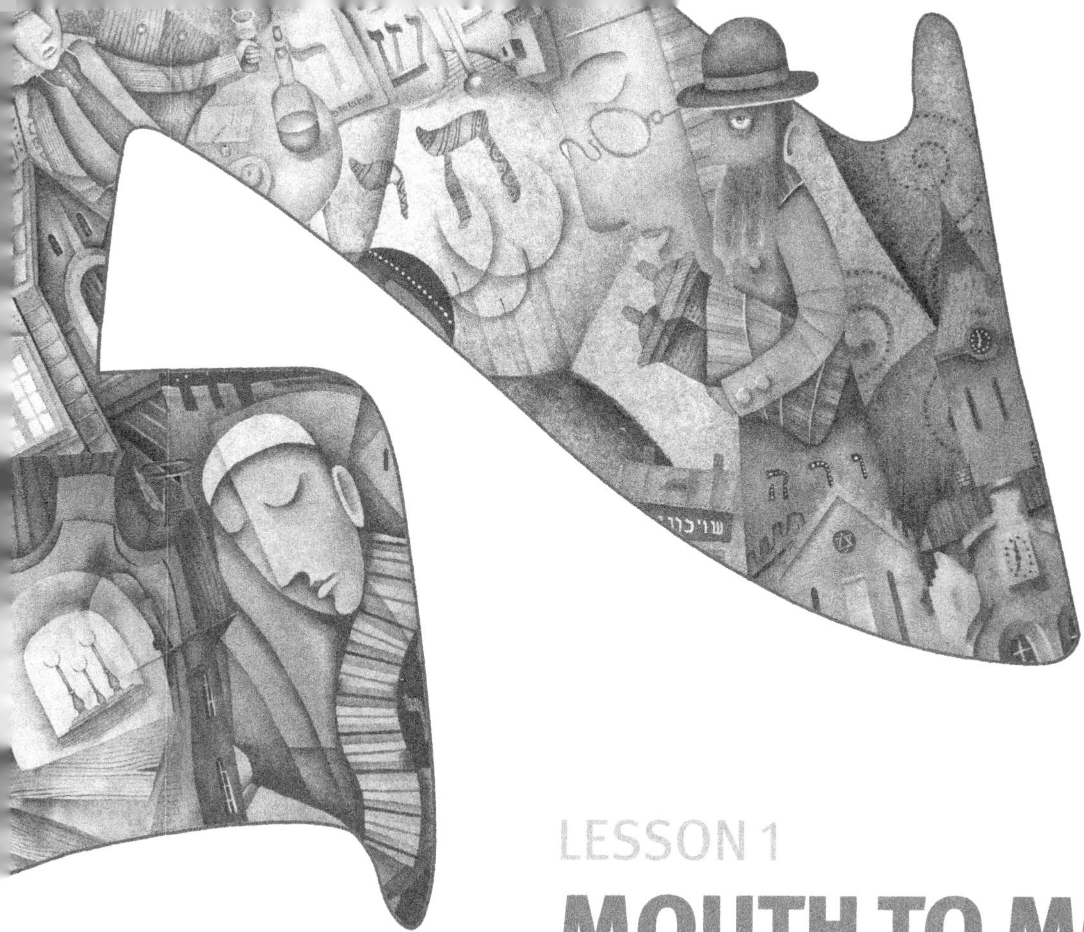

LESSON 1

MOUTH TO MOUTH

Jewish practice and observance, indeed the entire system of Jewish law (Halachah), is founded on more than Scripture alone. The other foundation is the "Oral Torah."

What is the Oral Torah? Who is its author? And why isn't the Bible sufficient?

After we answer these questions, we will have a few more: Why wasn't the Oral Torah written? And is it possible that it was accurately transmitted through the millennia?

Course Introduction

Text 1

Leviticus 16:29

וְהָיְתָה לָכֶם לְחֻקַּת עוֹלָם, בַּחֹדֶשׁ הַשְּׁבִיעִי בֶּעָשׂוֹר לַחֹדֶשׁ תְּעַנּוּ אֶת נַפְשֹׁתֵיכֶם, וְכָל מְלָאכָה לֹא תַעֲשׂוּ, הָאֶזְרָח וְהַגֵּר הַגָּר בְּתוֹכְכֶם.

It shall be as an eternal statute for you: in the seventh month, on the tenth of the month, you shall afflict yourselves, and you shall not do any work, neither the native nor the proselyte who dwells among you.

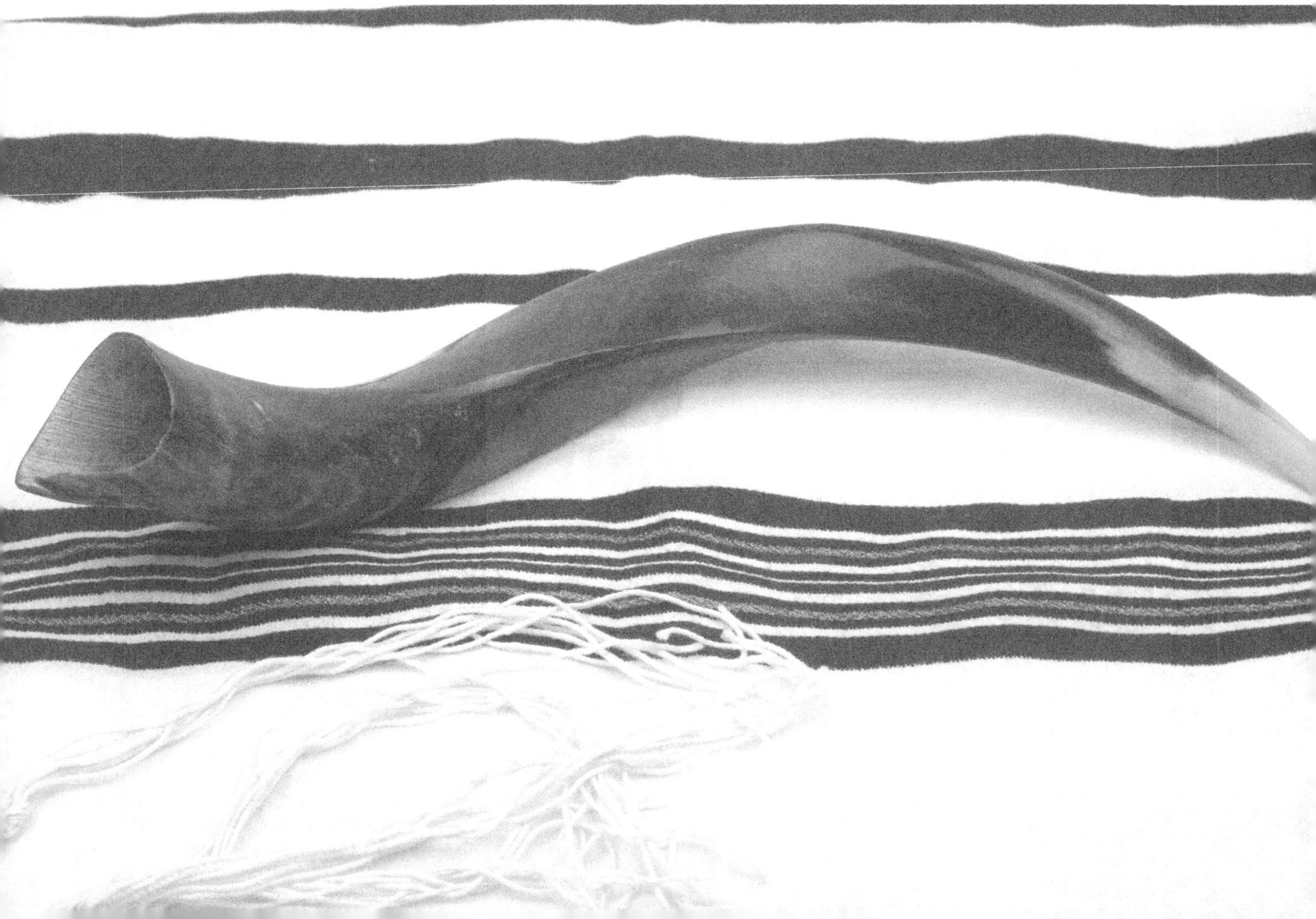

FIGURE 1.1

Words in the Bible from the Root Word A-N-H

Verse	Context
He said to Abram, “You shall surely know that your seed will be strangers in a land that is not theirs, and they will enslave them and **oppress [וְעִנּוּ]** them for four hundred years.” — Genesis 15:13	**God speaks to Abraham and informs him about the future Egyptian exile.**
If you **afflict [תְּעַנֶּה]** my daughters, or if you take wives besides my daughters, although no one is with us, see, God is witness between you and me. — Genesis 31:50	**Laban speaks to his son-in-law, Jacob, and makes a pact with him.**
Shechem, the son of Hamor, the Hivvite, the prince of the land, saw her; he took her, lay with her, and **violated her [וַיְעַנֶּהָ]**. — Genesis 34:2	**Shechem rapes Dinah, Jacob and Leah’s daughter.**
You shall not **oppress [תְעַנּוּן]** any widow or orphan. — Exodus 22:21	**In addition to the overall prohibition against oppressing any person, the Torah here issues an additional prohibition against oppressing the widow and orphan.**

Text 2

Talmud, Shabbat 31a

Babylonian Talmud

A literary work of monumental proportions that draws upon the legal, spiritual, intellectual, ethical, and historical traditions of Judaism. The 37 tractates of the Babylonian Talmud contain the teachings of the Jewish sages from the period after the destruction of the 2nd Temple through the 5th century CE. It has served as the primary vehicle for the transmission of the Oral Law and the education of Jews over the centuries; it is the entry point for all subsequent legal, ethical, and theological Jewish scholarship.

מַעֲשֶׂה בְּנָכְרִי אֶחָד שֶׁבָּא לִפְנֵי שַׁמַּאי. אָמַר לוֹ: כַּמָּה תּוֹרוֹת יֵשׁ לָכֶם?

אָמַר לוֹ: שְׁתַּיִם, תּוֹרָה שֶׁבִּכְתָב וְתוֹרָה שֶׁבְּעַל פֶּה.

אָמַר לוֹ: שֶׁבִּכְתָב - אֲנִי מַאֲמִינְךָ, וְשֶׁבְּעַל פֶּה - אֵינִי מַאֲמִינְךָ. גַּיְירֵנִי עַל מְנָת שֶׁתְּלַמְּדֵנִי תּוֹרָה שֶׁבִּכְתָב.

A non-Jew once came to Shamai and asked him, "How many Torahs do you have?"

Shamai replied, "Two—the Written Torah and the Oral Torah."

Said the man, "Regarding the Written, I trust you; but regarding the Oral, I do not trust you. Convert me on condition that you will teach me just the Written Torah."

QUESTION FOR DISCUSSION

Why was this prospective convert not willing to accept the Oral Torah?

FIGURE 1.2

Common Questions

1. Why is the Bible alone insufficient? What could be better than the word of God?
2. Who is the author of the Oral Torah? If it is the work of ancient rabbis, is it relevant to modern life? Weren't their ideas shaped by the knowledge and circumstances of their times?
3. Isn't the Oral Torah filled with debates, leaving us with unclear guidance and with the impression that Jewish law is all a matter of opinion?
4. Don't the debates in the Oral Torah indicate that it is not divine? After all, how can there be multiple opinions in a God-given system?
5. Do we have the original message? Is it possible for the Oral Torah to have been passed down accurately for so many years?

What Is the Oral Torah?

Text 3

Rabbi Moshe ben Maimon
(Maimonides, Rambam)
1135–1204

Halachist, philosopher, author, and physician. Maimonides was born in Cordoba, Spain. After the conquest of Cordoba by the Almohads, he fled Spain and eventually settled in Cairo, Egypt. There, he became the leader of the Jewish community and served as court physician to the vizier of Egypt. He is most noted for authoring the *Mishneh Torah*, an encyclopedic arrangement of Jewish law, and for his philosophical work, *Guide for the Perplexed*. His rulings on Jewish law are integral to the formation of halachic consensus.

Maimonides, Introduction to the Mishnah

שֶׁכָּל מִצְוָה שֶׁנָּתַן הַקָּדוֹשׁ בָּרוּךְ הוּא לְמֹשֶׁה רַבֵּינוּ נִיתְּנָה לוֹ עִם פֵּירוּשָׁהּ. הָיָה הַקָּדוֹשׁ בָּרוּךְ הוּא אוֹמֵר לוֹ הַמִּקְרָא וְאַחַר כַּךְ אוֹמֵר לוֹ פֵּירוּשׁוֹ וּבֵיאוּרוֹ וְכָל מַה שֶּׁכָּלַל אוֹתוֹ הַמִּקְרָא הַמְחוּכָּם.

Every mitzvah that God gave to Moses was given with its explanation. God would tell Moses the verse and then tell him its meaning, explanation, and all that was contained in the ingenious wording of the verse.

FIGURE 1.3

Categories of Oral Torah

1	**Received**	God-given explanations for each of the commandments
2		
3		
4		

Biblical Gaps

An Oral Tradition—Always

Text 4

Talmud, Shabbat 31a

יוֹמָא קַמָּא אָמַר לֵיהּ: א"ב ג"ד, לְמָחָר אַפִּיךְ לֵיהּ.

אָמַר לֵיהּ: וְהָא אֶתְמוֹל לֹא אָמַרְתְּ לִי הָכִי?

אָמַר לוֹ: לַאו עֲלַי דִידִי קָא סָמְכַתְּ? דְעַל פֶּה נַמִי סְמוֹךְ עֲלַי!

The first day, Hillel taught him *alef, bet, gimel, dalet*. The next day, Hillel reversed it.

Said the man, "But yesterday you didn't tell it to me that way!"

Hillel answered, "Are you not relying on me [to read the Written Torah]? Rely on me as well for the Oral Torah!"

Vowels

LEARNING EXERCISE 1

B—R—D

Write as many words as you can by adding only vowels to these three letters. Vowels may be added between, before, and after the letters, but the letters B—R—D must stay in that order.

____________	____________
____________	____________
____________	____________
____________	____________
____________	____________

Text 5

Exodus 23:19

רֵאשִׁית בִּכּוּרֵי אַדְמָתְךָ תָּבִיא בֵּית ה' אֱלֹקֶיךָ לֹא תְבַשֵּׁל גְּדִי בחלב אִמּוֹ.

The choicest of the first fruits of your soil you shall bring to the house of God. You shall not cook a kid in its mother's חלב.

LEARNING EXERCISE 2

"Woman without her man is nothing."

- ☐ I strongly agree with this statement.
- ☐ I somewhat agree with this statement.
- ☐ I somewhat disagree with this statement.
- ☐ I strongly disagree with this statement.

LEARNING EXERCISE 3

Punctuate the translation of the following verse (Exodus 25:34):

וּבַמְּנֹרָה אַרְבָּעָה גְבִעִים מְשֻׁקָּדִים כַּפְתֹּרֶיהָ וּפְרָחֶיהָ.	**On the menorah [shall be] four goblets decorated its knobs and its flowers.**

Getting the Message

Text 6

Deuteronomy 6:4–9

שְׁמַע יִשְׂרָאֵל ה' אֱלֹקֵינוּ ה' אֶחָד.

וְאָהַבְתָּ אֵת ה' אֱלֹקֶיךָ בְּכָל לְבָבְךָ וּבְכָל נַפְשְׁךָ וּבְכָל מְאֹדֶךָ.

וְהָיוּ הַדְּבָרִים הָאֵלֶּה אֲשֶׁר אָנֹכִי מְצַוְּךָ הַיּוֹם עַל לְבָבֶךָ.

וְשִׁנַּנְתָּם לְבָנֶיךָ וְדִבַּרְתָּ בָּם בְּשִׁבְתְּךָ בְּבֵיתֶךָ וּבְלֶכְתְּךָ בַדֶּרֶךְ וּבְשָׁכְבְּךָ וּבְקוּמֶךָ.

וּקְשַׁרְתָּם לְאוֹת עַל יָדֶךָ וְהָיוּ לְטֹטָפֹת בֵּין עֵינֶיךָ.

וּכְתַבְתָּם עַל מְזֻזוֹת בֵּיתֶךָ וּבִשְׁעָרֶיךָ.

Hear, O Israel, the Lord is our God, the Lord is one.

You shall love the Lord, your God, with all your heart and with all your soul and with all your might.

These words that I command you this day shall be upon your heart.

You shall teach them to your children and speak of them when you sit in your house, when you walk on the way, when you lie down, and when you rise up.

You shall bind them for a sign upon your hand, and they shall be for *totafot* between your eyes.

You shall inscribe them upon the doorposts of your house and upon your gates.

Text 7

Rabbi Yehudah Halevi, *Kuzari* 3:35

וְהִנֵּה זֶה סֵפֶר מֹשֶׁה הַפָּשׁוּט הֻצְרַכְנוּ בִּמְלוֹתָיו וּבַדִּבּוּר בּוֹ אֶל כַּמָּה
כִּתּוֹת מִן הַקַּבָּלָה, מִן הַנִּקּוּד, וּמִטַּעַם, וּמִפָּסוּק, וּמִמָּסֹרֶת, עַל אַחַת
כַּמָּה וְכַמָּה אָנוּ צְרִיכִים בְּעִנְיָנָיו, כִּי הָעִנְיָן רָחָב מִן הַמִּלּוֹת . . .

רְצוֹנִי לְהִשְׁתַּדֵּל, וְשֶׁיְּשִׁיבוּנִי תְּשׁוּבָה מְסַפֶּקֶת כַּאֲשֶׁר אֶשְׁאָלֵם, עַל מַה שֶּׁיַּתִּיר
הַחַי לֶאֱכֹל, וּמָה עִנְיַן הַזְּבִיחָה, וְשֶׁמָּא הִיא נְחִירָה אוֹ הֶרֶג כַּאֲשֶׁר יִזְדַּמֵּן . . .

וְהָיִיתִי רוֹצֶה שֶׁיְּבָאֵר לִי הַחֵלֶב הָאָסוּר, וְהוּא דָּבֵק עִם הַמֻּתָּר
בַּמֵּעַיִם וְהַקֵּבָה, וְזוּלַת זֶה מִנִּקּוּר הַבָּשָׂר . . .

וְהָיִיתִי רוֹצֶה שֶׁיִּתֵּן לִי גְּבוּל "אַל יֵצֵא אִישׁ מִמְּקוֹמוֹ" (שמות טז,כט) בְּיוֹם הַשַּׁבָּת,
אִם הוּא בֵּיתוֹ, אוֹ חֲצֵרוֹ, אוֹ רְשׁוּתוֹ אִם יִהְיוּ לוֹ חֲצֵרִים רַבִּים, אוֹ מְבוֹאוֹ, אוֹ
שְׁכוּנָתוֹ, אוֹ מְדִינָתוֹ, אוֹ מִגְרַשׁ עִירוֹ, אַחַר שֶׁתֵּבַת מָקוֹם סוֹבֶלֶת זֶה וְיוֹתֵר מִזֶּה.

וְהָיִיתִי רוֹצֶה שֶׁיַּרְאֶה לִי גֶּדֶר הַמְּלָאכָה הָאֲסוּרָה בַּשַּׁבָּת . . .

וְהַפָּשׁוּט שֶׁבַּתּוֹרָה הוּא סָתוּם, כָּל שֶׁכֵּן הַסָּתוּם, כִּי לֹא
הָיוּ סוֹמְכִים אֶלָּא עַל הַתּוֹרָה שֶׁבְּעַל פֶּה.

וְהָיִיתִי רוֹצֶה שֶׁאֶרְאֶה . . . אֵיכוּת הַמִּלָּה וְהַצִּיצִית וְהַסֻּכָּה.

וִיבָאֵר לִי . . . וְאֵיךְ הֵם דָּנִין בַּמִּצְוֹת הַדּוֹחוֹת זוֹ אֶת זוֹ, כְּמִלָּה
עִם הַשַּׁבָּת וְהַפֶּסַח עִם הַשַּׁבָּת, מִי נִדְחֶה מִפְּנֵי מִי.

וְזוּלַת זֶה מִמַּה שֶּׁיֶּאֱרַךְ סִפּוּר כְּלָלָיו כָּל שֶׁכֵּן פְּרָטָיו.

In order to read and pronounce the text of the Torah, we require traditions for the vowel signs, cantillations, divisions of sentences, and the spelling of certain words. Certainly, then, we require a tradition to comprehend the meaning of the text, which is a more difficult task. . . .

I want to ask the Karaites questions and hope they respond with satisfactory answers:

Rabbi Yehudah Halevi
ca. 1075–1141

Noted author, physician, and poet. Rabbi Yehudah Halevi is best known as the author of the *Kuzari*, a philosophical work, written in the form of a discussion between a Jew, a Christian, and a Muslim before the King of the Khazars. In addition to the *Kuzari*, he wrote thousands of poems, of which only a few hundred survive today.

What action must be taken to make an animal fit for consumption? What exactly [does the Torah mean in Deuteronomy 12:21 when it says that we should] slaughter the animal? Maybe it means simple puncturing of the animal, or any type of killing. . . .

I would like the Karaite to explain [Leviticus 3:17, which forbids the consumption of animal fat]. How would one distinguish between forbidden fats and permitted fats, considering that they connect in the intestine and stomach? Which fats must be removed? . . .

I desire a definition of the words: "Let no man go out of his place on Shabbat" (Exodus 16:29). Does "place" refer to one's house, courtyard, property (when one owns many adjoining courtyards), street, district, city, or suburbs of the city? The word "place" can refer to all of these or something else.

I should like to be shown how to define the prohibition of work on Shabbat [stated in Exodus 20:10]. . . .

That which appears plain in the Torah is yet obscure, and much more so are the obscure passages, because the oral supplement was relied upon.

I want to be shown . . . the details of circumcision [mentioned in Leviticus 12:3], fringes [mentioned in Numbers 15], and *sukah* [mentioned in Leviticus 23:42].

Explain to me . . . how to deal with laws that interfere with each other, such as circumcision or the Paschal lamb with Shabbat: which must yield to which?

There are many other such questions that I cannot enumerate in general, much less in detail.

Text 8

Deuteronomy 30:11–19

כִּי הַמִּצְוָה הַזֹּאת אֲשֶׁר אָנֹכִי מְצַוְּךָ הַיּוֹם, לֹא נִפְלֵאת הִוא מִמְּךָ וְלֹא רְחֹקָה הִוא.

לֹא בַשָּׁמַיִם הִוא, לֵאמֹר, מִי יַעֲלֶה לָּנוּ הַשָּׁמַיְמָה וְיִקָּחֶהָ לָּנוּ וְיַשְׁמִעֵנוּ אֹתָהּ וְנַעֲשֶׂנָּה.

וְלֹא מֵעֵבֶר לַיָּם הִוא, לֵאמֹר, מִי יַעֲבָר לָנוּ אֶל עֵבֶר
הַיָּם וְיִקָּחֶהָ לָּנוּ וְיַשְׁמִעֵנוּ אֹתָהּ וְנַעֲשֶׂנָּה.

כִּי קָרוֹב אֵלֶיךָ הַדָּבָר מְאֹד בְּפִיךָ וּבִלְבָבְךָ לַעֲשֹׂתוֹ.

רְאֵה נָתַתִּי לְפָנֶיךָ הַיּוֹם אֶת הַחַיִּים וְאֶת הַטּוֹב וְאֶת הַמָּוֶת וְאֶת
הָרָע . . . וּבָחַרְתָּ בַּחַיִּים לְמַעַן תִּחְיֶה אַתָּה וְזַרְעֶךָ.

The mitzvah that I am prescribing to you today is not too mysterious or remote from you.

It is not in heaven, so [that you should] say, "Who shall go up to heaven and bring it to us so that we can hear it and keep it?"

It is not over the sea so [that you should] say, "Who will cross the sea and get if for us, so that we will be able to hear it and keep it?"

It is something that is very close to you. It is in your mouth and in your heart, so that you can keep it.

See! Today I have set before you [a choice] between life and good [on one side], and death and evil [on the other]. . . . Choose life, so that you and your descendants will live.

Internal Evidence

Text 9

Deuteronomy 12:20–21

כִּי יַרְחִיב ה' אֱלֹקֶיךָ אֶת גְּבֻלְךָ כַּאֲשֶׁר דִּבֶּר לָךְ, וְאָמַרְתָּ אֹכְלָה בָשָׂר,
כִּי תְאַוֶּה נַפְשְׁךָ לֶאֱכֹל בָּשָׂר, בְּכָל אַוַּת נַפְשְׁךָ תֹּאכַל בָּשָׂר.

. . . וְזָבַחְתָּ מִבְּקָרְךָ וּמִצֹּאנְךָ אֲשֶׁר נָתַן ה' לְךָ כַּאֲשֶׁר
צִוִּיתִךָ, וְאָכַלְתָּ בִּשְׁעָרֶיךָ בְּכֹל אַוַּת נַפְשֶׁךָ.

When God expands your borders as He promised you and your natural desire to eat meat asserts itself so that you say, "I wish to eat meat"—you may eat as much meat as you wish.

. . . You need only slaughter your cattle and small animals that God will have given you in the manner that I have prescribed. You may then eat them in your settlements in any manner you desire.

The Benefits of *Oral* Torah

Why Not Write It All?

Text 10

Talmud, Gitin 60b

דְבָרִים שֶׁבְּעַל פֶּה אִי אַתָּה רַשָּׁאִי לְאוֹמְרָן בִּכְתָב.

You are not at liberty to speak the Oral Torah from a text.

QUESTION FOR DISCUSSION

What are some advantages of a system of oral transmission in comparison to studying from a written text?

Advantage #1: Avoiding Ambiguity

Text 11

Second Amendment, United States Constitution

A well-regulated Militia, being necessary to the security of a free State, the right of the people to keep and bear Arms, shall not be infringed.

QUESTIONS FOR DISCUSSION

1. **How is this amendment interpreted by those who maintain that the government can ban or severely restrict gun ownership and possession?**
2. **How is this amendment interpreted by those who maintain that the government can enact few if any restrictions on an individual's right to own and possess arms?**

LEARNING EXERCISE 4

Together with a few other participants, examine the following recipe from a fifteenth-century English cookbook. Translate it into modern English.

> Oyle Soppys.
>
> Take a gode quantyte of Oynonys, an mynse hem not to smale, an sethe in fayre Water: þan take hem vp, an take a gode quantite of Stale Ale, as .iij. galouns, an þer-to take a pynte of Oyle fryid, an caste þe Oynonys þer-to, an let boyle alle to-gederys a gode whyle; then caste þer-to Safroune, powder Peppr, Sugre, an Salt, an serue forth alle hote as tostes.

Thomas Austin, *Two Fifteenth-Century Cookery-Books* [London 1888], p. 12

Text 12

Rabbi Yosef Albo, *Sefer Ha'ikarim* 3:23

כָּל דָּבָר הַנִּכְתָּב מֵאֵיזֶה מִין שֶׁיִּהְיֶה, כְּבָר אֶפְשָׁר שֶׁיּוּבַן בִּשְׁתֵּי הֲבָנוֹת מִתְחַלְּפוֹת, עַד שֶׁאֶפְשָׁר שֶׁתִּהְיֶה הַהֲבָנָה הָאַחַת מַסְכֶּמֶת לְכַוָּנַת הָאוֹמֵר, וְהַשֵּׁנִית מִתְחַלֶּפֶת לָהּ מִכֹּל וָכֹל.

כְּמוֹ שֶׁכָּתַב הָרַמְבַּ"ם ז"ל בְּאִגֶּרֶת תְּחִיַּת הַמֵּתִים כִּי "שְׁמַע יִשְׂרָאֵל ה' אֱלֹקֵינוּ ה' אֶחָד" הָעִבְרִים יָבִינוּ מִמֶּנּוּ הָאַחְדוּת הַגְּמוּרָה, וְהַנּוֹצְרִים יְפָרְשׁוּ אוֹתוֹ עַל כַּוָּנַת הַשִּׁלּוּשׁ.

בַּעֲבוּר זֶה הָיָה מְחֻיָּב, כְּדֵי שֶׁתִּהְיֶה תּוֹרַת ה' תְּמִימָה וְתוּבַן עַל הַכַּוָּנָה הָרְאוּיָה, שֶׁבְּתֵת הַשֵּׁם יִתְבָּרֵךְ אוֹתָהּ אֶל מֹשֶׁה בִּכְתָב יְפָרֵשׁ אוֹתָהּ לוֹ עַל הַכַּוָּנָה הָרְאוּיָה, וְכֵן מֹשֶׁה לִיהוֹשֻׁעַ, וְכֵן יְהוֹשֻׁעַ לִזְקֵנִים, וּזְקֵנִים לִנְבִיאִים, וְכֵן דּוֹר אַחַר דּוֹר, כְּדֵי שֶׁלֹּא יִפֹּל שׁוּם סָפֵק בַּהֲבָנַת הַכְּתָב כְּפִי מַה שֶּׁרָאוּי.

וְלַפֵּרוּשׁ הַזֶּה . . . הוּא שֶׁקָּרְאוּ תּוֹרָה שֶׁבְּעַל פֶּה, לְפִי שֶׁאִי אֶפְשָׁר שֶׁבָּא הַפֵּרוּשׁ הַזֶּה בִּכְתָב, כִּי בִּכְתָב הַהוּא יִפֹּל גַּם כֵּן הַסָּפֵק שֶׁאָמַרְנוּ שֶׁיִּפֹּל בְּמִכְתָּב הָרִאשׁוֹן.

Anything that is written, regardless of the form, could possibly be interpreted in two different ways, to the extent that it is possible that one way will express the writer's intent, and the other way will convey the total opposite.

As Maimonides writes in his Epistle on Resurrection that while Jews understand "Hear, O Israel, the Lord is our God, the Lord is one" to mean that God is absolutely one, Christians interpret this verse to support the doctrine of the Trinity.

Therefore, in order for God's Torah to be complete and properly understood, it was necessary that when God gave the Torah to Moses that He also explained its true meaning to him. Moses did the same with Joshua, and Joshua

Rabbi Yosef Albo
ca. 1380–1444

Spanish rabbi and philosopher. A student of Rabbi Chasdai Crescas, Albo is renowned for his philosophical work *Sefer Ha'ikarim* (*Book of Fundamentals*). The work stresses three fundamental aspects of Jewish belief: the existence of God, Torah from Sinai, and reward and punishment.

with the prophets, and similarly with subsequent generations, so that there would be no doubt in understanding the text properly.

This explanation . . . is called Oral Torah because it is not supposed to be written. If it were written, it would be ambiguous, just like the text it is coming to explain.

Advantage #2: Superior Learning

Text 13

Rabbi Yehoshua Falk Hakohen Katz, Introduction to *Beit Yisrael* and *Sefer Me'irat Einayim*

וְנִצְטַוָה מֹשֶׁה מִסִינַי לְלַמֵד כָּל אֵלוּ לְיִשְׂרָאֵל עַל פֶּה וְלֹא בִּכְתָב . . . כְּדֵי שֶׁלֹא יִסְמְכוּ עַל מַה שֶׁכְּתוּבָה לִפְנֵיהֶן וְלֹא יַעַסְקוּ בָּה כָּל כַּךְ כְּמוֹ שֶׁצְרִיכִין לִיתֵּן לֵב כְּשֶׁיִלְמְדוּ בַּעַל פֶּה, שֶׁאָז צְרִיכִין לֶהָגוֹת בָּהֶן תָּמִיד כְּדֵי לִזְכּוֹר הַדְבָרִים וְלֹא יִשְׁכְּחוּהוּ.

Moses was commanded at Sinai to teach all of these laws orally and not to record them in writing . . . so that we would not rely on recorded information that would be readily available, as that would result in a laxity of study. When something is not recorded and its preservation requires of us to learn it by heart, we study it with more concentration, and we continuously contemplate the material in order to ensure we remember it and do not forget it.

Rabbi Yehoshua Falk Hakohen Katz
1555-1614

Polish rabbi, Talmudist, and authority on Jewish law. Rabbi Falk is best known for his *Perishah* and *Derishah* commentaries on the *Arba'ah Turim*, as well as *Sefer Me'irat Enayim* on the *Code of Jewish Law*. Rabbi Falk was a pupil of Rabbi Moshe Isserles and served as head of the yeshivah in Lemberg, as well as on the Council of Four Lands, a central body of Jewish authority in Poland.

Text 14

Rabbi Shne'ur Zalman of Liadi, *Tanya*, ch. 5

מֵאַחַר שֶׁכַּךְ עָלָה בִּרְצוֹנוֹ וְחָכְמָתוֹ שֶׁל הַקָּדוֹשׁ בָּרוּךְ הוּא, שֶׁאִם יִטְעוֹן זֶה כַּךְ וְזֶה כַּךְ יִהְיֶה הַפְּסַק כַּךְ, הֲרֵי כְּשֶׁאָדָם יוֹדֵעַ וּמַשִּׂיג בְּשִׂכְלוֹ פְּסַק זֶה . . . הֲרֵי זֶה מַשִּׂיג וְתוֹפֵס וּמַקִּיף בְּשִׂכְלוֹ רְצוֹנוֹ וְחָכְמָתוֹ שֶׁל הַקָּדוֹשׁ בָּרוּךְ הוּא . . . וְהוּא יִחוּד נִפְלָא . . .

Because it is the will and wisdom of God that in the event of a person's pleading this way, and the other [litigant] pleading that way, that the verdict shall be such and such; therefore, when we know and comprehend with our intellect this verdict . . . we have thus comprehended, grasped, and encompassed with our intellect the will and wisdom of God. . . . And this is a wondrous union. . . .

Rabbi Shne'ur Zalman of Liadi
(Alter Rebbe)
1745–1812

Chasidic rebbe, halachic authority, and founder of the Chabad movement. The Alter Rebbe was born in Liozna, Belarus, and was among the principal students of the Magid of Mezeritch. His numerous works include the *Tanya*, an early classic containing the fundamentals of Chabad Chasidism, and *Shulchan Aruch HaRav*, an expanded and reworked code of Jewish law.

Broken Telephone?

Text 15a

Talmud, Eiruvin 54b

כֵּיצַד סֵדֶר מִשְׁנָה?

מֹשֶׁה לָמַד מִפִּי הַגְּבוּרָה.

נִכְנַס אַהֲרֹן וְשָׁנָה לוֹ מֹשֶׁה פִּרְקוֹ. נִסְתַּלֵּק אַהֲרֹן וְיָשַׁב לִשְׂמֹאל מֹשֶׁה.

נִכְנְסוּ בָּנָיו וְשָׁנָה לָהֶן מֹשֶׁה פִּירְקָן. נִסְתַּלְּקוּ בָּנָיו, אֶלְעָזָר יָשַׁב לִימִין מֹשֶׁה וְאִיתָמָר לִשְׂמֹאל אַהֲרֹן . . .

נִכְנְסוּ זְקֵנִים וְשָׁנָה לָהֶן מֹשֶׁה פִּירְקָן. נִסְתַּלְּקוּ זְקֵנִים.

נִכְנְסוּ כָּל הָעָם וְשָׁנָה לָהֶן מֹשֶׁה פִּירְקָן . . .

נִסְתַּלֵּק מֹשֶׁה, וְשָׁנָה לָהֶן אַהֲרֹן פִּרְקוֹ. נִסְתַּלֵּק אַהֲרֹן, שָׁנוּ לָהֶן בָּנָיו פִּירְקָן. נִסְתַּלְּקוּ בָּנָיו, שָׁנוּ לָהֶן זְקֵנִים פִּירְקָן.

נִמְצָא בְּיַד הַכֹּל אַרְבָּעָה.

What was the order of learning the Oral Torah?

Moses learned directly from the Almighty.

Aaron would then enter and Moses would teach him; Aaron would then remove himself and sit to Moses' left.

Aaron's sons would enter and Moses would teach them; his sons would remove themselves—Elazar would sit to Moses' right and Ithamar to Aaron's left. . . .

The Seventy Elders would enter and Moses would teach them; the Elders would remove themselves.

Then all the people would enter and Moses would teach them. . . .

Moses would exit and Aaron would teach it to all those present; Aaron would exit and his sons would teach it to all those present; his sons would exit and the elders would teach it to all those present.

Thus, everyone learned it four times.

Text 15b

Maimonides, Introduction to the Mishnah

וּמִתְפַּזְּרִים הָעָם לְלַמֵּד זֶה לָזֶה מַה שֶּׁשָּׁמְעוּ מֵהַשָּׁלִיחַ. וְכוֹתְבִים הַמִּקְרָא בַּמְּגִלּוֹת.

וּמִתְפַּזְּרִים הַשָּׂרִים בְּכָל בֵּית יִשְׂרָאֵל לְלַמֵּד וּלְשַׁנֵּן עַד שֶׁיֵּדְעוּ אוֹתוֹ מִקְרָא וְיַשְׂכִּילוּ קְרִיאָתוֹ, וּמְלַמְּדִים אוֹתָם בֵּיאוּר אוֹתוֹ הַמִּקְרָא שֶׁנִּתַּן מֵאֵת ה׳ . . . וְהָיוּ כּוֹתְבִין הַמִּקְרָא וְזוֹכְרִים הַקַּבָּלָה עַל פֶּה.

Afterward, the people would disperse in order to review with one another what they had heard from Moses. And they would write the verse in scrolls.

Ministers spread out among all of the people to teach and review until everyone knew the verse and how to read it well; they would also teach the God-given explanation of the verse. . . . The people would write the verse and remember the explanation by heart.

Text 15c

Ibid.

וְכַאֲשֶׁר הִגִּיעַ סוֹף אַרְבָּעִים שָׁנָה, בְּרֹאשׁ חֹדֶשׁ שְׁבָט, הִקְהִילָם עָלָיו הַשָּׁלוֹם וְאָמַר לָהֶם: הֵן קָרְבוּ יָמַי לָמוּת, לָכֵן מִי שֶׁשָּׁמַע מִמֶּנִּי אֵיזֶה קַבָּלָה וְשָׁכְחָה, יָבוֹא וּנְבָרְרֶנָּה לוֹ, וּמִי שֶׁנִּסְתַּפְּקָה לוֹ אֵיזֶה שְׁאֵלָה, יָבוֹא וּנְבָאֲרֶנָּה לוֹ. אָמַר הַכָּתוּב (דְּבָרִים א,ה) "הוֹאִיל מֹשֶׁה בֵּאֵר אֶת הַתּוֹרָה הַזֹּאת לֵאמֹר", וְכָךְ אָמְרוּ חֲכָמִים בְּסִפְרֵי: כָּל מִי שֶׁשָּׁכַח הֲלָכָה אַחַת, יָבוֹא וְיִשְׁנֶה, וְכָל מִי שֶׁיֵּשׁ לוֹ לְפָרֵשׁ, יָבוֹא וִיפָרֵשׁ. וּבֵרְרוּ מִפִּיו הַקַּבָּלָה, וְלָמְדוּ הַפֵּרוּשִׁים כָּל אוֹתוֹ הַזְּמַן שֶׁמֵּרֹאשׁ חֹדֶשׁ שְׁבָט עַד שְׁבִיעִי בַּאֲדָר.

After forty years [in the desert], on the first of Shevat, Moses gathered the people and said, "The day of my death is near; therefore, whoever has heard from me something but forgot it shall come and clarify the matter, and whoever has a question shall come and I will explain." As the verse says, "Moses began to explain this law" (Deuteronomy 1:5), and the sages elucidate in *Sifrei*, [that Moses said], "Whoever forgot a law, come to me and I will teach it; whoever requires some explanation, come and I shall explain."

During this time—from the first of Shevat until the seventh of Adar—the Jewish people clarified with Moses the Received Oral Torah.

LEARNING EXERCISE 5

Pass on this message to your neighbor:

tsgl h2m2d & fotw

Key Points

TORAH Café™

Continue the JLI Learning Experience!

Visit www.TorahCafe.com/go/JD1

for a video lecture(s) related to the theme of this lesson.

1. The Oral Torah is relevant to every Jew because it constitutes the basis for virtually all modern-day Jewish observance and tradition.

2. There are multiple classes of Oral Torah. The "Received" Oral Torah refers to the laws and explanations that Moses received from God along with the Written Torah.

3. Every text requires some degree of oral tradition to be understood.

4. The lack of vowels and punctuation in the Written Torah renders many passages ambiguous and even unintelligible.

5. It is impossible to perform many *mitzvot* without the explanations and specifics provided by the Oral Torah. Because the Torah is meant to guide our lives, there must be a supplement that provides the missing details and specifics.

6. One reason why the Received Oral Torah was not written was because written texts are often ambiguous—especially as time elapses and language evolves—even when the authors intend to be clear. A proper system of oral transmission avoids this disadvantage.

7. A system of oral transmission compels us to study the Torah with greater rigor and frequency. The result is an enhanced understanding of the Torah and more moments of engaging God.

8. The system of oral transmission ensures that students learn from living examples, not just books.

9. The written text that accompanies the Received Oral Torah assists in the process of oral transmission and helps ensure its integrity and accuracy.

Appendix A

Glossary of Important Terms

Torah

The word Torah means "teaching" or "lesson." It is usually used to refer to the entire body of traditional Jewish scholarship—from the five books of Moses down to the scholarly responsa of today's rabbis. However, it is sometimes used to refer specifically to the five books of Moses. You can assume that when you hear the word "Torah," it is being used in the more general sense, unless the context tells you differently. When referring to the five books of Moses, people often say, "Chumash," or "Written Torah," or "Bible."

The term "Old Testament" is not valid from the Jewish point of view, because it implies that there is a valid "New Testament," which Judaism of course does not accept.

Chumash

Chumash refers to the five books of Moses, from the word "*chamesh*," which means "five." Some people call it Pentateuch.

Written Torah

The Written Torah refers to the entire set of the twenty-four books of the Bible. It is called in Hebrew "Tanach," which is an acronym for "Torah" (here meaning the five books of Moses), "Nevi'im" (the Prophets), and "Ketuvim" (the Writings).

Halachah

Halachah refers to Jewish law and practice. It comes from the word, "*halach*," which means "to go," or "to walk." This refers to "going" or "walking" in the path of divinely ordained conduct. In general, it refers to the entire range of works and decisions in Jewish law. When people ask, "what is the *halachah*?" they are trying to determine the conclusion of Jewish law about the issue at hand. The plural form is "*halachot*."

Mitzvot

The *mitzvot*, plural of "mitzvah," are more than just "good deeds"; they are divine commandments. Halachah describes how to perform the *mitzvot*.

Oral Torah

Oral Torah refers to the entire body of Torah (used here in the broader sense) except for the Written Torah. Although originally passed down in oral form, it was written down in later generations. The best-known work of the Oral Torah is the Talmud.

There are various categories of Oral Torah, and this course, *Judaism Decoded*, explores this topic at length.

Mishnah

Mishnah is the first comprehensive written compilation of the Oral Torah, redacted approximately in the year 3960 (200 CE) by Rabbi Yehudah Hanasi in the Land of Israel.

Talmud

The Talmud is the main work of the Oral Torah, set up as a commentary on the Mishnah. There are two Talmuds: The Jerusalem Talmud and the Babylonian Talmud. Unless specified otherwise, Talmud refers to the Babylonian Talmud, which is more authoritative in terms of Halachah. The Babylonian Talmud is a literary work of monumental proportions divided into thirty-seven tractates, and it contains the teachings of the Jewish sages through the 5th century CE. It has served as the primary vehicle for the transmission of the Oral Law and the education of Jews over the centuries.

The Torah from Sinai

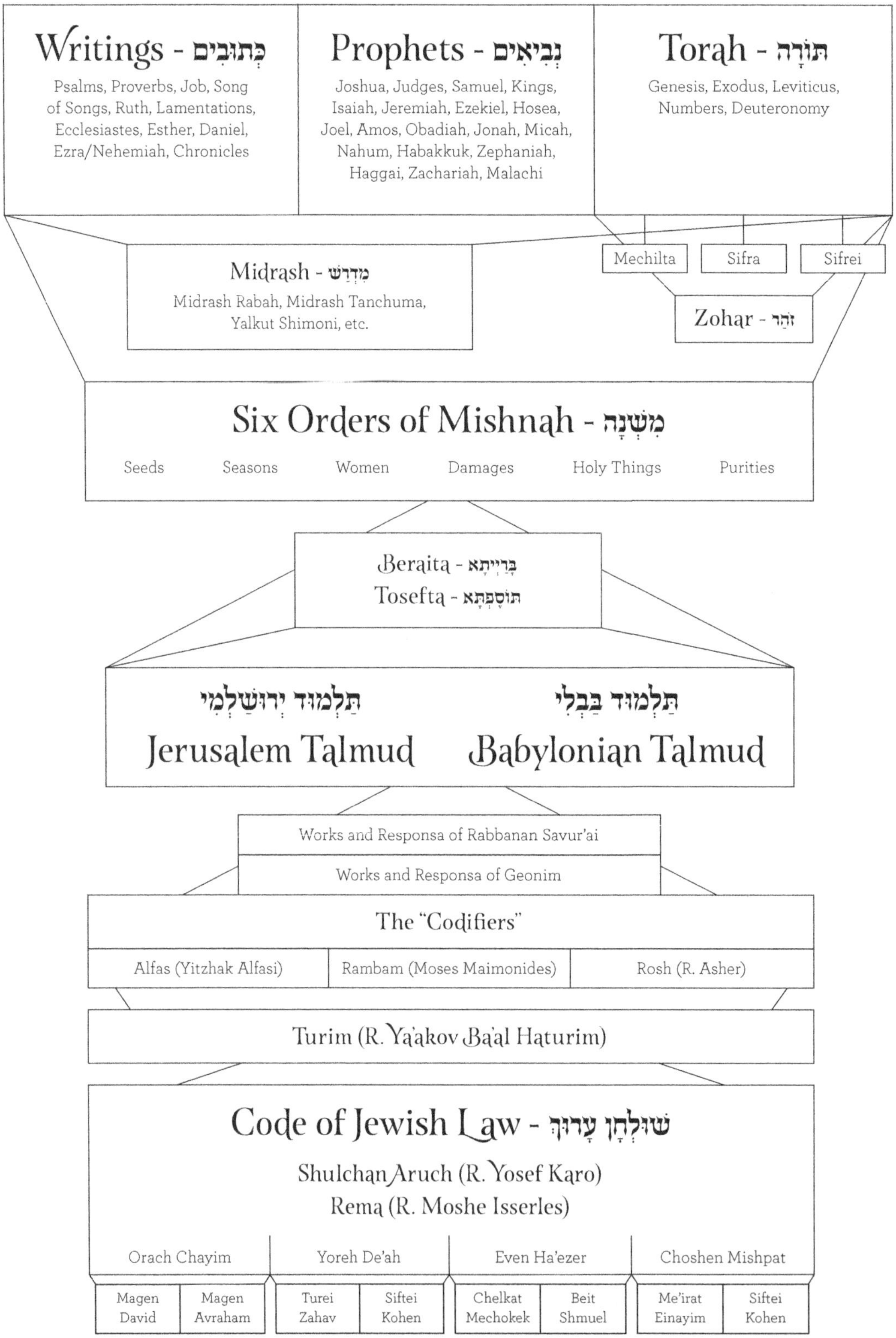

"Scripture, Mishnah, Talmud, Aggadah, even what young students will innovate in the future before their teacher, were all already said to Moses on Sinai." (Jerusalem Talmud, Pe'ah 2:4)

ADDITIONAL READINGS

RAMBAM'S INTRODUCTION[1] TO THE *MISHNEH TORAH*

TRANSLATED BY RABBI ELIYAHU TOUGER

"In the name of God, Lord of the world"[2] (Genesis 21:33).

"Then I will not be ashamed when I gaze at all Your mitzvot"[3] (Psalms 119:6).

The mitzvot given to Moses at Mount Sinai were all given together with their explanations,[4] as implied by [Exodus 24:12]: "And I will give you the tablets of stone, the Torah, and the mitzvah."

"The Torah" refers to the Written Law; "the mitzvah," to its explanation. [God] commanded us to fulfill "the Torah" according to [the instructions of] "the mitzvah."[5] "The mitzvah" is called the Oral Law.

Moses, our teacher, personally transcribed the entire Torah before he died. He gave a Torah scroll to each tribe and placed another scroll in the ark as a testimonial, as [Deuteronomy 31:26] states: "Take this Torah scroll and place it [beside the ark...] and it will be there as a testimonial."

"The mitzvah"— i.e., the explanation of the Torah— he did not transcribe.[6] Instead, he commanded it [verbally] to the elders, to Joshua, and to the totality of Israel,[7] as [Deuteronomy 13:1] states: "Be careful to observe everything that I prescribe to you." For this reason, it is called the Oral Law.

Even though the Oral Law was not transcribed, Moses, our teacher, taught it in its entirety in his court to the seventy elders. Elazar, Pinchas, and Joshua received the tradition from Moses. [In particular, Moses] transmitted the Oral Law to Joshua, who was his [primary] disciple, and instructed him regarding it.[8]

---

1 The heading "Introduction" is not found in any of the manuscript editions of the *Mishneh Torah* and appears to be a printer's addition. Note *Hilchot Shechitah* 1:4, where the Rambam refers to "...the Oral Law, which is called 'the mitzvah,' as we explained in the beginning of this text."
By referring to these passages as "the beginning" of the text and not "the introduction to the text," the Rambam implies that the subject matter contained in these passages is an essential part of the *Mishneh Torah* and not merely an author's preamble.

2 Though this verse is omitted by many printed editions of the *Mishneh Torah*, it is included in the manuscript editions. It is also found at the beginning of the Rambam's other works, the Commentary on the Mishnah, *Sefer HaMitzvot*, and the Guide to the Perplexed. The Rambam's intention is to clarify that he does not see this work as an expression of his individual efforts alone, but that it was composed "In the name of God, the Lord of the world."

3 The Rambam introduces every one of the books of the *Mishneh Torah* by quoting an appropriate verse from the Bible. It is possible to explain that he chose this verse for the introduction to the entire text in reply to objections he knew would arise to the *Mishneh Torah*. The Rambam's conception of his work as "a compilation of the entire Oral Law" would not be acceptable to many. Therefore, he begins by emphasizing that his actions were not presumptuous. There is no need for him to be "ashamed" at taking such a step. Since he can "gaze at all Your mitzvot"—i.e., has the knowledge of the entire Oral Law—he is obligated to try to communicate that knowledge to others, as stated in *Hilchot Talmud Torah 5:4 (Yayin Malchut)*.

4 By emphasizing that, at the revelation at Sinai, the mitzvot were given "together with their explanations," the Rambam stresses that the Written and Oral Laws cannot be viewed as two separate entities, but rather as two dimensions of a single whole. See also the Rambam's Introduction to his Commentary on the Mishnah, where he elaborates on the same concept.

5 See *Emunah V'De'ot* (Discourse 3, Chapter 3), where Rav Sa'adiah Gaon explains at length how the oral tradition is necessary to understand how to fulfill the mitzvot

6 Note *Gittin* 60b, which prohibits writing down the teachings of the Oral Law. Nevertheless, from the Rambam's statements here and in the Introduction to his Commentary on the Mishnah, it appears that the prohibition only applies to the composition of a text from which to teach, and not writing down notes for one's personal study.

7 See the Rambam's Introduction to his Commentary on the Mishnah, where he quotes Eruvin 54b, which describes the order in which Moses would teach Aharon, his sons, the elders, and then the entire Jewish people.

8 I.e., regarding its transmission to others *(Sifre, Pinchas)*.

Similarly, throughout his life Joshua taught the Oral Law. Many elders received the tradition from him.[9] Eli received the tradition from the elders and from Pinchas. Samuel received the tradition from Eli and his court. David received the tradition from Samuel and his court.

Achiah of Shiloh was one of those who experienced the exodus from Egypt.[10] He was a Levite and heard [teachings] from Moses. He was, however, of low stature in Moses' age. Afterwards, he received the tradition from David and his court. Elijah received the tradition from Achiah of Shiloh and his court. Elisha received the tradition from Elijah and his court.

Yehoyada, the priest, received the tradition from Elisha and his court. Zechariah received the tradition from Yehoyada and his court. Hoshea received the tradition from Zechariah and his court. Amos received the tradition from Hoshea and his court. Isaiah received the tradition from Amos and his court. Michah received the tradition from Isaiah and his court. Yoel received the tradition from Michah and his court. Nachum received the tradition from Yoel and his court. Chabbakuk received the tradition from Nachum and his court. Tzefaniah received the tradition from Chabbakuk and his court.

Jeremiah received the tradition from Tzefaniah and his court. Baruch ben Neriyah[11] received the tradition from Jeremiah and his court. Ezra and his court received the tradition from Baruch and his court. [The members of] Ezra's court are referred to as *Anshei K'nesset Hagedolah* (the men of the great assembly). They included Chaggai, Zechariah, Malachi, Daniel, Chananiah Mishael,Azariah, Nechemiah ben Chakaliah, Mordechai the linguist, Zerubavel and many other sages—120 elders in all.[12]

The last [surviving] member of this group was Shimon the Just. He was included among the 120 elders and received the Oral Law from all of them. He served as the High Priest after Ezra. Antignos of Socho and his court received the tradition from Shimon the Just and his court.

Yosse ben Yo'ezer of Tzreidah and Yosef ben Yochanan of Jerusalem[13] and their court received the tradition from Antignos and his court. Yehoshua ben Perachiah and Nittai of Arbel and their court received the tradition from Yosse ben Yo'ezer and Yosef ben Perachiah and their court. Yehudah ben Tabbai and Shimon ben Shatach and their court received the tradition from Yehoshua ben Perachiah and Nittai of Arbel and their court. Shemayah and Avtalion, who were righteous converts,[14] and their court re-

9 By listing the entire chain of tradition, the Rambam demonstrates how the Oral Law was transmitted in a continuous chain and was not the invention of the later Sages. However, beyond this obvious intent, the Rambam had another goal in mind. In his Introduction to *Sefer HaMitzvot* (where he outlines some of his deliberations about the composition of the *Mishneh Torah),* the Rambam writes:

> I chose to omit the supports and proofs [for the laws], and instead mention the major figures who transmitted the tradition. Thus, I will not say "These are the words of Rabbi—," or "Rabbi— says such and such" regarding each particular matter. Instead, I will mention all the sages of the Mishnah and the Talmud, of blessed memory, in general at the beginning of the text. I will state that all the judgments of the Torah— i.e., the Oral Law—were received and transmitted from so-and-so to so-and-so, until Ezra and until Moses. I will mention together with [the leading sage of the generation], who received the tradition, the other well-known personalities in his generation whose position in the chain of tradition is equivalent to his. All this [will be done] out of a desire for brevity.

The Rambam's willingness to sacrifice the mention of the sources for his decisions in favor of a brief and clear text became a major issue with regard to the acceptance of the Mishneh Torah by other rabbis. The Ra'avad writes:

> This author abandoned the practice of all the previous authors, who would bring supports for their statements and quote them in the name of their sources. This was of great benefit because, at times, a judge would presume to forbid or permit [something] based on a specific source. If he knew that a greater authority holds a different opinion, he would retract his. However, in this instance, I do not know why I should retract from the tradition I received and my sources because of [the statements] in this work by this author.

Afterwards, the Rambam himself regretted his original decision. In a responsum, he wrote that he desired to add the sources on which the decisions of the Mishneh Torah were based. Unfortunately, the Rambam himself never succeeded in composing such a text, and the task of discovering these sources has been left to the sages of subsequent generations.

10 See *Bava Batra* 121b.

11 Jeremiah and Baruch witnessed the destruction of the First Temple. After Jeremiah's death, Baruch went to Babylon and taught Torah to the exiles there.

12 The *Anshei K'nesset Hagedolah* presided over the return to Zion at the beginning of the Second Temple period and set the foundations for the reconstruction of the nation.

13 These two sages begin the line of *zugot* (pairs) mentioned in the first chapter of *Avot*. The first of the sages mentioned was the *nasi* (head of the academy), and the second the *av beit din* (head of the court).

14 See *Eduyot* 1:3 and *Gittin* ,57b. It is difficult to understand why the Rambam mentions Shemayah and Avtalion's ancestry. On the contrary, the fact that they were converts raises serious questions ceived the tradition from Yehudah and Shimon and their court.

Hillel and Shammai and their court received the tradition from Shemayah and Avtalion and their court. Rabban Yochanan ben Zakkai and Rabbi Shimon, the son of Hillel the elder, received the tradition from Hillel [and Shammai] and his [their] court[s].[15]

Rabban Yochanan ben Zakkai had five students [who were] great sages and received the tradition from him. They were: Rabbi Eleazar the great, Rabbi Yehoshua, Rabbi Yosse the priest, Rabbi Shimon ben Netanel and Rabbi Elazar ben Arach. Rabbi Akiva ben Yosef received from Rabbi Eleazar the great. Yosef, his father, was a righteous convert.

Rabbi Yishmael and Rabbi Meir, a son of righteous converts, received the tradition from Rabbi Akiva. Rabbi Meir and his colleagues also received the tradition from Rabbi Yishmael. The colleagues of Rabbi Meir include Rabbi Yehudah, Rabbi Yosse, Rabbi Shimon, Rabbi Nechemiah, Rabbi Elazar ben Shamu'a, Rabbi Yochanan the shoemaker, Shimon ben Azzai, and Rabbi Chananiah ben Teradion.[16]

Similarly, Rabbi Akiva's colleagues also received the tradition from Rabbi Eleazar the great. Rabbi Akiva's colleagues include Rabbi Tarfon—the teacher of Rabbi Yosse of the Galil—Rabbi Shimon ben Elazar, and Rabbi Yochanan ben Nuri.

Rabban Gamliel the elder received the tradition from Rabban Shimon, his father—the son of Hillel the elder. Rabban Shimon, his son, received the tradition from him. Rabban Gamliel, his son, received the tradition from him and Rabban Shimon, his son, received the tradition from him.

Rabbi Yehudah, the son of Rabban Shimon and referred to as Rabbenu Hakadosh ("our saintly teacher"),[17] received the tradition from his father, from Rabbi Elazar ben Shamu'a, and from Rabban Shimon and his colleagues.

Rabbenu Hakadosh composed the Mishnah. From the days of Moses, our teacher, until Rabbenu Hakadosh, no one had composed a text for the purpose of teaching the Oral Law in public. Instead, in each generation, the head of the court or the prophet of that generation would take notes of the teachings which he received from his masters for himself, and teach them verbally in public. Similarly, according to his own potential, each individual would write notes for himself of what he heard regarding the explanation of the Torah, its laws, and the new concepts that were deduced in each generation concerning laws that were not communicated by the oral tradition, but rather deduced using one of the thirteen principles of Biblical exegesis and accepted by the high court.

This situation continued until [the age of] Rabbenu Hakadosh. He collected all the teachings, all the laws, and all the explanations and commentaries that were heard from Moses, our teacher, and which were taught by the courts in each generation concerning the entire Torah. From all these, he composed the text of the Mishnah. He taught it to the Sages in public and revealed it to the Jewish people, who all wrote it down. They spread it in all places so that the Oral Law would not be forgotten by the Jewish people.

Why did Rabbenu Hakadosh make [such an innovation] instead of perpetuating the status quo? Because

as to why they were allowed to serve as *nasi* and *av beit din*. (See *Hilchot Melachim* 1:4 and the commentary in the Moznaim edition of that Halachah.)

15 Rabban Yochanan ben Zakkai witnessed the destruction of the Second Temple. Before the fall of Jerusalem, he escaped with his students to Yavneh and laid a new foundation for our people's spiritual growth.

16 The commentaries have noted some apparent contradictions between the Rambam's statements here and those in the Introduction to his Commentary on the Mishnah. For example, in the Introduction to his Commentary on the Mishnah, the Rambam states that Rabbi Meir and Rabbi Nechemiah were different names for the same person, while here he mentions them as separate individuals. Similarly, in the Introduction to his Commentary on the Mishnah, the Rambam places Rabbi Chananiah ben Teradion in the first generation of sages following the Temple's destruction, while here he places him in the third generation.
The Mishneh Torah is a later work, and it is possible that the Rambam changed his thinking on these particulars before its composition.

17 In the Introduction to his Commentary on the Mishnah, the Rambam explains that Rabbi Yehudah HaNasi merited the title Rabbenu Hakadosh (our saintly teacher), because "he possessed all the desired and good qualities."

he saw the students becoming fewer, new difficulties constantly arising, the Roman Empire[18] spreading itself throughout the world and becoming more powerful, and the Jewish people wandering and becoming dispersed to the far ends of the world. [Therefore,] he composed a single text that would be available to everyone, so that it could be studied quickly and would not be forgotten.[19] Throughout his entire life, he and his court taught the Mishnah to the masses.

These are the great Sages who were part of the court of Rabbenu Hakadosh and who received the tradition from him: His sons, Shimon and Gamliel, Rabbi Effess, Rabbi Chanina ben Chama, Rabbi Chiyya, Rav, Rabbi Yannai, bar Kafra, Shemuel, Rabbi Yochanan, Rabbi Hoshaia. Thousands and myriads of other sages received the tradition from [Rabbenu Hakadosh] together with these great sages.

Even though all of the eleven sages mentioned above received the tradition from Rabbenu Hakadosh and attended his study sessions, [there are differences between them. At that time,] Rabbi Yochanan was of lesser stature. Afterwards, he became a disciple of Rabbi Yannai and received instruction from him. Similarly, Rav received the tradition from Rabbi Yannai, and Shemuel received the tradition from Rabbi Chanina ben Chama.[20]

Rav composed the *Sifra* and the *Sifre* to explain the sources for the Mishnah. Rabbi Chiyya composed the *Tosefta*[21] to explain the subjects [discussed in] the Mishnah. Rabbi Hoshaia and bar Kafra composed *baraitot* to explain the matters [discussed in] the Mishnah. Rabbi Yochanan composed the Jerusalem Talmud in *Eretz Yisrael* approximately three hundred years after the destruction of the Temple.[22]

Among the great sages who received the tradition from Rav and Shemuel were:[23] Rav Huna, Rav Yehudah, Rav Nachman, and Rav Kahana. Among the great sages who received the tradition from Rabbi Yochanan[24] were: Ravvah bar bar Channah, Rav Ami, Rav Assi, Rav Dimi, and Rav Avin.

Among the Sages who received the tradition from Rav Huna and Rav Yehudah were Rabbah and Rav Yosef. Among the sages who received the tradition from Rabbah and Rav Yosef were Abbaye and Ravva. Both of them also received the tradition from Rav Nachman. Among the Sages who received the tradition from Ravva were Rav Ashi and Ravina. Mar bar Rav Ashi received the tradition from Rav Ashi, his father, and from Ravina.

Thus, there were forty generations from Rav Ashi back to Moses, our teacher, of blessed memory. They were:

1) Rav Ashi [received the tradition] from Ravva.

2) Ravva [received the tradition] from Rabbah.

3) Rabbah [received the tradition] from Rav Huna.

4) Rav Huna [received the tradition] from Rabbi Yochanan, Rav, and Shemuel.

5) Rabbi Yochanan, Rav, and Shemuel [received the tradition] from Rabbenu Hakadosh.

18 The Roman Empire systematically attempted to suppress the study of Torah in all the lands under its control.

19 Though Rabbi Yehudah HaNasi's composition of the Mishnah is a monumental achievement in its own right, perhaps the Rambam elaborates in his description of it because of the parallels to his own composition of the *Mishneh Torah*.

20 Rav and Shemuel represent the first generation of Amoraim, the age in which the center of Torah study shifted from *Eretz Yisrael* to Babylonia.

21 In the Introduction to his Commentary on the Mishnah, the Rambam explains Rabbi Chiyya's contribution as follows:
He followed his master's [Rabbi Yehudah HaNasi's] footsteps [in composing a text for the public] to explain the matters he saw to be confusing in his master's work.
This was called the *Tosefta*. Its intent was to explain the Mishnah and expound upon concepts that would require much effort to be derived from the Mishnah... to show how these ideas could be developed and deduced from the Mishnah.

22 Thus, according to the Rambam, the approximate date of the composition of the Jerusalem Talmud was the year 4025 (365 C.E.).
The commentaries have not found an explicit source supporting the Rambam's contention that Rabbi Yochanan composed the Jerusalem Talmud. Indeed, it appears that the final text of that work was composed by Rabbi Mannah and Rabbi Yosse ben Rabbi Bun approximately one hundred years after Rabbi Yochanan's death. Some commentaries explain that Rabbi Yochanan laid the foundation for the text that was completed by the later sages.

23 In Babylonia.

24 In *Eretz Yisrael*.

6) Rabbenu Hakadosh [received the tradition] from Rabbi Shimon, his father.

7) Rabbi Shimon [received the tradition] from Rabban Gamliel, his father.

8) Rabban Gamliel [received the tradition] from Rabban Shimon, his father.

9) Rabban Shimon [received the tradition] from Rabban Gamliel, the elder, his father.

10) Rabban Gamliel, the elder, [received the tradition] from Rabban Shimon, his father.

11) Rabban Shimon [received the Tradition] from Hillel, his father, and Shammai.

12) Hillel and Shammai [received the tradition] from Shemayah and Avtalion.

13) Shemayah and Avtalion [received the tradition] from Yehudah and Shimon [ben Shatach].

14) Yehudah and Shimon [received the tradition] from Yehoshua ben Perachiah and Nittai of Arbel.

15) Yehoshua and Nittai [received the tradition] from Yosse ben Yo'ezer and Yosef ben Yochanan.

16) Yosse ben Yo'ezer and Yosef ben Yochanan [received the tradition] from Antignos.

17) Antignos [received the tradition] from Shimon the Just.

18) Shimon the Just [received the tradition] from Ezra.

19) Ezra [received the tradition] from Baruch.

20) Baruch [received the tradition] from Jeremiah.

21) Jeremiah [received the tradition] from Tzefaniah.

22) Tzefaniah [received the tradition] from Chabbakuk.

23) Chabbakuk [received the tradition] from Nachum.

24) Nachum [received the tradition] from Yoel.

25) Yoel [received the tradition] from Michah.

26) Michah [received the tradition] from Isaiah.

27) Isaiah [received the tradition] from Amos.

28) Amos [received the tradition] from Hoshea.

29) Hoshea [received the tradition] from Zechariah.

30) Zechariah [received the tradition] from Yehoyada.

31) Yehoyada [received the tradition] from Elisha.

32) Elisha [received the tradition] from Elijah.

33) Elijah [received the tradition] from Achiah.

34) Achiah [received the tradition] from David.

35) David [received the tradition] from Shemuel.

36) Shemuel [received the tradition] from Eli.

37) Eli [received the tradition] from Pinchas.

38) Pinchas [received the tradition] from Joshua.

39) Joshua [received the tradition] from Moses, our teacher.

40) Moses, our teacher, [received the tradition] from the Almighty.

Thus, [the source of] all these people's knowledge is God, the Lord of Israel.

All the sages who were mentioned were the leaders of the generations. Among them were heads of academies, heads of the exile, and members of the great Sanhedrin. Together with them in each generation, there were thousands and myriads that heard their [teachings].

Ravina and Rav Ashi were the final generation of the Sages of the Talmud. Rav Ashi composed the Babylonian Talmud in Shin'ar approximately one hundred years after Rabbi Yochanan composed the Jerusalem Talmud.[25] The intent of both the Talmuds is to elucidate the words of the Mishnah, to explain its deeper points, and [to relate] the new matters that were developed by each court from the era of Rabbenu Hakadosh until the composition of the Talmud.

From the entire [body of knowledge stemming from] the two Talmuds, the *Tosefta,* the *Sifra,* and the *Sifre,* can be derived the forbidden and the permitted, the impure and the pure, the liable and those who are free of liability, the invalid and the valid as was received [in tradition], one person from another, [in a chain extending back] to Moses at Mount Sinai.

Also, [the sources mentioned above] relate those matters which were decreed by the sages and prophets in each generation in order to "build a fence around the Torah." We were explicitly taught about [this practice] by Moses, as [implied by Leviticus 18:30]: "And you shall observe My precepts," [which can be interpreted to mean]: "Make safeguards for My precepts."[26]

Similarly, it includes the customs and ordinances that were ordained or practiced in each generation according to [the judgment of] the governing court of that generation.[27] It is forbidden to deviate from [these decisions], as [implied by Deuteronomy 17:11]: "Do not deviate from the instructions that they will give you, left or right."

It also includes marvelous judgments and laws which were not received from Moses, but rather were derived by the courts of the [later] generations based on the principles of Biblical exegesis. The elders of those generations made these decisions and concluded that this was the law. Rav Ashi included in the Talmud this entire [body of knowledge, stemming] from the era of Moses, our teacher, until his [own] era.

The Sages of the Mishnah also composed other texts to explain the words of the Torah. Rabbi Hoshaia, the disciple of Rabbenu Hakadosh, composed an explanation of the book of Genesis.[28] Rabbi Yishmael [composed] an explanation beginning at "These are the names" [the beginning of the book of Exodus,] until the conclusion of the Torah. This is called the *Mechilta.* Rabbi Akiva also composed a *Mechilta.*[29] Other Sages of the following generations composed other [collections of the] interpretations [of verses] *(Medrashim).* All of these works were composed before the Babylonian Talmud.

Thus, Ravina, Rav Ashi, and their colleagues represent the final era of the great Sages of Israel who transmitted the Oral Law. They passed decrees, ordained practices, and put into effect customs. These decrees, ordinances, and customs spread out among the entire Jewish people in all the places where they lived.[30]

After the court of Rav Ashi composed the Talmud and completed it in the time of his son, the Jewish people became further dispersed throughout all the lands, reaching the distant extremes and the far removed islands. Strife sprung up throughout the world, and the paths of travel became endangered by

25 Thus, according to the Rambam, the approximate date of the composition of the Babylonian Talmud was 4125 (465 C.E.).
The commentaries point to *Bava Metzia* 86a, which relates that "Rav Ashi and Ravina were the final authorities with regard to instruction," as the source for the Rambam's statements. From the Rambam's later statements, it appears that in this instance as well, Rav Ashi laid the foundation for the Talmud. However, the composition of the text was completed by Ravina Zuta, Mar bar Rav Ashi, and Rav Yosse more than seventy years after Rav Ashi's death.

26 In the Introduction to his Commentary on the Mishnah, the Rambam deals with this subject at length, citing as examples, the prohibition of eating fowl together with milk and the eighteen decrees passed by the School of Hillel and the School of Shammai.

27 In the Introduction to his Commentary on the Mishnah, the Rambam also mentions these two categories, describing them as:
Laws that were established after meditation on the proper structure for interpersonal relations, without adding or detracting from the words of the Torah, or matters that [were instituted] for the spiritual betterment of mankind.
Among the examples of such laws he cites are: Hillel's institution of the *Pruzbul* and the ordinances of Ushia, which require a father to support his children. The Rambam also discusses these three categories of Rabbinic decrees in *Hilchot Mamrim,* Chapters 1 and 2.

28 The Rambam is referring to *Bereshit Rabbah.*

29 Today, this collection of teachings is known as Mechilta D'Rabbi Shimon bar Yochai.

30 Because these ordinances were universally accepted by the Jewish people, their observance became mandatory, as the Rambam explains further on.

troops. Torah study decreased and the Jews ceased entering their yeshivot in the thousands and myriads, as was customary previously.

Instead, individuals, the remnants whom God called, would gather in each city and country, occupy themselves in Torah study, and [devote themselves] to understanding the texts of the Sages and learning the path of judgment from them.

Every court that was established after the conclusion of the Talmud, regardless of the country in which it was established, issued decrees, enacted ordinances, and established customs for the people of that country—or those of several countries. These practices, however, were not accepted throughout the Jewish people, because of the distance between [their different] settlements and the disruption of communication [between them].

Since each of these courts were considered to be individuals—and the High Court of 71 judges had been defunct for many years before the composition of the Talmud—people in one country could not be compelled to follow the practices of another country, nor is one court required to sanction decrees which another court had declared in its locale. Similarly, if one of the Geonim interpreted the path of judgment in a certain way, while the court which arose afterward interpreted the proper approach to the matter in a different way, the [opinion of the] first [need] not be adhered to [absolutely]. Rather, whichever [position] appears to be correct—whether the first or the last—is accepted.

These [principles apply regarding] the judgments, decrees, ordinances, and customs which were established after the conclusion of the Talmud. However, all the matters mentioned by the Babylonian[31] Talmud are incumbent on the entire Jewish people to follow. We must compel each and every city and each country to accept all the customs that were put into practice by the Sages of the Talmud, to pass decrees paralleling their decrees, and to observe their ordinances, since all the matters in the Babylonian Talmud were accepted by the entire Jewish people.

The [Talmudic] Sages who established ordinances and decrees, put customs into practice, arrived at legal decisions, and taught [the people] concerning certain judgments represented the totality of the Sages of Israel or, at least, the majority of them. They received the tradition regarding the fundamental aspects of the Torah in its entirety, generation after generation, [in a chain beginning with] Moses, our teacher.

All the Sages who arose after the conclusion of the Talmud and comprehended its [wisdom] and whose prowess gained them a reputation are called the Geonim. All these Geonim that arose in Eretz Yisrael, Babylonia, Spain, and France taught the approach of the Talmud, revealing its hidden secrets and explaining its points, since [the Talmud's] manner of expression is very deep. Furthermore, it is composed in Aramaic, with a mixture of other tongues. This language was understood by the people of Babylonia in the era when the Talmud was composed. However, in other places, and even in Babylonia in the era of the Geonim, a person cannot understand this language unless he has studied it.[32]

The inhabitants of each city would ask many questions of each Gaon who lived in their age, to explain the difficult matters that existed in the Talmud. They would reply to them according to their wisdom. The people who had asked the questions would collect the replies and make texts from them, so that they could consider them in depth.[33] Also, the Geonim of each generation composed texts to explain the Talmud. Some of them explained only certain halachot. Others explained selected chapters that had created difficulty in their age. Still others explained entire tractates and orders. Also, [the Geonim] composed

[31] Perhaps by specifying "the Babylonian Talmud," the Rambam is alluding to the halachic principle that whenever there is a difference between the decisions of the Babylonian and the Jerusalem Talmuds, those of the Babylonian Talmud are followed.

[32] In his Introduction to *Sefer HaMitzvot*, the Rambam explains that he chose to compose the *Mishneh Torah* in Mishnaic Hebrew rather than in Aramaic in order to make it more accessible to the common man.

[33] The Rambam is referring to the body of responsa *(She'elot UTshuvot)* which began to accumulate from the many questions circulated among the different Jewish communities in the diaspora.

[texts recording] the decisions of Torah law regarding what is permitted and what is forbidden, when one is liable and when one is free of liability, with regard to subjects that were necessary at the time, so that they would be accessible to the grasp of a person who could not comprehend the depths of the Talmud.[34] This is the work of God, which was performed by all the Geonim of Israel from the completion of the Talmud until the present date, 1108 years after the destruction of the Temple, 4937 years after the creation of the world.[35]

At this time, we have been beset by additional difficulties, everyone feels [financial] pressure, the wisdom of our Sages has become lost, and the comprehension of our men of understanding has become hidden. Therefore, those explanations, laws, and replies which the Geonim composed and considered to be fully explained material have become difficult to grasp in our age, and only a select few comprehend these matters in the proper way.

Needless to say, [there is confusion] with regard to the Talmud itself—both the Jerusalem and Babylonian Talmuds—the *Sifra,* the *Sifre,* and the *Tosefta,* for they require a breadth of knowledge, a spirit of wisdom, and much time, for appreciating the proper path regarding what is permitted and forbidden, and the other laws of the Torah.

Therefore, I girded my loins—I, Moses, the son of Maimon, of Spain.[36] I relied upon the Rock, blessed be He. I contemplated all these texts and sought to compose [a work which would include the conclusions] derived from all these texts regarding the forbidden and the permitted, the impure and the pure, and the remainder of the Torah's laws, all in clear and concise terms, so that the entire Oral Law could be organized in each person's mouth without questions or objections.

Instead of [arguments], this one claiming such and another such, [this text will allow for] clear and correct statements based on the judgments that result from all the texts and explanations mentioned above, from the days of Rabbenu Hakadosh until the present. [This will make it possible] for all the laws to be revealed to both those of lesser stature and those of greater stature, regarding every single mitzvah, and also all the practices that were ordained by the Sages and the Prophets.

To summarize: [The intent of this text is] that a person will not need another text at all with regard to any Jewish law. Rather, this text will be a compilation of the entire Oral Law, including also the ordinances, customs, and decrees that were enacted from the time of Moses, our teacher, until the completion of the Talmud,[37] as were explained by the Geonim in the texts they composed after the Talmud.

Therefore, I have called this text, *Mishneh Torah* ["the second to the Torah,"[38] with the intent that] a person should first study the Written Law, and then study this text[39] and comprehend the entire Oral Law from it, without having to study any other text between the two.

I saw fit to divide this text into [separate] halachot[40] pertaining to each [particular] subject, and, with-

34 In the Introduction to his Commentary on the Mishnah, the Rambam mentions some of these texts: *Halachot Gedolot, Halachot Pesukot,* the *She'iltot* of Rav Achai Gaon, and the *Halachot* of Rav Yitzchak Alfasi.

35 This corresponds to the year 1177 C.E. Apparently, the Rambam composed the *Mishneh Torah* over a number of years, constantly revising his work. Thus, in *Hilchot Kiddush HaChodesh* 11:16, he mentions the date of the composition of the text as 4938, one year later, and in *Hilchot Shemitot V'Yovalot,* he mentions the date 4936, one year earlier.

36 Though the Rambam mentions his nationality when stating his name in some of his other works as well (see *Iggeret HaShmad),* it is possible that he had a specific intention in doing so here. Despite his desire and intention for the *Mishneh Torah* to be universally accepted, he knew that other customs were followed in the Ashkenazic community. By mentioning his country of origin, he could be alluding to the fact that some of the customs he mentioned were specific to Jews of that background *(Yayin Malchut).*

37 For it is only these laws that are binding on the entire Jewish people, as explained above.

38 As mentioned above, there were many rabbis who considered the Rambam's intention in the composition of this text and, in particular, the name he chose for it, as presumptuous. Indeed, for that reason the name *Mishneh Torah is* rarely used. Instead, the text is commonly referred to as the *Yad HaChazakah* ("The Strong Hand") [so called because the Hebrew is numerically equivalent to fourteen, the number of books in the *Mishneh Torah*], or simply "the Rambam."

39 The Rambam's statements imply that he desired the *Mishneh Torah* to be studied in the order in which it was composed, so that a reader can receive a full picture of the Oral Law.

40 These *halachot* are comparable to sections within a book.

in the context of a single subject, to divide those halachot into chapters. Each and every chapter is divided into smaller halachot so that they can be ordered in one's memory.

[Regarding] the halachot which pertain to specific subjects: Some of the halachot contain the laws governing only one mitzvah, this being a mitzvah that has many matters of the tradition [associated with it] and is a subject in its own right. Other halachot contain the laws governing many mitzvot, since they deal with the same subject matter, for I have divided this text according to topics, not according to the number of mitzvot, as will become clear to the reader.[41]

The number of mitzvot which are incumbent on us at all times[42] is 613. 248 are positive commandments; an allusion to their [number], the number of limbs in the human body.[43] 365 are negative commandments (prohibitions); an allusion to their [number,] the number of days in a solar year.[44]

Mishneh Torah [Moznaim Publishers: New York; Jerusalem, 2010]
Reprinted with permission

LOST IN TRANSLATION?

BY RABBI BEREL BELL

The first day of the Hebrew month of Sh'vat marks a memorable occasion of special importance to publications such as this one. On this day, approximately one month before his death, Moses "began to explain the Torah" in 70 languages. The Torah viewed this event in a positive light. In another situation, though, translating Torah was denounced in the harshest terms.

The Talmud relates that many years after Moses translated the Torah into 70 languages King Ptolemy requested that the Sages translate the Torah into Greek. It further states that, "This day was as bad for the Jewish people as the day on which the golden calf was made." It was so unfavorable, in fact, that in the past this day (the 8th of Tevet) was actually observed as a fast day.

How can these two statements be reconciled? Even if we find negative points in translating the Torah why should it be compared with something as bad as the golden calf?

If Only I Knew Hebrew

We must first make an observation that is obvious to a person who is fluent in Hebrew yet difficult to understand for someone who isn't. Simply put, the Five Books of Moses (chumash) in their Hebrew form, standing alone, are virtually incomprehensible.

This does not merely mean that without commentary one will gain superficial understanding but not appreciate the depth. Even more so, without commentary, one cannot achieve even a minimal understanding of the text. For this reason, it is inaccurate to call the Oral Tradition a "commentary" to the Written Torah. The English word "commentary" is usually

Rabbi Berel Bell. Rabbinical judge and pedagogue. Rabbi Bell is the founding dean of Bais Chaya Mushka Seminary in Montreal and is a member of the Rabbinical Court of Montreal. He is a sought-after educational consultant and the author of the JLI course *From Sinai to Cyberspace: How Ancient Wisdom Guides a Modern World.*

41 In his Introduction to *Sefer HaMitzvot*, the Rambam explains that he chose to structure the text in this manner in order to make the subject matter more accessible to the reader.

42 For there are some commandments—e.g., the requirement to dedicate the spoil taken from Midian (see Numbers, Chapter 31)—that were recorded in the Torah, but applied only in those specific circumstances.

43 In Sefer HaMitzvot, the Rambam quotes the *Midrash Tanchumah (Ki Tetzei)*, which states that it is as if each limb of the body is saying, "Do a mitzvah with me."

44 Thus, it is as if each day of the year is saying, "Do not commit a transgression on me" (*ibid.*).

used for something which gives greater understanding to something already at least partly understood. The Oral Tradition, on the other hand, gives us our basic understanding of the material. It might be better termed an "explanation," or a kind of "dictionary" used to decipher the Torah's words.

Let's take an example from this week's Torah portion. What was the fourth plague? A quick peek will reveal that it was (in Hebrew) arov. If you don't know the Hebrew, you need not feel too jealous, because knowing the translation of arov in not a great help.

The word means "a mixture." But a mixture of what? A mixture of burning cement and tar? Music played in different keys? Poison in the water supply? Armed with nothing more than Scripture and knowledge of Hebrew, the possibilities are endless.

Anyone with an English Chumash (or Hagaddah) knows by now that arov refers to a mixture of different wild beasts. To him, the verse is simple and straightforward. There is no room for question or misunderstanding.

One who studies the Hebrew, on the other hand, knows that the verse cannot be understood without the Oral Torah. According to the Oral Torah the word arov refers both to wild beasts and to flies!

Furthermore, he understands why the Torah indeed used a somewhat ambiguous word rather than clearly stating (in Hebrew, of course) "wild beasts." This is because the Torah also wants to allude to the flies.

He will not be surprised to learn that this word alludes to other matters as well. These other connotations make arov clearer; they help reveal why arov was used rather than a less ambiguous word. The ambiguity allows the Torah to communicate on many different levels simultaneously.

Institutionalized Ignorance

This dimension of the Torah is lost to one who studies it only in translation, for translations are clear and unambiguous. There is no doubt as to what is meant, and only rarely could a word be construed as alluding to more than one thing.

When he hears that the Midrash says that the word arov (also) refers to flies, he will find it hard to believe —he himself read the verse, and it says "wild beast" not "flies"!

He will perhaps wonder why the Midrash is so interested in making things difficult by putting in concepts which "aren't even written." Little does he realize that "wild beasts" are also not described in the verse, but just given as an explanation in the Oral Tradition for the word arov.

When learning in translation, people (erroneously) are sure they understand; in the original Hebrew, they know that they do not fully understand.

In translation, the Torah can be stripped of its holiness, and presented, G-d forbid, as archaic literature. With such a Torah, some people feel no need to look to it for guidance, nor to follow its laws. They are convinced that these laws are "commentary," and are somehow not really part of the Torah. "Where does it say I shouldn't drive on the Sabbath?" they claim. "All it says is that one should rest!"

For this reason, the Ptolemy translation was viewed as a potential tragedy. Such a word-for-word translation opened the door for ignorance and misunderstanding, for shaking off all the laws of the Torah.

Moses, on the other hand, did not just translate the Torah: he performed the task of "explaining" the Torah in all these languages. This is not just something positive, but a vitally important mission which remains binding to this very day.

From Sinai to Cyberspace [Jewish Learning Institute: New York, 2006], pp. 27–28

LESSON 2

DECIPHERING CODE

Our study of Torah is not limited to passive transmission of received teachings. Through a sophisticated system of interpretation, we are able to apply the Torah to new circumstances and technologies. This explains why an ancient Torah remains relevant to this very day.

What are the rules for interpreting the Torah and deriving new applications? Who is tasked with deriving new concepts and rulings? And how great a role does human innovation play in this process?

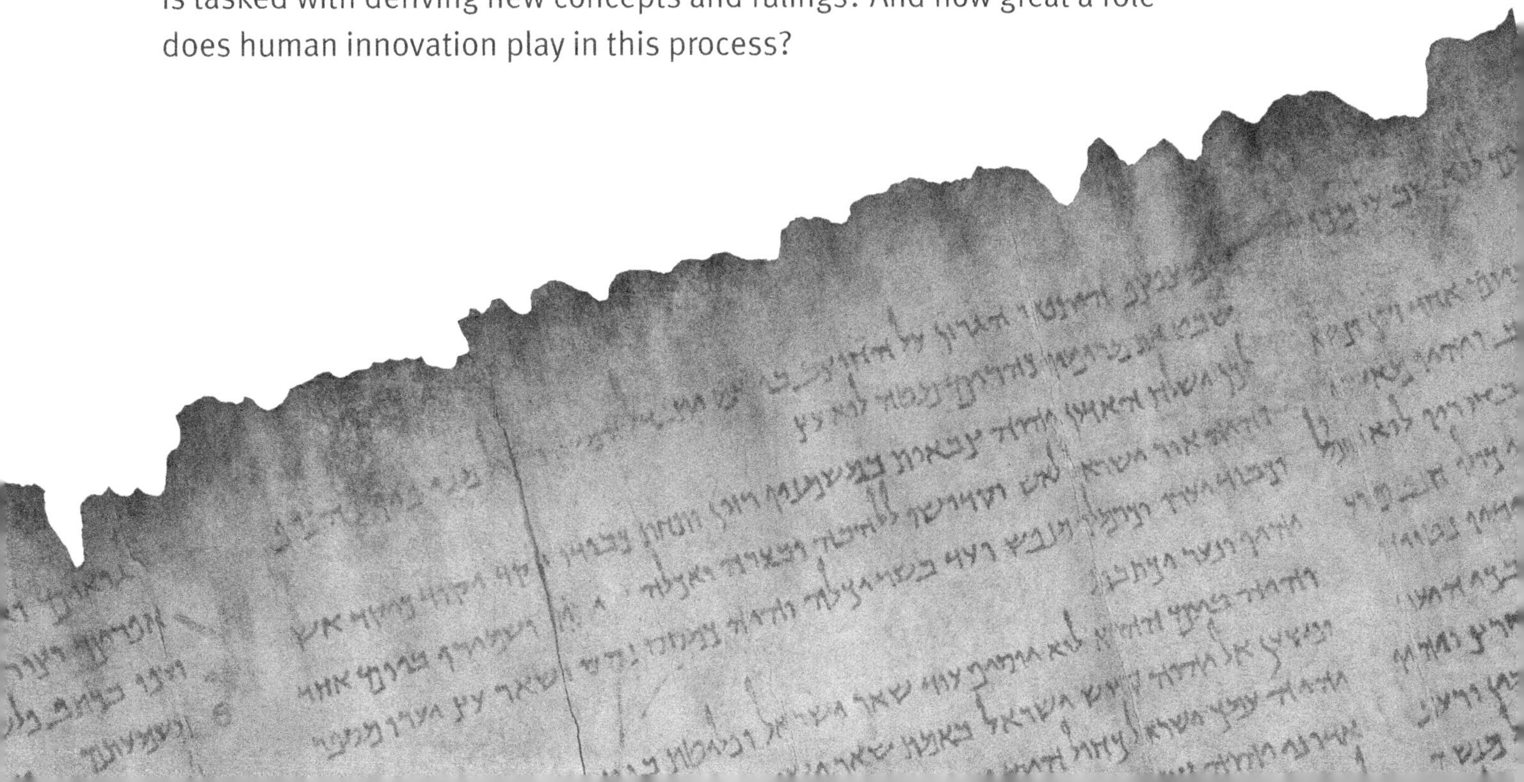

"Derived" Oral Torah

Wheat and Flax

Text 1

Midrash, *Eliyahu Zuta* 2

מִקְרָא וּמִשְׁנָה שְׁנֵיהֶם מִפִּי הַגְּבוּרָה נֶאֶמְרוּ. וּמַה בֵּין מִקְרָא לְמִשְׁנָה?

מָשְׁלוּ מָשָׁל, לְמָה הַדָּבָר דוֹמֶה, לְמֶלֶךְ בָּשָׂר וָדָם שֶׁהָיָה לוֹ שְׁנֵי עֲבָדִים, וְהָיָה אוֹהֲבָן אַהֲבָה גְדוֹלָה, וְנָתַן לָזֶה קַב חִטִּין וְלָזֶה קַב חִטִּין, וּלְכָל אֶחָד מֵהֶם נָתַן גַּם כֵּן אֲגוּדָה שֶׁל פִּשְׁתָּן. הַפִּקֵּחַ שֶׁבָּהֶן מַה עָשָׂה, נָטַל אֶת הַפִּשְׁתָּן וְאָרַג מַפָּה יָפָה, וְנָטַל אֶת הַחִטִּין וַעֲשָׂאָן סוֹלֶת, וּבֵרְרָה, וְטָחֲנָה, וְלָשָׁה, וַאֲפָאָה, וְסִידְּרָה עַל הַשֻּׁלְחָן, וּפֵרַס עָלֶיהָ מַפָּה יָפָה, וְהִנִּיחוֹ עַד שֶׁלֹּא בָּא הַמֶּלֶךְ. וְהַטִּפֵּשׁ שֶׁבָּהֶן לֹא עָשָׂה כְּלוּם.

לְיָמִים בָּא הַמֶּלֶךְ לְתוֹךְ בֵּיתוֹ וְאָמַר לִשְׁנֵי עֲבָדָיו, בָּנַי, הָבִיאוּ לִי מַה שֶּׁנָּתַתִּי לָכֶם. אֶחָד מֵהֶן הוֹצִיא אֶת הַפַּת שֶׁל סוֹלֶת עַל הַשֻּׁלְחָן וּמַפָּה הַיָּפָה פְּרוּסָה עָלָיו, וְאֶחָד הוֹצִיא אֶת הַחִטִּין בְּקוּפָּה, וַאֲגוּדָה שֶׁל פִּשְׁתָּן עֲלֵיהֶן. אוֹי לָהּ לְאוֹתָהּ בּוּשָׁה, וְאוֹי לָהּ לְאוֹתָהּ כְּלִימָה . . .

כְּשֶׁנָּתַן הַקָּדוֹשׁ בָּרוּךְ הוּא אֶת הַתּוֹרָה לְיִשְׂרָאֵל, לֹא נְתָנָהּ לָהֶם אֶלָּא כְּחִטִּין לְהוֹצִיא מֵהֶן סוֹלֶת, וּכְפִשְׁתָּן לֶאֱרוֹג מֵהֶן בֶּגֶד.

Tana Devei Eliyahu

A midrashic work, sometimes referred to as *Seder Eliyahu*. Midrash is the designation of a particular genre of rabbinic literature usually forming a running commentary on specific books of the Bible. This work deals with the divine precepts, their rationales, and the importance of knowledge of Torah, prayer, and repentance. The work is divided into two sections: *Seder Eliyahu Rabah* and *Seder Eliyahu Zuta*.

Both the Written Torah and the Oral Torah are God-given. What is the difference between them?

This can be compared to a king who had two subjects whom he loved very much and to whom he gave each a measure of wheat and a bundle of flax. The wise subject took the flax and wove a beautiful cloth. He took the wheat, turned it into fine flour, sifted it, ground it, kneaded it, baked it, set it upon the table, and spread the cloth over it until the king came. But the foolish subject did nothing at all with what he was given.

When the king returned to his palace, he said to his two subjects, "My sons, bring me what I gave you." The wise subject presented the bread made from fine flour with the cloth spread over it. The foolish subject presented raw wheat in a container with the raw flax on top of it. How great was his shame and disgrace! . . .

When God gave Israel the Torah, He presented it only in the form of wheat and flax, leaving us to extract fine flour and to weave a garment.

QUESTION FOR DISCUSSION

Is Text 1 consistent with our definition and understanding of Oral Torah as presented in Lesson One?

FIGURE 2.1

Categories of Oral Torah

1	**Received**	God-given explanations for each of the commandments
2	**Derived**	Laws that we derive from the Written Torah and the Received Oral Torah
3		
4		

Why "Received" Isn't Enough

Text 2

Maimonides, Introduction to the Mishnah

Rabbi Moshe ben Maimon
(Maimonides, Rambam)
1135–1204

Halachist, philosopher, author, and physician. Maimonides was born in Cordoba, Spain. After the conquest of Cordoba by the Almohads, he fled Spain and eventually settled in Cairo, Egypt. There, he became the leader of the Jewish community and served as court physician to the vizier of Egypt. He is most noted for authoring the *Mishneh Torah*, an encyclopedic arrangement of Jewish law, and for his philosophical work, *Guide for the Perplexed*. His rulings on Jewish law are integral to the formation of halachic consensus.

אָמַר לוֹ ה', "בַּסֻּכּוֹת תֵּשְׁבוּ שִׁבְעַת יָמִים" (וַיִּקְרָא כג,מב). וְגַם הוֹדִיעוֹ ה' יִתְעַלֶּה שֶׁסֻּכָּה זוּ חוֹבַת הַזְּכָרִים וְלֹא הַנְּקֵבוֹת. וְאֵינָהּ חוֹבָה לְחוֹלִים וְלֹא לְהוֹלְכֵי דְרָכִים. וְאֵין מְסַכְּכִין אוֹתָהּ אֶלָּא בְּדָבָר הַצּוֹמֵחַ מִן הָאָרֶץ. וְאֵין מְסַכְּכִין אוֹתָהּ לֹא בְצֶמֶר וְלֹא בְמֶשִׁי וְלֹא בְכֵלִים, וַאֲפִילוּ מִן הַצּוֹמֵחַ בָּאָרֶץ כְּגוֹן הַמַּחְצְלָאוֹת וְהַבְּגָדִים. וְהָאֲכִילָה וְהַשְּׁתִיָּה וְהַשֵּׁינָה יִהְיוּ בָּהּ כָּל שִׁבְעַת הַיָּמִים. וְלֹא יְהֵא חֲלָלָהּ פָּחוֹת מִשִּׁבְעָה טְפָחִים אוֹרֶךְ עַל שִׁבְעָה טְפָחִים רוֹחַב. וְלֹא יְהֵא גָבְהָהּ פָּחוֹת מֵעֲשָׂרָה טְפָחִים.

God told Moses [the written verse], "You shall live in booths for seven days" (Leviticus 23:42). He also told Moses that this mitzvah is obligatory for males but not for females; that the sick and travelers are not required to fulfill this mitzvah; that the roof of the *sukah* must be made of something that grows from the ground; that the roof cannot be made of wool, silk, or any other item that does not grow from the ground, nor from mats and clothing, even if they were made from something that grows from the ground; that one shall eat, drink, and sleep in the *sukah* for all seven days; that the size of the *sukah* shall be no smaller than seven handbreadths long by seven handbreadths wide; and that the *sukah* should be no less than ten handbreadths in height.

Text 3

Rabbi Yosef Albo, *Sefer Ha'ikarim* 3:23

לְפִי שֶׁאִי אֶפְשָׁר שֶׁתִּהְיֶה תּוֹרַת הַשֵּׁם יִתְבָּרֵךְ שְׁלֵמָה בְּאוֹפֶן שֶׁתַּסְפִּיק בְּכָל הַזְּמַנִּים. לְפִי שֶׁהַפְּרָטִים הַמִּתְחַדְּשִׁים תָּמִיד בְּעִנְיְנֵי הָאֲנָשִׁים בְּמִשְׁפָּטִים וְהַדְּבָרִים הַנִּפְעָלִים הֵם רַבִּים מְאֹד מִשֶּׁיִּכְלְלֵם סֵפֶר.

It is impossible that God's Torah could ever be complete in such a way that it would be sufficient for all times, for there are constantly new details, judgments, and events in human affairs, and [the laws about these matters] would be far too numerous to be enumerated.

Rabbi Yosef Albo
ca. 1380–1444

Spanish rabbi and philosopher. A student of Rabbi Chasdai Crescas, Albo is renowned for his philosophical work *Sefer Ha'ikarim* (*Book of Fundamentals*). The work stresses three fundamental aspects of Jewish belief: the existence of God, Torah from Sinai, and reward and punishment.

Rules of Derivation

The Need for a Framework

LEARNING EXERCISE 1

The Third Amendment to the United States Constitution states:

"No soldier shall, in time of peace be quartered in any house, without the consent of the Owner, nor in time of war, but in a manner to be prescribed by law."

Which of the following statements do you think can reasonably be derived from this amendment?

1. **It should be unconstitutional for a school to forbid teachers and principals from taking outside employment.**
   a. very reasonable derivation
   b. reasonable derivation
   c. not a reasonable derivation
   d. extremely unreasonable derivation

2. **It should be unconstitutional for the government to issue rent-control laws.**
   a. very reasonable derivation
   b. reasonable derivation
   c. not a reasonable derivation
   d. extremely unreasonable derivation

Text 4

Midrash, *Eliyahu Zuta* 2

מִקְרָא וּמִשְׁנָה שְׁנֵיהֶם מִפִּי הַגְּבוּרָה נֶאֱמְרוּ.

Both the Written Torah and the Oral Torah are God-given.

QUESTION FOR DISCUSSION

Can we assert that the Derived category of Oral Torah is God-given? What makes it so?

Text 5

Midrash Hagadol, Exodus 21:1

"וְאֵלֶּה הַמִּשְׁפָּטִים אֲשֶׁר תָּשִׂים לִפְנֵיהֶם" (שְׁמוֹת כא,א): רַבִּי יִשְׁמָעֵאל אוֹמֵר, אֵלּוּ שְׁלֹשׁ עֶשְׂרֵה מִדּוֹת שֶׁהַתּוֹרָה נִדְרֶשֶׁת בָּהֶן שֶׁנִּמְסְרוּ לוֹ לְמֹשֶׁה בְּסִינַי.

"These are the rules that you [Moses] shall set before them" (Exodus 21:1). Rabbi Yishmael says, "These are the thirteen hermeneutic rules of Torah derivation, which were given to Moses at Sinai."

Midrash Hagadol

A midrashic work on the five books of the Pentateuch. Midrash is the designation of a particular genre of rabbinic literature usually forming a running commentary on specific books of the Bible. *Midrash Hagadol* quotes widely from Talmud and other earlier midrashic works, serving as a valuable resource to reconstruct lost sections of Midrash. A traveler, Yaakov Sapir, first discovered the anonymous Midrash in Yemen in the middle of the 19th century. Some ascribe it to Rabbi Avraham, son of Maimonides.

FIGURE 2.2

Sudoku

				2	8		7	
			3					8
		8			1			4
	4					7		6
	8		7	5	6		4	
5		7					1	
9			8			6		
8					9			
	2		5	4				

Kal Vechomer

FIGURE 2.3

Kal Vechomer

Hebrew Name	Translation	Definition
Kal vechomer	Weak and strong; lenient and stringent; easy and hard	To infer from the less obvious case to the more obvious case; an *a fortiori* argument

Text 6a

Exodus 22:9–11

כִּי יִתֵּן אִישׁ אֶל רֵעֵהוּ חֲמוֹר אוֹ שׁוֹר אוֹ שֶׂה וְכָל בְּהֵמָה
לִשְׁמֹר וּמֵת אוֹ נִשְׁבַּר אוֹ נִשְׁבָּה . . . וְלֹא יְשַׁלֵּם.

וְאִם גָּנֹב יִגָּנֵב מֵעִמּוֹ יְשַׁלֵּם לִבְעָלָיו.

If a man gives his neighbor a donkey, a bull, a lamb, or any animal for safekeeping, and it dies, breaks a limb, or is captured . . . [the bailee] need not pay.

But if it is stolen from him, he shall pay its owner.

Text 6b

Exodus 22:13

וְכִי יִשְׁאַל אִישׁ מֵעִם רֵעֵהוּ וְנִשְׁבַּר אוֹ מֵת . . . שַׁלֵּם יְשַׁלֵּם.

If a person borrows [an animal] from his neighbor and it breaks a limb or dies . . . he shall surely pay.

LEARNING EXERCISE 2

Circle the correct answers per Text 6a and Text 6b.

	If the animal dies naturally . . .	If the animal is stolen . . .
Custodian	Liable Not liable Not sure	Liable Not liable Not sure
Borrower	Liable Not liable Not sure	Liable Not liable Not sure

Text 7a

Talmud, Bava Metsi'a 95a

מַה לִשְׁבוּרָה וּמֵתָה, דְלֹא אֶפְשָׁר לְמִיטְרַח וַאֲתוּיֵי, תֹּאמַר
בִּגְנֵיבָה וַאֲבֵידָה דְאֶפְשָׁר לְמִיטְרַח וַאֲתוּיֵי.

If the animal died or broke a limb, it is impossible for the owner to invest effort to retrieve it. But if the animal were stolen or lost, the owner can invest effort to retrieve it.

Babylonian Talmud

A literary work of monumental proportions that draws upon the legal, spiritual, intellectual, ethical, and historical traditions of Judaism. The 37 tractates of the Babylonian Talmud contain the teachings of the Jewish sages from the period after the destruction of the 2nd Temple through the 5th century CE. It has served as the primary vehicle for the transmission of the Oral Law and the education of Jews over the centuries; it is the entry point for all subsequent legal, ethical, and theological Jewish scholarship.

Text 7b

Ibid.

אַמַרְתְּ קַל וָחוֹמֶר:

וּמַה שׁוֹמֵר שָׂכָר, שֶׁפָּטוּר מִשְּׁבוּרָה וּמֵתָה, חַיָּיב בִּגְנֵיבָה וַאֲבֵידָה,
שׁוֹאֵל, שֶׁחַיָּיב בִּשְׁבוּרָה וּמֵתָה, אֵינוֹ דִין שֶׁחַיָּיב בִּגְנֵיבָה וַאֲבֵידָה.

וְזֶה הוּא קַל וָחוֹמֶר שֶׁאֵין עָלָיו תְּשׁוּבָה.

You shall say a *kal vechomer*:

If a paid custodian, who is exempt when the animal suffers a broken limb or death, is liable when the animal is stolen or lost, then a borrower, who is liable when the animal suffers a broken limb or death, is certainly liable when the animal is stolen or lost.

This *kal vechomer* is irrefutable.

Binyan Av

FIGURE 2.4

Binyan Av

Hebrew Name	Translation	Definition
Binyan av	A "parent" law from which a corollary is built	A law stated in one instance applies equally in different but similar instances.

Text 8a

Exodus 22:4

כִּי יַבְעֶר אִישׁ שָׂדֶה אוֹ כֶרֶם, וְשִׁלַּח אֶת בְּעִירֹה וּבִעֵר
בִּשְׂדֵה אַחֵר, מֵיטַב שָׂדֵהוּ וּמֵיטַב כַּרְמוֹ יְשַׁלֵּם.

If a person grazes [his livestock in] a field or a vineyard and lets his livestock loose so that it grazes in another's field, he must make restitution with the best of his field and the best of his vineyard.

Text 8b

Mechilta DeRabbi Shimon bar Yocha'i, ad loc.

"מֵיטַב שָׂדֵהוּ וּמֵיטַב כַּרְמוֹ יְשַׁלֵּם": זֶה בִּנְיַן אָב לְכָל
הַמְשַׁלֵּם קְנַס, שֶׁאֵין שָׁמִין לוֹ אֶלָּא מִן הָעִידִית.

"He must make restitution with the best of his field and the best of his vineyard." This is a *binyan av* for any case where someone pays restitution. The court appraises [and restitution is provided] from the offender's preferred field.

Mechilta DeRabbi Shimon bar Yocha'i

A midrashic text of unknown authorship on the Book of Exodus. Midrash is the designation of a particular genre of rabbinic literature usually forming a running commentary on specific books of the Bible. Only excerpts from *Mechilta DeRabbi Shimon bar Yocha'i* are still extant. The Midrash is named after Rabbi Shimon bar Yocha'i because he is the first sage mentioned in the text.

Text 9a

Deuteronomy 23:25

כִּי תָבֹא בְּכֶרֶם רֵעֶךָ וְאָכַלְתָּ עֲנָבִים כְּנַפְשְׁךָ שָׂבְעֶךָ וְאֶל כֶּלְיְךָ לֹא תִתֵּן.

When you come [to work] in your neighbor's vineyard, you may eat as many grapes as you desire to satisfy your hunger. However, you may not put any into your receptacle.

Text 9b

Talmud, Bava Metsi'a 87b

אַשְׁכְּחָן כֶּרֶם. כָּל מִילֵי מְנָא לָן?

גַּמְרִינָן מִכֶּרֶם.

מַה כֶּרֶם מְיוּחָד דָּבָר שֶׁגִּידוּלֵי קַרְקַע, וּבִשְׁעַת גְּמַר מְלָאכָה פּוֹעֵל אוֹכֵל בּוֹ, אַף כָּל דָּבָר שֶׁגִּידוּלֵי קַרְקַע, בִּשְׁעַת גְּמַר מְלָאכָה פּוֹעֵל אוֹכֵל בּוֹ.

We have [a biblical source for the case of] a vineyard. From where do we know that the law applies to all [fields]?

We derive it from the vineyard:

Just as with the vineyard, whose distinctive attribute is that it grows from soil, the law is that an employee is allowed to eat of it during the harvest; so too, every produce that grows from soil, an employee is allowed to eat of the harvest.

Text 9c

Ibid.

מַה לְּכֶרֶם - שֶׁכֵּן חַיָּיב בְּעוֹלֵלוֹת.

What comparison can you make to a vineyard, which is subject to the obligation of *olelot*?

An Ideal System

Text 10a

Midrash, *Shemot Rabah* 12:3

מָשָׁל לְמָה הַדָּבָר דּוֹמֶה, לְמֶלֶךְ שֶׁגָּזַר וְאָמַר: בְּנֵי רוֹמִי לֹא יֵרְדוּ לְסוּרְיָא, וּבְנֵי סוּרְיָא לֹא יַעֲלוּ לְרוֹמִי.

כַּךְ, כְּשֶׁבָּרָא הַקָּדוֹשׁ בָּרוּךְ הוּא אֶת הָעוֹלָם גָּזַר וְאָמַר, "הַשָּׁמַיִם שָׁמַיִם לַה', וְהָאָרֶץ נָתַן לִבְנֵי אָדָם" (תְּהִלִּים קטו,טז).

כְּשֶׁבִּקֵּשׁ לִיתֵּן הַתּוֹרָה, בִּטֵּל גְּזֵירָה רִאשׁוֹנָה וְאָמַר: הַתַּחְתּוֹנִים יַעֲלוּ לָעֶלְיוֹנִים, וְהָעֶלְיוֹנִים יֵרְדוּ לְתַּחְתּוֹנִים.

A parable: A king decreed, "The Romans may not go down to Syria and the Syrians may not go up to Rome."

Similarly, when God created the world, He decreed, "The heavens are the domain of God, and the earth He has given to the children of Adam" (Psalms 115:16).

But when God sought to give the Torah, He nullified the original decree and said, "Those below may ascend above, and those above may descend below."

Shemot Rabah

An early rabbinic commentary on the Book of Exodus. Midrash is the designation of a particular genre of rabbinic literature usually forming a running commentary on specific books of the Bible. *Shemot Rabah*, written mostly in Hebrew, provides textual exegeses, expounds upon the biblical narrative, and develops and illustrates moral principles. It was first published in Constantinople in 1512 together with four other midrashic works on the other four books of the Pentateuch.

Text 10b

The Lubavitcher Rebbe, Rabbi Menachem Mendel Schneerson, *Likutei Sichot* 19:5–6

דער חִילוּק צווישְׁן תּוֹרָה שֶׁבִּכְתָב און תּוֹרָה שֶׁבְּעַל פֶּה אִיז: תּוֹרָה שֶׁבִּכְתָב אִיז הַקָּבָּ"ה אוֹמֵר וּמֹשֶׁה כּוֹתֵב, זִי אִיז גֶעגֶעבְּן געוואָרעֶן אִינְגַאנְצְן מִלְמַעְלָה . . . תּוֹרָה שֶׁבְּעַל פֶּה . . . אִין אִיר דאַרְף זַיין "לְאַפָּשָׁה לָהּ" – דער לוֹמֵד דאַרְף האָרעֶוועֶן מִיט זַיין שֵׂכֶל צוּ אוֹפְטאָן און מְחַדֵּשׁ זַיין אִין תּוֹרָה . . .

דער אֱמֶת אִיז אָבּער אַז אויך תּוֹרָה שֶׁבְּעַל פֶּה אִיז גֶעגֶעבּעֶן גֶעוואָרעֶן בְּסִינַי, אויך דאָס וואָס נִבְרָאִים זַיינעֶן מַשִּׂיג מִיט זֵייעֶר שֵׂכֶל אִין תּוֹרָה, אִיז עֶס – תּוֹרַת ה' . . .

און אִין דעֶם פִּירְט זִיך אוֹיס דער מְכוּוָן פוּן מַתַּן תּוֹרָה, אַז סְ'זאָל זַיין דער חִיבּוּר "עֶלְיוֹן" וְ"תַחְתּוֹן". ווען אַ מעֶנְטְשׁ האָרעֶוועֶט אוֹיס מִיט זַיין שֵׂכֶל אַ סְבָרָא אִין תּוֹרָה, אִיז תּוֹרַת הוי' ווערְט נִקְרֵאת עַל שְׁמוֹ, תּוֹרָתוֹ, דאָס ווערְט זַיינעֶר אַן עִנְיָן.

The difference between the Written Torah and the Oral Torah is that God spoke the Written Torah and Moses wrote it—it was given completely from above; . . . whereas the Oral Torah . . . requires human contribution—a student must toil intellectually to introduce novel Torah ideas. . . .

The truth, however, is that the [Derived] Oral Torah was also given at Sinai. Meaning, even that which people comprehend with their own minds is God's Torah. . . .

Thereby, the purpose of the giving of the Torah is met—that there should be a bonding of the lofty with the mundane. When we introduce Torah concepts from our own minds, God's Torah becomes our Torah.

Rabbi Menachem Mendel Schneerson
1902–1994

The towering Jewish leader of the 20th century, known as "the Lubavitcher Rebbe," or simply as "the Rebbe." Born in southern Ukraine, the Rebbe escaped Nazi-occupied Europe, arriving in the U.S. in June 1941. The Rebbe inspired and guided the revival of traditional Judaism after the European devastation, impacting virtually every Jewish community the world over. The Rebbe often emphasized that the performance of just one additional good deed could usher in the era of Mashiach. The Rebbe's scholarly talks and writings have been printed in more than 200 volumes.

Text 11

Rabbi Shne'ur Zalman of Liadi, *Tanya*, *Igeret Hakodesh* 26

וְכָל אִישׁ יִשְׂרָאֵל יוּכַל לְגַלּוֹת תַּעֲלוּמוֹת חָכְמָה (לְגַלּוֹת) וּלְחַדֵּשׁ שֵׂכֶל חָדָשׁ, הֵן בַּהֲלָכוֹת, הֵן בַּאֲגָדוֹת, הֵן בְּנִגְלֶה, הֵן בְּנִסְתָּר . . . וּמְחוּיָיב בְּדָבָר לְהַשְׁלִים נִשְׁמָתוֹ.

Every one of us is able to reveal secrets of wisdom, (to reveal) and to innovate new insights in Halachah, *Agadah*, in the revealed dimensions of Torah, and in the Kabbalistic sphere. . . . Indeed, we are obliged to do so in order to perfect our souls.

Rabbi Shne'ur Zalman of Liadi
(Alter Rebbe)
1745–1812

Chasidic rebbe, halachic authority, and founder of the Chabad movement. The Alter Rebbe was born in Liozna, Belarus, and was among the principal students of the Magid of Mezeritch. His numerous works include the *Tanya*, an early classic containing the fundamentals of Chabad Chasidism, and *Shulchan Aruch HaRav*, an expanded and reworked code of Jewish law.

“Received” but “Derived”

Text 12a

Maimonides, *Mishneh Torah*, Laws of Rebels 2:9

הֲרֵי כָּתוּב בַּתּוֹרָה "לֹא תְבַשֵּׁל גְּדִי בַּחֲלֵב אִמּוֹ" (שְׁמוֹת כג,יט). מִפִּי הַשְּׁמוּעָה לָמְדוּ שֶׁזֶּה הַכָּתוּב אָסַר לְבַשֵּׁל וְלֶאֱכוֹל בָּשָׂר בְּחָלָב.

The Torah states (Exodus 23:19), “You shall not cook a kid in its mother’s milk.” The Received Oral Torah teaches us that this verse forbids both the cooking and eating of milk with meat.

Text 12b

Mechilta DeRabbi Shimon bar Yocha’i 34

"לֹא תְבַשֵּׁל גְּדִי בַּחֲלֵב אִמּוֹ" - הֲרֵי זֶה בָּא לֶאֱסוֹר בִּישּׁוּלוֹ. קַל וָחוֹמֶר אֲכִילָתוֹ.

“You shall not cook a kid in its mother’s milk.” This prohibits cooking [the mixture]. And through a *kal vechomer* we derive that one may not eat this mixture.

Text 12c

Maimonides, *Sefer Hamitzvot, Shoresh 2*

וְשֶׁיֵּשׁ שָׁם דִּינִין הֵם פֵּירוּשִׁים מְקוּבָּלִים מִמֹּשֶׁה . . . אֲבָל הֵם מְבִיאִים
רְאָיָה עֲלֵיהֶם בְּאַחַת מִשְּׁלֹשׁ עֶשְׂרֵה מִדּוֹת, כִּי מֵחָכְמַת הַכָּתוּב
שֶׁהוּא אֶפְשָׁר שֶׁיִּמָּצֵא בּוֹ רֶמֶז מוֹרֶה עַל הַפֵּירוּשׁ הַהוּא.

There are laws that were Received from Moses . . . but the sages proved them by means of the thirteen rules. The ingenious structure of a particular passage enables us to find hints for specific Received laws.

QUESTION FOR DISCUSSION

What is the benefit of Deriving laws that were already Received?

Key Points

TORAH Café™

Continue the JLI Learning Experience!

Visit www.TorahCafe.com/go/JD2

for a video lecture(s) related to the theme of this lesson.

1. God encoded in the Written Torah numerous laws and the answers to many questions. God asks of us to decode and reveal these encrypted messages, and when we do so, we discover His intent and will. This is the "Derived" class of the Oral Torah.

2. God provided us, through Moses, with specific tools for us to use in decoding the Torah: the hermeneutic rules. When we properly apply these laws and principles, we arrive at the messages and instructions that were "given" at Sinai, albeit in a concealed, potential state.

3. One of the hermeneutic rules is the *kal vechomer,* a device whereby we infer from a ruling in a less obvious case what the law would be in a more obvious case. Another rule is the *binyan av:* the application of a clause in one law to different laws that share similar features.

4. The world was created in order to allow for the harmonization and fusion of the holy and the mundane, the Creator with the created. The goal is not to find God by eschewing our own personality nor to be physical creatures with no spirituality; physical creatures and their personalities ought to express Godliness and His ideals.

5. When humans enact laws, the divine element is absent. When humans read, hear, and memorize divine laws, the human element is absent (to a degree). The perfect synthesis is accomplished when humans intellectually strive to discover and derive the divine intent embedded in the Torah.

6. Every Jew is obligated to participate in this process of the Derived Oral Torah and create cognitive harmony between God and humanity.

7. The sages derived many laws though they were already Received. One reason for this is to demonstrate the inherent unity of the Written and Received Torah.

ADDITIONAL READINGS

RABBI YISHMAEL'S THIRTEEN PRINCIPLES OF HERMENEUTICS

BY RABBI NISSAN MINDEL

The Beraitha of Rabbi Yishmael (taken from the Introduction to the *Sifra*, the Halachic Midrash on the Book of *Vayyikra*) appears in the Siddur as the last of the selections from the Torah, Mishnah, and Talmud, which have been included in the Siddur for reasons explained previously.

In this Beraitha, Rabbi Yishmael formulates the thirteen principles *(Middoth)* by which the Torah is interpreted. Its place at the beginning of the *Sifra* is explained by the fact that most of the Halachoth in this Halachic Midrash are derived from the application of these principles. However, these principles are frequently applied throughout the Talmud when it traces the sources of the various laws in the text of the Torah, both the laws which are explicitly mentioned in the Torah, as well as those laws which are implied in the text, and are inferred by means of any of the said thirteen principles.

It should be remembered that the Torah (the Five Books of the Pentateuch) which was given to the Jewish people through Mosheh Rabbenu, and written down by him (hence, *Torah shebiKthav*, "Written Torah") was given to, and transmitted by, Mosheh together with its interpretation. In other words, the Written Torah was given together with the Oral Torah *(Torah shebe'al Peh)*, or *Masorah* (Tradition). The latter was not written down by Mosheh, but transmitted orally by him to Joshua, who in turn transmitted it to the Elders, and they to the Prophets, and the latter to the Men of the Great Assembly, who handed it down to the *Tannaim*, the Sages of the Mishnah. In the last generation of the Tannaim, the whole body of the Oral Law was arranged and recorded by Rabbi Yehudah haNassi, in the form of the Six Orders of the Mishnah. Subsequently, the Mishnah itself was explained and expounded by the disciples of the Tannaim, called the *Amoruim*, and their disciples, as well as by subsequent generations of Torah scholars, called *Rabbanan Seburai*. When this vast accumulation of knowledge, called *Gemara*, was also recorded alongside with the Mishnah, the *Talmud* was completed. But although the Oral Law (the *Talmud Bavli* and *Talmud Yerushalmi, Midrashim*, etc.) was now also written down, it still retained its original title *Torah shebe'al-Peh* ("Oral Law") to distinguish it from the *Torah shebiKthav* ("Written Law").

Thus, the thirteen principles of interpretation were themselves part of the Oral Law, transmitted from generation to generation, since the time of Mosheh Rabbenu. Rabbi Yishmael merely formulated and defined them, and listed them. They follow below, together with a brief explanation :

1- *Kal vaChomer*: Deduction *from minor to major*, and *vice versa*.

An example of a simple *Kal vaChomer* is found in the passage where Mosheh says to G-d, "If the children of Israel did not listen to me, why should Pharaoh listen to me?"[2] Rashi comments on this verse that it

Rabbi Nissan Mindel, PhD 1912–1999 Secretary to the Lubavitcher Rebbe. Born in Latvia, Rabbi Mindel immigrated to the U.S. where he received a doctorate in Semitic languages from Columbia University. He translated many works into English, including the Tanya, the seminal text of Chabad philosophy, and was a prolific writer who authored numerous works including *Philosophy of Chabad and My Prayer*.

2 Exod. 6:12.

is one of ten instances of *Kal vaChomer* mentioned in the Torah.[3]

The actual application of this principle is based on the passage in the Torah,[4] speaking of Miriam's punishment for slandering her brother Mosheh. That passage, in effect, declares that "had Miriam angered her father to the extent of her father spitting in front of her, she would have been held in contempt and isolation outside the camp for seven days; how much more so when she angered G-d." By inference, she would be deserving of at least double the punishment, that is, expulsion from the camp for fourteen days. Yet G-d ordered her expelled for seven days only. Here the Torah reaches that in applying the *Kal vaChomer,* the *inference must be limited to the original premise;* no more and no less. In other words, if the law is such-and-such in a lighter case, it certainly could be no more lenient, but also *no more severe,* in a graver case.

The same principle applies in the reverse. If in a graver situation the Torah shows a certain leniency, we can infer that the leniency should certainly apply in a lighter case; again, no more and no less.[5]

2- *Gezerah Shavah*: Inference from a *similarity of words or phrases* in two different texts in the Torah.

This means that when an identical, or similar, word, or expression, is found in the Torah in two separate cases, it is an indication that there is an analogy between the two, and that one case complements the other. An example of the application of this principle is found in the law of prohibiting the tearing out of one's hair as a sign of mourning, in the manner of the heathen.[6] Elsewhere[7] a similar prohibition is stated in reference to *Kohanim.* In both cases the word *korcha* ("making baldness") is used. *According to Tradition,* this is a case where the principle of *Gezerah Shavah* is to be applied, to infer that just as in the case of Kohanim the prohibition refers to *any part* of the head, so in the case of ordinary Jews; and just as in the case of the latter, the prohibition refers to mourning after the dead, so it is also in the case of the Kohanim. We underscored "according to Tradition," because this principle (as also the others) cannot be used *freely,* but only where it has been transmitted by Tradition.

3- *Binyan Av*: The *establishment of a precedent,* or general rule, to be extended to similar cases.

For example, the Torah permits the preparation of food on the Festival of Pesach.[8] Since Pesach is the first of all the festivals, it serves as a precedent for all other festivals in regard to the permissibility of preparing food on any Yom Tov.

The said principle may be based on one text, as in the instance just mentioned, or on two texts. As an example of the latter may be cited the law regarding defects or deformities. The definition of physical defects is derived from two texts in the Torah, one dealing with defects in *humans,* which disqualify a Kohen from serving in the Beth Hamikdash,[9] the other specifying defects in *animals,* which disqualify them from being offered as sacrifices.[10] The texts are taken together to determine what constitutes a defect, whenever the word "defect" is mentioned in the Torah, be it in regard to animal or man.

4- A *general rule followed by a particular* (or particulars).

In this case, the general rule is qualified by, and limited to, the particulars, and no more. For example, it is written, "When any man of you bring a sacrifice unto G-d, of a beast, of cattle, or of sheep."[11] "Beast" is a general term which might include also kosher wild animals. But the general term "beast" is followed by specific particulars, namely, "cattle" and "sheep," and therefore limited to these only. Hence wild animals are excluded, and not permitted to be offered as sacrifices.

3 See Ber. Rabba ch. 32.

4 Num. 12:14.

5 E.g. Mishnah, Zevachim 49b.

6 Deut. 14:1.

7 Lev. 21:5.

8 Exod. 12:16.

9 Lev. 21:20.

10 Lev. 22:22.

11 Lev. 1:2.

5- *A particular term followed by a general term.*

In this case, the general term determines what is to be included. An example of this principle may be found in the law of returning lost property. It is written, "And so you shall do to his ass and to his garment."[12] These are specified categories which would rule out any other. However, the text continues, "and so you shall do to *any lost thing* of your brother," which is a general statement, making it a commandment to return any lost articles that could be identified by the owner.

6- A *general term, followed by particulars, followed again by a general term.*

Here the particulars specified in the text are not exclusive (as in No. 4), but they are considered as *collective* terms, to include anything which has similar characteristics, excluding things which lack these characteristics. A case in point is the law of safe-keeping, or trusteeship. It is written in the Torah, "If a man deliver unto his friend money or utensils to keep...."[13] The statement opens with a general proposition ("if a man deliver to his friend"), then continues with particulars ("money or utensils"), and again with a general term ("to keep"). Applying the above principle, the inference is that not *only* money or utensils are covered by this law, but also all such articles that have the characteristics of *money* and *utensils,* namely, (1) have intrinsic value, and (2) are movable. Accordingly, the law does *not* cover such things as a field, because it is immovable, nor a credit note, because it has no value *of its own* (except the "paper" on which it is written).

7- *A general proposition requiring a particular term to explain it,* and, conversely, a *particular term requiring a general rule to complete it.*

An example of the application of this principle can be found in the law about the consecration of the First-born. It is written in the Torah, "Sanctify unto Me all the first-born."[14] This is a general proposition which, by itself, would include also a female firstling. But elsewhere[15] the Torah specifies "male only." The question would still remain. Perhaps what is meant is the first of all the male babies, even though it was preceded by a female baby? So the text specifies further— "that openeth the womb"[16]; it must actually be the *first-born* baby, second to none. It might still be asked, The text implies the first baby born *naturally;* what if there was first a baby that was delivered by means of a caesarian operation? So the text makes it clear by insisting on it being a *firstling* (*Bechor).* Thus, the general term "first-born" is explained by the specific terms, to indicate that only such a first-born is consecrated which has all three conditions: (1) male, (2) delivered *naturally* and (3) an actual firstling.[17]

8- *When a subject which is already included in a general proposition is afterward mentioned separately in order to give some new information, it is not meant to be an isolated instance, but to clarify the general proposition as well.*

An example of the application of this principle is found in the law concerning the prohibition of work on Shabbos. It is written in the Torah, "You shall do no work (on Shabbos)."[18] Later, it is written, "You shall kindle no fire on the Shabbos day."[19] The kindling of fire is already included in the general prohibition of work (which covers 39 categories of work used in the building of the Sanctuary, as transmitted by Tradition); why, then, was the kindling of fire mentioned separately? The answer is: In order to establish a rule applying both to itself as well as to all other categories of work included in the general prohibition. This is to say: Just as the kindling of fire is one of the principal categories of work prohibited on Shabbos, which makes the absent-minded transgressor (who forgot that it was prohibited work) liable to bring a sin-offering *separately* (even when committed together with any other of the 39 types of

12 Deut. 22:23.

13 Exod. 22.

14 Exod. 13.

15 Deut. 15:19.

16 Exod. 13:2.

17 Berachot 19a.

18 Exod. 20:10.

19 Exod. 35:3.

work), so is any other of the 39 principal categories of work liable separately. In other words, on the basis of this principle, the law is that where a person performs two or more of the said 39 categories of work on Shabbos, forgetting that they were prohibited, he must bring a sin offering for each, and for as many, of the works which he so performed.

9- *When a subject already included in a general rule is mentioned separately in order to specify a certain point which is also included in the rule, this exception is intended to alleviate and not to aggravate this particular case.*

An example of the application of this principle may be found in the law concerning *nega'im* (blemishes, or symptoms of *tzara'at,* "leprosy").[20] The Torah begins with a general rule about skin blemishes,[21] specifying three *severe* symptoms, the first two of which being signs of *tumah* (defilement, i.e., that the person is definitely afflicted with the plague): (1) hair turned white in the blemish,[22] (2) quick raw flesh (open sore) in the swelling of the skin[23] and (3) if there has been no change in the skin blemish during the first week of isolation, a second week of isolation is required, at the end of which, if no change is noticeable, the person is declared *tahor* (ritually clean).[24] At the same time, the Torah specifies a "favorable" symptom, namely, a white discoloration of the entire skin.[25]

This general rule is followed in the Torah by two particular skin blemishes: (a) one that has developed in a "boil" which had healed,[26] and (b) one that has developed in a spot of the skin which had a burning by fire.[27] In each of the two cases, only one severe symptom is mentioned, namely, hair turning white.[28]

20 Sifra, on Lev. Ch. 13.
21 Lev. 13:2.
22 Lev. 13:3.
23 Lev. 13:10-11.
24 Lev. 13:5-6.
25 Lev. 13:12-13.
26 Lev. 13:8.
27 Lev. 13:24.
28 Lev. 13:20, 25.

According to the said principle, therefore, we say that the intent of each of these two exceptions is to alleviate the case, and not to aggravate it. This *is* to say, we apply to these cases the rule of the *favorable* symptom (whiteness of the whole skin), but not the rule of the *severe* symptoms (Nos. 2 and 3, mentioned above), except the one mentioned specifically (hair turning white).

10- *When a subject already included in a general rule is mentioned separately, in order to specify a certain point not covered by the general rule, the exception is intended to alleviate in some respects and to aggravate in other respects.*

An example of the application of this principle is found in connection with the law of *nega'im* (blemishes), when affecting the *head* or *beard.*[29] However, here the Torah introduces a *new* symptom, nor previously included in the general rule, namely, *yellow* hair as a sign of *tumah.*[30] Hence, according to the present principle, the Torah indicates that the purpose of the exception is *to* apply to it the severity of yellow hair, as a sign of *tumah,* while giving it the leniency of white hair *not* being a sign of *tumah* in this case (though white hair is a symptom of *tumah* in other skin blemishes) .

11- *A subject already included in a general rule and afterwards excepted in order to deal with a new matter, cannot be reincluded in the general rule unless the text expressly does this.*

By way of an example: A *metzora* ("leper"), having been cleared of his leprosy, had to bring certain sacrifices for atonement, among them a he-lamb as a guilt offering *(asham).* (One of the reasons for his requiring atonement was the fact that his being afflicted with the plague was a punishment for *lashon-hara,* evil tongue and defamation, whereby he isolated people from one another. He was, therefore, smitten with the plague and isolated from the community, so that during his isolation and affliction he could think and repent.) The Torah states that this he-lamb was

29 Lev. 13:29.
30 Lev. 13:30.

to be sacrificed in the same place where any sin-offering and burnt offering was sacrificed, that is, in the northerly corner of the altar. The text then goes on to say, "for as the sin-offering so is the guilt-offering."[31] Now, this general rule is already mentioned once.[32] It was, however, necessary to restate it because the case of the leper's guilt-offering was excepted from the general rule by the introduction of a new law attending it, namely, smearing some blood of the sacrifice on the right ear, thumb, and large toe of the cured leper[33] (a ceremony not required in the usual case of any other guilt-offering). Consequently, one might have thought that the exception applied also in other respects (e.g., burning of the fat on the altar, etc.). Hence the re-inclusion of this particular case into its original category, or general rule.

12- *A subject inferred from its context, or from the subsequent text.*

For example, one of the Ten Commandments is "You shall not steal."[34] Our Rabbis declare that this refers to stealing (kidnapping) a human being, which is punishable by death. They infer this from the fact that this "stealing" appears in the same context with "You shall not murder," etc., which the Torah (elsewhere) clearly makes a crime punishable by death. On the other hand, the text "You shall not steal, neither shall you deal falsely," etc.[35] refers to stealing money, or valuables, which is not subject to a death penalty.

An example of the application of the second part of this principle is found in the law concerning a plague on a house. It is written, "When you come in the land of Canaan . . . and I put a plague of leprosy in a house, in the land of your possession."[36] The Torah does not specify here as to what kind of a house, a wooden one, or a brick one. Later on, however, referring to the afflicted house, the text mentions specifically, "its stones, timber and mortar."[37] Thus the text later clarifies what type of a house is subject to this law.

13- *When two texts contradict each other, they can only be understood by a third text which reconciles them.*

For example, it is written, "And I will speak unto You (Mosheh) from above the *kapporeth*."[38] The *kapporeth* was the golden cover of the Ark in the *Holy of Holies*. Another text says, "And G-d spoke unto him from the tent of meeting."[39] The "tent of the meeting" (*ohel-moed)* was the *Sanctuary at large*. Thus, the two verses seem to contradict each other. However, the two texts are reconciled by a third, "And when Mosheh *came into the tent of the meeting*... he heard the *Voice speaking unto him from above the ark-cover (kapporeth)* that was upon the ark of testimony, from between the two cherubim; and He spoke unto him."[40] In other words, Mosheh was spoken to *in the Ohel-moed*, but the *Voice came* unto him from above the ark-cover in the Holy of Holies.

My Prayer [New York: Merkos L'Inyonei Chinuch, 1972], pp. 97–109
Reprinted with permission of the publisher

31 Lev. 14:13.
32 Lev. 7:1.
33 Lev. 14:14.
34 Exod. 20:30.
35 Lev. 19:11.
36 Lev. 14:34.

37 Lev. 14:45.
38 Exod. 25:22.
39 Lev. 1:1.
40 Num. 7:89.

MIDRASH (HALAKHIC EXEGESIS)

BY RABBI ADIN EVEN-ISRAEL STEINSALTZ

Midrash halakhah (from the root *darash,* meaning to enquire or investigate) is the body of literature that interprets Mosaic law, seeking evidence and suggestions within the text to further comprehension. It constitutes only a small proportion of the Mishnah itself, but in its efforts to elucidate the mishnaic sources, the Talmud often cites the *midrash.* It quotes extensively from midrashic compilations, some of which have survived to the present day, and other collections of *baraitot* (extraneous commentaries) preserved in the Talmud alone.

The basic problem of *midrash* is the question of whether examination of the biblical text and the various logical methods of interpretation are the true source of the legislation derived from it. Some important sages, led by Maimonides, believed that the *midrash,* or at least its large part, was not an authentic source of *halakhah.* It was their view that the main outlines of *halakhah* had been contained, by age-old tradition, in the oral law, which conveyed all the details of mishnaic *halakhah. Midrash,* they claimed, was nothing but a method, handed down from age to age, of linking the biblical text with the *halakhah* by finding associations and implications indicating the connection. According to this theory, the halakhic *midrash* is an important mnemotechnical instrument but cannot be regarded as constituting substantial evidence. Like so many of the statements formulated by Maimonides, this theory is distinguished by its clarity of thought, intellectual brilliance, and provision for the solution to many problems. It also created fresh problems, however, since analysis of the *midrashim* themselves does not always bear out his explanation.

Another theory, advocated by the classic talmudic commentators (Rashi, the *baalei tosafot,* and most of the Spanish commentators) distinguishes between true halakhic *midrashim* and *asmakhtot* (supports). According to this basic distinction, found in the Talmud, some *midrashim* are authentic sources of *halakhah,* while *asmakhtot* are merely aids to memory or devices for linking rabbinical legislation to scriptural texts and do not constitute true proof. The sages themselves sometimes said of biblical verses they cited as evidence, ". . . although there is no proof of this in the Bible." The difference between the two kinds of *midrash* is not always clear, since the mechanics may be almost identical, as was pointed out by the sages and the commentators.

There are certain hermeneutical rules for interpretation of the biblical text, usually enumerated according to the order established by Rabbi Ishmael, who formulated thirteen principles for interpretation. This list is not exhaustive, since not all the possible methods are encompassed, and there is an amplified list of thirty-two rules for aggadic interpretation, most of which also apply to the *halakhah.* But even this number does not cover all the details of interpretive methods in the Talmud, and in recent times these have been estimated at several hundred. At the same time, R. Ishmael's rules cover the fundamental methods, and several are widely utilized.

The most important exegetical principles are: *kal va-homer, gezerah shavah, binyan av, ketal uferat, davar ha-lamed me-inyano,* and *shnei ketuvim makhishim. Kal va-homer* is a simple method of deduction that exists in all methods of logic, permitting deduction from a minor to a major case or from a light to a severe case. The following example is cited in the Talmud, although for various reasons it is not considered totally satisfactory: according to Torah law, a man is forbidden to marry his daughter's daughter. From this we may deduce through *kal va-homer* that he is undoubtedly prohibited from marrying his daughter. This method is sometimes known, because

---

Rabbi Adin Even- Israel Steinsaltz (1937–) Talmudist, author, and philosopher. Rabbi Even-Israel Steinsaltz is considered one of the foremost Jewish thinkers of the 20th century. Praised by *Time* magazine as a "once-in-a-millennium scholar," he has been awarded the Israel Prize for his contributions to Jewish study. He lives in Jerusalem and is the founder of the Israel Institute for Talmudic Publications, a society dedicated to the translation and elucidation of the Talmud.

of its simplicity, as *din,* simple logical consideration, and the assumption is that any man may employ this method and derive new *halakhah* from it. There are many methods of restricting *kal va-homer,* whether by providing accurate proof of flaws in the basic logical structure or mechanism, or by proving the implausibility of the outcome. In the opinion of most sages, there is also a restrictive rule known as *dayo,* according to which the deduced fact is equalized to the case from which we infer and neither a stricter nor a more lenient view is taken. A clear proof of this rule is in the biblical text itself, where the sages found ten explicit references to *kal va-homer,* and this rule helps preserve a certain degree of logic and order.

Another basic hermeneutical principle is *gezerah shavah,* which may be defined as a philological measure. When the meaning of a word or *halakhah* is unclear, it is inferred by word analogy from another passage where the meaning is clear. *Gezerah shavah* is basically simple, but it is considerably elaborated in the halakhic *midrash* where a certain word may serve as the key to inference on different subjects. The logical structure resembles that of deciphering texts, various key words serving as the basis for interpretation of the entire sentence. This important exegetic rule may prove dangerous if employed indiscriminately, since many words appear in different sentences and any desired conclusion may be obtained. One basic qualification is that a man may not infer *gezerah shavah* unless he learned it from his teacher. Thus the method is a matter of traditional knowledge of key words, and it is necessary only to clarify the significance of the comparison between two related texts. There is an additional restriction: *gezerah shavah* is acceptable only if it can be proved that the key word in both passages was really inserted for this purpose and is superfluous to the text. The method is, therefore, utilized like the figures that denote footnotes, to designate the connection between the text and a note appearing elsewhere.

Binyan av resembles *gezerah shavah* in principle but differs in logical structure. It is an inductive method of proof, where an attempt is made to show that a certain *av* (case) serves as the basis for a whole series of other similar passages constructed in similar fashion. Here too there are several methods and several qualifications.

Ketal uferat takes many different forms, but the essence is that it is possible to draw conclusions from the way in which a passage is written, that is, where the generalization appears. When the general principle precedes the particular, we say that "there is nothing in the general principle that is not contained in the particular"; in other words, the general principle adds nothing but merely provides the logical structure. In the opposite case—for example, when it is stated in laws regarding losses: "In like manner shalt thou do with his ass and so shalt thou do with his raiment and with any lost thing of thy brother's"—where the general principle follows the particular, this implies that the details cited are mere examples, and that the precept applies to all types of losses, without exception.

Davar ha-lamed me-inyano is a relatively simple method of deduction from the text. For example, the commandment "Thou shalt not steal" appears twice. The first instance is in the Ten Commandments in a very solemn context (in proximity to the laws pertaining to murder and adultery), and it is therefore explained that the allusion is to kidnapping, for which the penalty is death. On the other occasion it appears among the various laws pertaining to fair trade and so forth and is interpreted there as a ban on the theft of property. Another of the basic hermeneutical rules is that pertaining to two contradictory passages, where the contradiction is either overt or hidden. In this case it is necessary to seek a third passage in order to decide the matter and to explain both in such a way that each is taken to refer to a different subject and the contradiction is prevented.

The halakhic *midrashim* employ a certain extremely precise exegetic method which derives from the assumption that every law or deed recorded in the Torah was formulated accurately and concisely, making each detail significant. Any word that appears superfluous—whether blatantly unnecessary or merely nonessential to the meaning—is a source of study, and superfluity is taken to imply emphasis. When two subjects are discussed in close proximity, it is possible to infer from one to the other to a certain extent, even if they do not deal with the same matter. Even superfluous letters have meaning; for example, if a sentence commences with the conjunctive letter *vav,* this may be regarded as a hint at some essential link with the preceding sentence.

Although *midrashic* methods are relatively simple, the *midrash* in general is not content with random interpretation, and one method is applied on top of another. Except for the laws of sacrifice—which cite, almost exclusively, primary evidence—the *midrash* compares various verses dealing with the same theme and explains each in its own way. The halakhic *midrash* is inflexible to a degree that appears relatively artificial, but in fact when the biblical text is regarded as a primary halakhic source, each word and phrase is important, as is the case with any text of vital legal significance where there is room for study of each minute detail.

There were various methods of interpretation: R. Ishmael's academy developed its own methods, while R. Akiva's developed detailed and comprehensive rules for itself, and the differences between various sages or schools of thought found expression in methods. For example, we find that the Babylonian Talmud cites halakhic proof only from the Torah, considering it to be the sole binding text from this point of view. Wherever evidence is cited from other books of the Bible, numerous qualifications are noted, and it usually appears only in support of other proof, as an *asmakhta.* The Jerusalem Talmud, on the other hand, tends to rely on the other books more, and thus offers simpler explanations of many of the involved theories of the Babylonian Talmud.

Although the basic rules for exegetic interpretation were simple, the mechanics of *midrash* and the interrelations between the various rules, as well as their exact definition and application (in some cases two rules may be applicable), are a subject that the Talmud peruses extensively, and the commentators on the Talmud and the *midrash* also devoted considerable attention and profound thought to it.

The Essential Talmud [New York: Basic Books, 2006], pp. 221–226
Reprinted with permission of the author

TYING SHOELACES AND OTHER DETAILS

BY SUSAN A. HANDELMAN , PhD

"R. Leib, son of Sarah, the hidden tzaddik who wandered over the earth, following the course of rivers, in order to redeems souls of the living and the dead said this: 'I did not go to the Maggid in order to hear Torah from him, but to see how he unlaces his felt shoes and laces them up again." So goes a well-known Chassidic story somewhat quaint and strange to our ears. What, one wonders, could one great tzaddik learn from the way another tied his shoes—and why concentrate on such trivia to begin with?

Susan Handelman, PhD. Dr. Handelman is a Chicago native and professor of English at Bar Ilan University. She is the author of *Fragments of Redemption, Slayers of Moses, and Make Yourself a Teacher.*

In fact, the modern Jew tends to ask the same question about much of the body of Jewish Law passed down to us in the *Shulchan Arukh* and various codes—that is, about halakha in general. Or perhaps we better say halakha in its "specifics"; what can one possible learn from it, and why concentrate on such trivia anyway? That mass of irritatingly minute prescriptions, which cover the pages of the *Shulchan Arukh,* is one of the greatest stumbling blocks for the modern Jew in search of her or himself. Its laws appear impossible, extreme. Here are directives about matters such as which shoe to put on first, when to wash your hands, when and when not to touch your spouse, how to sleep, eat, drink—even evacuate. Let alone the intricate directives concerning proper observance of the holidays, prayer, litigation, and so forth.

Nonetheless, says the Talmud: "Since the Temple was destroyed, G-d has no place left except the four cubits of halakha." What kind of G-d, one wonders, cares about my shoelaces? No one will argue about the need to strengthen Jewish "identity," "culture," "values" —but that we need to strengthen ourselves in abiding by Jewish law, in all its sticky specifics, is another matter.

What does it matter whether you drive to shul as long as you get there, or which shoe you put on first, and so forth. Justice, morality, being a good person, supporting Israel—these are the components of Judaism. Shabbat, kashrut, perhaps even mikveh make for a nice "lifestyle"; but let's not go too far; let's not be irrational, fanatic; and above all, let's not call it "law."

Halakha Unites Spiritual and Mundane

In fact, the popular term, "lifestyle," if we stretch it a bit, might serve as a roughly accurate translation of the Hebrew word halakha, which comes from the root *halakh,* meaning "to walk." The word does not specifically denote "law" (Hebrew *din* or *mishpat*), but "path," the "way to walk," the way to pattern one's life.

But there is more. Style is not always synonymous with substance. There is a profound insight in the popular cliché, "lifestyle"; we desperately search for lifestyle because we lack life-substance. Style can become a substitute for content. And so we try to pick and choose, amalgamate and discard, imitate and absorb bits and pieces of other people's lives, cultures, religions, philosophies, politics, struggling to sew some patchwork of ideas together to clothe our nakedness. Like the era which gave rise to Christianity, ours is one of great religious syncretism.

But halakha is more than style. Although it contains it own inner mechanism for dealing with the effects of temporal, cultural, and geographical change, the essence of halakha does not change. Precisely because the essence of halakha is the unity of the concrete actions it prescribes, with the "theoretical or conceptual" basis of the Torah, halakha is that which unites the most "spiritual" aspects of Judaism with the most physical, mundane details of life. Halakha is that unique religious expression which—leaping over the boundaries of other non-Jewish concepts of "spirituality" —somehow is able to connect G-d to... how you tie your shoelaces. Being good, ethical, spiritual, Zionist etc., is, halakha insists, somehow bound up with the way you eat, dress, cook, sleep, keep the Shabbat, and so on. Why?

Because in essence, the Torah teaches that nothing, literally nothing, is trivial for the Jew; that there is utterly no aspect of one's life which is unimportant; no action, word, thought, to which you can afford to be insensitive. There is no aspect or moment of life which the Jew does not seek to elevate and sanctify and penetrate with Jewishness. That is why in Judaism, soul and body, idea and action, the most metaphysical and the most mundane realms are not separate. And Halakha is this very unity of style and substance, soul and body, spirit and letter, daily life and the Divine. We have a G-d who "mishes in."

Halakha Should Not Be Modernized

Precisely in the detail does one find the whole, or to use more philosophical terminology, only though the particular does one reach the universal; concentrate and abstract cannot be separated, Precisely in the seeming small details, in the minutiae, in the concrete halakhot is the Torah expressed.

This concept is actually very contemporary. Twentieth century science teaches us the same lesson. The secret of nature, the ultimate strength and power of the universe lies not somewhere in the vast cosmic expanse, but within the infinitely small world of the atom. The biggest explosive force comes from a highly controlled reaction using the most minute nuclear components.

Those familiar with kabbalah will recognize that the term tzimtzum, meaning "contraction, condensation" is central to Jewish mystical thought. The idea is that G-d, so to speak, contracted himself to make space for the universe, and that he condensed his thought and will through immeasurable contractions into the physical letters and words of the Torah.

Halakha, for the mystic, is this greatly condensed wisdom of G-d, inseparable from the most abstract metaphysical speculation. And that explains why the very compiler and editor of the Shulchan Arukh was none other than the great mystic and kabbalist of the Safed circle, R. Yoseph Caro.

And R. Caro was not alone—our greatest speculative mystics were also our greatest Halakhists. This combination of law and mysticism is unique to Judaism. The most spiritually sensitive of our tradition were also the most attentive to the minutiae of halakha, for halakha is the body, the very concrete expression of the soul of Torah. Those who reached the highest levels sought not to abolish, alter, or "modernize" halakha, but to reinforce it.

We Must Seek Meaning in Halakha

Can halakha be attractive today? Yes, because halakha is the very concrete expression, the very ground and bedrock of Jewish "identity," "culture," "values," and all the other abstract words which don't exist in the Bible, because the word "Torah," meaning "teaching, instruction," includes and indissolubly binds together "religion," ethics," "politics" with one another and with the way one ties one's shoes. One can't separate them; separate halakha from the Torah, Jewish action from Jewish thought, and you separate the Jew from Judaism.

To be sure, some halakhot are not congruent with some contemporary styles of thought and behavior. That, however, is not a necessary reason for immediately doing away with them, and for rationalizing a Judaism which we adhere to only when it is comfortable for us to observe. And should not we, of all people, be most skeptical of the styles and conceptual fads of modern culture—did we not suffer most in the last century from the hands of those were most culturally and technologically advanced? Did not "liberal humanism" fail us miserably and does it not appear to beginning to fail us again? Instead of casting away halakha, let us search for its deeper meaning, its intricate and indissoluble connection to those aspects of Judaism unquestioningly meaningful to us and the world.

But let us search with Jewish eyes. The Torah deals not only with the beautiful and rational elements of ourselves, ignoring the rest, but also (and perhaps more importantly) with what is not beautiful and not rational, and what is spiritually intractable—with our physical behavior in the world of our everyday life, down to the last detail. For if one doesn't pay careful attention to those aspects of human behavior which are non-rational, they can easily become wildly, destructively irrational—rather than guides which can lead us above and beyond the limits of reason.

Even one who is concerned with beauty, proportion, and aesthetics will tell us that details are important. The artist, above all, knows that one incorrect line, awkward angle, off color, can destroy the painting; the poet agonizes over the exact word. Jewish beauty, however, is not ultimately embodied in plaster and paint and poetry, but in deeds, physical actions—the most minute, the most mundane—over which the Jew agonizes and meditates as deeply as does the artist over her or his composition. Meditation over the proper way to tie one's shoes merges into meditation on the secrets of creation, the *Shulchan Arukh* into the Kabbalah. In going to the tzaddik to learn how he ties his shoes, you learn all. For a Jew's life—way of "walking"—the specifics of halakha, constitute the essence of his or her art and the ultimate masterwork.

Feeding Among the Lilies: The Wellsprings Reader [New York: Kehot Publication Society, 1999]

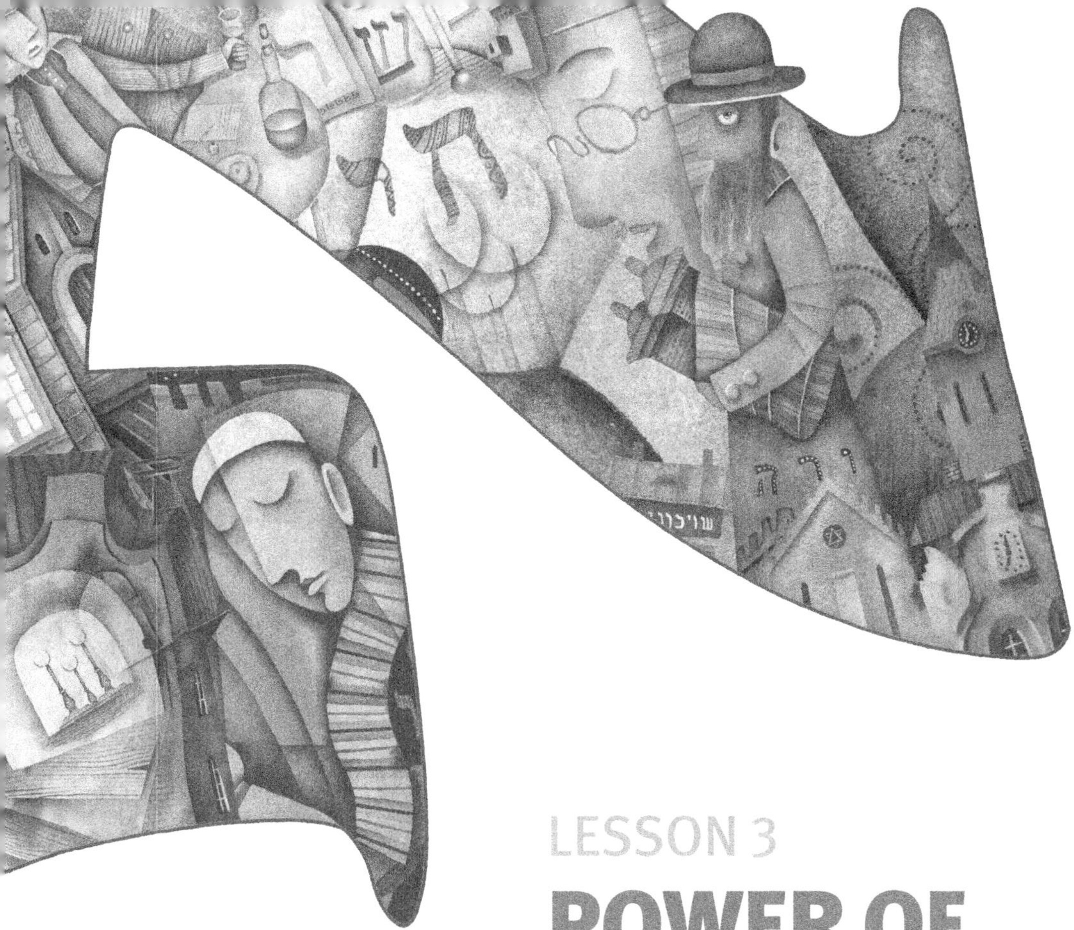

LESSON 3

POWER OF THE PEOPLE

The rabbis loom large in Jewish tradition; they have the authority to legislate new laws in addition to clarifying divine laws. Does God always concur with their decisions? Are there limits to what the rabbis can legislate? In which way are rabbinic enactments different from biblical law?

On the other end of the spectrum, what about the power of the people? What happens if a rabbinic enactment proves to be untenable for the masses? And do the behaviors and traditions that originate with the masses enjoy any legal or spiritual standing?

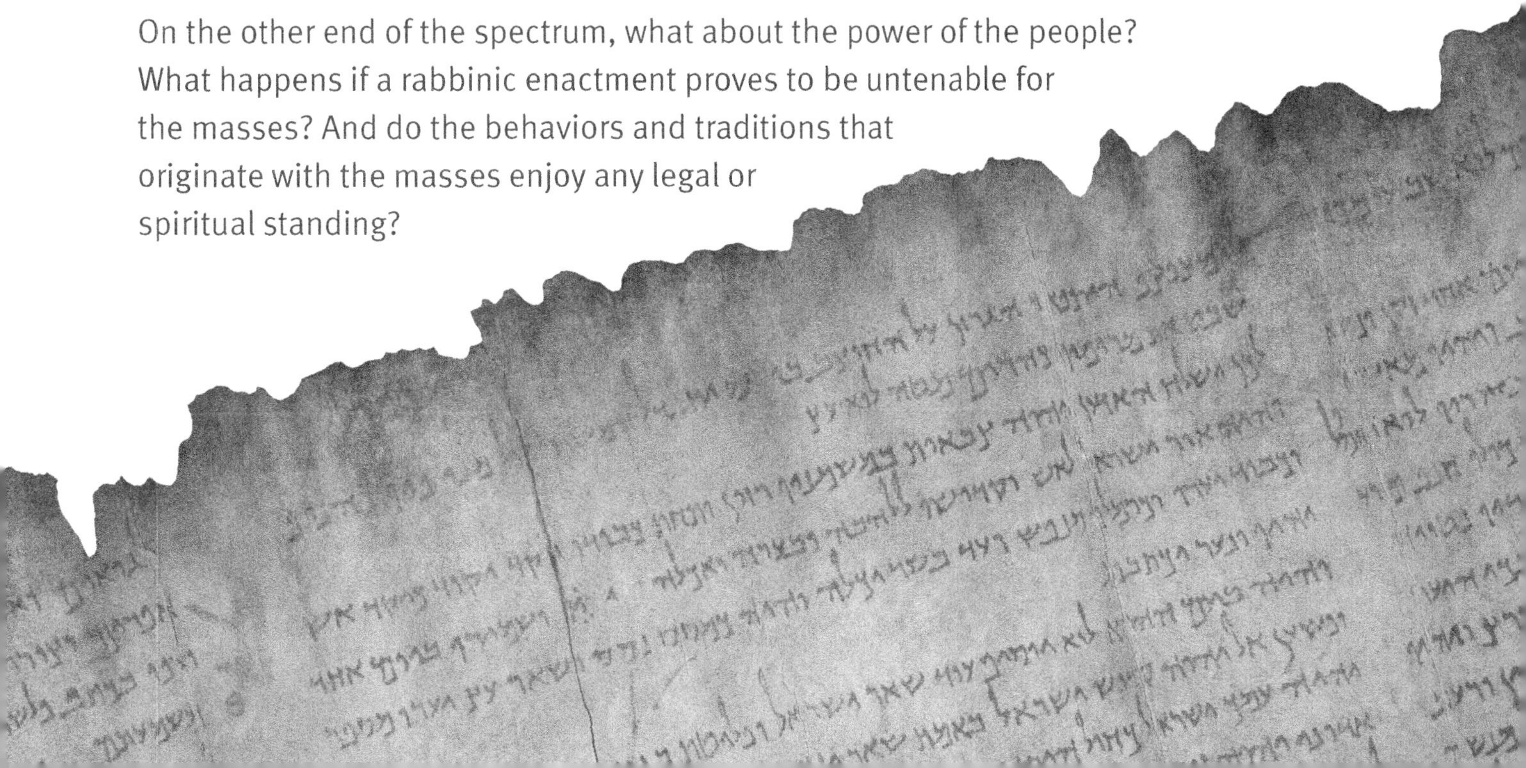

You Shall Not Divert

Legislative Powers

FIGURE 3.1

Three Ritual Blessings

בָּרוּךְ אַתָּה ה' אֱלֹקֵינוּ מֶלֶךְ הָעוֹלָם, אֲשֶׁר קִדְּשָׁנוּ בְּמִצְוֹתָיו, וְצִוָּנוּ לְהַדְלִיק נֵר שֶׁל שַׁבָּת קוֹדֶשׁ.	Blessed are You, Lord our God, King of the universe, Who has sanctified us with His commandments and commanded us to kindle the light of the holy Shabbat.
בָּרוּךְ אַתָּה ה' אֱלֹקֵינוּ מֶלֶךְ הָעוֹלָם, אֲשֶׁר קִדְּשָׁנוּ בְּמִצְוֹתָיו, וְצִוָּנוּ לְהַדְלִיק נֵר חֲנֻכָּה.	Blessed are You, Lord our God, King of the universe, Who has sanctified us with His commandments and commanded us to kindle the Chanukah light.
בָּרוּךְ אַתָּה ה' אֱלֹקֵינוּ מֶלֶךְ הָעוֹלָם, אֲשֶׁר קִדְּשָׁנוּ בְּמִצְווֹתָיו, וְצִוָּנוּ עַל נְטִילַת יָדָיִם.	Blessed are You, Lord our God, King of the universe, Who has sanctified us with His commandments and commanded us concerning the washing of the hands.

Text 1

Talmud, Shabbat 23a

מַאֵי מְבָרֵךְ?

מְבָרֵךְ "אֲשֶׁר קִדְּשָׁנוּ בְּמִצְוֹתָיו וְצִוָּנוּ לְהַדְלִיק נֵר שֶׁל חֲנוּכָּה".

וְהֵיכָן צִוָּנוּ?

רַב אַוְיָא אָמַר: מִ"לֹא תָסוּר" (דְּבָרִים יז,יא).

What blessing is recited [for kindling the menorah]?

One recites the blessing: "[Blessed are You, Lord our God, King of the universe,] Who has sanctified us with His commandments and commanded us to kindle the Chanukah light."

But where did He command us?

Rav Avya said, "In the verse, 'You shall not divert (Deuteronomy 17:11).'"

Babylonian Talmud

A literary work of monumental proportions that draws upon the legal, spiritual, intellectual, ethical, and historical traditions of Judaism. The 37 tractates of the Babylonian Talmud contain the teachings of the Jewish sages from the period after the destruction of the 2nd Temple through the 5th century CE. It has served as the primary vehicle for the transmission of the Oral Law and the education of Jews over the centuries; it is the entry point for all subsequent legal, ethical, and theological Jewish scholarship.

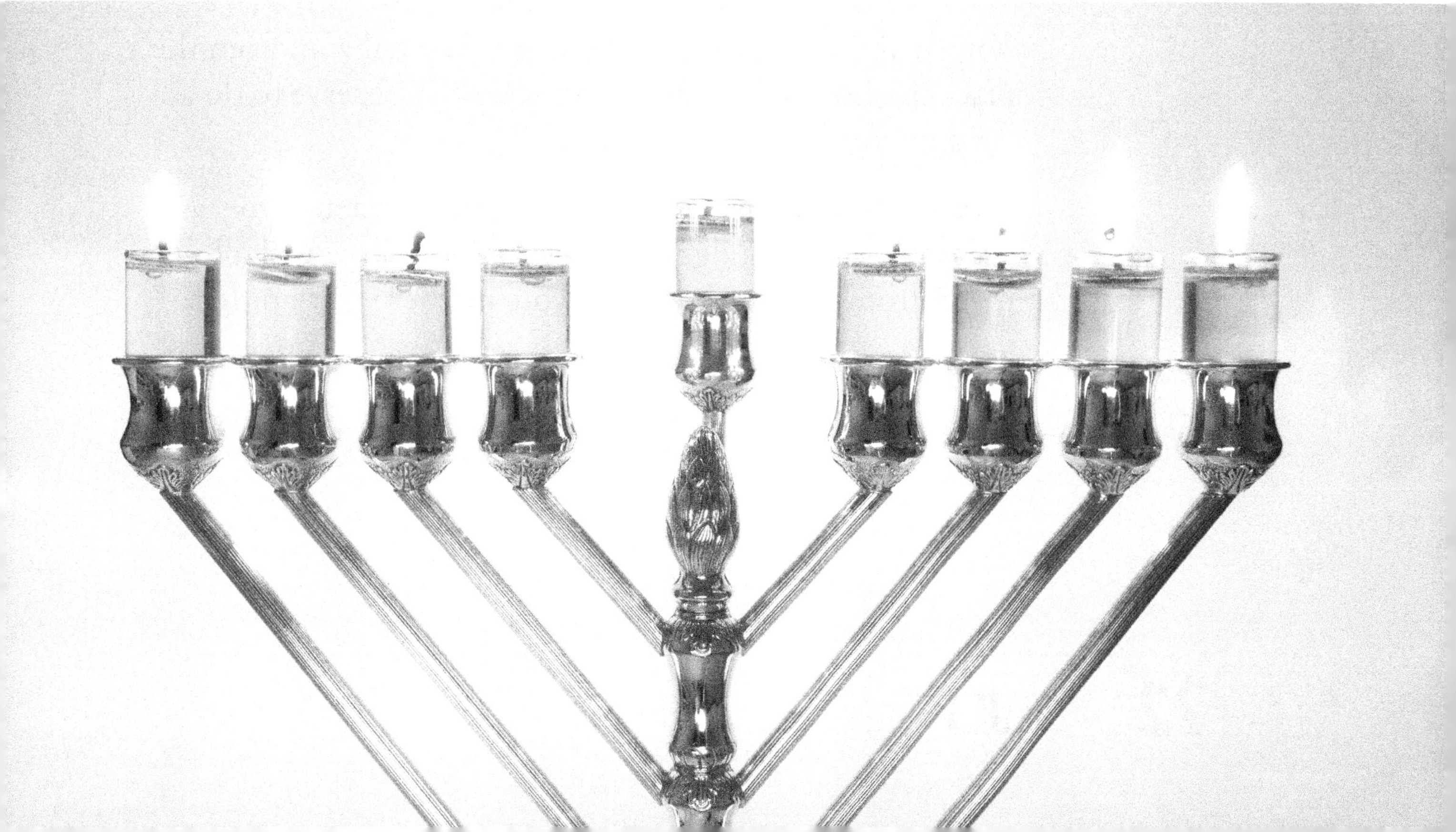

Text 2

Deuteronomy 17:8–11

כִּי יִפָּלֵא מִמְּךָ דָבָר לַמִּשְׁפָּט, בֵּין דָּם לְדָם, בֵּין דִּין לְדִין, וּבֵין נֶגַע לָנֶגַע, דִּבְרֵי
רִיבֹת בִּשְׁעָרֶיךָ, וְקַמְתָּ וְעָלִיתָ אֶל הַמָּקוֹם אֲשֶׁר יִבְחַר ה' אֱלֹקֶיךָ בּוֹ.

וּבָאתָ אֶל הַכֹּהֲנִים הַלְוִיִּם וְאֶל הַשֹּׁפֵט אֲשֶׁר יִהְיֶה בַּיָּמִים
הָהֵם, וְדָרַשְׁתָּ וְהִגִּידוּ לְךָ אֵת דְּבַר הַמִּשְׁפָּט.

וְעָשִׂיתָ עַל פִּי הַדָּבָר אֲשֶׁר יַגִּידוּ לְךָ מִן הַמָּקוֹם הַהוּא אֲשֶׁר
יִבְחַר ה', וְשָׁמַרְתָּ לַעֲשׂוֹת כְּכֹל אֲשֶׁר יוֹרוּךָ.

עַל פִּי הַתּוֹרָה אֲשֶׁר יוֹרוּךָ וְעַל הַמִּשְׁפָּט אֲשֶׁר יֹאמְרוּ לְךָ תַּעֲשֶׂה,
לֹא תָסוּר מִן הַדָּבָר אֲשֶׁר יַגִּידוּ לְךָ יָמִין וּשְׂמֹאל.

If a matter eludes you in a case involving capital punishment, litigation, leprous marks, a case where there is a dispute in your cities, then you shall set out and go up to the place that God your Lord shall choose.

You shall come to the Levitical priests and to the judge who will be in those days, and you shall inquire, and they will tell you the words of judgment.

You shall do according to the word they tell you, from the place the Lord will choose, and you shall observe to do according to all they instruct you.

You shall do according to the law they instruct you and according to the judgment they say to you; you shall not divert from the word they tell you, neither right nor left.

Text 3

Maimonides, *Mishneh Torah*, Laws of Blessings 11:3

נִמְצָא עִנְיַן הַדְּבָרִים וְהַצָּעָן כָּךְ הוּא: אֲשֶׁר קִדְּשָׁנוּ בְּמִצְוֹתָיו
שֶׁצִּיוָּה בָּהֶן לִשְׁמוֹעַ מֵאֵלּוּ שֶׁצִּוָּנוּ לְהַדְלִיק נֵר שֶׁל חֲנוּכָּה.

It follows, therefore, that we mean to say, "[Blessed are You . . .] Who has sanctified us with His commandments and commanded us to listen to those who commanded us to kindle the Chanukah light."

Rabbi Moshe ben Maimon
(Maimonides, Rambam)
1135–1204

Halachist, philosopher, author, and physician. Maimonides was born in Cordoba, Spain. After the conquest of Cordoba by the Almohads, he fled Spain and eventually settled in Cairo, Egypt. There, he became the leader of the Jewish community and served as court physician to the vizier of Egypt. He is most noted for authoring the *Mishneh Torah*, an encyclopedic arrangement of Jewish law, and for his philosophical work, *Guide for the Perplexed*. His rulings on Jewish law are integral to the formation of halachic consensus.

FIGURE 3.2

Categories of Oral Torah

1	**Received**	God-given explanations for each of the commandments
2	**Derived**	Laws that we derive from the Written Torah and the Received Oral Torah
3	**Legislated**	New laws legislated by rabbinic sages
4		

Does He Even Care?

Text 4

Midrash Tanchuma, Parashat Naso 29

לֹא יֹאמַר אָדָם אֵינִי מְקַיֵּים מִצְוֹת זְקֵנִים הוֹאִיל וְאֵינָן מִן הַתּוֹרָה. אָמַר לָהֶם הַקָּדוֹשׁ בָּרוּךְ הוּא: בָּנַי, אֵין אַתֶּם רַשָּׁאִין לוֹמַר כַּךְ, אֶלָּא כָּל מַה שֶׁגּוֹזְרִים עֲלֵיכֶם תִּהְיוּ מְקַיְּימִין, שֶׁנֶּאֱמַר "וְעָשִׂיתָ עַל פִּי הַתּוֹרָה אֲשֶׁר יוֹרוּךָ". לָמָּה? שֶׁאַף עַל דִּבְרֵיהֶם אֲנִי מַסְכִּים.

A person should not say, "I will not comply with the sages' enactments because they are not Torah laws." God tells such a person, "My child, it is not proper to say this. Rather, obey all that they tell you, as it says, 'You shall do according to the law they instruct you.' Why? Because I agree with their words."

Midrash Tanchuma

A midrashic work bearing the name of Rabbi Tanchuma, a 4th century Talmudic sage quoted often in this work. Midrash is the designation of a particular genre of rabbinic literature usually forming a running commentary on specific books of the Bible. *Midrash Tanchuma* provides textual exegeses, expounds upon the biblical narrative, and develops and illustrates moral principles. *Tanchuma* is unique in that many of its sections commence with a halachic discussion, which subsequently leads into non-halachic teachings.

A Sampling of Legislation

You Be a Sage

LEARNING EXERCISE 1

Case 1

It is the first century of the Common Era, and pirate activity on the Mediterranean is rampant. In addition to the plunder of personal property, the pirates sell the passengers and seamen into slavery. Representatives of Jewish communities around the Mediterranean endeavor to buy captive Jews in order to set them free. The pirates often demand that the Jews pay higher prices than what they usually charge slave buyers. While the community is committed to performing the mitzvah of redeeming captives, oftentimes the communal coffers cannot bear the burden. There are also rumors that the pirates are specifically targeting Jews.

Suggested Enactment	Arguments Against the Enactment	Vote
1.		
2.		
3.		

Case 2

It is during the lifetime of King David. Amnon, David's son, developed intense feelings of lust for his half sister Tamar. He pretended to be sick and asked Tamar to prepare and serve him food; but when they were alone, he raped her. Absalom, Tamar's brother, had Amnon murdered in revenge.

Suggested Enactment	Arguments Against the Enactment	Vote
1.		
2.		
3.		

Case 3

Jewish holidays are exciting and meaningful. However, it seems that many members of the community are so busy with their daily struggles that they are underprepared for the holidays. In addition, many people find it is hard to remember all of the holiday laws from year to year, such as the laws pertaining to building a *sukah* or baking matzah.

Suggested Enactment	Arguments Against the Enactment	Vote
1.		
2.		
3.		

Tikun Olam

Text 5

Mishnah, Gitin 4:6

אֵין פּוֹדִין אֶת הַשְּׁבוּיִים יֶתֶר עַל דְּמֵיהֶן, מִפְּנֵי תִּיקּוּן הָעוֹלָם.

For the purpose of *tikun olam* [societal remedy], we do not redeem captives for more than their worth.

Mishnah

The first authoritative work of Jewish law that was codified in writing. The Mishnah contains the oral traditions that were passed down from teacher to student; it supplements, clarifies, and systematizes the commandments of the Torah. Due to the continual persecution of the Jewish people, it became increasingly difficult to guarantee that these traditions would not be forgotten. Rabbi Yehudah Hanasi therefore redacted the Mishnah at the end of the 2nd century. It serves as the foundation for the Talmud.

Tikun Hadat: Building a Fence

Text 6

Maimonides, *Mishneh Torah*, Laws of Prohibited Relations 22:3

כְּשֶׁאֵירַע מַעֲשֵׂה אַמְנוֹן וְתָמָר, גָּזַר דָּוִד וּבֵית דִּינוֹ עַל יִיחוּד פְּנוּיָה.

When Amnon raped Tamar, King David and his court prohibited the seclusion of a man with an unmarried woman.

Text 7

Maimonides, *Mishneh Torah*, Laws of Rebels 2:9

גְּזֵרָה שֶׁלֹּא יָבֹא מִן הַדָּבָר חוֹבָה, וְיֹאמְרוּ הָעוֹף מוּתָּר מִפְּנֵי שֶׁלֹּא נִתְפָּרֵשׁ, כַּךְ . . . בְּשַׂר בְּהֵמָה מוּתֶּרֶת חוּץ מִן הָעֵז. וְיָבֹא אַחֵר לוֹמַר אַף בְּשַׂר הָעֵז . . . בַּחֲלֵב הָעֵז שֶׁאֵינָהּ אִמּוֹ מוּתָּר, שֶׁלֹּא נֶאֱמַר אֶלָּא "אִמּוֹ".

It is a decree, lest the matter lead to harm. People might say, "Fowl [with milk] is permitted, because the verse only forbids a 'kid in its mother's milk.' Similarly, then . . . the meat of all animals is permitted with the exception of a goat." Another will add, "Even the meat of a goat . . . is permitted with goat's milk as long as the milk is not from its mother, for the verse only says, 'its mother.'"

Text 8

Talmud, Yevamot 21a

"וּשְׁמַרְתֶּם אֶת מִשְׁמַרְתִּי" (וַיִּקְרָא יח,ל): עֲשׂוּ מִשְׁמֶרֶת לְמִשְׁמַרְתִּי.

"You shall safeguard My charge (Leviticus 18:30)": [This means,] "Make a fence around My charge."

Text 9

The Lubavitcher Rebbe, Rabbi Menachem Mendel Schneerson, *Likutei Sichot* 4:1076–1077

עַל דֶּרֶךְ זֶה אִיז אוֹיךְ דֶער טַעַם אוֹיף דִי פֶערשִׁיידֶענֶע גְדָרִים אוּן סְיָיגִים וואָס חַזַ"ל הָאָבְּן מְתַקֵן גֶעווען, בְּעִיקָר, אִין דֶער צַייט פוּן בַּיִת שֵׁנִי. אִין דֶעם זְמַן פוּן בַּיִת רִאשׁוֹן הָאָט דאָך מֵאִיר גֶעווען אֱלָקוּת בְּגִילוּי; אוֹיךְ אִין דִי זִיבּעֶצִיק יאָר וואָס נאָך דֶעם עֶרְשְׁטְן חוּרְבָּן, אִיז נאָךְ אַלְץ פַאַרְבְּלִיבְּן, אִין אֵיינִיגֶע פְּרָטִים, דֶער גִילוּי אֱלָקוּת ווִי עֶר אִיז גֶעווען אִין בַּיִת רִאשׁוֹן. אָבֶּער בִּזְמַן בַּיִת שֵׁנִי ווען עֶס הָאָט גֶעפֶעלְט אִין דֶעם גִילוּי פוּן דֶעם אוֹר הַקְדוּשָׁה אוּן מְצַד דֶעם אִיז דֶער חוֹשֶׁךְ פוּן לְעוּמַת זֶה פַאַרְשְׁטאַרְקְט גֶעוואָרְן, הָאָט מֶען דאָךְ מְתַקֵן גֶעווען דִי גְדָרִים וְסְיָיגִים בִּכְדֵי צוּ קֶענֶען בַּייקוּמֶען דֶעם גְרוֹיסְן חוֹשֶׁךְ פוּן לְעוּמַת זֶה.

אוּן דֶערִיבֶּער, אִיז פוּן דוֹר צוּ דוֹר, ווען דֶער חוֹשֶׁךְ אִיז וואָס ווַייטֶער גֶעוואָרְן אַלְץ גְרֶעסֶער, הָאָט מֶען אוֹיךְ אַלְץ מֶער אוּן מֶער צוּגֶעגֶעבְּן חוּמְרוֹת גְדָרִים אוּן סְיָיגִים.

There were many fences and boundaries that the sages enacted, mainly during the Second Temple era.

The era of the First Temple was marked by a revelation of God. This revelation remained, in some respects, even during the seventy years of exile. But during the Second Temple era, the sacred light was lacking and the darkness of opposing forces intensified. The sages therefore enacted fences and boundaries to overcome the great darkness.

Therefore, from one generation to the next, as the darkness intensifies, we correspondingly add protections and boundaries.

Rabbi Menachem Mendel Schneerson
1902–1994

The towering Jewish leader of the 20th century, known as "the Lubavitcher Rebbe," or simply as "the Rebbe." Born in southern Ukraine, the Rebbe escaped Nazi-occupied Europe, arriving in the U.S. in June 1941. The Rebbe inspired and guided the revival of traditional Judaism after the European devastation, impacting virtually every Jewish community the world over. The Rebbe often emphasized that the performance of just one additional good deed could usher in the era of Mashiach. The Rebbe's scholarly talks and writings have been printed in more than 200 volumes.

Tikun Hadat: Other Enactments

Text 10

Rabbi Shne'ur Zalman of Liadi, *Shulchan Aruch HaRav, Orach Chayim* 429:1

חֲכָמִים הָרִאשׁוֹנִים תִּקְנוּ בִּזְמַן שֶׁבֵּית הַמִּקְדָּשׁ הָיָה קַיָּים, שֶׁיַּתְחִילוּ
הַדַּרְשָׁנִים לִדְרוֹשׁ בָּרַבִּים הִלְכוֹת הָרֶגֶל שְׁלֹשִׁים יוֹם לִפְנֵי הָרֶגֶל.

While the Temple stood, the early sages legislated that lecturers should begin to publicly teach the laws of the holiday thirty days before the holiday begins.

Rabbi Shne'ur Zalman of Liadi
(Alter Rebbe)
1745-1812

Chasidic rebbe, halachic authority, and founder of the Chabad movement. The Alter Rebbe was born in Liozna, Belarus, and was among the principal students of the Magid of Mezeritch. His numerous works include the *Tanya*, an early classic containing the fundamentals of Chabad Chasidism, and *Shulchan Aruch HaRav*, an expanded and reworked code of Jewish law.

Text 11

Talmud, Berachot 48b

מֹשֶׁה תִּקֵּן לְיִשְׂרָאֵל בִּרְכַּת הַזָּן בְּשָׁעָה שֶׁיָּרַד לָהֶם מָן.

Upon the descent of the manna, Moses instituted the recitation of the first blessing of Grace after Meals.

Limitations

Do Not Add

Text 12

Deuteronomy 4:2

לֹא תֹסִפוּ עַל הַדָּבָר אֲשֶׁר אָנֹכִי מְצַוֶּה אֶתְכֶם וְלֹא תִגְרְעוּ מִמֶּנּוּ,
לִשְׁמֹר אֶת מִצְוֹת ה' אֱלֹקֵיכֶם אֲשֶׁר אָנֹכִי מְצַוֶּה אֶתְכֶם.

You shall not add to the word I command you, nor shall you subtract from it. You must keep all the commandments of God your Lord, which I am instructing you.

QUESTION FOR DISCUSSION

Is this verse reconcilable with the idea that the sages can enact new laws?

Text 13

Maimonides, *Mishneh Torah*, Laws of Rebels 2:9

אִם יָבוֹא בֵּית דִּין . . . וְאִם יֶאֱסוֹר בְּשַׂר הָעוֹף, וְיֹאמַר שֶׁהוּא בִּכְלַל הַגְּדִי וְהוּא אָסוּר מִן הַתּוֹרָה, הֲרֵי זֶה מוֹסִיף.

אֲבָל אִם אָמַר בְּשַׂר הָעוֹף מוּתָּר מִן הַתּוֹרָה, וְאָנוּ נֶאֱסוֹר אוֹתוֹ וְנוֹדִיעַ לָעָם שֶׁהוּא גְּזֵרָה שֶׁלֹּא יָבֹא מִן הַדָּבָר חוֹבָה . . . אֵין זֶה מוֹסִיף אֶלָּא עוֹשֶׂה סְיָיג לַתּוֹרָה.

If a *beit din* would . . . forbid fowl [with milk] saying that it is included in the category of "kid," and therefore biblically forbidden, it would be "adding" [to the Torah].

If, however, the *beit din* says, "The Torah permits fowl [with milk] but we are prohibiting it, and we will notify the people that this is a decree that aims to prevent transgression" . . . this is not called "adding," but "making a fence" around the Torah.

Text 14

Talmud, Beitsah 3b

וְכָל סְפֵיקָא דְאוֹרַיְיתָא לְחוּמְרָא . . . וְכָל סְפֵיקָא דְרַבָּנָן לְקוּלָא.

Any doubt regarding a biblical law is dealt with strictly . . . and any doubt regarding a rabbinic law is dealt with leniently.

With the People in Mind

Text 15

Talmud, Bava Batra 60b

אָמַר ר' יִשְׁמָעֵאל בֶּן אֱלִישָׁע: מִיּוֹם שֶׁחָרַב בֵּית הַמִּקְדָּשׁ, דִין הוּא שֶׁנִגְזוֹר עַל עַצְמֵנוּ שֶׁלֹא לֶאֱכוֹל בָּשָׂר וְלֹא לִשְׁתּוֹת יַיִן, אֶלָא אֵין גוֹזְרִין גְזֵרָה עַל הַצִּבּוּר אֶלָא אִם כֵּן רוֹב צִבּוּר יְכוֹלִין לַעֲמוֹד בָּהּ.

Rabbi Yishmael ben Elisha said: "From the day the Holy Temple was destroyed, it would have been proper to prohibit eating meat and drinking wine; but we do not issue a decree unless the majority of the public can stand by it."

Text 16

Maimonides, *Mishneh Torah*, Laws of Rebels 2:6

הֲרֵי שֶׁגָּזְרוּ בֵּית דִין גְזֵירָה, וְדִימוּ שֶׁרוֹב הַקָהָל יְכוֹלִין לַעֲמוֹד בָּהּ, וְאַחַר שֶׁגָּזְרוּהָ פִּקְפְּקוּ הָעָם בָּהּ, וְלֹא פָּשְׁטָה בְּרוֹב הַקָהָל, הֲרֵי זוּ בְּטֵלָה.

If a court issued a decree thinking that the majority of the community could stand by it, but after the decree was issued, the majority of the community had reservations about it and the practice did not spread throughout the majority of the community, the decree is nullified.

Customs

From the People

Text 17

Talmud, Pesachim 50b

בְּנֵי בֵּייְשָׁן נָהוּג דְלֹא הָווּ אָזְלִין מִצּוֹר לְצִידוֹן בְּמַעֲלֵי שַׁבְּתָא.

אָתוּ בְּנַיְיהוּ קַמֵּיה דְרַבִּי יוֹחָנָן, אָמְרוּ לוֹ: אַבְהָתִין אֶפְשָׁר לְהוּ, אֲנַן לֹא אֶפְשָׁר לָן.

אָמַר לְהוּ: כְּבָר קִיבְּלוּ אֲבוֹתֵיכֶם עֲלֵיהֶם, שֶׁנֶּאֱמַר (מִשְׁלֵי יא,א):
"שְׁמַע בְּנִי מוּסַר אָבִיךָ וְאַל תִּטֹּשׁ תּוֹרַת אִמֶּךָ".

The citizens of Beyshan had the custom not to go from Tyre to Sidon on Friday.

Their children went to Rabbi Yochanan and said to him, "For our ancestors, this was possible; for us, it is impossible."

Said he to them, "Your fathers have already taken this stringency upon themselves. And it says (Proverbs 11:1), 'Hear my child, the instruction of your father, and forsake not the teaching of your mother.'"

Text 18

Tosafot

A collection of French and German Talmudic commentaries written during the 12th and 13th centuries. Among the most famous authors of *Tosafot* are Rabbi Ya'akov Tam, Rabbi Shimshon ben Avraham of Sens, and Rabbi Yitschak ("the Ri"). Printed in almost all editions of the Talmud, these commentaries are fundamental to basic Talmudic study.

Tosafot, Menachot 20b

וּמִנְהָג אֲבוֹתֵינוּ תּוֹרָה הִיא.

A custom of our ancestors is [part of] Torah.

FIGURE 3.3

Some Notable Holiday Customs

Rosh Hashanah	Eating an apple dipped in honey
Yom Kippur	Wearing a white garment
Sukot	Taking a willow branch on the seventh day of the festival
Shemini Atseret	Celebrating the completion of the Torah, the dancing, etc.
Chanukah	Kindling an additional flame on the menorah each evening
Purim	Donning a costume
Passover	Refraining from eating legumes (Ashkenazic custom)
Shavu'ot	Eating dairy food

FIGURE 3.4

Categories of Oral Torah

1	**Received**	God-given explanations for each of the commandments
2	**Derived**	Laws that we derive from the Written Torah and the Received Oral Torah
3	**Legislated**	New laws legislated by rabbinic sages
4	**Customary**	Customs initiated by the people, intended to enhance an aspect of Judaism

Balance of Power

LEARNING EXERCISE 2

Each category of Torah features a distinct balance of divine and human contributions.

Using the letters W (Written), R (Received), D (Derived), L (Legislated), and C (Customary), indicate where each of these categories belongs on the scale below.

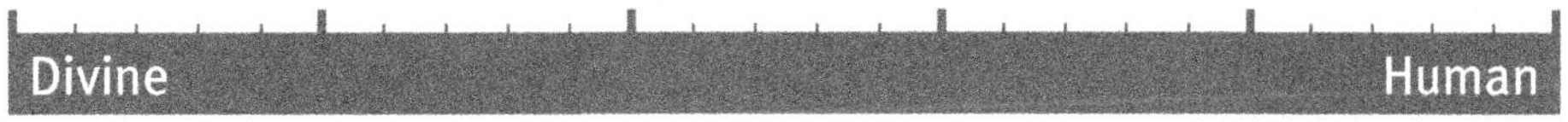

Text 19

The Lubavitcher Rebbe, Rabbi Menachem Mendel Schneerson, *Likutei Sichot* 19:385

דער תַּכְלִית הַכַּוָּונָה אִיז, אַז אִידְן זאָלן מאַכְן דִי דִירָה בְּתַחְתּוֹנִים
דוּרְךְ זַייעֶר אֵייגֶענֶער עֲבוֹדָה, עֲבוֹדָה בְּכֹחַ עַצְמָם . . .

אַף עַל פִּי אַז דִי "דִירָה", וואָס אִידְן שאַפְן בְּכֹחַ עַצְמָם, ווערְט אוֹיפְגֶעטאָן
דוּרְךְ דער עֲבוֹדָה פוּן כָּל הַתּוֹרָה וּמִצְוֹת בְּכָל פְּרָטֵיהֶם, שְׁטֵייט עֶס בְּגִילוּי
. . . אִין דעֶם עִנְיָן פוּן מִנְהָגֵי יִשְׂרָאֵל, הֱיוֹת אַז אוֹיף זֵיי אִיז נִיטאָ קֵיין צִיוּוּי
מִלְמַעֲלָה און בְּמֵילָא קוּמֶען זֵיי אִינְגאַנְצְן בְּכוֹחָם פוּן אִידְן אַלֵיין.

God's ultimate intention is for us to make this world into "a home" for God through our own effort and initiative. . . .

Although this is accomplished through all of Torah and *mitzvot,* this accomplishment is most apparent . . . when we observe Jewish customs, inasmuch as they are not commandments from above but initiated entirely by the Jewish people.

Three Stages of Love

Text 20

Rabbi Yanki Tauber, "Intuition," www.meaningfullife.com

The hallmark of a loving marriage is each partner's readiness to do the will of the other. If one partner expresses a desire for something, the other will do everything in his or her power to bring about its fulfillment.

A greater love is demonstrated when each partner also strives to fulfill the *implied* will of the other. To the truly devoted spouse, it makes no difference if a desire has been explicitly expressed or merely hinted at—he or she will carry it out with the same devotion and commitment to the loved one's gratification.

Finally, there are those very special marriages in which there is no need for even the merest of allusions. So deep is the bond between husband and wife that each intuitively knows what the other wants of him or her. Indeed, when two people love each other to such a degree, there is no greater joy than that experienced when one has succeeded in sensing and satisfying the other's desire all on one's own.

Rabbi Yanki Tauber
1965–

Chasidic scholar and author. A native of Brooklyn, NY, Rabbi Tauber is an internationally renowned author who specializes in adapting the teachings of the Lubavitcher Rebbe. He is a member of the JLI curriculum development team, and has written numerous articles and books, including *Once Upon a Chassid* and *Beyond the Letter of the Law*.

Key Points

TORAH Café™

Continue the JLI Learning Experience!

Visit www.TorahCafe.com/go/JD3

for a video lecture(s) related to the theme of this lesson.

1. In addition to authorizing the sages to enact laws and ordinances, God guides them so that they arrive at the proper conclusions. Hence, God concurs with each particular rabbinic enactment.

2. One type of rabbinic enactment is intended to fix a societal problem. For example, to combat the problem of slave traders targeting Jews, the sages decreed that when redeeming Jewish captives, we are not allowed to pay more than the slave-market value.

3. Another type of enactment is designed to safeguard against biblical transgression. Examples include the prohibitions of *yichud* and eating chicken with milk. Such enactments became more prevalent when overall spiritual sensitivity diminished.

4. Rabbinic enactments must be presented as such. If they are presented as new God-given instructions, it would constitute a transgression of the prohibition against adding to the commandments of the Torah.

5. The sages may not pass an enactment unless they assess that the majority of the population can tolerate it. If they passed a law based on this assessment and it turned out that the population did not accept it, the law is void.

6. Customs initiated by the people as a means of enhancing religious observance is an important element of the Torah tradition. In a certain respect, such customs reflect our deepest bond with God.

7. The categories of Torah that place greater emphasis on human discovery and initiative are crucial for fulfilling the ultimate purpose of Creation.

ADDITIONAL READINGS

CUSTOM

BY RABBI ARYEH KAPLAN

1. It is assumed that the Jewish people are given a degree of Divine Inspiration in ascertaining God's will, and therefore, custom strongly influences Jewish law.[1] Similarly, they are granted a degree of Divine Inspiration in creating customs.[2]

2. An accepted Jewish custom is known as a *minhag* (מנהג).[3]

3. The authority given to the Jewish people is such that even when the Sanhedrin passed legislation, it would not be binding until accepted by the populace.[4]

4. Customs were even instituted by the ancient prophets.[5] Likewise, in many cases, the Sanhedrin would formally ratify customs, making them as binding as any other rabbinical law.[6]

5. To a large degree, Jewish practice depends on custom as much as on law. Therefore, if one wishes to understand Judaism, one must understand the concept of Jewish customs.[7]

6. Throughout the world, different Jewish communities observe different customs.[8] Although this may make their observances appear very different in outward form, in essence, the differences are actually very minor. With regard to the basic observances of the laws of the Torah, all traditional Jewish communities are essentially the same.[9]

7. Every community differs in history and culture.[10] Individuals have different natures,[11] and so do cities and localities.[12] Just as each river flows along its natural path, so does each community.[13] The customs of

---

Rabbi Aryeh Kaplan (1934-1983) American rabbi, author, and physicist. Rabbi Kaplan authored more than 50 volumes on Torah, Talmud, Jewish mysticism, and philosophy, many of which have become modern- day classics. He is best known for his popular translation and elucidation of the Bible, *The Living Torah*, and his translation of the Ladino biblical commentary, *Me'am Lo'ez*.

1 See above, Chapter 12, note 11.

2 *Teshuvoth Maharik* 9:1, 54:1; Rabbi Yosef Halevi Nazir, *Teshuvot Matteh Yosef, Orach Chaim* 2 (Constantinople, 1717); *Pachad Yitzchak*, s.v. *Minhag* (137b).

3 Cf. 2 Kings 9:20; Targum on Ruth 4:7. Also see Rashi, *Taanith* 26b, s.v. *Ora'oy.*

4 See above, 11:46.

5 *Sukkah* 44a; Rashi *ad loc.* s.v. *Minhag; Teshuvoth HaGeonim, Shaarey Teshuvah* 307; *Halakhoth Pesukoth min HaGeonim* 180; Rabbi Yitzchak ibn Ghayyath, *Shaarey Simchah* (Furth, 1861), Volume 1, pp. 112,113; *HaManhig* 40 (Constantinople, 1519), p.70a; *Shibboley HaLeket* 369 *Sefer Yereyim* (Hashalem) 422. *Cf.* Ramban on Genesis 29:27. Also see below, note 94. The prophets had to institute the practice as a custom, since they could not institute laws; above, 8:31.

6 *Yad, Mamrim* 1:2,3 2:2,5. Cf. *Pri Megadim,* Introduction 1:41. See above, 11:40. Also see *Teshuvoth Rashba* 3:411, 1:729, 5:126; Rabbi Yaakov Reischer (author of Shevuth Yaakov), *Teshuvoth Minchath Yaakov* 1, at end of commentary on *Torath Chatath* (Prague, 1689). See *Lechem Mishneh, Talmud Torah* 6:14 11.

7 Rabbi Yosef Yozefa (ben Moshe) Kasman, *Nohag KeTz'on Yosef* (Hanau, 1718), Introduction.

8 Cf. *Sukkah* 3:11 (38a); *Pesachim* 119b; *Sofrim* 10:7. The most prominent division in custom was between the Ashkenazim and the Sepharadim; see above, Chapter 12, notes 53,54. Also see Obadiah 1:20; Rashi *ad loc.;* Meiri, *Magen Avoth* (London, 1909). For reasons for these divisions, see *Darkey HaHorah* 2 (in *Kithvey Maharatz* Chajas). pp. 244,245. Also see *Abudarham,* Introduction; Rabbi Yosef (beYitzchak) Ibn Ezra (author of *Atzmoth Yosef* on *Kiddushin). Maaseh Melekh* 7:15 (Salonika, 1601); *Kenesseth HaGedolah, Hagahoth al HaTur, Yoreh Deah* 214:31;
Pachad Yitzchak, s.v. *Devarim* (80c). Regarding the different customs in prayer, see *Pri Etz Chaim, Inyan Tefillah* (Koretz, 1782), p. 3d; *Shulchan Arukh HaAri,* Kavannoth HaTefillah 4; *Magen Avraham* 68:0; *Maggid Devarav LeYaakov* 141; *Teshuvoth Chatham Sofer, Orach Chaim* 15; *Teshuvoth Divrey Chaim, Orach Chaim* 2:8; *Teshuvoth Maharam Shik, Orach Chaim* 43; *Sedey Chemed, Mem* 38 (4:100).

9 *Beth Elohim, Shaar HaYesodoth* 38.

10 See *Darkey HaHorah* 2 (in *Kithvey Maharatz Chajas),* p. 225. Jewish communities are also influenced by their gentile surroundings; *Sefer Chasidim* 1101; *Sefer Chasidim* (from manuscript) 1301 (Berlin, 1891), p. 321. Cf. *Yad, Deyoth* 6:1; *Moreh Nevukhim* 3:46.

11 *Berakhoth* 58a; *Sanhedrin* 38a; *Yerushalmi, Berakhoth* 9:1; *BaMidbar Rabbah* 21:2; *Tanchuma, Pinchas* 10; *Yad, Deyoth* 1:1.

12 Cf. *Shabbath* 31a.

13 *Chulin* 18b, 57a; Rashi.ad *loc.* s.v. *Nahara; Arukh,* s.v. *Nahar.* Cf. *Gittin* 60b; Rashi *ad loc. s.v. BeMezil.* See *Teshuvoth Binyamin Zeev* 303.

each place thus tend to strengthen the Torah according to the character of that place.[14]

8. Customs usually involve practices that occur frequently or periodically.[15] Since habit becomes second nature,[16] these customs tend to reinforce Torah values in those areas.

9. Customs tend to create a strong bond between people, and therefore are a powerful force against assimilation.[17] Customs also tend to strengthen the bond between succeeding generations.[18]

10. In business matters, Torah law recognizes that people usually follow custom.[19] Therefore, where Torah law does not specifically cover a case, it is often decided on the basis of custom.[20]

11. There are two ways through which a person can obligate himself by his word: though an oath (*shevuah* שבעה)[21] and through a vow (נדר).[22] An oath obligates the person to keep his word, since if he does not, he will have been lying. A vow, on the other hand, gives a person a new obligation that he did not have before.[23]

12. It is forbidden to violate an oath or vow, as it is written, "When a man makes a vow to God, or makes an oath to make something forbidden to himself, he must not break his word; he must do all that he expresses" (Numbers 30:3).[24]

13. The concept of an oath parallels the oath through which Israel accepted the Torah.[25] Through vows, on the other hand, both individuals and communities can take upon themselves obligations which are not included in the Torah.[26]

14. Although Biblical law requires the verbal acceptance of a vow, rabbinical law renders any religious habit or custom binding as a vow, even without verbal acceptance. [27]

15. Therefore, if a person accustoms himself to observe any religious practice not required by law, he is obligated to adhere to his custom, just as if he actually made a vow to do so. [28]

14 *Darkey HaHorah 7* (p. 239). Cf. Rashi, *Betza* 25b, s.v. *Dathehem.*

15 See below, 13:50.

16 *Hergel naaseh teva;* Rabbi Shem Tov (ben Yosef) Falaquera, *HaMaaloth* 2 (Berlin, 1894); *Sheveiley Emunah* 4:5; Rabbi Shaul Halevi Mortira, *Giva'ath Shaul, Tazria* (Amsterdam, 1645); Rabbi Moshe (ben Menasheh) Chefetz (Gentile), *Melekheth Mach'sheveth Tazria* 2 (Venice, 1710); *Kitzur Shulchan Arukh* 32:8. Cf. *Yad, Deyoth* 2:2; *Yoma* 86b; *Moed Katan* 27b; *Sotah* 22a; *Arkhin* 30b; *Kiddushin* 20a, 40a.

17 *Darkey HaHorah 7* (p. 339). See above, Chapter 4, note 95.

18 *Teshuvoth Rashba* 3:41; *Kedushath Levi* on Genesis 15:8 (Jerusalem, 1958), p. 22. Cf. *Shabbath* 23a, *Sukkah* 46a, from Deuteronomy 32:7; *Midrash Lekach Tov, Emor,* p. 66a.

19 *Teshuvoth HaRosh* 55:10, 64:4; *Teshuvoth Rashbash* 562; *Teshuvoth Rashdam, Choshen Mishpat* 380; *Teshuvoth Chavath Yair* 91; Rabbi Yitzchak Stein on *Sefer Mitzvoth HaGadol,* Positive Commandments (Venice, 1547), p. 56c. Cf. Yerushalmi, *Kethuboth* 6:4 (40b). Also see *Teshuvoth Rashba* 4:142, 3:411; *Teshuvoth Rivash* 305; *Teshuvoth Tashbatz* 2:132, 2:239.

20 *Bava Metzia* 7:1 (83a); *Kethuboth* 6:4 (66b); *Tosefta, Bava Kama* 11:5 (end); *Tosefta, Kethuboth* 6:4; *Tosefta, Maasroth* 1:11; *Choshen Mishpat* 201:2; *Kenesseth HaGedolah ibid.; Pachad Yitzchak,* s.v. *Minhagey Mamon* (141d). In business law a custom can even take precedence over the law; *Yerushalmi, Bava Metzia* 7:1 (27b); *Peney Moshe ad loc.* s.v. *Zoth;* Rif, *Bava Metzia* 52a. See below, note 75.

21 Leviticus 19:12; *Yad, Shevuoth* 1:3; *Sefer HaMitzvoth,* Negative Commandment 61; *Sefer Mitzvoth HaGadol,* Negative Commandment 239; *Chinukh* 227.

22 Deuteronomy 23:24; *Yad, Nedarim* 1:4, *Sefer HaMitzvoth,* Positive Commandment 94; *Sefer Mitzvoth Gadol,* Positive Commandment 124; *Chinukh 575.*

23 Cf. *Rosh HaShanah* 6a; *Nedarim* 7a; *Yad, Nedarim* 1:1,2, *Shevuoth* 4:21. Whereas in the case of oaths there is only a negative commandment not to violate (note 21), in the case of vows, there is also a positive commandment to keep them (note 22). Furthermore, oaths primarily obligate the person *(gavra)*, while vows affect their object (cheftza); *Nedarim* 2b; Yad, *Nedarim* 3:7; Rashi, *Nedarim* 16b, s.v. *Eleh Amar; Tosafoth ibid.* s.v. Hah, *Shevuoth* 25a, s.v. *Hah;* Bertenoro, *Nedarim* 2:2; *Chinukh* 30.

24 Yad, *Nedarim* 1:5; *Sefer HaMitzvoth,* Negative Commandment 157; *Sefer Mitzvoth Gadol,* Negative Commandment 242; *Chinukh* 407.

25 See above, 5:13. Also see Bachya, Introduction to *Mattoth;* Alshekh on Numbers 30:3.

26 Hirsch on Numbers 30:2. Also see *Sifethey Cohen* on Numbers 30:3; Rabbi Eliezer Pappo, *Elef HaMagen ibid.* (Salonika, 1828). Cf. Rabbi Mordecai Yosef of Izbetza, *Mey HaShilo'ach, ibid.* (Vienna, 1860).

27 *Rosh, Pesachim* 4:3, *Nedarim* 2:4; Ran, *Nedarim* 81b, s.v. *MiShum; Yoreh Deah* 214:1; *Chayay Adam* 127:7; *Chokhmath Adam* 92:14; *Kitzur Shulchan Arukh* 67:7. Cf. *Sheiltoth* 67. This rule is derived from the verse, "He shall not break his word *(davar)*" (Numbers 30:3). The word *davar* also denotes a custom; Rashash, *Nedarim* 15a; *Targum* on 2 Kings 9:20; Rashi, *Pesachim* 54a. s.v. *Ama.*

28 *Rosh, Pesachim* 4:3, *Nedarim* 2 :4; Ran, *Nedarim* 81b, s.v. *MiShum; Yoreh Oeah* 214 :1; *Chayay Adam* 127:7; *Chokhmath Adam* 92: 14; *Kitzur Shulchan Arukh* 67:7. Cf. *Sheiltoth* 67. This rule is derived from the verse, "He shall not break his word *(davar)*" (Numbers 30:3). The word *davar* also denotes a custom; Rashash, *Nedarim* 15a; *Targum* on 2 Kings 9:20; Rashi, *Pesachim* 54a. s.v. *Ama.*

16. A religious practice is established as a binding personal custom as soon as it is performed once with the intent of doing so permanently.[29]

17. If a person wishes to stop observing a person custom he can formally annul it before a rabbinical court, just like any other vow.[30] Regret that one has adopted a custom binding as a vow is sufficient ground for its formal annulment.[31]

18. If a person wishes to adopt a personal custom without having it binding as a vow, he should expressly state this intent when he first begins to practice the customs.[32] Likewise, he should declare that he is only adopting the custom temporarily, and has no intention of making it a permanent practice.[33]

19. When a person adopts a personal custom, it is assumed that he does so anticipating certain contingencies that *temporarily* prevent him from observing his custom. Therefore, one may temporarily discontinue a custom because of illness[34] or a religious celebration[35] that prevents its observance. However, it is not assumed that one anticipates illness or other changes in plans which will necessitate him to discontinue a custom *permanently*. Therefore, in such a case, the custom must be formally annulled.[36]

20. An erroneous custom *(minhag ta'uth)* does not have to be annulled formally.[37]

21. Therefore, if a person erroneously assumes something to be forbidden and accustoms himself accordingly, upon discovering his error, he may abandon his custom without formal annulment.[38] The same is true if one adopts a custom as a safeguard to keep himself from what he erroneously thought to be a serious sin.[39]

22. Likewise, a foolish or unfounded custom, having no true religious significance, can be abandoned without formal annulment.[40]

23. Individual customs are only binding on the individuals who adopt them. Therefore, a person's children are not bound to abide by his personal customs, unless they themselves adopt them.[41] Similarly, a community is not bound by the personal customs of its religious leaders, unless they are adopted by the community itself.[42]

24. A community custom is binding on all members of the community for all times.[43]

---

29 Mordecai, *Pesachim* 602; *Hagahoth Maimonioth, Shevuoth* 12:12 3; *Hagahoth Asheri, Pesachim* 4:3; *Yoreh Deah* 214:1; *Beer Hetiv, Orach Chaim* 581:10; *Mishnah Berurah* 597:6. If he does not have specific intent, it becomes binding after three times; *Perishah, Yoreh Deah* 214:2; *Kitzur Shulchan Arukh* 67:7; *Pri Megadim, Eshel Avraham* 597:2; *Mishnah Berurah* 597:4. Cf. *Choshen Mishpat* 163:3 in *Hagah;* HaGra *ad loc.* 163:57, from *Yevamoth* 64b; *"Rav"Shulchan Arukh* 468:17. Also see *Terumath HaDeshen* 342; Rabbi Yaakov Castro (Maharikash), *Teshuvoth Ohaley Yaakov* 61 (end) (Livorno, 1783); *Nachalath Shivah* 27:6 (Warsaw, 1884), p. 70b; *Sedey Chemed, Mem* 37, s.v. *U'LeInyan* (4:75).

30 Mordecai, *Pesachim* 602; Rosh, *Pesachim* 4:3; *Hagahoth Maimonioth, Shevuoth* 12:12 3; *Yoreh Deah* 214:1; *Chayay Adam* 127:8,9; *Pri Chadash, Orach Chaim* 496, *Diney Minhagey Issur* 1; *Teshuvoth Tashbatz* 2:46; *Teshuvoth Radbaz* 3:527 (962). Other authorities, however, maintain that it cannot be annulled; *Yoreh Deah* 214:1, second opinion; *Teshuvoth Rashba* 3:236; Ran, *Pesachim* (Rif 17b, top); Ritva, *Pesachim* 51a; *Teshuvoth Rivash* 44; *Machzor Vitri*, p. 243 (end); *Otzar HaGaonim, Nedarim* 81b; cf. *Yerushalmi, Pesachim* 4:1 (25b); Rif, *Pesachim* 17a. See below, 13:51, 13:61.

31 *Yoreh Deah* 214:1; *Kitzur Shulchan Arukh* 67:7.

32 That is, he should say that he is doing it "without a vow" *(beli neder)*; *Yoreh Deah* 214:1.

33 *Kitzur Shulchan Arukh* 67:7. Cf. *Magen Avraham* 161:13; *Turey Zahav* 161:16.

34 *Dagul Me'rvavah, Yoreh Deah* 214:1; *Pith'chey Teshuvah ibid.* 214:1; *Magen Avraham* 581:12. *Beer Hetiv* 581:12. Other authorities, however, appear to maintain that even a temporary illness is not automatically anticipated; *Sifethey Cohen, Yoreh Deah* 214:2; *Chayay Adam* 127:8.

35 Cf. *Orach Chaim* 568:2 in *Hagah.*

36 *Yoreh Deah* 214:1.

37 Cf. Rashi, *Pesachim* 2b, s.v. *MiShaath.* See *Teshuvoth Rashbam, Orach Chaim* 1 (end).

38 *Yerushalmi, Pesachim* 4:1 (25b); *Yerushalmi, Taanith* 1:6 (6b); *Tosafoth, Pesachim* 51a, s.v. *Iy, Eruvin* 101b, s.v. *Rabbi Yosi, Megillah* 5b, s.v. *Devarim;* Ran, *Pesachim* (Rif 17a), s.v. *Tanya;* cf. *Chulin* 6b; *Yoreh Deah* 214:1, first opinion; HaGra *ad loc.* 214 :4; *Pri Chadash, Orach Chaim* 468:4; *Chayay Adam* 127:7. Others, however, require formal annulment in such a case; Mordecai, *Pesachim* 602; *Yoreh Deah* 214:1, second opinion; HaGra *ad loc.* 214:5. See second opinion above in note 30.

39 *Sifethey Cohen, Yoreh Deah* 214:5; *Chayay Adam* 127:7. Cf. *Yoreh Deah* 232:10.

40 See below, 13:33.

41 *Teshuvoth Chavath Yair* 126; *Pri Chadash, Orach Chaim* 496, *Diney Minhagey Issur* 7; *Beer Hetiv, Yoreh Deah* 214:5; *Pith'chey Teshuvah* ibid. 214:5; Rabbi Yosef Steinhart, *Zikhron Yosef, Teshuvoth, Yoreh Deah* 14 (Furth, 1733); *Chayay Adam* 127:11. Others, however, maintain that children are bound; *Maasah Melekh* 7:4; *Kenesseth HaGedolah, Yoreh Deah* 214:49; *Pachad Yitzchak*, s.v. *Devarim* (80d).

42 Original.

43 Ramban, *Mishpat HaCherem*, in *Teshuvoth Ramban* 288; *Kol Bo*, end; *Chidushey HaRamban* (Jerusalem, 1928), end of Volume 1; *Teshuvoth Rivash* 399. See next note. Also see Chapter 5, note 33. This is also binding as a vow; *Nedarim* 15a, *Pesachim* 51a, *Teshuvoth Chatham Sofer, Yoreh Deah* 107, s.v. *Shavti.*

25. Therefore, once a custom is established in a community, it is binding upon all future generations, as well as upon all newcomers to the community.[44] The community has the authority to enforce its customs.[45]

26. It is a commandment from Biblical tradition[46] to abide by all community customs, as it is written, "Hear, my son, your Father's instruction, and do not forsake your Mother's Torah" (Proverbs 1:8).[47] It is taught that "Father" in this verse refers to God,[48] while "Mother" refers to the nation of Israel.[49]

27. Our "Mother's Torah" is the Torah created by the Jewish people themselves, namely, their religious customs.[50] It is therefore taught, "A custom of Israel is Torah."[51] Moreover, just like the Torah itself, a custom is binding for all generations.[52]

28. Only a respectable custom *(minhag chashuv)* is universally binding.[53] This is a custom originated by Torah scholars even as the law itself was.[54] However, a custom initiated by the unlearned masses is considered an inferior custom *(minhag garua).*[55] Such a custom may be binding on those who observe it, just as any other personal custom, but it does not have the status of a community custom.[56]

29. An inferior custom is not binding on newcomers to the community[57] or on future generations[58] unless they themselves adopt the custom.[59]

30. Nevertheless, even an inferior custom should never be publicly violated. To do so would cause dis-

44 *Yoreh Deah* 214:2; *Teshuvoth Rivash* 399; *Teshuvoth Rashba* 3:411; *Teshuvoth Tashbatz* 2:132; *Teshuvoth Rabbi Moshe Alshakar* 49. Cf. *Pesachim* 50b.

45 The majority can impose the custom on the minority; *Massa Melekh* 7:12; *Kenesseth HaGedolah, Yoreh Deah* 214:25; *Pachad Yitzchak* s.v. *Devarim* (80c). In some cases, fines can also be imposed; *Yerushalmi, Pesachim* 4:3 (27a); *Tosafoth, Bekhoroth* 2a, s.v. *Konsim.* In some extreme cases, corporal punishment (flogging) can also be imposed; *Yerushalmi, Bikkurim* 1:5 (3b); *Yerushalmi, Kiddushin* 4:6 (46a).

46 *Divrey Kabbalah*, see above, Chapter 8, note 55. See *Chayay Adam* 127:11. Some say that it is an *asmakhta* (see above, Chapter 11, note 75); *Teshuvoth Chavath Yair* 126. See above, note 27. Also see *Chulin* 92a; *Gilyon HaShas, Pesachim* 55a; but see above 13:3.

47 *Pesachim* 50b; Ran *ad loc* (Rif 17b), s.v. *VeNimtzinu; Chulin* 93b; Rashi *ad loc.* s.v. *Al; She'iltoth* 67; *Halakhoth Gedolah, Megillah* (end); *Yalkut Shimoni* 1:892 (305c); *Chayay Adam* 127:1. See *Teshuvoth Rashdam, Orach Chaim* 35.

48 And not one's actual father, see above, note 41. Also see Rabbi Shlomo Eiger, *Gilyon Maharsha, Yoreh Deah* 214:2. Cf. *Sifri* on Deuteronomy 32:2; *Shemoth Rabbah* 30:5.

49 *Berakhoth* 35b; *Sanhedrin* 102a; *Yalkut Shimoni* 2:962; *Zohar* 2:85a, 3:213a. In this verse, the word for mother *ima* is said to denote one's nation, *umah; Tanchuma, Re'eh* 14; *Yalkut Shimoni* 1:892 (305c); Bachya, Introduction to *Avoth* (end) (4:526). Also see *Sifra* on Leviticus 9:1 (44c); *Shemoth Rabbah* 25:5; *BaMidbar Rabbah* 12:8; *Shir HaShirim Rabbah* 3:21; Rashi on Song of Songs 3:11; *Pesikta* 1 (4b); *Yalkut Shimoni* 2:986; from Isaiah 51:4; cf. *Minchath Shai ad loc. Cf.* Rashi *Berakhoth* 54a, s.v. *VeOmer;* Bertenoro on *Berakhoth* 9:5 (end). Some say that taking the value of the final Kaf (ך) to be 500, the numerical value of *ime-kha* in this verse is the same as that of *Yisrael; Sefer Chasidim* 970; Maharsha, *Berakhoth* 35b, s.v. *Lo Kushia.* Also see *Zohar* 3:55a, 3:197b, 3:277b.

50 Rashi *ad loc.* states that it also refers to rabbinical laws; *cf.* HaGra *ibid.* Also see Proverbs 6:20; *Sefer Chasidim* 970.

51 *Minhag Yisrael Torah Hi*; Teshuvoth Ramban 260: Rashba *Torath HaBayith* 2:3 (Yosefov, 1883), p. 34b; quoted in *Beth Yosef, Yoreh Deah* 39; *Darkey Moshe, Yoreh Deah* 116:5 (end); *Yoreh Deah* 242:14 in *Hagah; Matteh Ephraim* 610; *Beth Elohim, Shaar HaYesodoth* 38; *Teshuvoth Maharik* 54:1 Bachya, Introduction to *Avoth* (end) (4:526). There is a similar expression, "The custom of our fathers is Torah;" *Tosafoth, Minachoth* 20b, s.v. *Nifsal; Shiltey Gibborim, Berakhoth* (Rif 39b) 3; *Teshuvoth Maharik* 102:3, *Yoreh Deah* 376:4 in *Hagah.* Also *see* Rashi, *Pardes* 1,174 (Warsaw, 1870); *Teshuvoth Rivash* 44; *Teshuvoth Rashba* 3:326; below, note 108.

52 See above, note 43. Also see above, Chapter 5, note 33. See *Teshuvoth Rashba* 3:411; *Teshuvoth Rivash* 399; Pri Chadash, Orach Chaim 496, *Diney Minhagey Issur* 7; *Hagahoth Ben HaMechaber, Minchath Chinukh* 467; *"Rav" Shulchan Arukh* 468:9, *Cf.* Judges 21:1. Also see *Yoreh Deah* 228:35; *Beer HaGolah ad* loc. 228:79; HaGra *ad loc.* 228:99; *Teshuvoth HaRosh* 5:4.

53 There is a question as to whether this is the same as a *minhag vathikin;* see note 76.

54 *Cf.* Hirsch on Numbers 30:2.

55 *Cf.* Rashi, *Taanith* 26b, s.v. *Ora'oy; Teshuvoth Maharik* 171, *Teshuvoth Chavath Yair* 91. See Rashi, Pesachim 2b, s.v. *MiShaath.* Also see *Tosafoth, Eruvin* 62b, s.v. *U'Rabbi,* 72a, s.v. *Nagu, Pesachim* 103a, s.v. *VeAmar, Rosh HaShanah* 15b, s.v. *VeKhi, Kethuboth* 3b, s.v. *VeThu;* Maharatz Chajas, *Eruvin* 46b.

56 *Tosafoth , Pesachim* 51a; s.v. *Iy;* Rosh, *Pesachim* 4:3; Rabbenu Yerocham, *Toledoth Adam VeChavah* 3:5; Rabbi Yitzchak Stein on *Sefer Mitzvoth HaGadol,* Positive Commandments (56c); *Magen Avraham* 468:4; *Sifethey Cohen, Yoreh Deah* 214:7; *"Rav" Shulchan Arukh* 468:16. Others, however, consider all customs binding unless they are patently erroneous as described in 13:20, 13:33; Ran. *Pesachim* (Rif 16a), s.v. *Tanya,* (Rif 17b) s.v. *VeNimtzinu;* Raavad *ibid* (Rif 17a) 2; Ritva, *Pesachim* 51a. See second opinion in note 30. Also see *Tosafoth, Berakhoth* 52b, s.v. *Nahagu; Pachad Yitzchak,* s.v. *Minhag* (138c).

57 See note 56.

58 *Magen Avraham* 468:4; *Pri Megadim ad loc.; "Rav" Shulchan Arukh* 468:17.

59 *"Rav" Shulchan Arukh* 468:17.

sension and also result in the ignorant taking other laws and customs lightly.[60]

31. A newcomer to the community, however, may violate inferior customs in the presence of scholars, since it is assumed that these reasons do not apply.[61] Nevertheless, all native residents, including scholars, must abide even by inferior customs, unless they are formally annulled.[62]

32. Where it is not known whether a custom was originated by scholars or not, it is assumed that it was, and it is considered a respectable custom. This is especially true if the custom is of long standing.[63]

33. In order to qualify as a religious custom, a practice must have some justification, based on the Talmud, Midrash, or other sacred literature. A baseless observance has neither the status of a private or public custom, and may be abandoned without formal annulment.[64] This is especially true if such a practice may lead to a violation of a law.[65] It is also true if because of its stringency, the custom will tend to discourage religious observance.[66]

34. Where it is a custom to forbid something due to a *known* lack of information, the prohibition does not extend to newcomers in possession of the required information. Similarly, a resident of a community practicing such a prohibition need not keep it while visiting a community where the required information is available.[67] Nevertheless, the acquisition of the necessary information does not justify an entire community to abandon its custom, since it is possible that the custom also involved a safeguard against other prohibitions.[68]

35. Wherever there is any question of law and a local or regional custom exists, the custom should be followed.[69] The custom should be observed even if it follows the opinion of a single authority who is disputed by the majority.[70]

36. However, where observance of a local or regional custom results in the violation of any law, the custom should be abolished.[71]

60 *Tosafoth, Pesachim* 51a, s.v. *Iy; Sifethey Cohen, Yoreh Deah* 214:7. Cf. *Pesachim* 51a; *Yerushalmi, Pesachim* 4:1 (26a).

61 However, where there is a possibility of dissension, one should keep such customs even in the presence of scholars; *Sifethey Cohen, Yoreh Deah* 214:7.

62 *Tosafoth, Pesachim* 51a, s.v. *Iy; Sifethey Cohen, Yoreh Deah* 214:7; *"Rav", Shulchan Arukh* 268:16. Regarding annulment, see below, 13:51.

63 Rashba, *Chulin* 18b; *Teshuvoth Rashba* 98; *Pri Chadash, Orach Chaim* 496, *Diney Minhagey Issur* 3; *Massa Melekh* 7:1; *Kenesseth HaGedolah* 214:43; *Pachad Yitzchak*, s.v. *Devarim* (80d); *Birkey Yosef, Yoreh Deah* 214:2. Also see *Beth Yosef, Yoreh Deah* 194, s.v. *Kathav* (74a); Rabbi Elazar (ben Elazar) Kalir, *Or Chadash* on Pesachim 51a (Frankfort am Adar, 1771). Cf. *Teshuvoth Rivash* 44. See below, 13:45, 13:58.

64 *Pri Chadash, Orach Chaim* 496, *Diney Minhagey Issur* 15; *Idem., Orach Chaim* 468:3; from Ran, *Pesachim* (Rif 18a), s.v. *VeLaila; Maggid Mishneh* on *Yad, Yom Tov* 8:19; *Teshuvoth Rivash* 44; *Beth Yosef, Orach Chaim* 670 (end). *Cf.* Rambam on Mishnah, *Gittin* 5:8; *Yad, Issurey Biyah* 11:14,15. Also see *Teshuvoth Besamim Rosh* 19; *Teshuvoth Rashdam, Orach Chaim* 34; Rabbi Yosef Igres, *Teshuvoth Divrey Yosef* 1 (Livorno, 1742); *Sedey Chemed, Mem* 38, s.v. *U'VeLav* (4:104), s.v. *Shuv* (4:105).

65 *Ibid.* Cf. *Pesachim* 51a; Rabbi Chaim Palaggi, *Massa Chaim, Resh* 222 (Salonika, 1874). p. 60; *Kereithi U'Pelethi, Tifereth Yisrael, Yoreh Deah* 194:2; *Darkey Teshuvah* 194:7. See below, note 71.

66 Cf. *Sefer Chasidim* 362. Also see *Avoth deRabbi Nathan* 1:5.

67 *Chulin* 63a; Rosh, *Chulin* 3:60; *Yoreh Deah* 82:4; HaGra *ad loc.* 82:8; *Sifethey Cohen ad loc.* 82:10; *Turey Zahav* 82:5; *Chokhmath Adam* 36:7.

68 Rosh, *Chulin* 3:60; *Yoreh Deah* 82:5; HaGra *ad loc.* 82:9; *Sifethey Cohen* 82:11; *Turey Zahav* 82:6; *Yam Shel Shlomo, Chulin* 3:115; *Teshuvoth Nodeh BeYehudah, Tinyana, Yoreh Deah* 29; *Chokhmath Adam* 36:8. Cf. *Teshuvoth HaRosh* 20:20; *Maadney Yom Tov* on *Rosh, Chulin* 3:60 323. Other authorities, however, dispute this; cf. *Yoreh Deah* 82:5, HaGra *ad* loc. 82:9, from *Niddah* 7b.

69 *Yerushalmi, Peah* 7:5 (34b); *Yerushalmi, Maaser Sheni* 5:2 (30a); *Yerushalmi, Yevamoth* 7:3 (40a). Also see *Berakhoth* 45a; *Pesachim* 54a; *Menachoth* 35b; *Orach Chaim* 3:11 in *Hagah; Choshen Mishpat* 409:3 in *Hagah; Teshuvoth Rabbi Yaakov (Mahari) Weil* 7C (Venice, 1513); *Teshuvoth Maharik* 54:1, 102:2; *Teshuvoth Ramban* 260; Rashi, *Chulin* 18b, s.v. *Nahara; Pri Chadash, Orach Chaim* 496, *Diney Minhagey Issur* 10; Rabbi Chaim Abulafia, *Mikra'ey Kodesh, Orach Chaim* 496 (Ismir, 1729); Chida, *LeDavid Emeth, Kuntres Acharon* 21; *Sedey Chemed, Peh* 23 (4:463). See above, Chapter 12, note 12.

70 *Magen Avraham* 690:22; *Beer Hetiv* 690:14; *Pri Chadash, Orach Chaim* 496, *Diney Minhagey Issur* 11; *Teshuvoth Maharil* 37. See above, 12:33. Also see *Eruvin* 62b, 72a; *Rosh HaShanah* 15b; *Tosafoth ad* loc. s.v. *VeKhi; Darkey HaHorah* 3 (p. 226); Rabbi Aryeh Leib Tzintz, *Magen HaElef* (with *Sar HaElef, Shem Chadash*, Novidvar-Warsaw, 1817) 489; *Sedey Chemed, Mem* 38, s.v. *VeHisagti*, s.v. *VeAl* (4:90). Even scholars may keep such a custom; *Teshuvoth Rabbi David Cohen (Radakh)* 5. Others, however, dispute this, and maintain that the majority opinion must be followed completely; *Teshuvoth Rashbash* 419. In any case, this is true if the rabbis of a given region reach a decision in formal session: *Atereth Tz'vi, Mishpatey HaHorah* 5 (in *Kithvey Maharatz Chajas*), p. 380.

71 See above, note 65. Also see *Massa Meiekh* 7:7; *Pachad Yitzchak*, s.v. *Minhag* (137c.d); from *Pesachim* 51a; Rabbi Asher (ben Immanuel) Shalem, *Matteh Asher* (Salonika, 1748), p. 130d; *Sedey Chemed, Mem* 38, s.v. *VeHaRav* (4:87). Also see *Teshuvoth HaRosh* 56:5; *Binyamin Zeev* 159, 303, 361; *Teshuvoth Rama* 21; Rabbi Yitzchak Stein on *Sefer Mitzvoth HaGadol*, Positive Commandments (56c); *Magen Avraham* 468:4; Rabbi Barukh (ben Shlomo) Kaley, *Makar Barukh* 35 (Ismir, 1659); *Kenesseth HaGedolah, Yoreh Deah* 214:14; *Pachad Yitzchak*, s.v. *Devarim* (80b); *Chatham Safer, Orach Chaim* 66. Cf. *Massa Melekh* 7:5; *Pachad Yizchak*, s.v. *Minhag* (137c).

37. A local or regional custom should also be abolished if it opposes an unambiguous law.[72] This is even true if such action may result in strife.[73]

38. Even if a custom is based on the opinion of earlier authorities, it must be abandoned if present authorities deem it forbidden.[74]

39. There is a general principle that custom annuls a law (*minhag mebhatel halakhah*)[75] This, however, is only true of a custom of pious scholars *(minhag vathikin)*[76] and not of a custom initiated by the common people.[77]

40. The principle that custom takes precedent over law applies primarily to the case of business law, and not in questions of ritual law.[78] Where business law is concerned, a custom is like a mutually binding contract.[79]

41. Where ritual law is concerned, custom can take precedence over *halakhah* only in the case of a rab-

72 *Sifethey Cohen, Yoreh Deah* 259:8; *Pri Chadash, Orach Chaim* 496, *Diney Minhagey Issur* 10; *Chatham Sofer, Orach Chaim* 690:17; *Beur Halakhah ibid.* Also see *Tosafoth, Rosh HaShanah* 15b, s.v. *VeKhi;* Maharatz Chajas *ad loc.; Shiltey Gibborim, Pesachim* (Rif 17a) 1; *Teshuvoth Rivash* 49, 122, 388, 389, 390; *Darkey HaHorah* 3 (p. 226). This is certainly true where a Biblical law is violated by the custom; *Massa Melekh* 7:5; *Nachalath Shivah* 27:6; *Pachad Yitzchak,* s.v. *Minhag* (137c, 139d); *Sedey Chemed, Mem* 38, s.v. *U'VeDivrey* (4:89); *Arukh HaShulchan*
651:2, s.v. *VeDa; Pele Yoetz,* s.v. *Minhag.* Also see *Sedey Chemed, Mem* 38 (4:80). There are some cases where people try to justify serious sins on the basis of custom. Regarding this, it is taught that *minhag* spelled backwards is *Gehenom*; Rabbenu Tam, quoted in *Teshuvoth Rabbi Moshe Mintz* 67 (Cracow, 1617); *Teshuvoth Binyamin Zeev* 307; *Massa Chaim, Gimel* 29 (p. 49); *Chut HaShani* 56; *Teshuvoth Shevuth Yaakov* 2:6; *Teshuvoth Nachalath Shivah* 78; *Teshuvoth Rabbi Betzalel Ashkenazi* 24; Rabbi Yosef Zechariah (ben Nathan) Stern, *Zekher Yehosef, Drach Chaim* 20 (Warsaw, 1899), p. 36; *Sedey Chemed, Mem* 38, s.v. *Mah* (4:101), s.v. *U'LeKushioth* (4:91). Cf. Maharil, *Hilkhoth Pesach* (Jerusalem, 1969), p. 18b.

73 *Pri Chadash, Drach Chaim* 496, *Diney Minhagey Issur* 16; *Mishnah Berurah* 468:23 (end).

74 *Pri Chadash, Drach Chaim* 496, *Diney Minhagey Issur* 10, quoting *Teshuvoth Radbaz* 73.

75 In the case of business law; *Yerushalmi, Bava Metzia* 7:1 (27b); Rif, *Bava Metzia* 52a. In the case of ritual law; *Yerushalmi, Yevamoth* 12:1 (66a); *Sofrim* 14:18. Cf. *Tosefta, Shevi'ith* 2:8. See *Teshuvoth Maharik* 9:2, 102:2; *Darkey HaHorah* 4 (pp. 228, 230). Some authorities state that the Babylonian Talmud disputes the Yerushalmi; *Teshuvoth Rashbash* 562. However, Rabbenu Tam states explicitly that the Babylonian Talmud also maintains this view; *Sefer HaYashar* (Vienna, 1811), p. 43a; cf. Rif, *Bava Metzia* 52a; also see *Shabbath* 35b; *Eruv in* 104b; *Taanith* 28b. Some authorities dispute this principle completely; *Teshuvoth Rif* 13; *Teshuvoth Rivash* 44, from *Rosh HaShanah* 15b; *Teshuvoth Tashbatz* 3:160. Others say that a custom can only forbid something, but it cannot permit something; Ritva, *Pesachim* 51a; *Teshuvoth Radbaz* 1:359 (end), 3:645 (1070), 4:94 (1165) (end); *Kenesseth HaGedolah, Yoreh Deah* 214:4; *Pachad Yitzchak, s.v. Devarim* (80b); *Sedey Chemed, Mem* 38, s.v. *U'VeSethirath* (4:84), s.v. *Gam* (4:109). Cf. *Yad, Shevithath Assar* 3:3; *Teshuvoth Rabbi Yosef ibn Lev (Rival)* 3:14; *Teshuvoth Ralbtich* 2:11; *Massa Melekh* 7:14; *Kenesseth HaGedolah, Yoreh Deah* 214:4; *Pachad Yitzchak,* s.v. *Devarim* (80a).

76 Regarding the word *vathikin,* see *Berakhoth* 9b, 25b, 26a; *Rosh HaShanah* 32b; Rashi, *Berakhoth* 9b, s.v. *Vathikin; Sefer HaTishbi,* s.v. *Vathak; Maadney Yom Tov* on Rosh. *Berakhoth* 1:10, 70 (cf. Rashi, *Gittin* 70a, s.v. *Vathik);* Maharsha. *Shabbath* 105a, s.v. *Vathik.*

77 *Sofrim* 14:18; Mordecai, *Bava Metzia* 366; *Sefer HaAgudah* (Cracow, 1571), p. 228a; *Teshuvoth Maharik* 9:3, 54:2, 102:2; *Teshuvoth Binyamin Zeev* 303, *Tumath Yesharim* 120, 138; *Kenesseth HaGedolah, Yoreh Deah* 214:3; *Pachad Yitzchak,* s.v. *Devarim* (80a); *Teshuvoth Minchath Yaakov* 1 (in *Torath Chatath); Darkey HaHorah* 3 (p. 226). Some authorities write that a *minhas vathikin* is one that appears in the codes; *Teshuvath Nachalath Shivah* 38. There is also an important opinion that a *minhag vathikin* is only one formally instituted by leading rabbis; Ramban, *Bava Bathra* 144b, s.v. *DeAmrinan; Numukey Yosef, Bava Bathra* (Rif 67b, end); Ritva , *Kethuboth* 100a; *Bedek HaBayith , Choshen Mishpat* 368:6; *Teshuvoth* Radbaz 3:497 (932); *Massa Chaim* 13 (p. 47); Rabbi Eliahu (ben Moshe) Yisrael, *Kol Eliahu* 1, *Evven HaEzer* 14, s.v. *MeAtah* (Livorno, 1792), p. 66d; Rabbi Raphael Asher Covo, Shaar *Asher, Yoreh Deah* 11 (Salonika, 1877), p. 20c; *Sedey Chemed, Mem 37,* s.v. *U'LeBhatel* (4:76), *Mem* 38, s.v. *VeRa'ithi* (4:81). s.v. *U'BheSiyyum* (4:86). Cf. *Teshuvoth Nachalath Shivah* 78.

78 See above, 13:10. Some say that the rule applies *only* to business law; *Teshuvoth HaRosh* 55:10; *Teshuvoth Radbaz* 359 (end); *Teshuvoth Chavath* Yair 91; Rabbi Chaim Benveneste, *Ba'ay Chayay, Etz HaDaath, Yoreh Deah* 196 (end) (Salonika, 1788); Chidah, *Eyin Zokher, Mem* 19; Rabbi Chaim Palaggi, *Chaim VeShalom* 1:1 (Izmir, 1857); Rabbi Menasheh Sath'hon, *Kenesiah LeShem Shamayim* (Jerusalem, 1874), P: 55*; Sedey Chemed, Mem* 38, s.v. *Nachzor* (4:91), s.v. *Od* (4:108). Many authorities maintain that even in the case of business law, a custom must be formally enacted; Ramban *Nimukey Yosef,* quoted in note 77; Rabbi Nethanel (ben Aaron Yaakov) Segre, *Teshuvoth Afar Yaakov* 38 (Jewish Theological Seminary, Manuscript 791), quoted in *Pachad Yitzchak,* s.v. *Minhag* (140d); *Sedey Chemed, Mem* 38, s.v. *U'Mah* (4:108). According to these opinions, custom overrides law only when the law is in question; *Teshuvoth HaRosh* 55:10; Rabbi Yitzchak Stein on *Sefer Mitzvoth Gadol,* Positive Commandments (56c); see below, 13:41. Others write that in the case of ritual law, the Babylonian Talmud disputes the Yerushalmi; *Teshuvoth Rashbash* 562; see above, note 73. Some authorities, however, dispute this entire opinion, and state that custom overrides law even in the case of ritual law; *Teshuvoth Maharik* 9:3, from *Menachoth* 32a; *Magen Avraham* 690:22.

79 Teshuvoth *HaRosh* 64:4; *Teshuvoth Rashbash* 562; *Teshuvoth Rashdam, Choshen Mishpat* 380; Rabbi Yitzchak Stein on *Sefer Mitzvoth Gadol,* Positive Commandments (56c). See above, note 19.

binical law.[80] In the case of Biblical law, custom takes precedence only where the law itself is in question.[81]

42. Custom takes precedence only if it antedates the final decision of the law. Even when there was initially a question, once a law has been established, a custom cannot be introduced to oppose it.[82] This is especially true if the law has been established, in an accepted code.[83]

43. Therefore, even where ancient customs follow opinions disputed in the Talmud, they can be retained.[84] It can be assumed that in places where these customs prevail, the custom was in existence even before the Talmud was accepted by all Israel.[85]

44. Ancient customs should therefore be accorded great respect.[86] Wherever possible, effort should be made to justify them according to the law.[87]

45. If a custom has been kept by scholars and saints for many generations, it should be retained, even where it appears to contradict a law.[88] It is inconceivable that God would have allowed them constantly to do wrong.[89]

46. Hence, any custom followed by all Israel must be retained, even if it appears to go against the law.[90]

47. There are many customs which are based on a deeper understanding of the laws as found in the teachings of the Kabbalah. Since the Kabbalah is essentially based on Divine Inspiration, its decisions are not legally binding, and therefore such customs are no more obligatory than any other proper custom.[91]

48. Hence, when Kabbalistic customs are in conflict with laws based on the Talmudic authorities, the latter must be followed.[92] However, if there is a dispute

80 Raavad on *Yad, Maaser Sheni* 1:3; *Rashdam, Evven HaEzer* 129; *Teshuvoth Rabbi Moshe Mintz* 66:5; *Massa Melekh* 7:6; *Kenesseth HaGedolah, Yoreh Deah* 214:20; *Pachad Yitzchak*, s.v. *Devarim* (80b). Cf. *Teshuvoth Maharik* 9:2; *Maasa Melekh* 7:8; *Pachad Yitzchak*, s.v. *Minhag* (137d); *Sedey Chemed, Mem* 38, s.v. *VeGam* 4:91), s.v. *Gam* (4:108). Some authorities, however, maintain that the principle even applies to Biblical law; *Teshuvoth Tashbatz* 1:153; Rabbi Shimshon Morporgo, *Shemesh Tzadakah* 4 (end) (Venice, 1742), p. 26c, s.v. *Zoth; Ginath Veradim, Orach Chaim* 1:34; Rabbi Chaim Palaggi, *Semikha LeChaim* (Salonika, 1826), p. 9a, s.v. *Pash; Sedey Chemed, Mem* 38, s.v. *VeSefer*, s.v. *VeAl* (4:81), s.v. *U'Bhelnyan* (4:91), s. v. *Minhag* (4:80). Other authorities take the opposite opinion and maintain that it does not even apply in the case of a rabbinical law; *Pri Chadash, Orach Chaim* 496, *Diney Minhagey Issur* 10; cf. *Teshuvoth Rivash* 49, 122. This apparently would also be the opinion that a custom can never permit something, see above, note 75.

81 *Beer Sheva, Teshuvah* 22. See above, note 69.

82 *Teshuvoth Shevuth Yaakov* 2:6; Rabbi Mordecai Barukh Carabellio, *Tosafoth R'em, Chayay Yitzchak* (Livorno, 1761); *Matteh Asher* 28 (p. 136); *Darkey HaHorah* 3 (p. 226); *Sedey Chemed, Mem* 38, s.v. *VeHaHi* (4:90), s.v. *U'LeKushiath* (4:91). But see *Tosafoth, Chulin* 136b, s.v. *KeRabbi*.

83 See above, Chapter 12, note 14.

84 See above, Chapter 12, note 24. See *Darkey HaHorah* 2 (p. 224).

85 Rabbi Yitzchak Stein on *Sefer Mitzvoth Gadol*, Positive Commandments (56c). Cf. *Shabbath* 35b.

86 *Teshuvoth Maharik* 54:2,3; *Orach Chaim* 690:17 in *Hagah; Beth Yosef, Orach Chaim* 690, s.v. *Kathav* (371a); *Magen Avraham* 690:22; *Pachad Yitzchak*, s.v. *Minhag* (13d, 137a); *Darkey HaHorah* 6 (p. 235). *Cf.* Rambam, *Tosefoth Yom Tov*, on *Berakhoth* 9:5 (end).

87 *Teshuvoth Rabbi Meir (ben Yitzchak) Katzanelenbogen of Padua* 78 (beginning) (with *Teshuvoth Rabbi Yehudah* Mintz, Venice, 1553); *Massa Chaim* 258; Rabbi Moshe Yisrael, *Masath Moshe* 1, Yoreh Deah 17 (Constantinople, 1734); Rabbi Aaron (ben Chaim Avraham) Perachiah HaCohen; *Perach Matteh Aaron* 1:21 (Amsterdam, 1703); Rabbi Chaim HaCohen Rappaport, *Mayim Chaim, Orach Chaim* 12, s.v. *U'Me'acher; Teshuvoth Rashdam, Yoreh Deah* 193; *Sedey Chemed, Mem* 37, s.v. *Im* (4:78), *Mem* 38, s.v. *VeAfilu* (4:103). Cf. *Tosafoth, Berakhoth* 2a, s.v. *MeEmathai, Shabbath* 48a, s. v. *Deleythim*. Also see *Beth Hillel, Yoreh Deah* 364:4; *Shemesh Tzadakah, Orach Chaim* 4, s.v. *LeKol; Teshuvoth Chatham Safer, Orach Chaim* 51, s.v. *Omer*.

88 Mordecai, *Bava Metzia* 366; *Magen Avraham* 690:22; *Teshuvoth Radbaz* 3:532 (967). Cf. *Shabbath* 35b; *Eruvin* 104b; *Taanith* 28b; *Teshuvoth Maharik* 54:2; Rabbi Yitzchak Stein on *Sefer Mitzvoth Gadol*, Positive Commandments (56c); *Orach Chaim* 68; *Sedey Chemed, Mem* 38, s.v. *VeAf* (4:102).

89 *Teshuvoth Maharik* 54:4. See *Yevamoth* 99b; *Kethuboth* 28b; Gitlin 7a; *Chulin* 5b, 6a, 7a. Cf. *Teshuvoth HaRosh* 55:10.

90 *Teshuvoth Maharik* 54; Rabbi Shmuel (ben Moshe) Kaley, *Mishpatey Sh'muel* 92 (Venice, 1599); *Kenesseth HaGedolah, Yoreh Deah* 214:13; *Ibid., Hagahoth Beth Yosef, Choshen Mishpat* 201; *Pachad Yitzchak*, s.v. *Devarim* (80a,b); Rabbi Yitzchak Abulafia of Damascus, *Peney Yitzchak* 1:7 (Aram Tzova [Aleppo], 1871), p. 31, s.v. *Hiney: Teshuvoth Chatham Safer, Orach Chaim* 68. Cf. *Yevamoth* 102a; *Menachoth* 32a; *Berakhoth* 22a; *Chulin* 136b. Some authorities maintain that a custom in a major community is as strong as a universal custom; *Tumath Yesharim*
120; *Teshuvoth Chatham Safer, Orach Chaim* 66.

91 See above, note 5.

92 *Teshuvoth Radbaz* 4:80 (1151); *Beth Yosef, Orach Chaim* 25 s. v. *VeYeBharekh; Kenesseth HaGedolah, Orach Chaim, Kelaley HaPoskim* 1: *Turey Zahav, Orach Chaim* 274:1; *Magen Avraham* 25:20; *Beer Hetiv* 25:14; *Mishnah Berurah* 25:42; *"Rav" Shulchan Arukh* 25:48. Some say, however, that if a law is not mentioned expressly in the Talmud, one may follow the *Zohar*, even against later halakhic authorities; *Beth Yosef, Orach Chaim* 141, s.v. *U'MiTokh* (123b); *Sefer HaYuch'sin* 1, s.v. *Rabbi Shimon* (Jerusalem, 1962), p. 22a. If the *Yerushalmi* dispute the *Zohar*, we follow the *Yerushalmi;* Rabbi Chaim Binyamin Pontromoli, *Pethach HaDevir*, Volume 1 (Izmir, 1855), p. 46c; *Sedey Chemed, Kelaley HaPoskim* 2:9 (9:130). Also see *Pachad Yitzchak*, s.v. *Gemara* (69b).

among the Talmudic authorities, then the Kabbalistic custom may be followed,[93] just as any other custom.[94]

49. A practice only found in the Kabbalah, and not mentioned by Talmudic authorities, may be followed by individuals.[95] However, it cannot be forced upon the community unless it is already an established custom.[96]

50. For a practice to be considered a custom, it must occur fairly commonly. However, practices and decisions that are established in individual occurring cases do not establish a custom.[97]

51. Any community custom, whether adopted formally or spontaneously, can be annulled.[98] The annulment is accomplished by the common consent of the majority of the community[99] or their elected leaders.[100] Such action requires neither formal grounds[101] nor action by a rabbinical court.[102]

52. Just as a community can annul customs initiated by themselves, later generations can annul customs initiated by their ancestors.[103]

53. A custom is only binding on the community as a whole. Therefore, when the majority of the community agrees to annul a custom, it is no longer binding on the dissenting minority.[104]

54. Under no condition can an individual or the minority of a community exempt themselves from a community custom by formal annulment.[105]

---

93 *Teshuvoth Radbaz* 4:36 (1111); *Kenesseth HaGedolah, Orach Chaim, Kelaley HaPoskim* 2; *Magen Avraham* 25:20. Also see Rabbi Chaim Chizkiahu Medini *Mikhtav LeChizkiahu, Teshuvah* 3 (Izmir, 1866); *Idem., Or Li* 69 (Izmir, 1874) *Pethach HaDevir* 1:46a, 1:115a; Rabbi Chaim Palaggi, *Kol HaChaim* (Izmir, 1834), p. 26b; *Sedey Chemed, Kelaley HaPoskim* 2:13 (9:131), 15:9 (9:173).

94 See above, 13:35.

95 *Teshuvoth Radbaz* 4:80; *Teshuvoth Rabbi Yaakov HaLevi* 41 (Venice, 1514), *Kenesseth HaGedolah, Orach Chaim, Kelaley HaPoskim* 2; *Teshuvoth Chakham Tzvi* 36; *Shaarey Teshuvah, Orach Chaim* 25:11.

96 Rabbi Eliahu Mizrachi, *Teshuvoth She'eloth* 1:1 (Constantinople, 1560); *Kenesseth HaGedolah, Orach Chaim, Kelaley HaPoskim* 2; *Magen Avraham* 25:20.

97 *Terumath HaDeshen* 342; *Teshuvoth Rashdam, Choshen Mishpat* 436; *Teshuvoth Rabbi Yosef ibn Lev (Rival)* 3:30; *Kenesseth HaGedoiah, Yoreh Deah* 214:39; *Pri Chadash, Orach Chaim* 496, *Diney Minhagey Issur* 17; *Pachad Yitzchak*, s.v *Minhag* (136d), s.v. *Devarim* (80c end); *Sedey Chemed, Mem* 37, s.v. *VeKath* (4:75). Cf. *Tosafoth, Berakhoth* 22b, s.v. *VeNechzey; Yad, Shechitah* 11:3; *Teshuvoth Rivash* 463; *Choshen Mishpat* 331:1 in *Hagah*. A custom must also be unambiguous; *Teshuvoth Rivash* 475; *Teshuvoth Rashdam, Choshen Mishpat* 33. Regarding the case where there is a question involving the existence of a custom, see *Birkey Yosef, Yoreh Deah* 214:2; *Massa Chaim* 158 (p. 58); *Nishmath Kol Chai, Yoreh Deah* 66 (103b); *Sedey Chemed, Mem* 37, s.v. *Velm* (4:76), s.v. *Velm* (4:77) However, see *Tosafoth, Pesachim* 55a, s.v. *Amar.*

98 *Yerushalmi, Pesachim* 4:1 (26a); *Tosafoth, Shevuoth* 29b, s.v. *Ki;* Rosh, *Pesachim* 4:3; *Teshuvoth Rashba* 5:234; *Yoreh Deah* 228:25; *Teshuvoth Chavath Yair* 126; *Pri Chadash, Orach Chaim* 496, *Diney Minhagey Issur* 4; *Chayay Adam* 127:9. Also see *Teshuvoth HaGeonim, Shaarey Teshuvah* 139; Raavad, *Tamim Deyim* 192 (Lvov, 1812); *Otzar HaGeonim*, Gitlin 36a. There is, however, an opinion that a custom can only be annulled if it involves an error in law; *Teshuvoth Radbaz* 3:527 (962); see second opinion in note 30. If a custom is formally adopted by a community as a safeguard *(seyag)* to prevent a violation of law, all agree that it cannot be annulled; *Teshuvath Rivash* 178; *Yoreh Deah* 228:28; *Chayay Adam* 127:11. Cf. *Yoreh Deah* 228:15, from *Yerushalmi, Nedarim* 5:4 (18b). The distinction between a spontaneous and a formally adopted custom only applies to those who initiate the custom. Later generations, however, are considered as having spontaneously adopted their fathers' customs, unless they specifically adopted them, or unless the custom was specifically initiated on the condition that it should be binding on future generations; *Teshuvoth HaRosh* 5:4; *Yoreh Deah* 228:35; *Sifethey Cohen ad loc.* 228:94; *Teshuvoth Rabbi Moshe Alshakar* 49; *Chayay Adam* 127:12.

99 *Pri Chadash, Orach Chaim* 496, *Diney Minhagey Issur* 5; *Yoreh Deah* 228:31. Cf. *Horioth* 3b. Also see *Teshuvoth HaRosh* 5:4, 7:5; *Teshuvoth Rivash* 73; *Teshuvoth Tashbatz* 1:123, *Teshuvoth Chavath Yair* 127.

100 Ramban, *Mishpat HaCherem* (see note 43); *Teshuvoth Rashba* 5:234 , *Yoreh Deah* 228:31 in *Hagah;* from *Yerushalmi, Megillah* 3:2 (24a). Cf. *Teshuvoth Shevuth Yaakov* 1:74.

101 *Yoreh Deah* 228:25; Rosh, *Shevuoth* 3:23. Cf. *Yoreh Deah* 228:8, HaGra *ad loc.* 228:76.

102 Rosh, *Shevuoth* 3:23; *Teshuvoth Rashba* 5:234; *Yoreh Deah* 228:25. Also see Raavad, *Tamim Deyim* 213; *Teshuvoth Rabbi Yose f ibn Lev* (Rival) 2:72; *Teshuvoth Rabbi Yosef (ben Moshe) Trani (Maharit)* 1:69 (end) (Constantinople, 1641); *Teshuvoth Rabbi Moshe Alshekh* 75; *Teshuvoth Rashdam, Yoreh Deah* 26; *Mishpatey Sh'muel* 69.

103 *Yerushalmi, Pesachim* 4:1 (26a); *Karban HaEdah ad loc.* s.v. *U'Pharekh;* Rosh, *Pesachim* 4:3; *Karban Nethanel ad loc.* 5, 8; *Pri Chadash, Orach Chaim* 496, *Diney Minhagey Issur* 8; Rabbi Raphael Meldul a, *Teshuvoth Mayim Rabbim, Yoreh Deah* 65, 66 (Amsterdam, 1737); Rabbi Yosef Steinhart, *Teshuvoth Zikhron Yosef, Yoreh Deah* 14 (Furth, 1773); *Teshuvoth Chavath Yair* 126; *Pith'chey Teshuvah, Yoreh Deah* 228:30; *Chayay Adam* 127:7. Some authorities maintain that children cannot annul their parents' customs if the custom was initiated as a safeguard *(seyag);* Raavad, *Pesachim* (Rif 16b) 1; *Teshuvoth Rashdam, Yoreh Deah* 40. See above, note 98.

104 Rabbi Meir (ben Shem Tov) Melamed, *Mishpat Tzedek* 2:47 (Salonika, 1615); *Kenesseth HaGedolah, Yoreh Deah* 214:46; *Pachad Yitzchak*, s.v. *Devarim* (80d); *Pri Chadash, Orach Chaim* 496, *Diney Minhagey Issur* 5. A formally adopted custom, on the other hand, is only annulled to those who agree to annul it. Those who dissent from the annulment remain bound, even if they are a minority of the community; *Teshuvoth HaRosh* 5:4, 7:5; *Teshuvoth Rivash* 73; *Yoreh Deah* 228:31. Cf. *Yoreh Deah* 229:2; Ran, *Nedarim* 27a, s.v. *VeKathav* (end); *Teshuvoth Rivash* 94.

105 *Massa Melekh* 7:6; *Kenesseth HaGedolah, Yoreh Deah* 214:21; Pri *Chadash, Orach Chaim* 496, *Diney Minhagey Issur* 5; *Pachad Yitzchak*, s.v. *Devarim* (80b); *Chayay Adam* 127:9; *Mishnah Berurah* 468:11.

55. Similarly, a community cannot exempt itself from a custom that is observed over a larger geographical area.[106]

56. If a custom is accepted among all Jews, it cannot be annulled in any manner.[107] Such customs are as binding as is the Torah itself.[108]

57. If a custom was initiated for a well known specific reason, it is automatically annulled when the reason ceases to exist.[109] This is only true, however, when there is no likelihood of the recurring need for the custom.[110]

58. Any custom of long standing should be highly respected and not annulled.[111] This is especially true if it is endorsed by accepted authorities.[112]

59. Therefore, long standing customs should not be annulled even if they include practices that normally would not be condoned.[113] Concerning such venerable customs it is written; "Do not remove the ancient landmark which your fathers have set" (Proverbs 22:28).[114]

60. If something is forbidden only because of cust om, it can be permitted in case of emergency or illness, even when there is no actual danger.[115]

61. If a community has a practice to follow a certain opinion in a question of law, it is considered the acceptance of that opinion as law, rather than as mere custom.[116] Therefore, such a practice can never be annulled.[117] However, since every community is bound to follow its own religious leadership,[118] it can abandon such a practice on the basis of its rabbi's judgment.[119]

62. If a community has an established custom to follow the opinion of one authority, it may do so, even when that opinion is the lenient one and opposes a majority.[120] Nevertheless, a community should not initially adopt a minority opinion as their common practice.[121]

106 *Teshuvoth Chavath Yair* 126; Rabbi Shlomo Eiger, *Gilyon Maharsha, Yoreh Deah* 214:1. To be a regional custom, a practice must be generally observed throughout the entire region; *Yad, Ishuth* 23:12. However, if it is observed in the majority of the region, it is assumed to be observed throughout the region; *Teshuvoth HaRosh* 79:4; *Beth Yosef, Choshen Mishpat* 42:21.

107 *Teshuvoth Maharshal* 7; *Sifethey Cohen, Yoreh Deah* 214:4; *Kenesseth HaGedolah, Yoreh Deah* 214:10; *Pri Chadash, Orach Chaim* 496, *Diney Minhagey Issur* 6; *Pachad Yitzchak,* s.v. *Devarim* (80a); *Chayay Adam* 127:9. Cf. *Teshuvoth Rivash* 99. Also see *Betza* 4b; *Yevamoth* 102a; *Yad, Kiddush HaChodesh* 5:5. Such a custom cannot be annulled by even the greatest rabbis; *Teshuvoth Maharik* 54:4, from *Taanith* 28b; cf. *Sedey Chemed, Mem* 3S, s.v. *VeAin* (4:101). Only the Sanhedrin had this power; *Yad,* Mamrim 1:2,3.

108 *Teshuvoth Rashba* 3:236; *Teshuvoth Rivash* 44. Cf. *Chulin* 92b; *Pesachim* 3la, S3b; *Bereshith Rabbah* 78:9; above, note 51.

109 *Teshuvoth Maharik* 144; *Teshuvoth Rama* 21; *Magen Avraham* 690:22; *Beer Hetiv* 690:15; *Darkey HaHorah* 5 (p. 232). Cf. *Yoreh Deah* 228:29. See above, 11:55.

110 *Betza* 4b. There is an indication, however, that there was specific legislation to retain this custom; *Yad, Kiddush HaChodesh* 5:5. However, see *Lechem Mishneh, Talmud Torah* 6:14 11.

111 Yerushalmi, *Eruvin* 3:9 (26b); *Yerushalmi, Taanith* 1:6 (6a); *Bereshith Rabbah* 94:4; *Orach Chaim* 690:16 in *Hagah.* It is assumed that such customs were instituted by the sages of old; *Teshuvoth Ramban* 51; *Teshuvoth HaRosh* 55:10; *Teshuvoth Maharik* 102:3. Such respect should be regarded to even a local custom; *Massa Moshe* 7:6; *Kenesseth HaGedolah, Yoreh Deah* 114:37; *Pachad Yitzchak,* s.v. *Devarim* (80c).

112 *Teshuvoth Maharik* 142; *Teshuvoth Rama* 21; *Magen Avraham* 690:22.

113 Cf. *Shabbath* 35b; *Eruvin* 104b; *Taanith* 2Sb; *Tosafoth, Taanith* 2a, s.v. *MeEimathai.* See above, note 86.

114 *Midrash Mishley,* Rashi, *ad loc.; Yalkut Shimoni* 2:960; *Sefer Chasidim* 114; *Magen Avraham* 68:0; cf. *Peah* 5:6, 7:3; *Tanchuma, VaYishlach* 10. See above Chapter 11, note 95. Other sources derive this from Deuteronomy 19:14, *Torah Temimah ad loc.; Tur, Choshen Mishpat* 368 (end); *Teshuvoth HaGeonim, Shaarey Tzedek* 20 (32a); *Otzar HaGeonim, Bava Kama* 114a (p. 108); *Teshuvoth Chut HaMeshulash* 3:24; *Sefer Chasidim* 114; cf. *Shabbath* 85a; Rif, *Bava Kama* 37b.

115 *Massa Melekh* 7:1; *Kenesseth HaGedolah, Yoreh Deah* 214:42; *Pachad Yitzchak,* s.v. *Devarim* (80d); *Chayay Adam* 127:6. Also see Rabbi Avraham (ben Nachman) HaCohen, *Tohorath HaMayim* 49 (Leghorn, 1879), p. 95; Rabbi Sh'muel Yitzchak, *Ne'eman Sh'muel* 10 (Salonika, 1723); *Sedey Chemed, Mem* 37, s.v. *Davar* (4:80). Cf. *Orach Chaim* 462:4 in *Hagah; Chayay Adam* 126:7; and *Orach Chaim* 686:1 in *Hagah,* from *Taanith* 14a. See above, 13:19.

116 C f. *Sifethey Cohen, Choshen Mishpat* 25:10.

117 Ran, *Pesachim* (Rif 17b); s.v. *VeNimtzinu;* Ritva, *Pesachim* 51a; *Massa Melekh* 7:1; *Kenesseth HaGedolah, Yoreh Deah* 114:11; *Pachad Yitzchak,* s.v. *Devarim* (80a), s.v. *Minhag* (137c); *Pri Chadash, Orach Chaim* 496, *Diney Minhagey Issur* 2; *Chayay Adam* 127:10. Cf. *Teshuvoth Rashba* 3:236; *Teshuvoth Rashdam, Yoreh Deah* 40, 129. Some authorities, however, maintain that even such a custom can be annulled; *Teshuvoth Rabbi Sh'lomo (ben Avraham) Cohen (Rashakh)* 1:178; *Mishpat Tzedek* 1:32.

118 See above, 12:30.

119 *Teshuvoth Radbaz* 359 (end); *Pri Chadash, Orach Chaim* 496, *Diney Minhagey Issur* 2. Cf. *Chulin* 6b. See above, note 107, that no rabbi can annul a universal custom.

120 *Pri Chadash, Orach Chaim* 496, *Diney Minhagey Issur* 11; *Magen Avraham* 690:22; *Beer Hetiv* 690:14. Cf. *Rosh HaShanah* 15b.

121 *Pri Chadash, lac. cit.* Cf. *Taanith* 26b.

63. In all cases, a community is bound to abide by the decisions of its duly chosen religious leaders,[122] and their opinions are binding as a custom even after their death.[123] In such cases, however, a later rabbi can overturn the decisions of his predecessors.[124]

64. A person must always abide by the customs of his home community even while temporarily residing elsewhere.[125]

65. Similarly, a person is exempt from abiding by the customs of any community where he may be visiting or residing temporarily,[126] as long as he has the intention of returning home.[127]

66. Although a visitor or temporary resident is not bound by the customs of the community in which he is staying, he must nevertheless have respect for the sensibilities of the people.[128] Therefore, he should refrain from violating any local customs in the presence of any area residents.[129] Similarly, he should refrain from publicly observing his own customs,[130] unless he can do so unobtrusively.[131]

67. Activities which cannot be effectively concealed, such as manual labor, may not be done in violation of local custom, even in private.[132] However, they are permitted outside the city,[133] or away from Jewish habitation.[134]

68. When a person establishes permanent residence in a community he is considered a member of that community with regard to all questions of custom[135] and practice.[136]

69. Therefore, when s person moves to a new community, he must abide by all its customs.[137] He is likewise absolved from the observances of the customs of the community from which he came.[138]

70. If a person intends to settle in a new community and never return home, he establishes residence as soon as he enters the suburbs of the city to which he is moving.[139] Similarly, he establishes residence in a nation as soon as he reaches the first inhabited area,[140] even if it is inhabited by non-Jews.[141]

122 *Ibid.* See above, 12:30.

123 *Shiltey Gibborim, Avodah Zarah* (Rif 2a).

124 *Pri Chadash, lac. cit.* See above, 12:31.

125 *Pesachim* 4:1 (50a), 51a; *Chulin* 18b, 117a; *Tosafoth, Chulin* 93b, s.v. *MiShum;* Ran, *Pesachim* (Rif 16b), s.v. *HaHolekh;* Rosh, *Pesachim* 4:4; *Shiltey Gibborim, Avodah Zarah* (Rif 2a); *Yad, Yom Tov* 8:20; *Orach Chaim* 468:4, 574:1; *Chayay Adam* 127:9; *M ishnah Berurah* 468:13,14.

126 *Pri Chadash* 468:4; *"Rav" Shulchan Arukh* 468:10. Others, however, distinguish between a visitor and a temporary resident in this case; *Teshuvoth Radbaz* 73.

127 There are various opinions regarding this; *Beur Halakhah* 468:4, s.v. *HaHolekh.*

128 *Pesachim* 4:1 (86b): *Bava Metzia* 86b; *Bereshith Rabbah* 48:16; *Shemoth Rabbah* 47:6; *Tanchuma, VaYera* 11; *Zohar* 1:144a.

129 *Tosafoth, Pesachim* 51a, s.v. *Iy;* Ran, *Pesachim* (Rif 16b), s.v. *HaHolekh,* (Rif 16b,), s.v. *U'Rabbah,* s.v. *VeNimtzinu; HaMaor HaKatan, Pesachim* (Rif 16b), s.v. *Makom;* Rosh , *Pesachim* 4:4; Yad, *Yom Tov* 8:20; *Orach Chaim* 486:4; *Magen Avraham* 468:10; *"Rav" Shulchan Arukh* 468:11; *Mishnah Berurah* 468:13. Cf. *Orach Chaim* 572:2; *Magen Avraham,* 574:2.

130 Yad, *Yom Tov* 8:20; Rosh, *Pesachim* 4:4; *Magen Avraham* 468:11; *"Rav" Shulchan Arukh* 468:13.

131 Cf. *Pesachim* 51b.

132 *Tosafoth, Pesachim* 52a, s.v. *BaYishuv;* Ran , *Pesachim* (Rif 17b), s.v. U'Rabbah; *Orach Chaim* 468:4; *Magen Avraham* 468:7,12; *"Rav" Shulchan Arukh* 468:10; *Mishnah Berurah* 468:13, 17.

133 *Pesachim* 52a; *Magen Avraham* 468:8; *Mishnah Berurah* 468:18.

134 *Magen Avraham* 496:5; *Mishnah Berurah* 496:10.

135 *Pesachim* 51a; *Chulin* 18b; Ran, *Pesachim* (Rif 17a), s.v. *U'Rabbah; Orach Chaim* 468:4, 496:3; *Yoreh Deah* 214:2.

136 *Shiltey Gibborim, Avodah Zarah* (Rif 2a); *Teshuvoth Rabbi David Cohen (Radakh)* 14.

137 This does not include inferior customs, see above, 13:29-31.

138 *Kenesseth HaGedolah, Yoreh Deah* 214:12; *Pachad Yitzchak,* s.v. *Devarim* (80a); *Magen Avraham* 468:9,12; HaGra *ibid.; "Rav" Shulchan Arukh.* 468:9,12; *Mishnah Berurah* 468:13; *Beur Halakhah* ibid. Others,however, maintain that one is never absolved of his native customs; *Tosafoth, Chulin* 18b, s.v. *Ham; Sifethey Cohen, Yoreh Deah* 214:8; *Pri Chadash, Orach Chaim* 468:4; *Pri Megadim, Eshel Avraham* 468:9; *Beur Halakhah loc. cit.; Iggereth Moshe, Orach Chaim* 158. Some say that where it does not cause dissent, one should keep his native stringencies; *Massa Melekh* 7:40; *Kenesseth HaGedolah, Yoreh Deah* 214:22; *Pachad Yitzchak,* s.v. *Devarim* (80b).

139 *Magen Avraham* 468:8, 496:5; *Mishnah Berurah* 468:13, 496:10. Cf. *Chulin* 110a; Ran, *Pesachim* (Rif 17a), s.v. *U'Rabbah; HaMaor HaKatan, Pesachim* (Rif 16b), s.v. *Avel.* Also see *Teshuvoth Rashba* 3:414; *Yerushalmi, Yoma* 6:6 (34b); *Gilyoney HaShas, Pesachim* 51a. Some say that there are cases where one must live in an area for twelve months before accepting its leniencies; *Teshuvoth Geoney Mizrach U'Maarev* 39; *Maaseh HaGeonim* 31 (p. 47); *Otzar HaGeonim,* Pesachim 51a (p. 72); cf. *Teshuvoth Rashba* 337. See *Bava Bathra* 1:5 (7b); *Pachad Yitzchak* s.v. *Ore'ach* (39c).

140 *Orach Chaim* 496:3; *Teshuvoth Radbaz* 4:73; *Teshuvoth Rashdam, Orach Chaim* 15; *Teshuvoth Mabit* 2:149; *Magen Avraham* 496:4. Cf. *Pesachim* 52a; Ran, Pesachim (Rif 17a), s.v. *U'Rabbah; HaMaor HaKatan, Pesachim* (Rif 16b), s.v. *Avel.*

141 *Teshuvoth Radbaz* 4:73; *Magen Avraham* 496:6; *Mishnah Berurah* 496:11. Some authorities dispute this; cf. *Bigdey Yesha ibid.*

71. As soon as a person establishes residence in a community he is bound by all its customs, even if he immediately leaves the area.[142]

72. When a family moves its complete household to a new community, they establish residence there even if they plan to return to their home community.[143] Nevertheless, a person can make a permanent move and establish new residence even if he is not accompanied by his family.[144]

73. A student retains the residence of his parents, even though he may be away at school for many years.[145] However, if he has clear intentions of permanently residing where he is studying, he can establish residence there.[146]

74. When a woman marries, she adopts the customs of her husband.[147]

75. A person is absolved from keeping his home town customs only when there is a definite alternate custom in the place where he establishes residence. However, if a definite custom does not exist, he must adhere to the custom of his home community.[148]

76. Therefore, if people settle where there is no existing[149] Jewish community, they must adhere to the customs of their place of origin.[150] If they come from places with different customs, they must adhere to the custom of the majority.[151] If there is no clear majority, each group may follow its native customs until an agreement is reached, or until an indigenous custom develops.[152]

77. However, if any Jewish community at all exists in a place, all newcomers are obliged by its customs, even if the newcomers vastly outnumber the original inhabitants.[153]

78. If many people from one community settle in another, and wish to maintain their identity, they may form a separate congregation where they can adhere to their original customs.[154] Under no conditions, however, may they impose their customs on the original inhabitants of the community, even if the newcomers vastly outnumber them.[155]

79. Every congregation is considered to be a separate community and each may therefore have its own customs.[156] Therefore, as soon as a person joins a congregation, he must abide by all its customs.[157]

80. In order to qualify as an autonomous community, a place must have a quorum *(minyan)* of observant adult males, as well as its own synagogue and rabbi. Otherwise, the community is not considered auton-

142 *"Rav" Shulchan Arukh* 468:10; *Mishnah Berurah* 468:14.

143 *Teshuvoth Radbaz* 4:73; *Magen Avraham* 496:7; *Pri Chadash* 468:4; *"Rav" Shulchan Arukh* 496:10; *Beer Hetiv* 496:5; *Mishnah Berurah* 496:13. Also see Ran, *Pesachim* (Rif 17b), s.v. *VeNimtzinu*; *Teshuvoth Ginath Veradim, Orach Chaim* 4:17; Rabbi Avraham Yitzchaki; *Teshuvoth Zera Avraham, Orach Chaim* 9, 10 (Constantinople, 1732); *Teshuvoth Rabbi Yosef Trani (Maharit)* 19; *Teshuvoth Rabbi Shlomo Cohen (Rashakh)* 2:26; *Teshuvoth Rabbi Shlomo (ben Yitzchak) HaLevi* 68 (Salonika, 1690). However, if they have definite, established plans to return, they may retain their native customs.

144 *Teshuvoth Mishpat Tzedek* 2:49; *Magen Avraham* 496:7; *Pri Chadash* 468:4.

145 *Teshuvoth Radbaz* 73; *Magen Avraham* 468:12; *Teshuvoth Halakhoth Ketanoth* 4.

146 *Shaarey Teshuvah, Orach Chaim* 496:2.

147 Rabbi Moshe Feinstein, *Iggereth Moshe, Orach Chaim* 158. See Rabbi Yaakov ben Abba Mari, *Sefer HaMelamed*, quoted in *Kol Bo* 73 (beginning).

148 *Teshuvoth Rabbi Yosef Trani (Maharit)* 19; *Pri Chadash, Orach Chaim* 468:4; *"Rav" Shulchan Arukh* 468:15; *Beur Halakhah* 468:4, s.v. *VeChomrey*. Cf. Yerushalmi, Berakhoth 2:2 (19b).

149 Regarding the rule when an earlier community existed but was destroyed or abandoned, see *Shiltey Gibborim, Avodah Zarah* (Rif 2a); *Magen Avraham* 493:6; *Pri Megadim, Eshel Avraham* 468:12; *Beer Hetiv, Yoreh Deah* 214:5; *Beur Halakhah* 468:4; *Teshuvoth Chavath Yair* 126.

150 *Bava Metzia* 83b; Rashba, Ran, *ad loc.*; *Choshen Mishpat* 331:1 in *Hagah*. Cf. *Yerushalmi, Pesachim* 4:1 (26a); *Pri Chadash, Orach Chaim* 496, *Diney Minhagey Issur* 19; *Massa Melekh* 7:11; *Pachad Yitzchak*, s.v. Minhag (137d); *Teshuvoth Maharik* 102:2.

151 *Nimukey Yosef, Bava Metzia* (Rif 52a), s.v. *BeLikutey*.

152 *Pri Chadash, Orach Chaim* 496, *Diney Minhagey Issur* 19; from *Bava Metzia* 83b.

153 *Teshuvoth Rabbi Yosef ibn Lev (Rival)* 3:14; *Massa Melekh* 7:11; *Kenesseth HaGedolah, YorehDeah* 214:9; *Pri Chadash, Orach Chaim* 496, *Diney Minhagey Issur* 19; *Pachad Yitzchak*, s.v. *Devarim* (80a), s.v. *Minhag* (137d).

154 *Ibid.* Also see Rabbi Eliahu Mizrachi, *Teshuvoth She'eloth* 1:13; *Teshuvoth Rabbi Yosef ibn Lev (Rival)* 3:10; *Teshuvoth Rashdam, Yoreh Deah* 40. The same is true in a new community where many groups come from different places; *Tumath Yesharim* 168; *Kenesseth HaGedolah, Yoreh Deah* 214:7.

155 *Teshuvoth Rabbi David Cohen (Radakh)* 13; Rabbi Yitzchak (ben Sh'muel) Adrabi, *Divrey Rivoth* 162 (Salonika, 1582); *Pri Chadash, Orach Chaim* 496, *Diney Minhagey Issur* 19; *Pachad Yitzchak*, s.v. *Lo Thithgodedu* (8a). See above, 12:37.

156 Above, 12:37.

157 Rabbi Eliahu Mizrachi, *Teshuvoth She'eloth* 1:13; *Magen Avraham* 493:6; *Pri Chadash, Orach Chaim* 496, *Diney Minhagey Issur* 20.

omous, and must follow the customs of the nearest large community.[158]

81. In each community, everyone is obliged to abide by the customs of the majority.[159] However, if it is a practice for some to observe stricter customs out of personal piety, they may do so, as long as there is no danger of dissension.[160]

82. There are many lofty concepts that seem highly desirable in theory, but work out very poorly in practice. Judaism, however, consists of practice rather than theory, and therefore, God decreed that its final form be established by those who practice it. It is for this reason that we are constantly warned to abide by custom.

83. It is also for this reason that we are warned of the great punishment for ignoring a custom.[161] The initial breaking of minor customs often led entire communities completely away from Torah and Judaism.[162]

84. One of the fundamental unvoiced concepts of Judaism is that God reveals His will to us, not only through prophecy, but in the common destiny of all who seek Him. Therefore, even such seemingly prosaic concepts as legal decisions and customs partake of God's continuous process of revelation.[163]

The Handbook of Jewish Thought, vol. 1 [Moznaim Publishers: New York, 1979], pp. 261–286
Reprinted with permission of the publisher

158 *Beur Halakhah* 468:4, s.v. *HaHolekh.*

159 See above, 12:39.

160 *Magen Avraham* 493:6; *Eshel Avraham ad loc.* Cf. *Teshuvoth Rabbi Yosef ibn Lev (Rival)* 3:14; *Teshuvoth Ralbach* 2:11; *Massa Melekh* 7:14; *Kenesseth HaGedolah, Yoreh Deah* 214:4; *Pachad Yitzchak,* s.v. *Devarim (80a), s.v. Minhag* (138a).

161 *Sefer Chasidim* 607; *Sefer Maharil, Hilkhoth* Yom *Kippur* (47b); Rabbi Mikhel of Arapchik, *Minchah Chadashah* on *Avoth,* end (Cracow, 1576); *Maaver Yaakov, Minchath Aaron* 7. There is also a curse that he be bitten by a snake (Ecclesiastes 10:8); Rashba, *Torath HaBayith* 2:3 (34a); *Yoreh Deah* 196:13 in *Hagah.* See above, 11:29. Also see *Pesachim* 52a; *Yad, Talmud Torah* 6:14 11; *Lechem Mishneh ad loc.*

162 Cf. *Teshuvoth Ralbach, Chatham Safer, Orach Chaim* 28; *Beur Halakhah* 150:5, s.v. *BeEmtza.*

163 163. Cf. *Tanchuma, Shemoth* 18.

INTUITION

BY RABBI YANKI TAUBER

The hallmark of a loving marriage is each partner's readiness to do the will of the other. If one partner expresses a desire for something, the other will do everything in his or her power to bring about its fulfillment.

A greater love is demonstrated when each partner also strives to fulfill the *implied* will of the other. To the truly devoted spouse, it makes no difference if a desire has been explicitly expressed or merely hinted at—he or she will carry it out with the same devotion and commitment to the loved one's gratification.

Finally, there are those very special marriages in which there is no need for even the merest of allusions. So deep is the bond between husband and wife that each intuitively knows what the other wants of him or her. Indeed, when two people love each other to such a degree, there is no greater joy than that experienced when one has succeeded in sensing and satisfying the other's desire all on one's own.

Three Degrees of Commandment

The month of Tishrei is a month replete with mitzvot—with opportunities for carrying out the divine will. For thirty days, the Jew's every thought and moment is filled with praying, repenting, fasting, feasting, dancing, building a *sukkah*, acquiring a *lulav* and *etrog* or a bundle of *hoshaanot*, and dozens of other mitzvot, customs and observances.

The observances of Tishrei fall into three general categories. There are "biblical precepts"—commandments that are explicitly stated in the Torah. These include mitzvot such as sounding the *shofar*, fasting on Yom Kippur, or eating in the *sukkah*. There are also a number of "rabbinical mitzvot"—observances instituted by the prophets and the sages by the authority vested in them by the Torah. For example, the five prayer services held on Yom Kippur and the taking of the "Four Kinds" on all but the first day of Sukkot are all rabbinical institutions.

Finally, the month of Tishrei has many *minhagim* or "customs," such as eating an apple dipped in honey on the first night of Rosh HaShanah or conducting the *kapparot* in the wee hours of the morning on the day before Yom Kippur. The *minhagim* are not mandated by biblical or rabbinical law, but by force of custom: these are things that we ourselves have initiated as ways to enhance our service of our Creator.

The climax of the month of Tishrei, the point at which our celebration of G-d's festivals attains the very pinnacle of joy, is during the *hakkafot* of Simchat Torah, when we take the Torah scrolls in hand and dance with them around the reading table in the synagogue. Most amazingly, the *hakkafot* are neither a biblical nor a rabbinical precept; they are "merely" a custom.

For it is with our observance of the customs that we express the depth of our love for G-d. The biblical commandments might be compared to the explicitly expressed desires between two people bound in marriage. The rabbinical mitzvot, which G-d did not directly instruct us but which nevertheless constitute expressions of the divine will,[1] resemble the implied requests between spouses. But the *minhagim* represent those areas in which we intuitively sense how we might cause G-d pleasure—and in this lies our greatest joy.

www.Meaningfullife.com
Reprinted with permission of the Meaningful Life Center

[1] Before performing a rabbinical mitzvah, we recite a blessing that begins with the words, "Blessed are You, G-d... Who has sanctified us with His commandments and commanded us to...." For since G-d commanded us to fulfill the mitzvot instituted by the sages, these are divine commandments; the difference between the biblical and rabbinical mitzvot is only in that the former are more explicitly the expressed will of G-d. Thus, fulfilling a rabbinical precept is a greater show of commitment, for we thereby exhibit our equal devotion to those divine desires which G-d has not directly related to us.

IS IT REALLY THE TORAH, OR IS IT JUST THE RABBIS?

BY RABBI TZVI FREEMAN

Question:
I believe in my heart that the Five Books of Moses and the Prophets are from G-d. When it comes to the Talmud, however, I am beginning to believe it was made up over the centuries to control the Jewish believer with all its added laws. The rabbis add scores of laws to each of the 613 commandment and you end up having to obey all kinds of things that were never part of Judaism when it all started.

I guess what I'm saying is that although we claim to believe in the Bible, in reality we are controlled by a small group of old men and their Talmud.

Answer:
I appreciate your concern, since this is the trap institutionalized religions have fallen into time and time again: It starts off with a lot of good ideas, and then come along a priestly cult to hijack those ideas for their own benefit.

The question is, does Judaism include some mechanism to avoid this trap? If, as we say, the Torah is truly a Divine document, you would expect it to foresee all obstacles to its own survival—including this one—and to include some safeguard to prevent it from happening.

The answer, it seems to me, is that this is why G-d chose Moses, of all men, to be the agent by which Torah would enter earth-space.

Moses was the first populist civil rights leader. Already at a young age, he demonstrated his contempt for abuse of power when he struck and killed an Egyptian taskmaster. He was well aware of the dangers of a hierarchical religious cult, familiar as he was with the priestly cult of ancient Egypt. He cared for the people and empathized with them—so much so, that he even took G-d Himself to task in Egypt, demanding, "Why have you done evil to this people? Why did you send me?" More than his wisdom, more than his courage, it was this trait of Moses that made him a faithful shepherd of his people. And for this, he was chosen to bring Torah to them.

Moses, the Populist
They say that a prophet hears the voice of G-d speaking in his own voice.[1] In the story of the Exodus and the giving of the Torah, we see how G-d works with Moses in accordance with Moses' own style.

Other prophets came and told the people, "This is what G-d told me. Trust me." G-d tells Moses to gather all the people at the foot of Mount Sinai, to hear for themselves the revelation that he hears. When the people complain that they cannot bear such revelation—"You go find out what He wants and tell us"—Moses is sincerely disappointed. G-d must console him, telling him that this is good, that they should be in such awe—and all Moses has to do is to tell them what G-d wants and they will do it.

But Moses is not satisfied with that. When he teaches the people—we're told that all the people participated—he does it publicly, repeatedly, disclosing everything he hears and explaining in further detail. He tells them to teach it to one another and to their children, to speak of it "when you sit in your house and when you go on the road, when you lie down and when you get up." He asks the people to bring to him those that they choose as their judges, from the people and of the people, who will judge each case according to the law he has taught them.[2] He even

Rabbi Tzvi Freeman (1955–) Rabbi, computer scientist, and writer. A published expert, consultant, and lecturer in the field of educational technology, Rabbi Freeman held posts at the University of British Columbia and the Digipen School of Computer Gaming. Rabbi Freeman is the author of Bringing Heaven Down to Earth and *Men, Women & Kabbalah*. He is a senior editor at Chabad.org.

[1] See Rabbi Chaim Vital, Shaar HaNevua.

[2] Deuteronomy 1:13.

urges each person to write down the entire law for himself, so that he can study from it and know it well.

Typical of the Moses approach is the book of Leviticus. In Ancient Egypt, the priesthood was an occult, with mysterious rituals and secret knowledge. In Leviticus, that scheme is deliberately overturned. Everything is spelled out in black and white for every Jew to read. The initiation ceremonies are performed before the entire community. The punishments due to the priestly class for improper performance of their duties is spelled out clearly. Any five-year-old would be able to yell out, "Hey, that kohen didn't sprinkle the blood the way it says in the Torah!" The priests of any society throughout history would have considered this ludicrous and self-defeating. But this was G-d speaking through Moses the populist, restructuring society.

Pop-Culture

Similarly, with all the legislation of Torah: Moses commands the people again and again to learn all these laws and to know them well. He tells them to write them down and study from the written word. And so, the Jewish people became the first literate society in history—and remained such until the advent of popular literacy in the modern era.

A fascinating tidbit of history: We know that the ancient Egyptians had a sophisticated system of writing, known to us as hieroglyphics, using graphic symbols to represent words and phrases. So complex was their system—using over 2,000 distinct glyphs—that only the initiated few were able to decipher the meanings. Phonetic writing, representing the sounds of the words individually—with only 22 letters—appears first in Canaan. When it spread, it revolutionized culture and thought by making the written word accessible to the general populace. All of the hundreds of historical phonetic alphabets, including our present day alphabet, can easily be traced back to that original aleph-bet. There's even a vestigial remnant—the letter "Q", which is useless in Latin and Greek, but represents the Semitic guttural "Quf" (originally made deep in the throat).

What's not so well known is that the Egyptian hieroglyphs also comprised a complete set of 24 consonants, quite similar to the 22 letters of the Hebrew alphabet. To us, in retrospect, it seems quite puzzling: What prevented them from making the logical step of rejecting all those esoteric symbols and reducing their printing needs to a small and simple set?

To us, a bewildering puzzle. To Pharaoh's priests, however, it is the question that would be most bewildering: "Why on earth," they would retort, "would we want to make our hidden code more accessible?"

As the great anthropologist, Claude Levi Strauss, writes, ancient writing's main function was, "to facilitate the enslavement of other human beings."

To take that great step needed not a genius but a revolutionary. When Moses transmitted G-d's message to his people that they were to be "a nation of priests" and committed the Torah to phonetic writing, he was creating *the* most significant watershed event in the history of populism: The flattening of the hierarchy of knowledge with the advent of public education and literacy.

Everyone a Moses

If he had stopped there, Moses would without a doubt have been the greatest social revolutionary of all time. But he didn't. It wasn't enough for Moses that all Jews be educated. He wanted them to be participants as well, everyone involved in the debate. That's why he deliberately devised an institution of Torah study and debate, to circumvent just those issues you mention.

Moses didn't have to go this far. He could have written the book, handed it to his brothers, the Levites, and told them to ensure the masses follow the law. Perhaps the common people would read it as well, even write each man his own copy. But they would read it only as one reads a holy incantation, a script to follow, a path to walk down straightly, without stopping to examine its cobblestones. He could have preserved the hierarchy: The law comes from Above, and the people receive it below.

And what if some new circumstance would arise, the solution for which could not be found in this written Torah? Once again, Moses would have to go to the Divine Authority and ask—as he did in several instances. When he saw that his time of passing was near, he could have appointed his children and confidants to discuss among themselves any difficulties that would arise and issue new rulings in accordance with what he had been taught.

Sure, G-d told him to teach the people, to ensure that they knew the dos and do nots. But who says he had to empower them to decide new laws, and to incite them to discuss and debate? He could have claimed that this way, the law would remain pure and intact, as received, the Divine Word from Above.

But Moses knew that was a lie. He knew that knowledge in the hands of a minority corrupts both the minority and the knowledge. He knew that truth is only truth when it can sprout forth from the grassroots of the populace. So he urged his people not just to learn the rules, but to debate and discuss, to dig deep into the details and nuances of every word and to find there new meanings, new applications, new wonders of G-d's infinite wisdom and its relevance at every time. He taught them the way of the Talmud.

This what Rabbi Yossi, son of Rabbi Chanina, explained.[3] He said that in truth, G-d only gave the Torah to Moses and his descendants. After all, when G-d told Moses to write the second tablets, He told him, "Write *for yourself* two tablets of stone...".

The other rabbis argued with Rabbi Yossi, "But didn't G-d tell Moses to teach the Torah to all the Children of Israel?"

But what Rabbi Yossi meant was, as I said, that the instructions of the Torah—"do this and don't do that"—were for all the Jews. But the power to deduce one thing from another, to examine deeply and unfold the inner workings of the Torah—that was meant for Moses and his progeny alone.

[3] Talmud, Nedarim 38a.

But this was Moses, a man who began his career by striking down the taskmaster to rescue the slave. Who, when his disciple Joshua attempted to muzzle "those who prophesied in the camp," protested, "Would it be that all the people should be prophets!"[4] Who, when told by G-d that the Jewish nation, having sinned with the golden calf, would have to be erased and rebuilt from Moses' own progeny, replied, "If this is the way Your story goes, you can erase me from the script!"[5] Moses, who smashed the tablets of G-d to save his people.[6]

So what did Moses do? He determined that every Jew should be his progeny—just as he had brought every Jew to hear G-d at Mount Sinai to hear what he heard. They would not only hear the voice, they would participate in knowing it, in resonating with it and in amplifying it further.

In effect, Moses deemed that the collective consciousness of the Jewish nation should be Moses, through whom G-d's voice is heard.

Moses and Rabbi Akiva

Moses' dream was perhaps best realized in a much later leader of popular revolution, a man also from the people and of the people: The famed Rabbi Akiva, a man of humble beginnings who lived his life by humble means, and stood behind the Bar Kochba revolt against the Romans. Rabbi Akiva, when making a crucial decision would take serious account of popular custom, saying, "Let's go out and see what the people do."

The Talmud illustrates the relationship of Rabbi Akiva to Moses in the form of a story[7]:

They told that when Moses went above to receive the Torah, he found the Holy One, blessed be He, sitting and attaching crowns to the letters. (Of course, G-d doesn't sit, neither does He need to use cut and paste when composing the Torah. Once you get used to the

[4] Numbers 11:27

[5] Exodus 32:32.

[6] See Rashi to Exodus 34:1

[7] Menachot 29b.

style of the Talmud, you learn to take these things figuratively. But without them, the story is very dry.)

Apparently, Moses didn't see any need for these crowns. He asked, "Master of the Universe! Who forces You to go to such extremes?"

G-d answered, "There is a man who will live many generations after you and his name is Akiva, son of Yosef. He will examine every single spike of every letter and draw from them piles upon piles of halachot."

So Moses asked, "Master of the Universe! Show him to me!"

G-d replied, "Step backwards."

And Moses stepped back until he found himself standing in the 18th row of Rabbi Akiva's class. You see, the students were arranged in this class by order of their understanding. It seems the only thing left after the eighteenth row was out in the hallway.

So Moses stood there and listened—and was unable to follow a thing that was said. He became weak with despair. Until finally, the story tells, a ruling came up for which Rabbi Akiva could provide no source. A student asked of Rabbi Akiva, "Where do you learn this from?"

Rabbi Akiva responded, "This is an oral tradition passed down from Moses."

By those words, Moses was set at ease.

You see, when Moses heard Rabbi Akiva teaching, he was concerned. How could he know for certain that this was the Torah as he had received it? But once he heard that this man was not one to take credit for himself, but rather to quote in Moses' name, he understood that Rabbi Akiva's teachings were pure, unadulterated Torah, the same Torah Moses was to receive, only unfolded and unpacked.[8]

[8] See Rashi ad loc.

Pop-Tradition

Back to Moses' "power to the people" revolution: This populist approach was also the distinction between the Sadducees and Pharisees. The Sadducees were an elite class, removed from the common people, whereas the Pharisees—who later were known as the *Chachamim*—were well integrated with the working class. Most were working people themselves. This is why, after the destruction of the Second Temple, the Romans saw the *Chachamim* as the only true spokesmen of the people and chose to deal exclusively with them (see Lawrence Schiffman's "From Text to Tradition").

That the Chachamim continued this tradition of populism is evident in the tradition that no greater a scholar than Hillel the Elder earned his living as a woodchopper.[9] So did Rabbi Akiva.[10] The tradition was still intact centuries later when Rav Huna, while head of the academy of Sura in Babylonia, earned his livelihood as a water carrier.[11] Similarly, the Talmud provides accounts of the menial trades and crafts of many other respected rabbis.

Consider the context of the era, when menial labor was considered by Greeks and Romans as odious and degrading. Cicero wrote to his son, "Vulgar are the means of livelihood of all hired workmen."[12] Members of the Roman upper class were precluded by law to engage in any craft. Work, in their view, was for slaves, not for men. Rabbi Judah the princely leader of the Sanhedrin at that time, on the other hand, taught, "Studying Torah without working will produce nothing and only brings to sin."[13] Indeed, the work ethic extends back to King David himself, "Work with your hands that you may eat, you will be glad and it is good for you.[14]"

So it continued, up until most recent times, that we were an anomaly among the nations. Through-

[9] According to the version of Yoma 35 cited in the Kessef Mishna, as well as the commentary of Maimonides to Avot 4:5.

[10] Avot D'Rabbi Nathan, 6.

[11] Ketubot 105a.

[12] On Duties, 1:151.

[13] Avot 2:2.

[14] Psalms 168:2.

out most of history, whatever bodies of lawmakers we had appointed were not from an elite class, but composed of men active within common society, concerned with the needs of the common man and sympathetic to his plight. Throughout our history, the rabbis were men who struggled with the same poverty, prejudice and persecution as the rest of us.

How To Make a New Law

This social dynamic is reflected in the method by which legislation is passed in the Talmud and later. Although complex, we can distinguish three encompassing principles that define what makes new halachic legislation binding:

1. The legislation is passed after discussion and debate by a governing body or appointed individual whose authority has been established by consensus of the people.[15] At one time, this body was the *Sanhedrin*, which was composed of scholars and judges who had been accepted by the people in their particular communities and gradually moved up to the highest authoritative body. The decisions of the *Sanhedrin* were made by majority rule.

At a later date, this authority became the *Gaonim* of Babylon. Since the times of the early *Rishonim*, halachic decisions have been the product of intense discussion and debate between diverse opinions on an international scale. Who debates? Whoever has the knowledge and wits.

2. The legislation must be based on strong precedent. No Jewish court ever said, "Let's make up a new law today" out of the blue. An educated populace would never accept such a law. Rather, as every student of the Talmud can see, every law is either:

a) a clarification of an ambiguous matter of accepted law

b) a stamp of approval on an accepted custom

c) an establishment of required stringency due to extenuating circumstances

This is all clarified in Maimonides' introduction to Sefer HaMitzvot, as well as in his introduction to his Commentary on the Mishnah.[16]

This is the way of the Talmud when dealing with a new circumstance: Plunge the depths of the original text of Moses, examining every nuance, following the principles of exegesis that were passed down to us in his name. Compare every known ruling on similar cases, searching for the reasoning behind each one and seeking a harmony between them. Discuss, debate, build and tear down, until an opinion arises that can be accepted by a majority.

If I can provide my own parallel: The process of devising a new halachah is not much different than the process of good environmental design. It's perfectly possible to build a factory in the middle of a forest without adversely impacting the ecology of the wildlife and resources—it just takes a thorough knowledge of the dynamics of that ecology and a desire to leave no footprint behind. Similarly, any decision in halachah can only be enacted after weighing into consideration the entire gamut of pre-existing Jewish law and custom. One can say that halachah grows organically, without grafting or genetic modification.

3. Perhaps most significant: Every new legislation is contingent upon its acceptance by the Jewish community at large. A striking example (real brief): At one point in the history of the Sanhedrin, the Schools of Shammai and Hillel passed several key points of legislation, including a prohibition against using the olive oil of a gentile. They also declared that none of this legislation could ever be overturned. Yet, years later, the Bet Din of Rabbi Judah the Prince overturned their ruling and ruled that this oil was permissible. How were they able to do this? Simply because they saw that the original legislation had never become accepted by the community.[17]

15 See Maimonides, Laws of the Sanhedrin, chapters 1–2.

16 The Letter of Rabbi Sherira Gaon is also an important document in understanding the formation of halachah. Those interested in understanding further are urged to read the popular work, "The Essential Talmud" by Adin Steinsaltz.

17 Avoda Zara 36a.

Similarly, in each community, there are rulings made by the accepted authoritative body of that particular community. Not only do these rulings not apply to another community, but if they are not accepted by the members of that particular community, they are subject to reversal.

And we are not speaking of ignorant masses. In every community, whosoever has the mind to do so is urged to learn the ways of the Talmud from his youth, so he, too, can fathom the rationale of any decision.

Under Divine Authority

In sum, the process of halachah is a populist dynamic, by the people, for the people, yet simultaneously, on the authority of Divine Law.

This is the answer to your question, where do these rabbis get the authority to make such laws to begin with? The answer is that they receive it from three sources: From G-d, from Moses and from the people.

From G-d, because the Torah itself provides ample authority to the seventy elders and to the "priests and the wise men who will be in your times" to answer "all that is difficult for you" to the point that "you should not turn from their words to the left nor to the right."[18]

From Moses, as we have seen, that he decided those wise men should be from the masses, and that all the people should learn to be wise. It was Moses, after all, who declared that the Torah is no longer in heaven "that you should say, 'who will go up to heaven and get it for us?'"[19]

And from the people, as we have seen, that it is the people who establish these rabbis as their authority, not out of ignorance or apathy or blind faith, but within the context of a literate and educated society.

Finding G-d in the Details

And here is my vital point: Torah, you see, is not a staid book, nor is it a malleable plastic, but a living organism. An organism adapts, but doesn't change. As the weather changes and so, too, its environment, the polar bear, the dolphin and the bacterial cell find the keys within their own DNA to cope with the new and survive. Similarly, as the Jewish people travel through the vicissitudes of history, storming every form of culture and society ever known to humankind, they look in the Torah and find, "Yes! Here is the solution for this particular situation. All was foreseen, everything was provided for us, by He by whose word all things come to be."

For this, the Maharal of Prague provided another parable. He likens our situation to a man who moves into a home built by a master architect. The man finds all in place, in exquisite design and order. Yet, in one place, it seems a door is missing. There is a lintel, there are doorposts, even hinges in place. Within is a room that needs to be shut off from the rest of the house. So the man fashions a door, in accordance with every other door in the house, to match the fittings of the open doorway.

So, too, says the Maharal, when the story of Esther occurred and the rabbis established the festival of Purim; when merchants began to trade on the Shabbat and the rabbis established the laws of *muktzah*; when Jewish society became primarily mercantile and the rabbis established the *pruzbul*. And in our day, as we deal in medical halachah and supervision of the food industry—at each step along the way, we find the lintel, the doorposts and the hinges awaiting our finishing touches.

And whose door are we placing? Not our own, says the Maharal, but that of the Master Architect. For all is His design, only that He has provided us the privilege of being His partner in completing His world.

This was precisely Moses' intent: That Torah should come from within, not from without, from below, not from above. He recognized that, even though he had not been Divinely instructed so, this was the true intent. It's just that you can't direct a populist revolution from above, so it had to come from Moses himself.

18 Deuteronomy 17:8-12.
19 Deuteronomy 30:12

That is why what we do is called Judaism—and not "Scripturalism" or "Torahism" (there was such a movement, called Karaism). Judaism believes in the Jews, meaning, in the Torah that is revealed through the Jewish People. Because G-d relies upon our communal understanding through history to unfold His wisdom in the world. He knows that if He tells us, "an eye for an eye," we will understand from the context that He really meant monetary compensation. He knows that if He tells us to study Torah, we will read it in public three times a week and dance with it at the end of the cycle. He looks at those stringencies and customs of ours and says, "Yes! They got the idea!" He sees our collective consciousness not as an obstacle to His wisdom, but rather as its conduit, since, as the Zohar teaches, "no place is void of him"—not even the human mind.[20]

[20] Further reading: See *Likutei Sichot*, vol. 19, pp. 252-255; *Sefer Hasichot* 5752, vol. 2, pp. 504-510

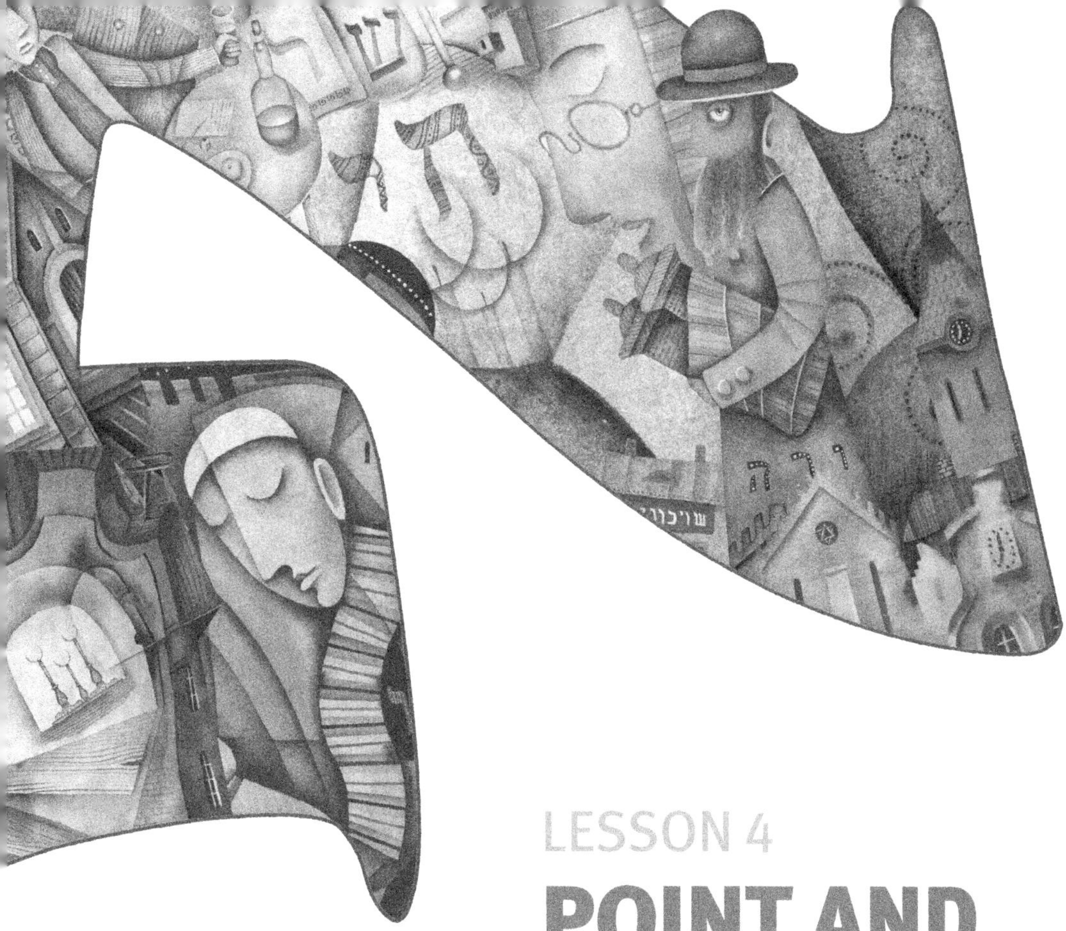

LESSON 4

POINT AND COUNTERPOINT

For many, Talmud is synonymous with debate. It is indeed a matter of fact that Jewish law abounds with disagreements and dissenting opinions. Does that mean Jewish law is just a matter of opinion? Furthermore, do the debates indicate that the system is not divine? How can there be multiple opinions in a God-given Torah? Is Talmudic debate unfortunate or ideal? Lastly, how is a final *halachah* determined in the event of differing opinions?

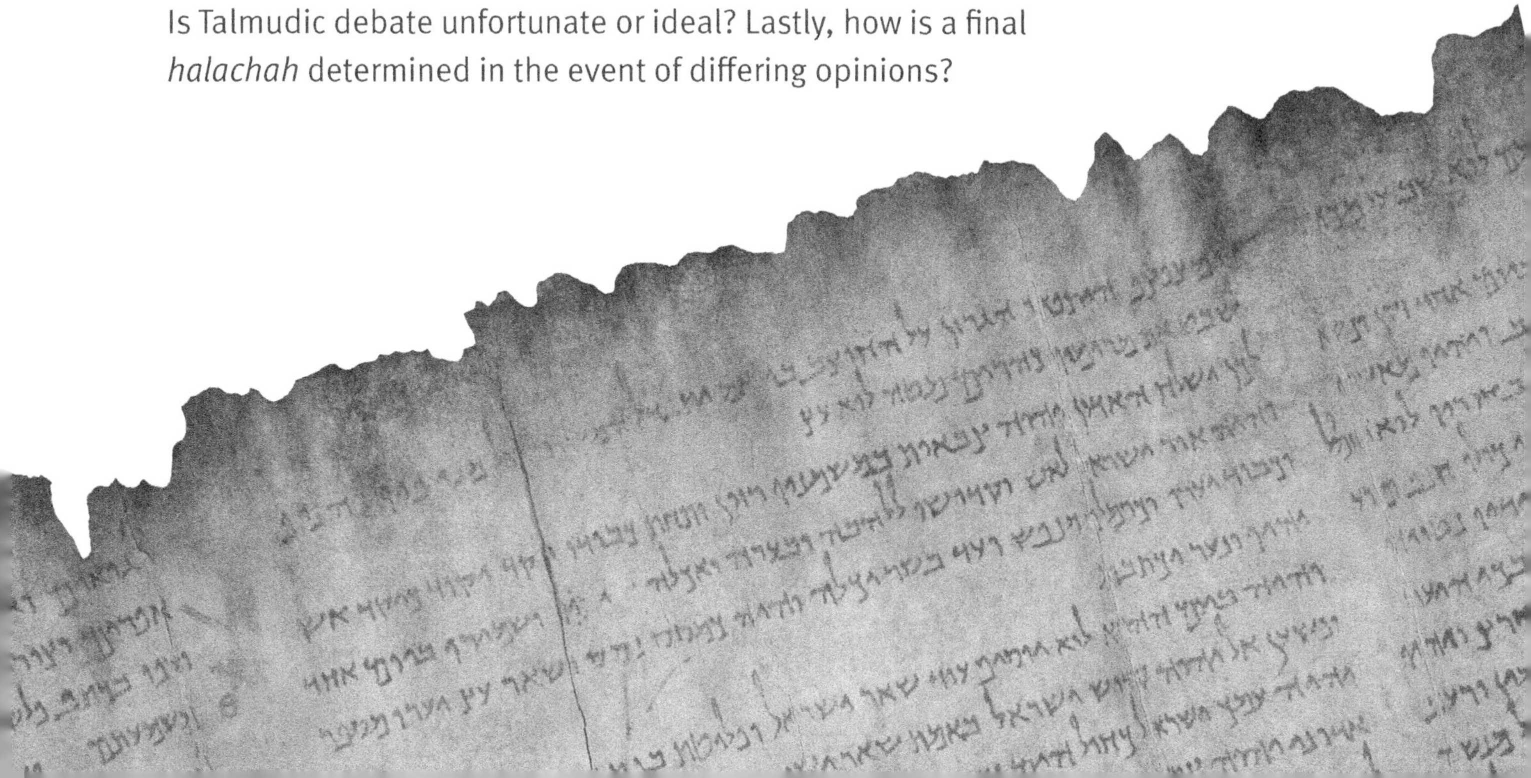

To Share, or Not to Share

Text 1

Marc Lacey and Salvador Rodriguez, "A Hiker's Plight: How to Help When Water Runs Low," *New York Times*, September 1, 2011

With their packs full, their canteens overflowing and their reserve bottles filled to the brim, outdoorsy Arizonans set out on foot this time of year under the scorching sun. But as they navigate the state's picturesque trails, they face not only physical challenges but ethical ones, like how much water to share with strangers who have miles to go and not a drop to drink.

The question comes up on South Mountain, an urban refuge in southern Phoenix, on the four-mile hike down into Fossil Springs a couple of hours north and, most definitely, along the steep pathways that descend into the Grand Canyon. Wherever it is, hikers regularly encounter strangers gasping trailside from the heat.

"If it came down to having enough for myself or helping someone, I'd have to drink my own water," said Laura Craig, a Phoenix businesswoman who shared some of her extra water with distressed strangers on a recent hike at Fossil Springs. "It's an ethical decision. You hate to think of things like survival of the fittest, but it does come down to that."

A hiker who had run out of water died in the Grand Canyon last weekend after some backpackers he had encountered, who were parched themselves, shared some of their water with him.

But the hiker continued on alone, ignoring the strangers' entreaties for him to turn back toward the Colorado River, where hikers replenish their water supplies. . . .

"If giving up water would endanger myself to the point that I would also become a heat casualty, I would not share," [another hiker] said. "Rather, I would search for help before one unfortunate hiker turned into two."

This kind of situation has happened before. Shannan D. Marcak, a spokeswoman at the Grand Canyon National Park, said park veterans recalled at least one case in which someone died "trying to provide more help than they could physically afford to provide."

Ms. Craig said that looking out for oneself first makes sense.

"It's just like in an airplane when a stewardess tells you to secure your own mask before you help people," she said. "It sounds selfish, but it's right."

QUESTIONS FOR DISCUSSION

1. **"It sounds selfish, but it's right." Do you agree? Why?**
2. **Is there anything amiss with people disagreeing about the answer to this question? Does this surprise you?**
3. **Is there anything amiss with Talmudic sages debating this matter? Does it surprise you?**

FIGURE 4.1

Key Questions

1. Why don't the Talmudic debates undermine the validity of the entire system of Halachah?
2. Which areas of Jewish law are subject to debate and difference of opinion?
3. Why is there disagreement? Why would God want and/or allow this?
4. How are the debates resolved?

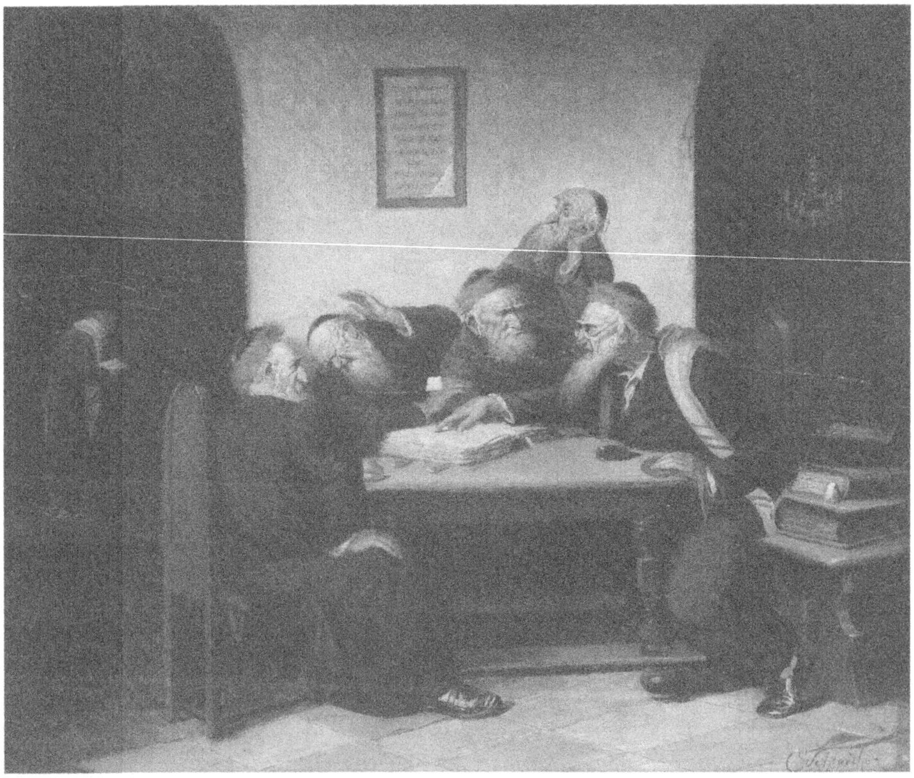

Debates and the Categories of Torah

Debate-Free Zone

LEARNING EXERCISE 1

Which of the following categories of Torah are more conducive to the existence of debate and difference of opinion? Rate each category on a scale of 1 to 5, with 5 indicating a strong likelihood for debate, and 1 indicating a strong likelihood for unanimity.

Category	Definition	Likelihood for debate
1. Received	God-given explanations for each of the commandments	1 2 3 4 5
2. Derived	Laws that we derive from the Written Torah and the Received Oral Torah	1 2 3 4 5
3. Legislated	New laws legislated by rabbinic sages	1 2 3 4 5
4. Customary	Customs initiated by the people, intended to enhance an aspect of Judaism	1 2 3 4 5

Text 2a

Maimonides, Introduction to the Mishnah

שֶׁהַפֵּירוּשִׁים הַמְקוּבָּלִים מִמֹּשֶׁה אֵין בָּהֶם מַחֲלוֹקֶת כְּלָל.

לְפִי שֶׁעַד עַכְשָׁיו לֹא מָצָאנוּ שֶׁנָּפְלָה מַחֲלוֹקֶת בֵּין הַחֲכָמִים בְּשׁוּם זְמַן מִן הַזְּמַנִּים,
מִמֹּשֶׁה רַבֵּינוּ עַד רַב אַשִׁי, שֶׁאֶחָד אָמַר שֶׁמִּי שֶׁסִּימָּא עֵין אָדָם מְסַמִּין אֶת עֵינוֹ,
כְּמַאֲמָר ה' יִתְעַלֶּה עַיִן בְּעַיִן (שְׁמוֹת כא,כד), וְאַחֵר אָמַר דָּמִים בִּלְבָד הוּא חַיָּיב.

גַּם לֹא מָצָאנוּ מַחֲלוֹקֶת בְּמַה שֶּׁאָמַר הַכָּתוּב "פְּרִי עֵץ הָדָר" (וַיִּקְרָא כג,מ)
שֶׁאֶחָד אָמַר שֶׁהוּא הָאֶתְרוֹג, וְאַחֵר אָמַר שֶׁהוּא הַפָּרִישׁ אוֹ הָרִמּוֹן אוֹ
זוּלָתָם. גַּם לֹא מָצָאנוּ מַחֲלוֹקֶת בְּ"עֵץ עָבוֹת" (שָׁם) שֶׁהוּא הַהָדָס . . .

וְכֵן כָּל כַּיּוֹצֵא בָּזֶה בְּכָל הַמִּצְוֹת אֵין בָּהֶן מַחֲלוֹקֶת,
לְפִי שֶׁהֵם פֵּירוּשִׁים מְקוּבָּלִים מִמֹּשֶׁה.

There are no debates at all with regard to the explanations we received from Moses.

There never has arisen a debate among the sages of any era—from Moses until Rav Ashi [who redacted the Talmud]—in which one sage said "an eye for an eye (Exodus 21:24)" means literal retaliation and another sage said the Torah is only referring to monetary compensation.

Likewise, there never arose a dispute over the meaning of the verse, "On the first day you shall take the fruit of a *hadar* tree (Leviticus 23:40)," whereby one sage said that this fruit was an *etrog,* and another said that it referred to a quince, a pomegranate, or some other fruit.

Nor have we come across any disagreement whether "*anaf ets avot* (ibid.)" refers to myrtle branches. . . .

Rabbi Moshe ben Maimon
(Maimonides, Rambam)
1135–1204

Halachist, philosopher, author, and physician. Maimonides was born in Cordoba, Spain. After the conquest of Cordoba by the Almohads, he fled Spain and eventually settled in Cairo, Egypt. There, he became the leader of the Jewish community and served as court physician to the vizier of Egypt. He is most noted for authoring the *Mishneh Torah*, an encyclopedic arrangement of Jewish law, and for his philosophical work, *Guide for the Perplexed*. His rulings on Jewish law are integral to the formation of halachic consensus.

Text 2b

Ibid.

אֲבָל סְבָרַת מִי שֶׁחָשַׁב שֶׁגַּם הַדִּינִים שֶׁיֵּשׁ בָּהֶם מַחֲלוֹקֶת קַבָּלָה מִמֹּשֶׁה, וְנָפְלָה בָּהֶם מַחֲלוֹקֶת מֵחֲמַת טָעוּת בְּקַבָּלָה אוֹ שִׁכְחָה, וְשֶׁהָאֶחָד צוֹדֵק בְּקַבָּלָתוֹ וְהַשֵּׁנִי טָעָה בְּקַבָּלָתוֹ, אוֹ שֶׁשָּׁכַח, אוֹ שֶׁלֹּא שָׁמַע מֵרַבּוֹ כָּל מַה שֶּׁצָּרִיךְ לִשְׁמוֹעַ . . . הִנֵּה זֶה חַי ה' דָּבָר מְגוּנֶּה וּמוּזָר מְאֹד, וְהוּא דָּבָר בִּלְתִּי נָכוֹן וְלֹא מַתְאִים לִכְלָלִים. וְחוֹשֵׁד בַּאֲנָשִׁים שֶׁמֵּהֶם קִבַּלְנוּ אֶת הַתּוֹרָה, וְכָל זֶה בָּטֵל.

וְהֵבִיא אוֹתָם לִידֵי הַשְׁקָפָה נִפְסֶדֶת זוֹ מִיעוּט יְדִיעַת דִּבְרֵי חֲכָמִים הַנִּמְצָאִים בְּתַלְמוּד . . . הֵם לֹא הִבְדִּילוּ בֵּין הַכְּלָלִים הַמְקוּבָּלִים וְהַחִדּוּשִׁים שֶׁנִּלְמְדוּ בְּדַרְכֵי הָעִיּוּן.

It would be very strange and disgraceful for a person to think that the Talmudic disagreements are about laws received from Moses, and that the debates ensued from forgetfulness or error, where one person's tradition was correct but the other did not receive it properly, forgot it, or did not study sufficiently from teachers. . . . This view is incorrect and inconsistent with the principles of Judaism. It slurs the people from whom we received the Torah and it amounts to empty talk.

What brings people to believe such faulty ideas is that they are insufficiently versed in the words of the Talmudic sages. . . . They therefore fail to draw a distinction between the basic explanations [that we received from Moses] and the laws that the sages derived through analysis.

FIGURE 4.2

Categories of Oral Torah

Category	Definition	Multiple Opinions
1. Received	God-given explanations for each of the commandments	No
2. Derived	Laws that we derive from the Written Torah and the Received Oral Torah	Sometimes
3. Legislated	New laws legislated by rabbinic sages	Sometimes
4. Customary	Customs initiated by the people, intended to enhance an aspect of Judaism	Sometimes

Debate in Derived

Text 3a

Leviticus 25:35–36

וְכִי יָמוּךְ אָחִיךָ וּמָטָה יָדוֹ עִמָּךְ וְהֶחֱזַקְתָּ בּוֹ גֵּר וְתוֹשָׁב וָחַי עִמָּךְ׃

אַל תִּקַּח מֵאִתּוֹ נֶשֶׁךְ וְתַרְבִּית וְיָרֵאתָ מֵאֱלֹקֶיךָ וְחֵי אָחִיךָ עִמָּךְ׃

When your brother becomes destitute and his hand falters beside you, you shall support him, [whether] a convert or a resident, so that he can live with you.

You shall not take interest from him. Fear your God, and let your brother live with you.

LEARNING EXERCISE 2

Think about this passage for a moment. Together with the person next to you, discuss how you might apply it to the situation described in Text 1. Which word or phrase supports your view?

Text 3b

Sifra, Parashat Behar 5:3

שְׁנַיִם שֶׁהָיוּ הוֹלְכִים בַּמִּדְבָּר, וְאֵין בְּיַד אֶחָד אֶלָּא קִיתוֹן שֶׁל מַיִם, אִם שׁוֹתֵהוּ אֶחָד, מַגִּיעַ לְיִישׁוּב, וְאִם שׁוֹתִים אוֹתוֹ שְׁנַיִם, שְׁנֵיהֶם מֵתִים.

דָּרַשׁ בֶּן פַּטִירִי: יִשְׁתּוּ שְׁתֵּיהֶם וְיָמוּתוּ, שֶׁנֶּאֱמַר "וְחֵי אָחִיךָ עִמָּךְ".

אָמַר לוֹ רַבִּי עֲקִיבָא: "וְחֵי אָחִיךָ עִמָּךְ" - חַיֶּיךָ קוֹדְמִים לְחַיֵּי חֲבֵירְךָ.

Two people were traveling in the desert, and one of them has only a flask of water. If he drinks it, he will reach town; if both of them drink it, they will both die.

Ben Petura derived that both should drink from it and die, as it says, "Let your brother live with you."

Rabbi Akiva said to him, "Let your brother live *with* you"—implying, your life takes precedence over the life of another.

Sifra
(*Torat Kohanim*)

An ancient rabbinic exegesis on the Book of Leviticus. The subject matter of this work is predominately Temple-era-related laws inasmuch as much of the Book of Leviticus focuses on the Temple service. According to Maimonides, the compiler and editor of this work was the Talmudic sage Rav (175–247 CE). Others attribute it to an earlier redactor. The work is quoted often in the Talmud.

Debate in Derived-Received

Text 4

Maimonides, Introduction to the Mishnah

וּכְשֶׁתִּרְאֶה בְּתַלְמוּד נוֹשְׂאִים וְנוֹתְנִים וְנֶחֱלָקִים עַל דֶּרֶךְ הָעִיּוּן וּמְבִיאִים רְאָיָה עַל אֶחָד מִן הַפֵּירוּשִׁים הַלָּלוּ וְדוֹמֵיהֶם, כְּמוֹ שֶׁאָמְרוּ (סֻכָּה לה,א) עַל אָמְרוֹ יִתְעַלֶּה "פְּרִי עֵץ הָדָר", וְאוּלַי הוּא הַרִמּוֹן אוֹ הַפָּרִישׁ אוֹ זוּלָתָן? עַד שֶׁהֵבִיאוּ רְאָיָה מֵאָמְרוֹ "פְּרִי עֵץ", וְאָמְרוּ עֵץ שֶׁטַּעַם עֵצוֹ וּפִרְיוֹ שָׁוִין, וְאָמַר אַחֵר פְּרִי הַדָּר בְּאִילָנוֹ מִשָּׁנָה לְשָׁנָה, וְאָמַר אַחֵר פְּרִי הַדָּר עַל כָּל מַיִם, אֵין זֶה מִפְּנֵי שֶׁהַדָּבָר סָפֵק אֶצְלָם עַד שֶׁלָּמְדוּ עָלָיו בִּרְאָיוֹת אֵלּוּ, אֶלָּא רָאִינוּ בְּלִי סָפֵק מִיהוֹשֻׁעַ עַד עַכְשָׁו שֶׁהָאֶתְרוֹג הוּא הַנִּטָּל עִם הַלּוּלָב בְּכָל שָׁנָה, וְאֵין מַחֲלֹקֶת בְּכָךְ, וְרַק חָקְרוּ עַל הַהוֹרָאָה שֶׁיֵּשׁ בַּמִּקְרָא לַפֵּרוּשׁ הַמְקֻבָּל הַזֶּה.

When you find Talmudic sages discussing, debating, and bringing proofs for any of these Received explanations or others like it [they are not arguing over the validity or the nature of the Received law, but rather how it might be Derived from the biblical text].

For example, the sages discuss (Talmud, Sukah 35a) the "fruit of a *hadar* tree," and ask, "But maybe it refers to some fruit other than the *etrog*?" They then bring proof from the words "fruit" and "tree" to indicate that it must be fruit of a tree whose bark tastes the same as its fruit, which is true of the *etrog*. Another sage finds a hint for the *etrog* in the word *hadar*, explaining that the word *hadar* can also mean "to dwell," indicating that it is a fruit that can dwell on the tree from one year to the next, which is a characteristic of the *etrog*. A third sage [noting the similarity between *hadar* and the Greek *hydor*, meaning water] says this indicates it is a fruit that grows on much water, which is true of the *etrog*.

The sages did not offer these derivations because they were not sure of what the Torah meant by "fruit of a *hadar* tree." From the days of Joshua until today, Jews took a *lulav* and an *etrog*, year after year, without debate. The sages were merely investigating the biblical allusion for this Received tradition.

Jewish coinage from the period of the Bar Kochba Revolt (ca. 132–135 CE) depicting a *lulav* and *etrog*

Text 5

Mishnah, Keritot 3:9

אָמַר רַבִּי עֲקִיבָא: אִם הֲלָכָה נְקַבֵּל; וְאִם לַדִּין, יֵשׁ תְּשׁוּבָה.

Rabbi Akiva said, "If it is a law [passed down from Sinai], we will accept it. But if you are deriving it, it can be disproved."

Mishnah

The first authoritative work of Jewish law that was codified in writing. The Mishnah contains the oral traditions that were passed down from teacher to student; it supplements, clarifies, and systematizes the commandments of the Torah. Due to the continual persecution of the Jewish people, it became increasingly difficult to guarantee that these traditions would not be forgotten. Rabbi Yehudah Hanasi therefore redacted the Mishnah at the end of the 2nd century. It serves as the foundation for the Talmud.

Debate in Legislated and Customary

Text 6

Maimonides, Introduction to the Mishnah

הַדִּינִים שֶׁקְּבָעוּם הַנְּבִיאִים וְהַחֲכָמִים שֶׁבְּכָל דּוֹר וָדוֹר עַל דֶּרֶךְ הַגָּדֵר וְהַסְּיָג לַתּוֹרָה . . . וְגַם בָּהֶם יֵשׁ שֶׁתִּהְיֶה מַחֲלֹקֶת, כְּגוֹן שֶׁיֵּרָאֶה לָאָדָם לֶאֱסוֹר כָּךְ מִשּׁוּם כָּךְ, וְאַחֵר לֹא יֵרָאֶה לוֹ. וְזֶה הַרְבֵּה בַּתַּלְמוּד, ר' פְּלוֹנִי גָּזַר מִשּׁוּם כָּךְ וְכָךְ, ור' פְּלוֹנִי לֹא גָּזַר.

It is also possible for there to be debate . . . with regard to the laws that were established by the prophets and sages in each generation, when they enacted measures to protect people from violating a prohibition in the Torah. One sage might prohibit something for a particular reason whereas another one could disagree. You find this often in the Talmud, where it says, "This rabbi prohibited such-and-such because of this-and-that, and another rabbi did not issue this prohibition."

Text 7

Rabbi Yosef Caro, Shulchan Aruch, *Even Ha'ezer* 1:10

רַבֵּינוּ גֵּרְשׁוֹם הֶחֱרִים עַל הַנּוֹשֵׂא עַל אִשְׁתּוֹ . . . וְלֹא פָּשְׁטָה תַּקָּנָתוֹ בְּכָל הָאֲרָצוֹת.

Rabbeinu Gershom declared excommunication upon a polygamous man . . . but his enactment did not take hold in all lands.

Rabbi Yosef Caro
(Maran, *Beit Yosef*)
1488–1575

Halachic authority and author. Rabbi Caro was born in Spain, but was forced to flee during the expulsion in 1492 and eventually settled in Safed, Israel. He authored many works including the *Beit Yosef*, *Kesef Mishneh*, and a mystical work, *Magid Meisharim*. Rabbi Caro's magnum opus, the Shulchan Aruch (Code of Jewish Law), has been universally accepted as the basis for modern Jewish law.

Profundity in Debate

Returning to the Opening Question

Text 8

Midrash, *Eliyahu Zuta* 2

מִקְרָא וּמִשְׁנָה שְׁנֵיהֶם מִפִּי הַגְּבוּרָה נֶאֶמְרוּ.

Both the Written Torah and the Oral Torah are God-given.

Tana Devei Eliyahu

A midrashic work, sometimes referred to as *Seder Eliyahu*. Midrash is the designation of a particular genre of rabbinic literature usually forming a running commentary on specific books of the Bible. This work deals with the divine precepts, their rationales, and the importance of knowledge of Torah, prayer, and repentance. The work is divided into two sections: *Seder Eliyahu Rabah* and *Seder Eliyahu Zuta*.

Divine Debate

Text 9a

Talmud, Chagigah 3b

הַלָּלוּ מְטַמְּאִין וְהַלָּלוּ מְטַהֲרִין, הַלָּלוּ אוֹסְרִין וְהַלָּלוּ מַתִּירִין, הַלָּלוּ פּוֹסְלִין וְהַלָּלוּ מַכְשִׁירִין.

שֶׁמָּא יֹאמַר אָדָם: הֵאַךְ אֲנִי לָמֵד תּוֹרָה מֵעַתָּה?

תַּלְמוּד לוֹמַר: "כֻּלָּם נִתְּנוּ מֵרֹעֶה אֶחָד" (קֹהֶלֶת יב,יא). אֵ-ל אֶחָד נְתָנָן, פַּרְנֵס אֶחָד אֲמָרָן מִפִּי אֲדוֹן כָּל הַמַּעֲשִׂים בָּרוּךְ הוּא. דִּכְתִיב (שְׁמוֹת כ,א) "וַיְדַבֵּר אֱלֹקִים אֵת כָּל הַדְּבָרִים הָאֵלֶּה".

Some sages rule [that an object is ritually] impure, and others rule [that it is] pure; some forbid while others permit; some disqualify while others declare fit.

A person might ask, "Why study Torah under such circumstances?"

The verse therefore says, (Ecclesiastes 12:11), "All were given from one shepherd." One God gave them; one leader communicated them from the mouth of God. As it is written (Exodus 20:1), "And God spoke all these words."

Babylonian Talmud

A literary work of monumental proportions that draws upon the legal, spiritual, intellectual, ethical, and historical traditions of Judaism. The 37 tractates of the Babylonian Talmud contain the teachings of the Jewish sages from the period after the destruction of the 2nd Temple through the 5th century CE. It has served as the primary vehicle for the transmission of the Oral Law and the education of Jews over the centuries; it is the entry point for all subsequent legal, ethical, and theological Jewish scholarship.

Text 9b

Midrash Tehilim 12

Midrash Tehilim

A rabbinic commentary on the Book of Psalms. Midrash is the designation of a particular genre of rabbinic literature usually forming a running commentary on specific books of the Bible. This particular Midrash provides textual exegeses and develops and illustrates the principles of the Book of Psalms.

עַל כָּל דִּבּוּר שֶׁהָיָה אוֹמֵר הַקָּדוֹשׁ בָּרוּךְ הוּא לְמֹשֶׁה הָיָה
אוֹמֵר מ"ט פָּנִים טָהוֹר, ומ"ט פָּנִים טָמֵא.

For each law that God told Moses, He would enumerate forty-nine arguments for ruling that an object was ritually pure, and forty-nine arguments for ruling that the object was ritually impure.

Text 9c

Talmud, Eiruvin 13b

שָׁלֹשׁ שָׁנִים נֶחֶלְקוּ בֵּית שַׁמַּאי וּבֵית הִלֵּל. הַלָּלוּ אוֹמְרִים:
הֲלָכָה כְּמוֹתֵנוּ, וְהַלָּלוּ אוֹמְרִים: הֲלָכָה כְּמוֹתֵנוּ.

יָצְאָה בַּת קוֹל וְאָמְרָה: אֵלּוּ וְאֵלּוּ דִּבְרֵי אֱלֹקִים חַיִּים הֵן.

For three years, there was a dispute between Beit Shamai and Beit Hillel, the former asserting, "The *halachah* is in agreement with our views" and the latter contending, "The *halachah* is in agreement with our views."

A heavenly voice declared, "These and these are the words of the living God."

Text 10

Rabbi Yehuda Loew, *Be'er Hagolah* 1

כִּי כָּל דָּבָר וְדָבָר אִי אֶפְשָׁר שֶׁלֹּא יְהֵא בְּחִינָה יוֹתֵר מֵאַחַת לְדָבָר אֶחָד. שֶׁאַף אִם הַדָּבָר טָמֵא, אִי אֶפְשָׁר שֶׁלֹּא יִהְיֶה לוֹ צַד בְּחִינָה אֶל טָהֳרָה שֶׁל מַה, וְכֵן אִם הַדָּבָר טָהוֹר, אִי אֶפְשָׁר שֶׁלֹּא יִהְיֶה לוֹ בְּחִינָה מַה שֶׁל טוּמְאָה . . . שֶׁדִּין זֶה יֵשׁ בּוֹ בְּחִינָה לִזְכוּת וְיֵשׁ בּוֹ בְּחִינָה לְחוֹבָה, וְדִין שֶׁל אִיסּוּר וְהֶיתֵּר יֵשׁ בְּדִין זֶה בְּחִינָה לְהֶיתֵּר וְיֵשׁ כַּאן בְּחִינָה לֶאֱסוֹר, וְכֵן כָּשֵׁר וּפָסוּל יֵשׁ בְּחִינָה אַחַת הֵפֶךְ הָאַחֶרֶת.

כְּמוֹ שֶׁבָּעוֹלָם נִמְצָא דָּבָר מוּרְכָּב מֵהֲפָכִים, וְתוּכַל לוֹמַר עַל הָעֵץ שֶׁהוּא מִתְיַחֵס אֶל יְסוֹד הַמַּיִם, וְכֵן הוּא הָאֱמֶת שֶׁיֵּשׁ בּוֹ מִן הַמַּיִם, וְתוּכַל לוֹמַר שֶׁיֵּשׁ בּוֹ מִן יְסוֹד הָאֲוִיר, וְכֵן הוּא הָאֱמֶת שֶׁיֵּשׁ בּוֹ יְסוֹד הָאֲוִיר . . . וְכַאֲשֶׁר אֶחָד לִמֵּד עַל דָּבָר אֶחָד טָהוֹר וְנָתַן טַעֲמוֹ וְשִׂכְלוֹ לְטָהֳרָה, הֲרֵי אָמַר בְּחִינָה אַחַת כְּפִי מַה שֶׁהוּא, וְהָאוֹמֵר טָמֵא וְאָמַר טַעֲמוֹ, זֶה אָמַר גַּם כֵּן בְּחִינָה אַחַת . . .

רַק לְעִנְיַן הֲלָכָה לְמַעֲשֶׂה אֵין סָפֵק שֶׁהָאֶחָד יוֹתֵר עִיקָּר מִן הַשֵּׁנִי . . . אַף שֶׁיֵּשׁ לְדָבָר אֶחָד בְּחִינוֹת מִתְחַלְּפוֹת כּוּלָּם נִתְּנוּ מִן הַשֵּׁם יִתְבָּרַךְ, רַק כִּי אֶחָד מֵהֶם יוֹתֵר עִיקָּר, וְהוּא מַכְרִיעַ וְהוּא הֲלָכָה.

מִכָּל מָקוֹם אַל תֹּאמַר כִּי דָּבָר שֶׁאֵינוֹ עִיקָּר אֵינוֹ נֶחְשָׁב כְּלוּם, זֶה אֵינוֹ, כִּי הַשּׁוֹמֵעַ כָּל הַדֵּעוֹת הֲרֵי הִשִּׂיג הַדָּבָר כְּפִי מָה שֶׁיֵּשׁ לְדָבָר בְּחִינוֹת מִתְחַלְּפוֹת, וַהֲרֵי לָמַד תּוֹרָה כְּפִי מָה שֶׁהוּא הַדָּבָר שֶׁיֵּשׁ לוֹ בְּחִינוֹת מִתְחַלְּפוֹת. רַק לְעִנְיַן הֲלָכָה אֶחָד מַכְרִיעַ עַל הַשֵּׁנִי.

It is not possible for anything in this world to have just one aspect to it. Even if something is ritually impure, it must contain an aspect of ritual purity; and when something is ritually pure, it must have an aspect of ritual impurity. . . . One feature of a particular case can elicit a verdict of innocence and another feature a verdict of guilt. One facet of a particular item or action can indicate permitted while another facet indicates prohibited. The same applies with regard to an item or action that is either valid or invalid.

Rabbi Yehudah Loew (Maharal of Prague)
1525–1609

Talmudist and philosopher. Maharal rose to prominence as leader of the famed Jewish community of Prague. He is the author of more than a dozen works of original philosophic thought, including *Tiferet Yisrael* and *Netsach Yisrael*. He also authored *Gur Aryeh*, a supercommentary to Rashi's biblical commentary, and a commentary on the non-legal passages of the Talmud. He is buried in the Old Jewish Cemetery of Prague.

This is true in general for the world we inhabit, where objects are comprised of multiple elements. One can say about a tree that it is comprised of water, and another can say it is comprised of oxygen—and both are speaking truth. . . .

When someone declares an item ritually pure and presents arguments to prove it, this person has demonstrated only one aspect of reality. Similarly, when one declares it ritually impure, it reflects only one aspect of reality. . . .

There is no doubt, however, that for the purpose of practical *halachah*, one aspect is more important than the other. . . . Although God created things with multiple facets, one of them is more significant, and this is what determines the actual *halachah*.

Still, do not say that the less significant aspects are wholly unimportant. This is not true. For when we hear all of the opinions, we comprehend the item in its totality, with all of its features and components, as spelled out in the Torah. It is only with regard to the practical final ruling that one feature outweighs the others.

Text 11

Rabbi Yechiel Michel Epstein, *Aruch Hashulchan*, introduction to *Choshen Mishpat*

וְכָל הַתּוֹרָה כּוּלָּהּ נִקְרֵאת שִׁירָה, וְתִפְאֶרֶת הַשִּׁיר הִיא כְּשֶׁהַקּוֹלוֹת
מְשׁוּנִּים זֶה מִזֶּה. וְזֶהוּ עִיקַּר הַנְּעִימוּת. וּמִי שֶׁמְּשׁוֹטֵט בְּיַם הַתַּלְמוּד
יִרְאֶה נְעִימוּת מְשׁוּנּוֹת בְּכָל הַקּוֹלוֹת הַמְשׁוּנּוֹת זֶה מִזֶּה.

The Torah is called a melody. The beauty of melody is when the sounds are different from each other; this is the primary pleasantness of song.

One who swims in the sea of Talmud will find pleasure in each of its differing sounds.

Rabbi Yechiel Michel Halevi Epstein
1829–1908

Noted author on Jewish law. Rabbi Epstein lived in Czarist Lithuania and was chief rabbi of Novozypkov, a town near Minsk, and later, of Navahrudak, where he served until his death. A prolific writer, his primary work is *Aruch Hashulchan*, an expanded and reworked code of Jewish law.

Reaching a Ruling

Text 12

Midrash Tehilim 12

עַל כָּל דִּבּוּר שֶׁהָיָה אוֹמֵר הַקָּדוֹשׁ בָּרוּךְ הוּא לְמֹשֶׁה הָיָה אוֹמֵר מ"ט פָּנִים טָהוֹר, ומ"ט פָּנִים טָמֵא.

אָמַר לְפָנָיו: רִבּוֹנוֹ שֶׁל עוֹלָם, עַד מָתַי נַעֲמוֹד עַל בֵּירוּרוֹ שֶׁל דָּבָר?

אָמַר לֵיהּ: "אַחֲרֵי רַבִּים לְהַטּוֹת" (שְׁמוֹת כג,ב). רָבּוּ הַמְטַמְּאִין, טָמֵא, רָבּוּ הַמְטַהֲרִין, טָהוֹר.

For each law that God told Moses, He would enumerate forty-nine arguments for ruling that an object was ritually pure and forty-nine arguments for ruling that the object was ritually impure.

Moses said before Him, "Master of the universe, how will we be able to reach the practical conclusion?"

God responded, "'Follow the majority (Exodus 23:2).' If the majority rules it is ritually impure, it is impure; if the majority rules pure, it is pure."

Text 13

Maimonides, *Mishneh Torah*, Laws of Rebels 1:4

כְּשֶׁהָיָה בֵּית דִּין הַגָּדוֹל קַיָּים, לֹא הָיְתָה מַחֲלוֹקֶת בְּיִשְׂרָאֵל.

אֶלָּא כָּל דִּין שֶׁנּוֹלַד בּוֹ סָפֵק לְאֶחָד מִיִּשְׂרָאֵל, שׁוֹאֵל לְבֵית דִּין שֶׁבְּעִירוֹ. אִם יָדְעוּ אָמְרוּ לוֹ, אִם לַאו, הֲרֵי הַשּׁוֹאֵל עִם אוֹתוֹ בֵּית דִּין אוֹ עִם שְׁלוּחָיו עוֹלִין לִירוּשָׁלַיִם וְשׁוֹאֲלִין לְבֵית דִּין שֶׁבְּהַר הַבַּיִת. אִם יָדְעוּ אָמְרוּ לוֹ, אִם לַאו, הַכֹּל בָּאִין לְבֵית דִּין שֶׁעַל פֶּתַח הָעֲזָרָה. אִם יָדְעוּ, אָמְרוּ לָהֶן, וְאִם לַאו הַכֹּל בָּאִין לְלִשְׁכַּת הַגָּזִית לְבֵית דִּין הַגָּדוֹל וְשׁוֹאֲלִין.

אִם הָיָה הַדָּבָר שֶׁנּוֹלַד בּוֹ הַסָּפֵק לְכָל יָדוּעַ אֵצֶל בֵּית דִּין הַגָּדוֹל, בֵּין מִפִּי הַקַּבָּלָה בֵּין מִפִּי הַמִּדָּה שֶׁדָּנוּ בָּהּ, אוֹמְרִים מִיָּד. אִם לֹא הָיָה הַדָּבָר בָּרוּר אֵצֶל בֵּית דִּין הַגָּדוֹל, דָּנִין בּוֹ בְּשַׁעְתָּן, וְנוֹשְׂאִין וְנוֹתְנִין בַּדָּבָר עַד שֶׁיַּסְכִּימוּ כּוּלָּן, אוֹ יַעַמְדוּ לַמִּנְיָן, וְיֵלְכוּ אַחַר הָרוֹב.

מִשֶּׁבָּטֵל בֵּית דִּין הַגָּדוֹל רָבְתָה מַחֲלוֹקֶת בְּיִשְׂרָאֵל: זֶה מְטַמֵּא וְנוֹתֵן טַעַם לִדְבָרָיו, וְזֶה מְטַהֵר וְנוֹתֵן טַעַם לִדְבָרָיו, זֶה אוֹסֵר וְזֶה מַתִּיר.

As long as the Sanhedrin was in existence, there were no [enduring halachic] debates among the Jewish people.

A Jew who had a doubt about a particular law would inquire of the local *beit din*. If its judges knew the answer, they would tell him; if not, the questioner would go together with the *beit din*, or its representatives, to Jerusalem and ask the *beit din* that sat on the Temple Mount. If its judges knew the answer, they would tell him; if not, they would all go to the *beit din* that sat by the entrance to the Temple courtyard. If its judges knew the answer, they would tell them; if not, they would all go to the chamber of hewn stone where the Sanhedrin convened.

If the Sanhedrin knew the answer—because it had a Received tradition about it or because it had Derived it—it would say so immediately. If the answer was not immediately clear to the Sanhedrin, its members would discuss it until everyone agreed; or they would put it to a vote and the law would follow the majority.

But once the Sanhedrin ceased to exist, divergent opinions proliferated. One sage would rule that an article is ritually impure and support this ruling with a rationale, and another would rule that it is pure and support this ruling with a rationale. One would rule an article is forbidden and another that it is permitted.

Text 14

Maimonides, Introduction to *Mishneh Torah*

כָּל הַדְּבָרִים שֶׁבַּגְּמָרָא הַבַּבְלִי חַיָּבִין כָּל יִשְׂרָאֵל לָלֶכֶת בָּהֶם, וְכוֹפִין כָּל עִיר וָעִיר וְכָל מְדִינָה וּמְדִינָה לִנְהוֹג בְּכָל הַמִּנְהָגוֹת שֶׁנָּהֲגוּ חַכְמֵי הַגְּמָרָא, וְלִגְזוֹר גְּזֵירוֹתָם, וְלָלֶכֶת בְּתַקָּנוֹתָם, הוֹאִיל וְכָל אוֹתָם הַדְּבָרִים שֶׁבַּגְּמָרָא הִסְכִּימוּ עֲלֵיהֶם כָּל יִשְׂרָאֵל. וְאוֹתָם הַחֲכָמִים שֶׁהִתְקִינוּ אוֹ שֶׁגָּזְרוּ אוֹ שֶׁהִנְהִיגוּ אוֹ שֶׁדָּנוּ דִּין וְלָמְדוּ שֶׁהַמִּשְׁפָּט כַּךְ הוּא, הֵם כָּל חַכְמֵי יִשְׂרָאֵל אוֹ רוּבָּם.

It is incumbent upon all Jews to follow all the rulings recorded in the Babylonian Talmud. Each city and each province must follow the customs endorsed by the Talmud and must enforce all rabbinic legislation mentioned therein. This is because the Jewish people agreed to all of these rulings, and because all of the Jewish sages—or at least a majority of them—issued those decrees and edicts, endorsed those customs, derived those new applications, and handed down those final halachic rulings.

Unity from Diversity

Text 15

Mishnah, Uktsin 3:12

לֹא מָצָא הַקָּדוֹשׁ בָּרוּךְ הוּא כְּלִי מַחֲזִיק בְּרָכָה לְיִשְׂרָאֵל אֶלָּא הַשָּׁלוֹם.
שֶׁנֶּאֱמַר (תְּהִלִּים כט,יא), "ה' עוֹז לְעַמּוֹ יִתֵּן ה' יְבָרֵךְ אֶת עַמּוֹ בַשָּׁלוֹם".

God found no better vessel than peace to hold blessing for the Jewish people. For it says, (Psalms 29:11), "The Lord shall grant strength to His people; the Lord shall bless His people with peace."

Key Points

TORAH Café™

Continue the JLI Learning Experience!

Visit www.TorahCafe.com/go/JD4

for a video lecture(s) related to the theme of this lesson.

1. We do not find rabbinic debates regarding the Received Oral Torah—that is, the basic meaning of the *mitzvot*. When a sage asserted that a certain law was Received, the students would unconditionally accept it as such.

2. It is common for debates to appear in the Derived category of Oral Torah.

3. When the sages choose to Derive a Received law, they could disagree about the correct derivation while agreeing on the nature of the Received law.

4. There can be difference of opinion between sages regarding the Legislated and Customary categories of Torah.

5. At times, God embedded in the Torah multiple clues leading to variant outcomes. Therefore, dissenting opinions in the sphere of the Derived Torah are both "the words of the living God."

6. Conflicting Torah opinions are both true, because each Derived halachic opinion reflects a divine perspective regarding the case under discussion. Through all of the perspectives, we come to learn about the object or case in its entirety.

7. The final *halachah* was determined by the majority of the Sanhedrin, and it reflected the most important and dominant perspective on a given item or case.

8. The Talmud represents final and binding *halachah* for all Jews, inasmuch as the majority of Jewish sages of its day ratified its decisions.

9. Rabbinic debates are a paradigm of peaceful relations. Peace requires divergent viewpoints and perspectives that then peacefully resolve. When the Sanhedrin was operational, a halachic dispute ideally ended with the minority agreeing with the majority ruling.

ADDITIONAL READINGS

MIAMONIDES' INTRODUCTION TO THE MISHNAH: THE ORAL TORAH

TRANSLATED BY FRED ROSNER, MD

Know[1] that every commandment which the Holy One Blessed Be He gave to Moses our Teacher, may he rest in peace,[2] was given with its clarification. First He told him the commandment and then He expounded on its explanation and content, including all that which is included in the Torah. The manner of its transmittal to Israel occurred as stated in the Gemara:[3] Moses entered into the tent, and first Aaron entered unto him. Moses then stated to him a single time the commandment he had received, and taught him its explanation, (following which) Aaron retreated to the right of Moses, our teacher. Thereupon, Elazar and Ithamar, Aaron's sons, entered and Moses told them what he had told Aaron, and then they stepped back. One sat to the left of Moses, our Teacher, and the other on the right of Aaron. Then the seventy Elders arrived, and Moses taught them, just as he had taught Aaron and his sons. Following this came the masses of people and everyone seeking God, and he (Moses) placed before them that commandment, until all had heard it from his mouth. The result is that Aaron, heart that precept from the mouth of Moses four times, his sons three times, the Elders twice, and the remainder of the populace once. Moses then left and Aaron repeated the explanation of that commandment which he had learned, having heard it from the mouth of Moses four times as we have mentioned, to all those present. Aaron then left, after his sons had heard the precept four times; three times from Moses, and once from Aaron. After Aaron had departed, Elazar and Ithamar repeated and taught that commandment to the entire populace that was present, and then ceased their teaching. Thus we find that the seventy Elders heard the precept four times; twice from Moses, once from Aaron, and once from Elazar and Ithamar. The Elders themselves then repeated and expounded the commandment to the populace once and, (as a result), we find that the entire congregation heard the precept in question four times; once from Moses, once from Aaron, a third time from his sons, and the fourth time from the Elders. After this, all the people went to teach one another what they had heard from Moses and to write that commandment on scrolls. The leaders roamed over all of Israel to (ensure that the people) learn and apply themselves until they would know the traditional version of that commandment and were fluent in reading it. They would then teach the explanations of that God-given precept. That explanation would include all aspects, and they would write the precept and learn by heart the oral tradition.[4]

Thus, our Sages, of Blessed Memory, said in the *Beraitha*:[5] *And the Lord spoke unto Moses at Mount Sinai.*[6] Why does the teaching state specifically *at Mount Sinai?* Was not the entire Torah given[7] at Sinai? But (the lesson is) to tell us that just as the law

---

1 This introduction to Tractate Berachoth serves as the general introduction to the entire Commentary on the Mishnah. It is sometimes spoken of as the introduction to Seder Zeraim since Maimonides wrote separate introductions for the other sections or orders of the Mishnah.

2 Lit: peace be upon him.

3 Tractate Erubin 54b.

4 This oral transmittal of precepts and their explanation comprise the "oral law" *(Torah She-B'al Peh)* and is extant today as the Talmud (Mishnah & *Gemara)*. This is in contradistinction to the "written Law" *(Torah She-Bichetav)* which is the Pentateuch.

5 *Torath Kohanim*, a *halachik* Commentary on Leviticus.

6 Levit. 25,1.

7 Lit: said.

of *Shemita*[8] was stated with its generalities, specifics and fine details at Sinai, so too all the commandments were stated with their generalities, specifics and fine details at Sinai. You have an example of this when the Holy One Blessed Be He told Moses: *Ye shall dwell in booths for seven days,*[9] following which He informed him that this *Succah*[10] is an obligation upon males and not females, and that sick people are not so obligated, nor travelers; also the covering of the *Succah* should only be of that which grows from the earth, and that one should not use wool or silk or utensils for a covering even when these utensils are made of products which grow from the earth, such as mattresses, pillows and clothing. He (God) also clearly indicated that eating, drinking and sleeping therein are all obligatory for the entire seven (days of *Succoth).* Furthermore, its (interior) space should not be less than seven handbreadths in length by seven handbreadths in width, nor shall the height of the *Succah* be less than ten handbreadths. And when the prophet (Moses), may he rest in peace, came, he was given this commandment with its explanation, and so too the 613 precepts with their explanations; the commandments in writing, and the explanations by oral transmission.

And it came to pass in the fortieth year, in the eleventh month[11] on the day of the New Moon of the month of Shebat, that he (Moses) gathered the people and told them: *The time of my death has arrived. If there is anyone among you who heard a law and forgot it, let him come and ask me and I will explain it. Also, let anyone to whom a question remains in doubt come and I will clarify it* as it is written: *Moses began to explain this Torah saying....*[12] Thus too did the Sages state in *Sifre:*[13] "Let he who has forgotten (even) one single law come and relearn it and whoever is in need of explanation, let him come and it will be explained".[14] From his (Moses) mouth they received clarification of the law and learned the explanations during the entire period, from the New Moon of Shebat till the seventh of Adar.[15] When he was close to death he began to write the Torah on scrolls,[16] and wrote thirteen Torah scrolls, all of rolled parchment, from the (letter) *Beth* of *Bereishith*[17] to the (last) *Lamed* of *L'ainai Kol Yisrael.*[18] He gave one scroll to each tribe to conduct itself accordingly, and to follow its laws. He gave the thirteenth scroll to the Levites and told them: *Take this book of the law,*[19] *after which he ascended the Mount at noon*[20] *of the seventh day*[21] *of the month of Adar,*[22] *as tradition has deduced. We would consider that particular process*[23] *which occurred to him death, because we lost him and missed him. However, he lives in the glory of the (greater) height to which he ascended. So too is it stated "Moses our Teacher, did not die; rather he ascended and is serving in heaven."*[24] *Discussions in these matters (of death) can be extremely lengthy, and this is not the place (to expound upon the details). He died, may he rest in peace, after having bequeathed to Joshua that which was endowed to him (Joshua), in the way of interpretation and wisdom, and he became wise. And Joshua and the people of his generation studied it.*

Of all that he (Joshua) or one of the Elders received from Moses, there was no need for further discussion, since no disagreement occurred thereon. He who did not hear the decision, directly from the prophet (Moses), of blessed-memory, concerning questions arising therefrom,[25] derived the laws by means of reasoning or by means of the thirteen principles given at Mount Sinai through which the Torah may be expounded.[26] These interpreted laws were sometimes

---

8 Resting of the soil and cancellation of debts in the Sabbatical year.

9 Levit. 23,42.

10 Booth or hut or tabernacle.

11 Deut. 1,3.

12 Deut.1,5.

13 Maimonides explains *Beraitha, Sifra* & *Sifre* later in his Introduction to the Commentary.

14 *Sifre,* Deut. 1,5.

15 One month and seven days.

16 lit: books.

17 The first word in the Torah.

18 The last three words in the Torah. They begin and end with the letter *lamed.* See Tractate Baba Bathra 15a.

19 Deut. 31, 26.

20 lit: half.

21 *Sifre* Deut. 32,1.

22 Tractate Megillah 13b.

23 The death of Moses.

24 Tractate Sotah 13b.

25 Questions whose answers can be derived from the explicit law.

26 *Sifra* 1, also known as the *Beraitha* of Rabbi Ishmael which enunciates the thirteen principles of Rabbinic exegesis. See Hertz, *Authorized Daily Prayer Book.* New York. Bloch Publishers, 1959, p. 43.

free of argumentation, everyone agreeing (to a single view). On some of them, however, differences of opinion occurred between two views, the one stating thusly and the other thusly, the former deducing his view and, by means of reason, strengthening it in his own mind, and the latter also presenting reason to strengthen his opinion. It is because of the pitfall of analogy[27] by means of reasoning that this happening (i.e. the difference) in their opinions occurs. When such a difference of opinion does occur, then one follows, the (ruling of the) majority as it is written: *Thou shalt follow the majority....*[28]

When Joshua, the son of Nun, died, may he rest in peace, he transmitted[29] to the Elders all the explanations (of the Torah) that he had received (from Moses), and also all the laws that were inferred in his lifetime, concerning which no argument existed. However, where there was a difference of opinion, the final ruling was in accordance with (the view of) the majority of the Elders. Concerning them does Scriptures state: *(And Israel served the Lord all the days of Joshua), and all the days of the Elders who outlived Joshua.*[30] Following this, these Elders taught what they had received from the mouth of Joshua to the prophets, may they rest in peace, and the prophets taught (these laws and their elaborations) to one another. No generation went by[31] in which there was no investigation or delving into these matters. The Sages of every generation would consider the teachings[32] of their predecessors as fundamental, and would learn their texts from them, and would generate new ideas. The basic[33] fundamentals were never subject to differences of opinion. (The transmission of the Torah teachings proceeded in this manner) until the period of the men of the Great Assembly was reached.[34] These were Haggai, Zachariah, Malachi, Daniel, Hananiah, Mishael, Azariah, Ezra the Scribe, Nehemiah the son of Chachaliah, Mordechai and Zerubabel the son of Sh'altee'el. To these prophets were added elders from among the craftsmen and smiths[35] and the like to make up the remainder of the 120 (of the Great Assembly). These, too, deliberated, as did their predecessors, and they proclaimed decrees and enacted ordinations. The last of that Holy[36] group is the first of the Sages mentioned in the Mishnah, namely, Simeon the Righteous who was the High Priest of that generation.

Time passed until the last of them[37], (Rabbi Judah the Patriarch), our Holy Rabbi, may he rest in peace, who was the outstanding one in his generation, and unique in his time; a man in whom were found all precious attributes and virtuous traits, so much so that he became worthy, in the eyes of the people of his generation, to be called (simply) Our Holy Rabbi. His name was Judah. He was the epitome of wisdom and greatness, as they stated: "From the time of Moses our Teacher until Rebbe,[38] we have not seen Torah and greatness in one place".[39] He was unsurpassed in righteousness, humility and abstinence from (worldly) pleasures, as they (the Sages) also stated: "When Rebbe died, true humility and fear of sin disappeared".[40] He was also eloquent and more knowledgeable in the Holy Tongue[41] than any other man, so much so, that the Sages of blessed memory came to learn the explanation of words[42] of Scriptures which were unclear to them[43] from the words of his slaves and servants. This is well-known in the Talmud.[44] He was also endowed with great wealth and property and great means[45], to the point that it was said: "The House Steward of Rebbe was wealthier

27 Between two Biblical laws.

28 Exodus 23, 2.

29 Lit: taught.

30 Joshua 24,31.

31 Lit: there was not time.

32 Lit: words.

33 Lit: accepted or transmitted.

34 Approximately the fifth century BCE. The last Head of this Assembly was Simeon, the righteous.

35 Second Kings 24,16 and Tractate Gittin 88a.

36 lit: pure.

37 The sages of the Mishnah, also called *Tannaim*.

38 Rabbi Judah the Patriarch, Our Holy Rabbi.

39 He was supreme in both Torah and secular matters. Tractate Gittin 59a.

40 Tractate Sotah 49a. Although this statement is in the Mishnah it must have been added later since Rebbe himself compiled the Mishnah.

41 Hebrew.

42 Lit: letters.

43 Lit: into which errors had fallen.

44 Tractate Rosh Hashana 26b.

45 Lit: capabilities.

than King Shapur".[46] He was generous with people of learning, and with those who sought it, and he spread Torah in Israel. He collected all the legal decisions and discussions of the Sages as well as the differences of opinion which had been transmitted (through the generations) from the days of Moses our Teacher until his time. He himself was one of those who received (these traditions), since he acquired them from his father Simeon, and Simeon from his father Gamliel (who received them) from Simeon (who acquired them) from Hillel (who received them) from his teachers Shemaiah and Abtalion. The latter (received the Torah traditions) from Judah the son of Tabbai and Simeon the son of Shetach; they from Joshua the son of Perachiah and Nitai the Arbelite, and they from Yose the son of Yoezer, of Tz'raidah, and Yose the son of Yochanan, they from Antignos of Socho, and he from Simeon the Righteous, he from Ezra who was the teacher of the men of the Great Assembly, and Ezra from his teacher Baruch, the son of Neriah, and Baruch from Jeremiah.[47]

Undoubtedly, in a similar manner did Jeremiah receive it from the prophets who preceded him, (and they), prophet from prophet, until the Elders, who received it from Joshua, the son of Nun, and he from Moses.

When he[48] had collected all the views and opinions, he commenced to redact the Mishnah which incorporates the explanations of all the commandments written in the Torah. Of these, some are teachings received directly from the mouth of Moses; others are views derived from logical reasoning and concerning which no difference of opinion exists. Others yet are those regarding which argumentation occurs between two views; these he included with the debate saying: "This one states thusly, and that one states differently". If one (Sage) is in disagreement with many, the opinion of the one as well as the view of the majority are recorded. This (recording of the opinion of a single person) was done in many discussions to good purpose, as is enumerated in the Mishnah in (tractate) Edduyoth.[49] I will mention these, but only after (mentioning) a fundamental principle that I see fit to describe here, and that is that a person could ask: "If these explanations of the Torah, as we have established them, were received from Moses, as we have stated, in the name of the Sages, that the entire Tora including its generalities, specifics and minutiae were given at Sinai, then what are these special laws that are referred to as Verbal Mosaic Tradition?"[50] The following principle should be understood in its depth,[51] namely that the explanations received from Moses, as we have stated, in the name of the Sages, are without controversy whatsoever. From then until now we have never found a difference of opinion amongst the Sages at any time from the days of Moses until Rav Ashi, such that one would say: "He who blinds[52] the eye of his friend shall have his eye removed as it is written *An eye for an eye*[53], and the other would say "He is only obligated to pay indemnity (for the blinded eye)". We have also not found any difference of opinion in (the interpretation of the) Scriptural verse: *The fruit of splendid trees*[54], so that some would say it refers to the *ethrog*[55] and another (sage) would say it refers to quinces or pomegranates or something else. We have further never found a difference of opinion that the *Aboth Tree*[56] refers to anything other than the myrtle.[57] We have found no dispute in the interpretation of the verse *Thou shalt cut off her hand*[58] that it refers to indemnity; and also

46 Tractate Baba Metzia 85a. King Shapur the First reigned over Persia in the third century.

47 In his Introduction to the *Mishneh Torah* (Code of Maimonides), he continues the lineage as follows:

> Jeremiah from Zephaniah, Zephaniah from Habbakuk, Habbakuk from Nahum, Nahum from Joel, Joel from Michah, Michah from Isaiah, Isaiah from Amos, Amos from Hosea, Hosea from Zachariah, Zachariah from Jehojadah, Jehojadah from Elisha, Elisha from Elijah, Elijah from Achiyah, Achiyah from David, David from Samuel, Samuel from Eli, Eli from Pinchas, Pinchas from Joshua, Joshua from Moses our teacher, Moses our teacher, the teacher of all prophets, from the Eternal, God of Israel.
> Thus from Rav Ashi, compiler of the Gemara, through Rebbe, redactor of the Mishnah, until Moses was a total of forty generations.

48 Rebbe, compiler of the Mishnah.

49 Chapter 1.

50 Lit: *Halachah* of Moses from Sinai.

51 Lit: stand on its secret.

52 Lit: takes out.

53 Exod. 21, 24 and Levit. 24, 20.

54 Levit. 23,40.

55 A type of citrus fruit used together with the festive wreath on the Festival of *Sukkoth* (Booths).

56 Levit. 23, 40.

57 Hebrew: *Hadass*.

58 Deut. 25, 12.

not in what Scripture states: *And the daughter of a priest, if she profane herself by becoming a harlot, (she profaneth her father); she shall be burnt with fire*[59], that such an edict cannot be decreed by us unless she is at least bound to a husband.[60]

Similarly, regarding the Biblical exegesis of *a damsel in whom the tokens of virginity were not found (during the consummation of the marriage)* and who must then be *stoned,*[61] we have not found anyone from Moses till now who disagrees with the one who interprets that this (punishment) occurs only if she was a married woman and witnesses testified that she committed adultery after betrothal, in the presence of witnesses, after she had been warned. In a similar manner, in the totality of precepts (of the Torah), there is no controversy that all their explanations were received from Moses. Regarding these and similar instances did the Sages say: "The entire Torah with its generalities, specifics and fine details are all from Sinai".[62]

However, although these (laws) are accepted (through tradition), and no difference of opinion exists concerning them, it is possible for us to extract these explanations through the wisdom of the Torah given to us, through one of the types of deductive reasoning, through hints from the Biblical text,[63] or demonstration or suggestion that may be found in the Scriptural phrase. Thus, one sees the (Rabbis) in the Talmud theorizing and arguing with one another in a course of investigation, and bringing proofs for each of these interpretations and the like, as exemplified by what they stated regarding the scriptural phrase *The fruit of splendid trees:*[64] perhaps these are pomegranates or quinces or the like, until they brought proof for this (deduction) from the quotation itself.[65] "The fruit of a splendid tree" means a tree whose wood[66] and fruit taste equally (good).[67] Another (Sage) says that this (Scriptural phrase) refers to a fruit that dwells in its tree from year to year,[68] i.e., perennial. Yet another (Sage) says it refers to a fruit which always grows near water[69]. All these proofs were not adduced because the matter was unclear to them until they deduced them from one of these proofs. Indeed, we have unquestionably seen from (the time of) Joshua until the present that it is the *ethrog*[70] that was taken with the *lulav*[71] every year. No difference of opinion exists regarding this. Rather, they (the Sages) sought the Scriptural hint which pointed to the accepted meaning.

In a similar manner did they offer their proof regarding the myrtle tree[72], as well as the laws of (damaged) limbs for which financial compensation must be paid.[73] The latter refers to what one is obligated to pay one's neighbor whom he has injured in any limb. Similarly, the Sages' proof concerning a Priest's daughter, as (in the case) mentioned above, (to show that the verse) refers to a married woman.[74] All similar instances abide by this fundamental principle.

This is the intent of their statement: "Its generalities and specifics", which refers to the matters of law which can be derived through a general proposition, followed by a specifying particular, or through any of the other thirteen principles through which the Torah may be expounded.[75] These matters of law were received from Moses from Sinai, yet, though received from Moses, are not called verbal Mosaic Tradition.[76]

---

59 Levit. 21, 9.

60 The *Gemara* in Tractate Sanhedrin 50a–51b has a lengthy discussion as to whether this edict refers to an engaged or married woman, but all agree that the Scriptural verse refers to infidelity on the part of a priest's daughter who has marital sex.

61 Deut. 22, 20–21.

62 *Beraitha* in *Torath Kohanim*.

63 Hebrew: *A smachta*. Scriptural text used as a support for a rabbinical enactment; intimation.

64 Levit: 23, 40.

65 Tractate Sukkah 35a.

66 The Hebrew word *Eitz* means both wood and tree.

67 Heb: *Hadar* meaning good.

68 Heb: *Hadar* meaning lives or dwells, deduced from the infinitive *Ladur* which means to live.

69 Greek: *Hydras* meaning water.

70 A type of citrus fruit used together with the festive wreath on the Festival of *Sukkoth* (Booths).

71 Date palm, one of the components of the festive wreath.

72 Tractate Sukkah 32a.

73 Tractate Baba Kamma 83b.

74 Tractate Sanhedrin 52a.

75 The 13 principles of Rabbinic Exegesis. See Hertz, *Authorized Daily Prayer Book*, New York. Bloch, 1959 p. 43.

76 Lit: *Halachah* to Moses from Sinai. i.e. traditional interpretation of a written law.

It is incorrect to say that "the fruit of a splendid tree", meaning the *ethrog*, is a verbal Mosaic Tradition, or that the law providing that he who injures his neighbor must pay indemnity is a verbal Mosaic Tradition. This is because it has already been clarified to us that these explanations were all transmitted through Moses, and all have either suggestions in Scripture, or can be derived by some type of deductive reasoning, as we have mentioned. Therefore, only something which has no Scriptural allusion, nor is it linked thereto, and which cannot be derived from the Torah by any manner of deductive reasoning, is called verbal Mosaic Tradition.

For this reason, when we stated that measurements are a Verbal Mosaic Tradition, it was asked of us:[77] Why do you say that these laws are a Verbal Mosaic Tradition? Are not the (laws of) measurements alluded to in Scriptures when it states: *A land of wheat and barley (and vines and fig trees and pomegranates, a land of olive oil and honey)?*[78] The answer is that they are really Verbal Mosaic Tradition, and that the idea of measurements does not manifest a fundamental principle that can be derived from this verse through deductive reasoning. Further, they are not alluded to anywhere in the Torah. This commandment is associated with this Scriptural phrase as a device to make it known and remembered, but is not of the subject matter of the phrase itself.[79] This is the meaning of the statement "The Scriptural verse is merely a suggestive support" in the many places where it is found....[80]

As a result, the classification of laws ordained in the Torah comprises five categories, according to the aforementioned principles.

THE FIRST CATEGORY (consists of) explanations which were received from Moses[81], which are alluded to in Scriptures, and may be derived by deductive reasoning.[82] Here no difference of opinion exists; rather if someone states: "Thusly I have received it", one should not question it further.[83]

THE SECOND CATEGORY (consists of) laws which have been called Verbal Mosaic Tradition, and no support exists for them, as we have mentioned (above). This, too, is something without controversy.

THE THIRD CATEGORY (consists of) laws which are derived through methods of deductive reasoning[84], and concerning which dispute occurs, as we have mentioned. The final ruling in these cases is according to (the opinion of) the majority. Such a (dispute) occurs because the understanding of the law changes. For this reason it is stated: "If this is a *Halacha,*[85] we shall accept it, but if it is only an inference, an objection may be raised".[86] However, (in reality), there is dispute and theorizing, only in something that was not heard to be *Halacha.*[87] Thus we find throughout the Talmud that they (the Sages) delve into the reasons underlying a deductive derivation which is the cause for the argumentation among the disputants, and they (the Sages) state: "What are they arguing about?", or "What is the reason of Rabbi so and so?", or "What is (the point of difference) between them?" They approach (the problem) in this manner in most places, and then mention the reason which underlies the controversy, such as if they say: "Rabbi so and so employs such and such an argument whereas (Rabbi) so and so relies on such and such an argument", and the like.

However (there are) those who think that the laws which are in controversy were also received from Moses, and who (further) believe that the controversy arose by way of errors in the (traditionally received) *Halachoth,* or (because of) forgetfulness, or because one of the (Sages) received the correct tradi-

[77] Tractate Berachoth 41a; Erubin 4a and Sukkah 5b.

[78] Deut. 8, 8.

[79] i.e. this Biblical phrase only enumerates types of fruit, but does not mean to give measurements.

[80] e.g. Tractate Sukkah 6a.

[81] Lit: from the mouth of Moses.

[82] Through one of the 13 principles of Rabbinic exegesis.

[83] Lit: speak of it.

[84] Through one of the 13 principles of Rabbinic exegesis.

[85] i.e. received by tradition.

[86] Tractate Yebamoth 76b. In other words, if this law is one of those received from Moses which is alluded to in Scripture, or a Verbal Mosaic Tradition, we will accept it. However, if it is a law derived only through logical reasoning, we can argue thereon.

[87] i.e. received by tradition.

tion whereas the other[88] was mistaken in (the understanding of) what he received, or forgot, or did not understand all that which he was supposed to understand from his teacher. They[89] bring evidence for this (contention) with the statement "When the disciples of Shammai and Hillel who had insufficiently served (their teachers)[90] multiplied, controversy increased in Israel and the Torah became as two Torahs".[91] This type of contention is, by my life, an extremely depraved thing. These are words of someone without understanding, one who has no (knowledge of) fundamentals and who blemishes (the honor of those) people through whom the commandments were received. All this (type of reasoning) is false and void. That which brought one to believe in this depraved[92] conviction was a paucity of contemplation into the words of the Sages that are found in the Talmud. They found the sense of every explanation (of a law of the Torah) that was received from Moses to be true, as they did not differentiate between (traditionally) received fundamentals and the secondary teachings derived by deliberation.

Indeed, do not bring any doubt into your heart concerning the controversy between Beth Shammai and Beth Hillel[93] whether: "(After the meal) they sweep the floor[94] and then wash their hands"[95], or "They wash their hands and then sweep the floor";[96] (do not) think that one of these two views was not received by Moses at Sinai. The reason which is the basis for their argument is that which is mentioned in the Talmud,[97] namely, one of them (Beth Hillel) forbids the use of an unlearned attendant[98] (to remove bread crumbs), whereas the other (Beth Shammai) permits it. The same is true of all controversies similar to this, which are ramifications.

However, that which they (the Sages) stated: "When the disciples of Shammai and Hillel who had insufficiently served (their teachers)[99] multiplied, controversy increased in Israel", is a matter which can be simply explained. That is, wherever two people are equal in understanding, in deliberative capacity, and in knowledge of fundamentals (of the Torah) from which to derive their, deduced opinions, no controversy at all arises[100] in regard to their reasoning. Should this happen,[101] it will be minute indeed; and thus we do not find a difference of opinion between Shammai and Hillel, save in (a few) specific *Halachoth*. This is because the opinions of both are similar in all that they derive by way of deductive reasoning. The fundamentals, too, given to one are the same as the fundamentals given to the other. However, when the diligence of their disciples in (the search for) wisdom diminished, and when their power of correct deduction weakened, as compared with the reasoning of their teachers Hillel and Shammai, then controversy arose between them during deliberation of many subjects, as each one's opinion was molded by his understanding and the fundamentals which he was familiar.

In spite of this, one should not condemn them, because we cannot compel two wise men who are discussing a theory to propound it with the understanding of Joshua or Pinchas.[102] We should not doubt (the validity of) what they[103] argue just because they are not as (capable as) Shammai and Hillel, or like one who is greater (in knowledge) than they.[104] The Holy One Blessed be He did not command us to serve Him in this manner[105], but instructed us to listen to the Sages of our generation as it is stated: *To the judge who shall be in those days.*[106] It is in this manner that controversies arose, and not because they[107] erred in

88 Lit: the second.
89 The aforementioned thinkers.
90 i.e. insufficiently studied the Torah.
91 i.e. many conflicting rulings arose. Tractate Sanhedrin 88b.
92 i.e, faulty or damaging.
93 Tractate Berachoth 51b.
94 Lit: the house.
95 Referring to the latter water before Grace.
96 Beth Shammai hold the former, Beth Hillel the latter.
97 Tractate Berachoth 52b.
98 Hebrew: *Am Haaretz* or ignoramus.
99 i.e. insufficiently studied the Torah.
100 Lit: falls between them.
101 i.e. controversy and dispute between two such people.
102 Each can only discuss at a level of intelligence with which God endowed him.
103 The disciples of Hillel and Shammai.
104 Such as Joshua & Pinchas.
105 i.e. to think derogatorily of Sages because their predecessors were more learned than they.
106 Deut. 17, 9.
107 The disciples of Hillel and Shammai.

Halacha, and that one is saying the truth, the other a falsity. How much clearer this subject will become to all who delve into it and what a precious and great principle of our commandments this is!

THE FOURTH CATEGORY (consists of) decrees ordained by the prophets and Sages of every generation in order to make a protective fence around the Torah.[108] In regard to these (Biblical laws), the Holy One Blessed be He commanded to make the (protective laws), and this is what is meant by the all inclusive statement: *And ye shall keep my charge,*[109] which is traditionally interpreted to mean, "Provide protection for my observances."[110] The Sages call these (restrictive measures) "decrees".[111] Sometimes controversy may arise, therefrom, because one Sage may prohibit something for a specific reason, whereas the other Sage disagrees. This occurs frequently in the Talmud, where it is stated that Rabbi so and so decreed such (and such) because of such and such, whereas Rabbi so and so did not so decree. This, too, is one of the causes of controversies (among Sages in the Talmud).

Thus (for example, the prohibition of eating) flesh of fowl with milk is a Rabbinical decree to keep one far from transgression. However, the Torah only prohibits (milk with) flesh of cattle[112] and beasts[113], whereas the Sages (decreed the additional) prohibition of flesh of fowl (with milk) to keep one far from (transgressing) an interdiction.[114] There are some who did not ordain this decree, like Rabbi Jose the Galilean who permitted (the consumption of) flesh of fowl with milk, and all the inhabitants of his town ate this (combination), as is well publicized in the Talmud.[115] Where complete agreement prevails regarding one of the decrees, no one argues thereon in any respect. If a prohibition has spread throughout Israel, then no one should dispute such a decree. Even the prophets themselves were not permitted to void it. Thus it is stated in the Talmud[116] that (even) Elijah, of blessed memory, could not abrogate one of the eighteen items which Beth Shammai and Beth Hillel decreed. The reason which is quoted[117] for this is that these prohibitions have spread among all of Israel.

THE FIFTH CATEGORY consists of laws based on (empirical) investigation regarding the social behavior of individuals in those matters which do not constitute an addition to or detraction from a (Biblical) commandment[118] –or regarding things which are efficacious for people[119] with respect to the observance of the laws[120] of the Torah. These are called "ordinances"[121], and customs. It is prohibited to transgress any one of these. (King) Solomon of blessed memory has already stated regarding him who transgresses anyone of these ordinances[122]: *And whosoever breaketh through a fence will be bitten by a snake.*[123]

These decrees are extremely numerous and are described in the Talmud and Mishnah. Some are related to the topic of the forbidden and permitted (foods, marriages, etc.), and others pertain to civil law.[124] Some of these decrees were ordained by the prophets, such as the decrees of Moses, Joshua and Ezra, as they (the Sages) have stated: "Moses ordained to the Israelites that they should discuss[125] the laws of Passover in the season of Passover".[126] They further stated: "Moses decreed (the benediction) 'Who feeds'[127] at the time when the Manna was de-

108 A Rabbinic prohibition to protect a person from transgressing a Biblical injunction.

109 Levit. 18, 30.

110 Tractate Yebamoth 21a; i.e. add restrictions to safeguard the original precepts. There is a play on words here. The Hebrew word *Shomor* means to observe but also means to protect.

111 Hebrew: *Gezeroth.*

112 Such as cows.

113 Such as a deer. Many manuscripts and some texts substitute flesh of cleat; animals for cattle and beasts.

114 i.e. one should not erroneously eat cattle flesh with milk by comparing it with flesh of fowl which is permitted in the Torah.

115 Tractate Shabbath 130a.

116 Tractate Aboda Zara 36a.

117 Lit: brought.

118 Both are prohibited in Deut. 4, 2.

119 Lit: for the children of man.

120 Lit: words.

121 Hebrew: *Takanoth.*

122 i.e. social reforms.

123 Eccles. 10, 8.

124 Lit: money matters.

125 Lit: ask and seek.

126 Tractate Megillah 4a.

127 The first benediction of the Grace after meals. Hertz *Prayer Book* (see footnote 55) p. 967.

scending for the Israelites".[128] The decrees of Joshua and Ezra, however, are many (and will, therefore, not be enumerated here). Yet other decrees (of this social reform type) are attributed to individual Sages as they stated: "Hillel instituted *Pruzbul*";[129] "Rabban Gamliel the Elder decreed"[130] "Rabbi Yochanan ben Zakkai ordained";[131] and often in the Talmud (it is stated) "Rabbi so and so decreed", or Rabbi so and so ordained". (Finally), there are some decrees attributed to a multitude of Sages[132], as they stated: "(The Sanhedrin) in Usha decreed"[133], or as it is written "The Sages ordained", or "A decree of the Sages". Similar instances are very common.

Thus, all the laws enumerated in the Mishnah are subdivide into these five categories; some are interpretations received from Moses which are alluded to in Scripture, or can be derived through deductive reasoning;[134] others are Verbal Mosaic Tradition (which cannot be proved either directly from Scriptures or by deduction); others yet are (laws) derived by comparisons[135] and reasoning concerning which differences of opinion may arise. Some of these (laws) are decrees[136], and others are ordinances.[137]

I will now mention the reason he[138] saw necessary to record (both sides of) a controversy that arises between two viewpoints. If these legal decisions[139] were written as final rulings[140], without the controversy, and if the opinion of the Sage whose view is not the finally accepted one were omitted, then it is possible that at a later time someone will come along who learned[141] the very opposite of the statement of the final ruling. (This he learned) from the Sage who disputes that view, or from someone who is inclined to agree with his[142] opinion. Thus a doubt is raised in our minds, and we might say: How could this person, a trustworthy man, have learned that such and such a thing is prohibited if the Mishnah (specifically) states that it is permitted, or vice versa? Because of this, if (all) these opinions will be written down for us, this danger will be averted[143], since when the receiver (of knowledge from his teachers) will say: "I have heard that such and such is prohibited", we can say to him: "You speak correctly, and it is the view of so and so, but many disagree with him", or "so and so disagrees with him, and the final ruling is according to the dissenting viewpoint", either because its deductive reasoning is more plausible, or because we have found proof that supports it.[144] On the other hand, the reason why he[145] found it necessary to record the opinion of a single person against the many is that it is possible that the final ruling should be according to (the opinion of) the single person and, therefore he[146] teaches us that if an argument is convincing[147], even if it be that of a single person, it is accepted[148], although many may argue with him.[149]

There is a reason for recording the opinion of one man though he later withdrew from that opinion. One sees this, for example, when the (Sages) stated: "Beth Shammai say such and such whereas Beth Hillel say such and such, and Beth Hillel reconsidered and taught according to the opinion of Beth Shammai":[150] to demonstrate their love for the truth and that righteousness and honesty prevail. Thus, when these honored pious, noble people of eminent schol-

128 Tractate Berachoth 48b.

129 Mishnah Shebiith, Chapter 10, Mishnah 3. *Pruzbul* is a device which prevents remission of debts in the Sabbatical year by entrusting the court with the collection of the debt. A complete discussion of *Pruzbul* can be found in Tractate Gittin 36a-37b.

130 Tractate Gittin 34b. A man should write his true name on a divorce document, and not an adopted name.

131 a) Tractate Betzah 5a. Testimony concerning the appearance of the New Moon is admitted the whole day, even in the evening.
b) Tractate Rosh Hashana 30b. During the whole day of the waving of the *Omer* (the sheaf of barley offered on the 16th of Nissan prior to which new cereals of that year were forbidden. Levit. 23, 10), the new corn is forbidden.

132 As opposed to an individual sage.

133 Tractate Kethuboth 49b. A man must sustain his sons and daughters while they are young.

134 Using the 13 principles of Rabbinic exegesis.

135 Hebrew: *Hekesh*.

136 Hebrew: *Gezeroth*.

137 Hebrew: *Takanoth*.

138 Rebbe, compiler of the Mishnah.

139 Hebrew: *Halachoth*.

140 As in the Code of Jewish Law, the *Shulchan Aruch*.

141 Lit: received, by oral tradition.

142 the dissenting sage.

143 lit: this breach will be fenced.

144 Mishnah Edduyoth, Chapter 1, Mishnah 6.

145 Rebbe, compiler of the Mishnah.

146 Rebbe, compiler of the Mishnah.

147 Lit: a viewpoint is simpler. i.e. logical and understandable.

148 Lit: listened to.

149 Mishnah Edduyoth, Chapter 1, Mishnah 5.

150 *ibid.* Mishnah 4 and Mishnah 12.

arship[151] saw that the opinions of him who argues with them are better than their own and that his[152] deliberations are correct, they would admit to him and change to his viewpoint. All the more so should other people, when seeing the truth, lean toward their opponent, likewise turn to this truth (and accept it) without being stubborn.[153] This is the meaning of the Scriptural phrase *Justice, justice shalt thou follow.*[154] It is concerning this (matter) that the Sages stated, "Acknowledge the truth"[155], meaning that even if you could save face[156] with (sophisticated) counterarguments, if you know that your friend's viewpoint is the correct one, although your argument may be clearer due to his weakness (in expressing himself), or because of your ability to pervert the truth, withdraw to his viewpoint and abandon the fight.[157]

Maimonides' Introduction to His Commentary on the Mishnah [New Jersey: Ktav Publishers, 1995], pp. 40–44, 63–70, 74–83
Reprinted with permission of the publisher

151 Such as Beth Shammai and Beth Hillel.
152 The dissenter.
153 Lit: hard-necked.
154 Deut. 16, 20.
155 Mishnah Aboth, Chapter 5, Mishnah 7.
156 Lit: save your soul.
157 i.e. admit defeat with dignity.

LOVE AND TRUTH CONVERGE

AN ANALYSIS OF THE DIFFERENT CHARACTERISTICS OF THE SCHOOLS OF HILLEL AND SHAMMAI

ADAPTED FROM THE WORKS OF THE LUBAVITCHER REBBE, RABBI MENACHEM MENDEL SCHNEERSON

Out of the One, Many

The Talmud[1] states:

> It is written:[2] "The words of the wise are like spurs, and like nails well driven in are [the words of] the masters of collections; they are given from one Shepherd...."
>
> "The masters of collections"—these are the students of the Sages who sit in different groups and engage themselves in Torah study. Some will rule [that an object is] impure, and others will rule [that it is pure]. Some will declare [an object] unacceptable, and others will declare [it] acceptable.
>
> If a person will ask: "How is it possible for me to study the Torah under such circumstances?"—the verse continues: "[These words] were given from one Shepherd." One G-d gave them, and one master[3] communicated them.

The concept of variety and difference within the Torah is also reflected in our Sages' account of the very source of our Torah heritage, the communication of the Oral Law to Moshe on Mount Sinai. Our Sages relate:[4]

> On each law, [the Holy One, blessed be He,] would teach [Moshe] 49 perspectives [leading to the ruling that an object is] impure, and 49 perspectives [leading to the ruling that it is] pure.
>
> Moshe exclaimed: "Master of the World, when will I be able to reach the clarification of these matters?"
>
> The Holy One, blessed be He, told him: "Follow the majority.[5] If the majority rules that it is impure, it is impure. If the majority rules that it is pure, it is pure."

The Torah is spiritual truth, existing on a level above worldly existence.[6] And yet, it is not intended to remain on that lofty plane, but rather to descend and relate to our experience in this world. Nevertheless, because it is lofty and abstract, this process of descent leads to a variety of conceptions. As pure light takes on many colors when filtered through a prism, so too, as the Torah's truth comes in contact with material existence, different perspectives arise. For the same principle can motivate two opposite conclusions.

To cite an example: Before the Flood,[7] "G-d saw that... every impulse of the thoughts of [man's] heart was only for evil... And G-d said, 'I will obliterate mankind.'" After the Flood, when Noach offered sacrifices, G-d said:[8] "I will not continue to curse the earth, because of man, for the impulse of man's heart is evil." One factor, the yetzer hara's constant temptation of man, serves as the rationale calling for both the Flood, and for G-d's promise never to repeat such disasters.

Rabbi Menachem Mendel Schneerson (1902–1994) The towering Jewish leader of the 20th century, known as "the Lubavitcher Rebbe," or simply as "the Rebbe." Born in southern Ukraine, the Rebbe escaped Nazi-occupied Europe, arriving in the U.S. in June 1941. The Rebbe inspired and guided the revival of traditional Judaism after the European devastation, impacting virtually every Jewish community the world over. The Rebbe often emphasized that the performance of just one additional good deed could usher in the era of Mashiach. The Rebbe's scholarly talks and writings have been printed in more than 200 volumes.

1 Chagigah 3b.

2 Koheles 12:11.

3 Moshe (Rashi's commentary, loc. cit.).

4 Jerusalem Talmud, Sanhedrin 4:2; Midrash Tehillim 12:7.

5 See Shmos 23:2 and commentaries; Rambam, Mishneh Torah, Hilchos Sanhedrin 8:1.

6 See Bereishis Rabbah 8:2, et al., which states that the Torah predated the world.

7 Bereishis 6:5-6.

8 Ibid., 8:21.

In a similar way, each of the Tannaim and Amoraim would view the Torah's laws as they exist in their spiritual source. Nevertheless, to determine a ruling regarding a particular situation, a Sage would have to sift through the relevant legal principles and apply them to the circumstances at hand. And for every Sage, this process of analysis was guided by the thrust of his spiritual personality. As his awareness of the spiritual motivation for the law became intertwined with his appreciation of the germane factors, the Sage's decision would shape and form.

Often the decisions reached by the Sages would differ, for the processes of determination that characterized one would vary from that of the other. And with regard to these differences, it is said:[9] "These and these are the words of the living G-d." For the truth of Torah contains the potential for manifold expressions. This dictum was applied, however, only in the realm of theory. With regard to practice, the Torah tradition has always sought uniformity,[10] and when differences of opinion arise, the halachah is established according to the majority.[11]

Introspection and Outreach

The above concepts apply not only with regard to the Oral Tradition as a whole, but with regard to particular phases in its transmission. For example, Hillel and Shammai received the Oral Tradition from the same masters, Shemayah and Avtalyon.[12] Nevertheless, they—and to a greater extent, their students—developed these thoughts in different directions. And thus throughout the Talmud, we find differences of opinion between the School of Shammai and the School of Hillel.

In most instances, the School of Hillel would rule more leniently and the School of Shammai more stringently. What was the source for these differences?[13] Hillel's approach was characterized by the attribute of Chesed, kindness, while Shammai's was distinguished by the attribute of Gevurah, might, which tends toward severity.

Gevurah has an inward thrust, as reflected in our Sages' statement:[14] "Who is a gibbor (mighty man)? One who conquers his inclination." And according to the Kabbalah, the attribute of Gevurah is identified with din, judgment. A person who tends toward Gevurah has unalterable standards of truth to which he personally endeavors to conform and which he desires to see reflected in the world at large. This is implied by the name Shammai, which relates to the Hebrew phrase:[15] hasham orchosov, "He evaluates his ways,"[16] i.e., he is constantly subjecting his conduct to rigorous introspection.

Chesed, by contrast, reflects an outward orientation. Others are one's primary concern. A person motivated by chesed extends himself and gives, following the path Hillel outlines,[17] "Loving peace and pursuing peace; loving the created beings[18] and drawing them close to the Torah." This approach also relates to Hillel's name which is associated with the phrase behilo neiro,[15] "When His candle shined forth."[19] For this approach emphasizes disseminating light, with the expectation that it will effortlessly cause darkness to shrink. And as light diffuses into wider peripheries, it attracts people and motivates them to change.

"The Rest Is Commentary"

These character thrusts are reflected in the classic story[20] of the potential convert who approached Shammai and asked him to teach him the entire Torah while he stood on one foot. Shammai "drove him away with a measuring rod." When, however, the person came to Hillel with the same request, Hillel

9 Eruvin 13b.

10 See Ta'amei HaMitzvos (of the AriZal), Parshas Ki Seitzei, which states that "every (Sage) would relate the truth as perceived by his spiritual rung. Halachah is determined according to the nature of the time."

11 The determination of Torah law also involves a respect for precedents. A later court cannot change a ruling adopted by a previous court unless "it is greater than its predecessors in wisdom and in the number of adherents it has" (Rambam, Mishneh Torah, Hilchos Mamrim 2:1-2).

12 Avos 1:12; See Hemshech 5672, Vol. I, p. 20ff.

13 Zohar, Vol. III, p. 245a, 281a; Tanya, Iggeres HaKodesh, Epistle 13.

14 Avos 4:1.

15 Likkutei Torah, Shir HaShirim, p. 48b ff.

16 Moed Kattan 5a.

17 Avos 1:12.

18 I.e., this includes even such individuals whose only redeeming quality is that they are G-d's creations (see Tanya, ch. 32).

19 Iyov 29:3.

20 Shabbos 31a.

told him to stand, and taught him: "What is hateful to you, do not do to your colleague. This is the entire Torah; the rest is commentary. Go and learn."

Shammai was demanding of himself, and to the same degree, he was demanding of others. This is implied by the phrase: "he drove him away with a measuring rod." As he stood before Shammai, the potential convert did not measure up to the expectations which Shammai had of his students.

Hillel, by contrast, was willing to patiently extend himself. He appreciated the potential convert's spiritual state as Shammai had, but he also saw a possibility for growth. Therefore, he communicated a fundamental Torah concept to the potential convert on a level to which he could relate. And it had an effect; the man converted and began proceeding on the Torah's unending path of personal development.

"To Draw Close with the Right Hand and Rebuff with the Left"

A similar pattern is reflected in the general thrust of the halachic rulings of these Sages and their disciples. Because Hillel's spiritual thrust was characterized by kindness, he would take a patient look at every situation, seeing whether there was a way it could serve the purpose of holiness. If he could discover such a possibility, he would rule leniently.

Shammai, by contrast, guarded the standards of holiness with meticulous rigor, and if it appeared that an object did not meet those standards, he ruled stringently. Rather than risk the possibility of spiritual decline, he forbade contact with such objects, and thus forestalled any negative repercussions.

It must, however, be emphasized that neither Hillel nor Shammai—nor any of the other Sages of the Talmud—solely followed their own personal tendencies when delivering halachic rulings. On the contrary, our Sages described[21] the differences of opinion between Hillel and Shammai as being maintained "for the sake of Heaven." In a desire to ascertain G-d's law, they sought to rise above their personal tendencies, and to be objective. Accordingly, Hillel would sometimes arrive at a more stringent ruling and Shammai would occasionally rule more leniently.

Nevertheless, by and large, the Sages would perceive the truth as filtered through their natural spiritual thrust. And therefore, Hillel and his students would predominantly rule more leniently, and Shammai and his students, more stringently.

Towards a More Comprehensive Understanding

The above concepts are reflected, not only in the overall thrusts toward leniency and stringency evident in the rulings of the Schools of Shammai and Hillel, but also in theoretical constructs of a middle range, i.e., motifs that connect seemingly unrelated rulings throughout the Talmud. A particular difference of opinion mentioned in one source appears not as an isolated phenomenon but as part of a paradigm of a more general scope. To use the terminology employed by the Talmud in certain instances, azlinan lishitoso, "we follow his pattern of logic."

The following are several examples of such patterns: With regard to the blessing recited over the candle during the havdalah ceremony:[22] The School of Shammai rules that the conclusion of the blessing should be: borei maor haeish, praising G-d as "the Creator of the light of fire." The School of Hillel, by contrast, rules that the text of the blessing should be: borei meorei haeish, "the Creator of the lights of fire," employing a plural form.

We cannot say that the difference of opinion focuses on a point of actual fact: whether there are several lights in a flame or just one light, for it is obvious that there are several colors in a flame. There is no way that the School of Shammai can dispute this.[23] Instead, the difference of opinion is: which aspect of the flame is of primary concern?

---

21 Avos 5:17.

22 Berachos 51b. There the Mishnah states the two conflicting rulings; see also the explanation in the Gemara, 52b.

23 Indeed, for reasons such as this, an effort is always made to explain how a difference of opinion between Sages stems not from a point of fact, which can be verified, but rather from a point of theory, so that there will not be a machlokes bimetzius.

To explain: When one sees a flame, one immediately sees light. Afterwards, as one looks more closely, one sees that this light is comprised of several different colors. The School of Shammai puts the emphasis on one's initial perception, while the School of Hillel, by contrast, highlights the conception that one would reach after a more patient look.

Appreciating a Bride's Beauty

A similar motif is reflected in the praise which is traditionally given a bride.[24] The School of Shammai maintains that a bride should be praised according to the positive qualities which she personally possesses,[25] while the School of Hillel states that all brides should be praised as being "beautiful and gracious."

The School of Shammai asked the School of Hillel: "If a bride limps or is blind, should one praise her as being 'beautiful and gracious'? Has not the Torah told us,[26] 'Keep your distance from falsehood'?"

The School of Hillel responded: "When a person buys an inferior article in the market, should one praise it in his presence, or should one find fault with it in his presence? It appears to us that one should praise it for him." As the Talmud concludes, the thrust of the School of Hillel was to be considerate of others and their feelings.

The School of Hillel was not stating that one should lie and praise a bride with qualities which she did not possess. Their perspective is that every groom surely considers his bride as "beautiful and gracious." And if a person wants to make a friend feel gratified by praising his bride, the person offering the praise should be patient enough to think over the matter carefully until he appreciates the qualities which cause her groom to see her as "beautiful and gracious."

The School of Shammai, by contrast, does not require a person to make such an involved and careful analysis. A person should endeavor to make a groom feel happy, and emphasize the positive qualities which a bride possesses that are overtly obvious. One should not, however, make statements which do not appear to be true.

As in the previous instance, the School of Shammai gives priority to a person's initial perception. The School of Hillel, by contrast, underscores the need for extending oneself, and taking a more involved and more detailed look at the situation at hand.

Looking at the Cover, or at What's Inside It

A third example of this pattern can be seen in the Rogachover Gaon's interpretation[27] of the difference of opinion between the School of Shammai and the School of Hillel with regard to whether or not the covers of sacred scrolls are susceptible to the contraction of ritual impurity.[28] The School of Shammai maintains that regardless of whether the cover of a scroll is embroidered with ornamental patterns or not, the cover is susceptible to ritual impurity.

The ruling of the School of Hillel is based on the principle that it is functional articles, not ornaments, which are susceptible to ritual impurity. As such, an ordinary cover is considered as an article which serves a purpose, and therefore is susceptible to ritual impurity. The primary purpose of an embroidered cover, however, is considered its aesthetic dimension, and not the function it serves. Hence, such a cover is not susceptible to ritual impurity.

The Rogatchover Gaon explains[29] why the School of Shammai does not make a distinction between one type of cover and the other. Since at first glance, both types of covers appear the same, no differentiation is made between the rulings that apply to them. The School of Hillel, by contrast, accentuates the particular characteristics of each type of cover, and accordingly, places them in different categories. In this instance as well, the School of Hillel's approach is

24 Kesubbos 16b ff.

25 See the interpretation of Tosafos.

26 Shmos 23:7.

27 Tzafnas Paneach Responsa (New York), Responsum 136, cited in Tzafnas Paneach al HaTorah, Parshas Shemini, p. 106.

28 Keilim 28:4.

29 Based on the Raavad's gloss to Toras Kohanim, Parshas Shemini. The Rambam, the Rosh, and Rav Ovadiah of Bartenura offer different interpretations of this Mishnah that do not conform as closely to this conception of the difference in interpretation between the Schools of Shammai and Hillel.

characterized by a patient process of distinction that focuses on the particulars, while the approach of the School of Shammai focuses on the general impression[30] that immediately arises.[31]

The Potential for Light

Another general pattern which characterizes several of the differences of opinion between the School of Shammai and the School of Hillel can be seen in their rulings regarding the order of the kindling of Chanukah lights.[32] The School of Shammai rules that on the first night, eight candles should be lit, on the second night seven, each night reducing the number. The School of Hillel, by contrast, maintains that on the first night, one candle should be lit, on the second night, two, and it is only on the last night that eight candles are lit.

What is the rationale which motivates their different rulings?[33] The School of Shammai focuses on the potential (the ko'ach, in yeshivah terminology). On the first night of Chanukah, there is a potential for eight days; every night, the potential is reduced. The School of Hillel, by contrast, focuses on the actual (the poel, in yeshivah terminology). On the first night, there is only one day of Chanukah which is actually being celebrated. Each day, another day is added, until on the eighth day, the full potential of the holiday has been expressed in actual practice. Accordingly, eight candles are lit.

The Time of the Redemption

To cite another example of this pattern: The School of Shammai maintains[34] that during the recitation of the Hallel at the Pesach Seder, we should recite only the first psalm, Hallelu avdei HaShem, before partaking of the meal. The School of Hillel, by contrast, maintains that we should also recite the second psalm, B'tzeis Yisrael MiMitzrayim, "When Israel left Egypt," before partaking of the meal.

In explanation of their difference of opinion, the Jerusalem Talmud relates:[35]

The School of Shammai said to them: "Why mention the exodus from Egypt [at this point]? Did the children of Israel leave Egypt [before partaking of the Paschal sacrifice]?"

The School of Hillel responded to them: "Even if you were to wait until the rooster's crow, you would not reach halfway to [the time of] the Redemption.... For they did not leave until noon."

The School of Shammai maintains that the potential for the Redemption came with the eating of the Paschal sacrifice. Hence, after partaking of that sacrifice, it is fit to recite "When Israel left Egypt." The School of Hillel, by contrast, maintains that since the actual exodus did not take place until midday, there is no point in delaying recitation of the psalm, and it should be recited even before partaking of the Paschal sacrifice.

30 The intent is not that the School of Shammai does not have the ability to discern particulars. On the contrary, our Sages (Yevamos 14a; Tosafos, Eruvin 6b) describe them as being "sharper and more astute" than the School of Hillel. Nevertheless, their powers of discernment were focused on abstracting a general conception from the particulars, and not on appreciating the particulars per se.

31 The same pattern is reflected in the story of the convert cited above (and in two similar narratives quoted in Shabbos, loc. cit.). Shammai related to the potential convert according to the general impression he initially projected, while Hillel patiently considered the full picture into which the person could blossom. Similarly, there are other examples of this pattern in the Talmud. The rulings cited above were intended to serve as prototypes of this conception to which other parallels can be found.

[Trans. note: Here we see a connection to Hillel's dominant trait of Chesed (kindness) and Shammai's traits of Gevurah (might) and Din (judgment). Following the principle (Sanhedrin 6b) that: "A judge [takes into consideration] only what is perceivable to his eyes," the School of Shammai would make their determination according to the factors which were obvious, and a person or object which did not meet their standards would be firmly rejected. With patient kindness, the School of Hillel would, by contrast, consider all the factors of a situation, and contemplate the full range of realizable means of expression, and when possible, underscore the positive dimensions.]

32 Shabbos 21b.

33 See the explanation of parallel concepts in Beis Otzar by R. Yosef Engel (Os Alef, sec. 27; Os Beis, sec. 2) and LeOr HaHalachah by R. Shlomo Y. Zevin. The example cited above and those to follow are not the only reflections of this pattern throughout the Talmud, but rather paradigms that clearly express the theme of each school.

[Trans. note: Here, too, a connection can be drawn to the attributes of Din (judgment) and Chesed (kindness). For Shammai's emphasis on the potential relates to the objective standard of Din, according to which every situation is judged. Hillel's emphasis on the actual reflects the tendency of Chesed to encourage the full manifestation of all potentials.]

34 Pesachim 116b.

35 Pesachim 10:5; Tosefta, Pesachim 10:6.

The Conclusion of the *Talmud*

Another example of this difference in approach can be seen in the laws which conclude the entire Talmud. The Mishnah[36] states:

Fish: when do they become susceptible to the contraction of ritual impurity?[37] The School of Shammai states: "When they are caught." The School of Hillel states: "When they die."...

Honeycombs: when do they become considered as liquids [which make other foods] fit to contract ritual impurity?[38] The School of Shammai states: "When one thinks about [removing the honey]."[39] The School of Hillel states: "When one crushes [the honeycomb]."

Since fish will die shortly after they are caught and removed from the water, the School of Shammai maintains that they are susceptible to ritual impurity as soon as they are caught. From this time onward, there is the potential to use them as food, and this makes them susceptible to impurity. The School of Hillel, by contrast, maintains that until the fish actually die, they are not considered as food, nor are they susceptible to impurity.

Similarly, with regard to honeycombs, since the potential exists for the honey to be removed from them, the School of Shammai maintains that as soon as one decides to take this step,[40] the honey is considered as a liquid. The School of Hillel, by contrast, maintains that until one actually crushes the honeycomb to remove the honey, it is not considered as a liquid.

36 Uktzin 3:9, 11.

37 A living being never contracts ritual impurity while foods do. The question is: At which point are fish considered to have become food?

38 Produce is not susceptible to ritual impurity until it comes in contact with one of seven liquids: water, wine, oil, milk, honey, dew, or blood. The question in this mishnah is: When is the honey in the honeycombs considered as a liquid?

39 This version is found in the texts of Rabbeinu Hai, Rabbeinu Shimon, Rabbeinu Asher, and others. The standard printed texts, the Aruch, the Rambam, and others, follow a different version which states: "When one creates smoke" for the purpose of driving away the bees (the Aruch) or heating the honeycomb to remove the honey (the Rambam).

40 Or according to the other versions of the mishnah, as soon as one begins the preliminary activities for this purpose.

Heaven or Earth

The fact that this difference of opinion between the School of Shammai and the School of Hillel was chosen as the subject for the final laws to be discussed by the Mishnah[41] indicates that it is of general importance. And indeed, we find the same thrust motivating two passages that quote differences of opinion between the Schools of Hillel and Shammai, which relate to the purpose of the creation and the purpose of man.

With regard to the purpose of creation, it is stated:[42]

The School of Shammai says: "The heavens were created first, and then the earth...." The School of Hillel says: "The earth was created first, and then the heavens."

The Alter Rebbe explains[43] that with regard to the order of creation, the heavens—the spiritual worlds—were created before this material world, and indeed, it is the spiritual realms that convey the life energy which brings this world into being. Nevertheless, the purpose of creation is our material world; to borrow a phrase,[44] "Last in deed, first in [G-d's] thought." Or, to refer to an analogy, when one constructs a building, it is the ultimate product which reflects the builder's original intent.

This resolution requires further explanation, for it implies that the School of Hillel and the School of Shammai are speaking about different aspects of the creation—the School of Shammai, the order of creation, and the School of Hillel, the intent—and there is no difference of opinion between them. The form of the quotation: "The School of Shammai says:.... The School of Hillel says:..." however, implies that they do not accept each other's positions.

41 The Mishnah concludes with a teaching describing the reward the righteous will receive in the Era of the Redemption. This teaching is not directly connected to the halachic concepts that precede it, but is included so that the Mishnah will conclude with a positive theme.

42 Chagigah 12a; Bereishis Rabbah 1:15.

43 Torah Or, at the beginning of Parshas Vayigash.

44 The Lecha Dodi hymn, Shabbos liturgy, Siddur Tehillat HaShem, p. 132.

Upon what does their difference of opinion revolve? Not on their opinions with regard to chronological precedence, but rather upon their conception of what is of primary importance. According to the School of Hillel, the earth is of paramount importance—it is in this material realm that G-d's intent for creation is expressed. The School of Shammai maintains that, although G-d's intent is expressed in this material world, the intent is first manifest in the heavens—in spiritual reality. And the entire thrust of our Divine service is to elevate material existence to the point that it can reflect this spiritual reality. The School of Hillel is thus putting the emphasis on the actual expression of the intent for creation (the poel), while the School of Shammai is highlighting the spiritual truths that enable this intent to be expressed (the ko'ach).[45]

This concept also enables us to understand why in all matters, the School of Shammai places the emphasis on the ko'ach. Since they conceive of the purpose of creation as elevating the material to the spiritual, it is the spiritual conception — the ko'ach — which receives priority. The School of Hillel, by contrast, conceives of the intent of creation as having spiritual truth made manifest in our material world. Hence, their emphasis is on actual expression — the poel.[46]

To Be, or Not To Be

Similar concepts apply with regard to the purpose of the creation of man. Our Sages state:[47]

For two and a half years, there was a difference of opinion between the School of Shammai and the School of Hillel. These (the School of Shammai)[48] would say: "It is better for a person not to have been born than to have been born." And these (the School of Hillel) would say: "It is better for a person to have been born than not to have been born."

The School of Shammai, who highlights the potential, says that it is better for a person not to have been born because the potential for personal fulfillment already exists in the spiritual realms. A person's existence in this world is—at its best—merely an expression of his spiritual potential. This is essential to fulfill G-d's purpose in creation, but "for a person," i.e., from his own individual standpoint, it is preferable that he not have been created.

The School of Hillel, who focuses on actual expression, maintains that it is through the descent into this world that a soul reaches the heights of fulfillment. For the observance of the Torah and its mitzvos on this material plane lifts a person to a level above his or her previous rung in the spiritual realms. Therefore, it is preferable for the person to have been born.

This leads to a further point. Since the School of Shammai puts the emphasis on G-d's desire and not man's, man's Divine service is characterized by self-nullification, the negation of his own will. As such, it is "better for a person not to have been born." The School of Hillel, by contrast, sees man's fulfillment as a personal goal. G-d's intent in creation, the establishment of a dwelling in this material world, is not merely an objective to which we should strive, but one which should be internalized within our own selves. And as this motive blossoms into fulfillment, every person can perceive its benefits; his existence is thus "better for him."

Perceiving Truth that Transcends Intellect

As mentioned at the outset, although the Torah leaves room for a variety of theoretical approaches, with regard to actual practice, our halachic tradition

45 Here also we see a connection to the attributes of Chesed and Gevurah. For Gevurah is characterized by he'elem, concealment, which relates to the ko'ach, for, by definition, a potential is not overtly evident. Chesed, by contrast, is characterized by gilui, revelation. This relates to the poel, for it is the actual expression that brings a subject into revelation.

46 This also reflects how the thrusts of Divine service expressed by these two schools are outgrowths of the attributes of Chesed and Gevurah. The attribute of Gevurah is characterized by a movement towards ascent in Divine service, elevating and refining the material realm so that it reflects the spiritual. Conversely, the attribute of Chesed is characterized by a downward thrust in Divine service, bringing the spiritual into manifestation within our material world.

47 Eruvin 13b.

48 The Talmud states that this passage reflects a difference of opinion between the School of Shammai and the School of Hillel, but does not state explicitly which school made which statement. Nevertheless, since throughout the Talmud the opinion of the School of Shammai is cited before the School of Hillel, it is likely that this pattern is followed in this instance as well. See the gloss of the Ritva to Eruvin, loc. cit., and the gloss of the Radbaz to Rambam, Mishneh Torah, Hilchos Maaser Sheni 6:3.

has always striven toward uniformity. In this vein, our Sages teach:[49]

From three years, there was a difference of opinion between the School of Shammai and the School of Hillel. These would say, "The halachah follows our perspective," and these would say, "The halachah follows our perspective."

A heavenly voice issued forth: "These and these are the words of the living G-d; the halachah follows the School of Hillel."

The passage continues:

Why did the School of Hillel merit to have the halachah follow their perspective? Because they were patient and humble, and would cite the statements of the School of Shammai before their own.

The latter passage is difficult to understand. Our Sages state that the students of the School of Shammai were more astute and discriminating[50] than the students of the School of Hillel. Since the comprehension of Torah law depends on intellectual understanding, seemingly it would be appropriate for the halachah to follow their perspective. Moreover, the rationale given by the Talmud, that the students of the School of Hillel were "patient and humble" is problematic. What connection do these virtues have with the determination of law?

These difficulties can, however, be resolved by differentiating between Torah study and other fields of wisdom. The Torah is not merely knowledge; the Torah is unbounded G-dly truth. Its intellectual dimension is merely a garb that enables man to internalize his connection with this truth.

Wisdom can be grasped through intellect. To develop a connection with the Torah's unbounded truth, however, intellect is not sufficient: bittul, self-transcending commitment, is necessary. The patience and humility of the School of Hillel reflects such bittul. And for this reason, it is their perspective which determines the halachah.

Determining *Halachah*

To offer an explanation of the above passage that relates more closely to the principles of Torah law:[51] The halachah follows the School of Hillel because, except for several isolated instances, a majority of Sages followed their understanding. Nevertheless, since the School of Shammai were more astute, the Sages doubted whether they should rely on the majority vote. And it was not until the proclamation of the heavenly voice that these doubts were silenced.[52]

One might ask: If the Sages of the School of Shammai were more astute, why didn't the majority of Sages accept their rulings? Because a ruling of Torah law must be understood thoroughly by the Sage delivering it. Although the Sages of the School of Shammai were more astute, the majority of the Sages could not thoroughly comprehend their logic, and therefore they could not rule accordingly. To cite a parallel example—extending the wording slightly beyond its literal context, our Sages state:[53]

There was no one in Rabbi Meir's generation of his stature. Why then was the halachah not established according to his perspective? Because his colleagues could not comprehend the full breadth of his knowledge.

Because the logic advanced by Rabbi Meir and the School of Shammai could not be grasped fully by their colleagues, the rulings they rendered were not accepted as law.

Also, from a spiritual perspective, the approach of the School of Hillel—spreading light—is vital in the present age to elevate mankind and the world at large. It is true that this endeavor presents challenges. The words of caution of the School of Shammai

49 Eruvin, loc. cit.

50 Yevamos 14a; Tosafos, Eruvin 6b.

51 See Tosafos, loc. cit.

52 Although halachah cannot be determined on the basis of a heavenly voice (Bava Metzia 59b), this principle applies when the heavenly voice contradicts the ruling of the majority and not when it supports it (Tosafos).

53 Eruvin 13b.

must be, therefore, included within our spiritual consciousness, but our overriding attitude should be one of positive activity.

Looking Toward the Horizon

Although in the present age, the halachah follows the School of Hillel, in the Era of the Redemption, the halachah will follow the School of Shammai.[54] In that era, "the Jews will be great sages and will know the hidden matters."[55] The majority of the Sages will thus comprehend the perspective of the School of Shammai, and therefore, the halachah will change.[56] Moreover, since Mashiach will "perfect the entire world,"[57] the task of refinement given the Jewish people will be different in that era, and the more elevated standard required by the School of Shammai will be accessible to people at large.

At the present time, short moments before the dawning of that future era, we should yearn to be able to apply the lofty standards of refinement taught by the School of Shammai. Simultaneously, however, we must realize that the means to hasten the coming of that era is the warm and humble outreach exemplified by the School of Hillel.[58]

Beacons on the Talmud's Sea [Brooklyn, N.Y.: Sichos in English, 1997]
Reprinted with permission of the publisher

54 Mikdash Melech to Zohar, Vol. I, 17b; Likkutei Torah, Korach, p. 54b ff.

55 Rambam, Mishneh Torah, Hilchos Melachim 12:5.

56 For although as stated above (note 11), a later court cannot change a ruling adopted by a previous court unless "it is greater than its predecessors in wisdom and in the number of adherents it has," the Sanhedrin to be convened by Mashiach will surely meet those qualifications.

57 Rambam, Mishneh Torah, loc. cit. 11:4.

58 Adapted from *Likkutei Sichos*, Vol. II, p. 321ff.; Vol. IV, p. 1121; Vol. VI, p. 69ff.; Vol. XVI, p. 312ff.; Vol. XXI, p.115ff.; Vol. XXII, p. 47ff.; *Toras Menachem Hadranim*, p. 375; *Sefer HaSichos 5751*, Vol. II, p. 566ff.; *Sichos Shabbos Parshas Bamidbar*, 5734.

LESSON 5

THE MORE THINGS CHANGE

Are there areas of Jewish law that can use change or repeal? If yes, who has the authority to amend or revoke? A heavenly voice? A prophet? A sage? Is modifying rabbinic enactments a simple process? After all, what human beings create, they should be able to abrogate.

A deeper understanding of the nature of Torah law and its ultimate objective will help us navigate these thorny questions.

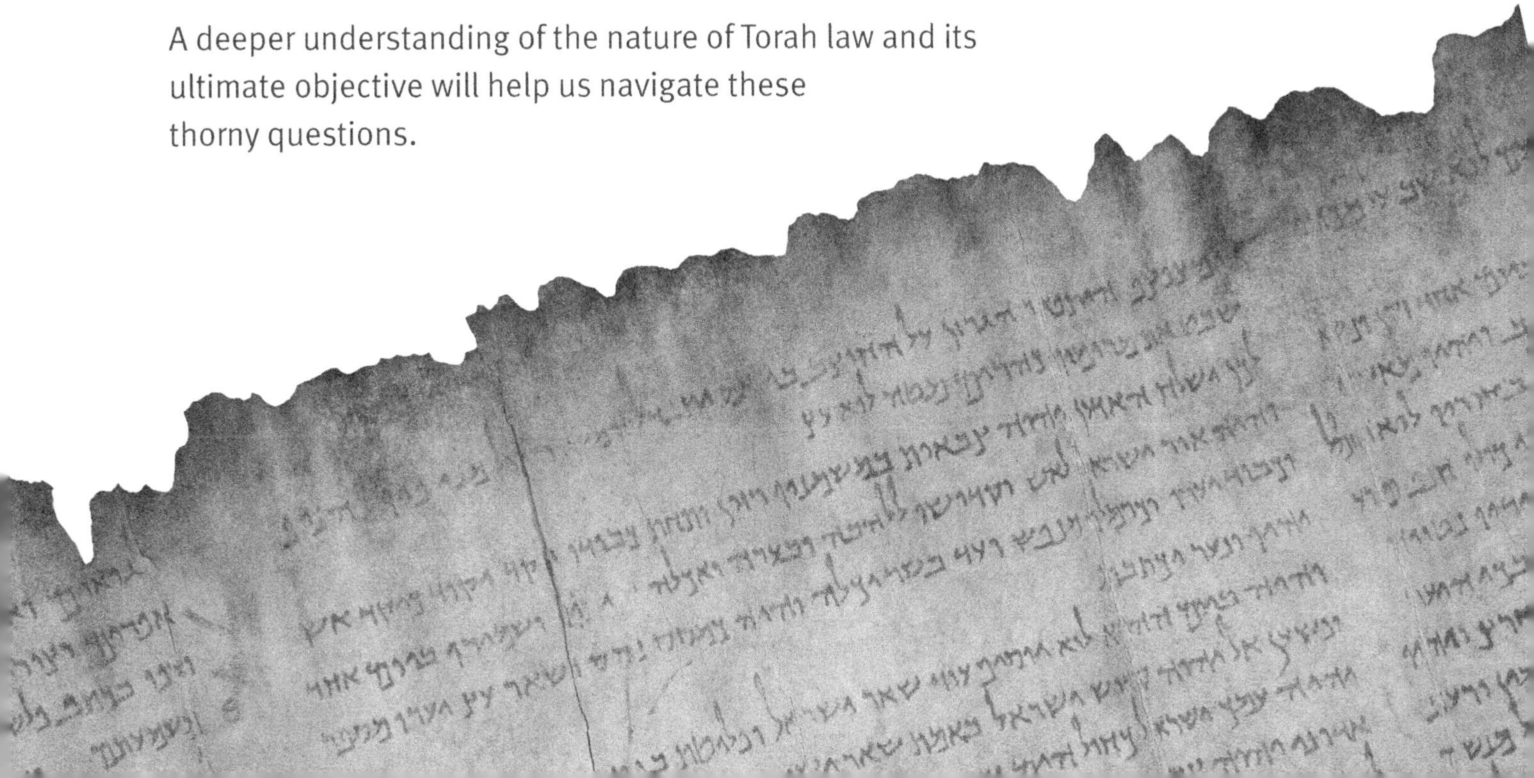

A Question of Change

LEARNING EXERCISE 1

In which of the following categories of Torah should we have the authority to make changes?

Category	Definition	Ability to Change
1. Received	God-given explanations for each of the commandments	Yes / No
2. Derived	Laws that we derive from the Written Torah and the Received Oral Torah	Yes / No
3. Legislated	New laws legislated by rabbinic sages	Yes / No
4. Customary	Customs initiated by the people, intended to enhance an aspect of Judaism	Yes / No

Written and Received

An Everlasting Statute

Text 1a

Maimonides, *Mishneh Torah*, Laws of the Foundations of the Torah 9:1

דָּבָר בָּרוּר וּמְפוֹרָשׁ בַּתּוֹרָה שֶׁהִיא מִצְוָה עוֹמֶדֶת לְעוֹלָם וּלְעוֹלְמֵי עוֹלָמִים, אֵין לָהּ לֹא שִׁנּוּי, וְלֹא גֵּרָעוֹן, וְלֹא תּוֹסֶפֶת. שֶׁנֶּאֱמַר (דְּבָרִים יג,א): "אֶת כָּל הַדָּבָר אֲשֶׁר אָנֹכִי מְצַוֶּה אֶתְכֶם אוֹתוֹ תִּשְׁמְרוּן לַעֲשׂוֹת לֹא תוֹסֵף עָלָיו וְלֹא תִגְרַע מִמֶּנּוּ". וְנֶאֱמַר (דְּבָרִים כט,כח): "וְהַנִּגְלֹות לָנוּ וּלְבָנֵינוּ עַד עוֹלָם לַעֲשׂוֹת אֶת כָּל דִּבְרֵי הַתּוֹרָה הַזֹּאת". הָא לָמַדְתָּ שֶׁכָּל דִּבְרֵי תּוֹרָה מְצוּוִּין אָנוּ לַעֲשׂוֹתָן עַד עוֹלָם. וְכֵן הוּא אוֹמֵר (וַיִּקְרָא ג, יז): "חוּקַּת עוֹלָם לְדוֹרוֹתֵיכֶם".

It is clear and explicit in the Torah that its commandments remain forever, without change, diminishment, or addition. As it states (Deuteronomy 13:1), "You shall be careful to perform all of these matters that I command to you. You may not add to it or diminish from it." And it says (Deuteronomy 29:28), "What God revealed to us is for us and our children forever, to carry out all the words of this Torah." This teaches us that we are commanded to fulfill all the Torah's directives forever. It also says (Leviticus 3:17), "It is an everlasting statute for all your generations."

Rabbi Moshe ben Maimon
(Maimonides, Rambam)
1135–1204

Halachist, philosopher, author, and physician. Maimonides was born in Cordoba, Spain. After the conquest of Cordoba by the Almohads, he fled Spain and eventually settled in Cairo, Egypt. There, he became the leader of the Jewish community and served as court physician to the vizier of Egypt. He is most noted for authoring the *Mishneh Torah*, an encyclopedic arrangement of Jewish law, and for his philosophical work, *Guide for the Perplexed*. His rulings on Jewish law are integral to the formation of halachic consensus.

Text 1b

Maimonides, Introduction to *Perek Chelek*

וְיסוֹד הַתְּשִׁיעִי הַבִּטּוּל. וְהוּא שֶׁזּוּ תּוֹרַת מֹשֶׁה לֹא תְּבָטֵל, וְלֹא תָּבוֹא תּוֹרָה
מֵאֵת ה' זוּלָתָהּ, וְלֹא יִתּוֹסֵף בָּהּ וְלֹא יִגְרַע מִמֶּנָּה לֹא בַּכָּתוּב וְלֹא בַּפֵּרוּשׁ.

The ninth fundamental principle concerns nullification—that the Torah of Moses will not be abolished and that God will not give another Torah. There will be no additions to the Torah, nor any subtractions from it—neither in its text nor in its Received explanation.

His Wisdom, Will, and Blueprint

Text 2

Rabbi Shne'ur Zalman of Liadi, *Tanya*, ch. 4

Rabbi Shne'ur Zalman of Liadi (Alter Rebbe)
1745–1812

Chasidic rebbe, halachic authority, and founder of the Chabad movement. The Alter Rebbe was born in Liozna, Belarus, and was among the principal students of the Magid of Mezeritch. His numerous works include the *Tanya*, an early classic containing the fundamentals of Chabad Chasidism, and *Shulchan Aruch HaRav*, an expanded and reworked code of Jewish law.

שֶׁכָּתוּב בַּזֹּהַר דְּאוֹרַיְיתָא וְקוּדְשָׁא בְּרִיךְ הוּא כּוּלָּא חַד. פֵּרוּשׁ:
דְּאוֹרַיְיתָא הִיא חָכְמָתוֹ וּרְצוֹנוֹ שֶׁל הַקָּדוֹשׁ בָּרוּךְ הוּא . . .

וְצִמְצֵם הַקָּדוֹשׁ בָּרוּךְ הוּא רְצוֹנוֹ וְחָכְמָתוֹ בְּתַרְיַ"ג מִצְוֹת הַתּוֹרָה וּבְהִלְכוֹתֵיהֶן . . .
בִּכְדֵי שֶׁכָּל הַנְּשָׁמָה אוֹ רוּחַ וְנֶפֶשׁ שֶׁבְּגוּף הָאָדָם תּוּכַל לְהַשִּׂיגָן בְּדַעְתָּהּ, וּלְקַיְּימָן כָּל
מַה שֶּׁאֶפְשָׁר לְקַיֵּם מֵהֶן בְּמַעֲשֶׂה דִּבּוּר וּמַחֲשָׁבָה . . .
וּמֵאַחַר שֶׁהַתּוֹרָה וּמִצְוֹתֶיהָ מַלְבִּישִׁים כָּל עֶשֶׂר בְּחִינוֹת הַנֶּפֶשׁ . . .
הֲרֵי כּוּלָּהּ צְרוּרָה בִּצְרוֹר הַחַיִּים אֶת ה' מַמָּשׁ.

The Zohar states that the Torah and God are one. This means that the Torah is [nothing other than the expression of] God's wisdom and will. . . .

God "compressed" His will and wisdom within the 613 commandments of the Torah and their laws. . . . He did this so that each soul, though invested in a human body, should be able to intellectually comprehend His wisdom and will, and live accordingly, in action, speech, and thought. . . . [When this occurs,] the Torah and its commandments encompass the whole person . . . and the person is completely and literally bound up with God in the "Bundle of Life."

Text 3

Zohar 2:161a

וְכַד בָּעָא קוּדְשָׁא בְּרִיךְ הוּא לְמִבְרֵי עָלְמָא, הֲוָה מִסְתַּכֵּל בָּהּ בְּאוֹרַיְיתָא, בְּכָל מִלָּה וּמִלָּה, וְעָבֵד לְקָבְלָהּ אוּמְנוּתָא דְעָלְמָא.

When God resolved to create the world, He looked into the Torah, into its every word, and fashioned the world accordingly.

Zohar

The seminal work of Kabbalah, Jewish mysticism. The Zohar is a mystical commentary on the Torah, written in Aramaic and Hebrew. According to Arizal, the Zohar contains the teachings of Rabbi Shimon bar Yocha'i who lived in the Land of Israel during the 2nd century. The Zohar has become one of the indispensable texts of traditional Judaism, alongside and nearly equal in stature to the Mishnah and Talmud.

A Prophet or Prophetess

Text 4

Deuteronomy 18:15

נָבִיא מִקִּרְבְּךָ מֵאַחֶיךָ כָּמֹנִי יָקִים לְךָ ה' אֱלֹקֶיךָ אֵלָיו תִּשְׁמָעוּן.

God will set up for you a prophet like me from among your brethren, and to him you must listen.

Text 5

Maimonides, *Mishneh Torah*, Laws of the Foundations of the Torah 9:1

אִם יַעֲמֹד אִישׁ, בֵּין מִן הָאוּמוֹת בֵּין מִיִּשְׂרָאֵל, וְיַעֲשֶׂה אוֹת וּמוֹפֵת, וְיֹאמַר שֶׁה' שְׁלָחוֹ לְהוֹסִיף מִצְוָה אוֹ לִגְרוֹעַ מִצְוָה אוֹ לְפָרֵשׁ בְּמִצְוָה מִן הַמִּצְוֹת פֵּרוּשׁ שֶׁלֹּא שָׁמַעְנוּ מִמֹּשֶׁה, אוֹ שֶׁאָמַר שֶׁאוֹתָן הַמִּצְוֹת שֶׁנִּצְטַוּוּ בָּהֶן יִשְׂרָאֵל אֵינָן לְעוֹלָם וּלְדוֹרֵי דוֹרוֹת אֶלָּא מִצְוֹת לְפִי זְמַן הָיוּ, הֲרֵי זֶה נָבִיא שֶׁקֶר . . . שֶׁהוּא בָּרוּךְ שְׁמוֹ צִוָּה לְמֹשֶׁה שֶׁהַמִּצְוָה הַזֹּאת "לָנוּ וּלְבָנֵינוּ עַד עוֹלָם".

If a person will arise, Jew or Gentile, and perform a sign or wonder and say that God sent him to add a mitzvah, withdraw a mitzvah, explain a mitzvah in a manner that differs from the tradition Received from Moses, or that the *mitzvot* are not forever but were given for a limited time—this person is a false prophet. . . . For God instructed Moses that this commandment is "for us and our children forever."

Text 6

Rav Sa'adia Ga'on, *Emunot Vede'ot* 3

שֶׁהֵם אוֹמְרִים כְּמוֹ שֶׁהָיְתָה סִבַּת הֶאֱמִין בְּמֹשֶׁה הֶעֱמִידוֹ הָאוֹתוֹת וְהַמּוֹפְתִים,
כֵּן חַיָּיב שֶׁתִּהְיֶה הַסִּבָּה לְהַאֲמִין בְּזוּלָתוֹ הָאוֹתוֹת וְהַמּוֹפְתִים.

וְתָמַהְתִּי בְּעֵת שָׁמְעִי זֶה תָּמֵהַּ גָּדוֹל, הוּא, שֶׁסִּבַּת הַאֲמִינֵנוּ בְּמֹשֶׁה לֹא הָיְתָה
הָאוֹתוֹת וְהַמּוֹפְתִים בִּלְבַד, אֲבָל סִבַּת הַאֲמִינֵנוּ בּוֹ וּבְכָל נָבִיא, שֶׁקְּרָאָנוּ תְּחִלָּה
אֶל מָה שֶׁיֻּכְשַׁר, וְכַאֲשֶׁר נִשְׁמַע דְּבָרוֹ וְנִרְאֶה אוֹתוֹ שֶׁיֻּכְשַׁר, נְבַקֵּשׁ מִמֶּנּוּ
הַמּוֹפְתִים עָלָיו, וְכַאֲשֶׁר יַעֲמִידֵם נַאֲמִין בּוֹ, וְאִם נִשְׁמַע טַעֲנָתוֹ מִתְּחִלָּתָהּ
וְנִרְאֶה שֶׁלֹּא תֻכְשַׁר, לֹא נְבַקֵּשׁ מִמֶּנּוּ מוֹפְתִים, כִּי אֵין מוֹפֵת עַל נִמְנָע.

וְהַדֶּרֶךְ בְּאֵלֶּה הַשְּׁנֵי עִנְיָנִים, כִּרְאוּבֵן וְשִׁמְעוֹן עָמְדוּ לִפְנֵי הַדִּין, וְאִם יִטְעוֹן
רְאוּבֵן מַה שֶּׁאֶפְשָׁר כָּמוֹהוּ, כְּאִלּוּ אָמַר יֵשׁ לִי עָלָיו אֶלֶף דִּינָר יְבַקֵּשׁ מִמֶּנּוּ
הַדַּיָּן עֵדִים; וְכַאֲשֶׁר יָעִידוּ הָעֵדִים יִתְחַיֵּב לוֹ הַמָּמוֹן. וְאִם יִטְעוֹן עָלָיו מַה
שֶּׁאִי אֶפְשָׁר, כְּאִלּוּ אָמַר יֵשׁ לִי עָלָיו חִדֶּקֶל, תִּהְיֶה טַעֲנָתוֹ מֵעִקָּרָהּ בְּטֵלָה,
שֶׁאֵין חִדֶּקֶל בִּרְשׁוּת אָדָם, וְלֹא יִתָּכֵן שֶׁיְּבַקֵּשׁ הַדַּיָּן עֵדִים עַל זֶה.

כֵּן הַדֶּרֶךְ עִם כָּל טוֹעֵן בִּנְבוּאָה, אִם יֹאמַר לָנוּ שֶׁאֱלֹקִים מְצַוֶּה אֶתְכֶם
שֶׁתָּצוּמוּ יוֹם כָּךְ, נְבַקֵּשׁ מִמֶּנּוּ אוֹתוֹת וְכַאֲשֶׁר נִרְאֶה אוֹתָם נַאֲמִין וְנָצוּם.
וְאִם יֹאמַר אֱלֹקַי יְצַוֶּה אֶתְכֶם בִּנְאוּף וְלִגְנוֹב . . . לֹא נְבַקֵּשׁ מִמֶּנּוּ אוֹת,
מִפְּנֵי שֶׁקְּרָאָנוּ לְמַה שֶּׁלֹּא יַכְשִׁירֵהוּ הַשֵּׂכֶל, אוֹ הַגָּדָה נֶאֱמֶנֶת.

Some say that in the same way we believed Moses because he performed wonders and miracles, so we must believe a prophet [who wants to abrogate the Torah] if he performs wonders and miracles.

I was greatly astonished when I heard this remark. We did not believe Moses only because of his miracles; we believed him and all other prophets because they called upon us to do something that did not go against one of our fundamental beliefs. When we heard their words and they met this criterion, we asked for signs; and when they provided signs, we believed them. But if someone calls upon us to do that

Rav Sa'adia Ga'on (Rasag)
882–942

Rabbinic scholar, philosopher, and exegete. Rav Sa'adia Ga'on was born in Egypt and came to the forefront of the rabbinic scene through his active opposition to Karaism, a divergent sect that denied the divinity of the Oral Law. In 928, the exilarch David ben Zakai invited him to head the illustrious yeshivah in Sura, Babylonia, thereby bestowing upon him the honorific title, "Ga'on." He is renowned for his works on the Torah, Hebrew linguistics, Jewish philosophy, and his redaction of a *sidur*.

which goes against one of our fundamental beliefs, we do not ask for any signs. No sign can support the impossible.

This is similar to two people, Reuven and Shimon, appearing at trial. If Reuven claims from Shimon something in the realm of possibility, for example, "He owes me 1,000 dinar," the judge will ask him to produce witnesses, and if he does so, the money will be awarded to him. But if he claims something in the realm of the impossible, such as, "He owes me the Tigris River," his claim will be void from the outset because nobody owns the Tigris. It is inconceivable that a judge would even ask for witnesses to substantiate this claim.

So it is with anyone who claims to be a prophet. If he tells us, "God commands you to fast today," we ask him for signs, and if they are realized, we believe him and we fast. But if he says, "God commands you to commit adultery and to steal," . . . we shall not ask him for a sign because he has told us an impossibility, something no true prophet would say.

Text 7

Rabbi Moshe Sofer, *Responsa Chatam Sofer* 1:208

הָא דְ"לֹא בַשָּׁמַיִם הִיא" וְשֶׁ"אֵין הַנָּבִיא רַשַּׁאי לְחַדֵּשׁ דָּבָר מֵעַתָּה" (שַׁבָּת קד, א) הוּא יְסוֹד וְשֹׁרֶשׁ כָּל הַתּוֹרָה כֻּלָּהּ. דְּאִי לַאו הָכִי, אֵין כַּאן תּוֹרָה כְּלַל.

דְּהֲרֵי כְּבָר הָיָה לָעוֹלָמִים בְּשַׁבָּת קי"ו ע"ב, דְּאָמַר הַהוּא מִנָּא, מִיּוֹמָא דְּגָלִיתוּן מֵאַרְעֲכוֹן אִתְנַטָּלוּ אוֹרַיְיתָא דְּמֹשֶׁה וְאִתְיְהִיב אוֹרַיְיתָא אַחֲרִיתִי, עַיֵּן שָׁם. וְאֶפְשָׁר יַעֲשֶׂה אוֹתוֹת וּמוֹפְתִים עַל יְדֵי תַּחְבּוּלוֹת וְכִשּׁוּף. וְנָבִיא הַיִּשְׁמְעֵאלִים עָשָׂה כֵּן. וְשַׁבְּתַי צְבִי תר"ו אָמַר שֶׁנִּתְהַפְּכוּ הַמִּצְוֹת וְנַעֲשׂוּ מֵעֲשִׂיִּין לַאוִין וּמִלַּאוִין עֲשִׂיִּין. וַאֲפִלּוּ אִם לֹא נַאֲמִין כֵּן בִּכְלָלוּת הַתּוֹרָה, מִכָּל מָקוֹם אֵין שׁוּם מִצְוָה שֶׁתִּשָּׁאֵר בְּמַתְכּוּנְתָּהּ. כָּל אֶחָד יֹאמַר חָלַמְתִּי חֲלוֹם שֶׁחֵלֶב זֶה אָסוּר וְזֶה מֻתָּר, וְזֶה יֹאמַר כָּךְ וְזֶה כָּךְ, וְתָפוּג תּוֹרָה.

The notion that "the Torah is not in heaven (Deuteronomy 30:12)" and that "a prophet may not innovate anything after Sinai (Talmud, Shabbat 104a)" is the foundation and root of the entire Torah. If not for this principle, we would be left without any Torah at all.

I refer you to the anecdote recorded in the Talmud (Shabbat 116b) where a heretic argued that since the Jews were exiled from their land, the Torah of Moses was revoked and a different Torah was given in its place. Possibly, such people could perform signs and miracles by means of deception or sorcery. In fact, the prophet of the Ishmaelites did so. And Shabtai Tsvi said that Torah prohibitions became required *mitzvot*, and required *mitzvot* became forbidden. Even if we would not believe this [to nullify] the entire Torah at once, [if we would believe such people] not a single commandment would remain unaltered. Every individual would say, "I had a dream that this type of fat is prohibited and the other permitted," and so on; and the Torah would fade away.

Rabbi Moshe Sofer
(Chatam Sofer)
1762–1839

A leading rabbinical authority of the 19th century. Born in Frankfurt am Main, *Chatam Sofer* ultimately accepted the rabbinate of Pressburg (now Bratislava), Slovakia. Serving as rabbi and head of the yeshivah that he established, Rabbi Sofer maintained a strong traditionalist perspective, opposing deviation from Jewish tradition. *Chatam Sofer* is the title of his collection of halachic responsa and his commentary to the Talmud.

Debating Heaven

Text 8a

Talmud, Bava Metsi'a 59a–b

חֲתָכוֹ חֻלְיוֹת וְנָתַן חוֹל בֵּין חוּלְיָא לְחוּלְיָא, רַבִּי אֱלִיעֶזֶר מְטַהֵר וַחֲכָמִים מְטַמְּאִין. וְזֶה הוּא תַּנּוּר שֶׁל עַכְנַאי.

If an oven is constructed out of layers of clay coils and sand is placed between each layer—Rabbi Eliezer declares that oven to be [permanently] pure, while the sages declare it to be [susceptible to] ritual impurity. And this is the *achna'i* oven.

Babylonian Talmud

A literary work of monumental proportions that draws upon the legal, spiritual, intellectual, ethical, and historical traditions of Judaism. The 37 tractates of the Babylonian Talmud contain the teachings of the Jewish sages from the period after the destruction of the 2nd Temple through the 5th century CE. It has served as the primary vehicle for the transmission of the Oral Law and the education of Jews over the centuries; it is the entry point for all subsequent legal, ethical, and theological Jewish scholarship.

Text 8b

Ibid., 59b

בְּאוֹתוֹ הַיּוֹם הֵשִׁיב רַבִּי אֱלִיעֶזֶר כָּל תְּשׁוּבוֹת שֶׁבָּעוֹלָם וְלֹא קִבְּלוּ הֵימֶנּוּ.

אָמַר לָהֶם, אִם הֲלָכָה כְּמוֹתִי, חָרוּב זֶה יוֹכִיחַ.

נֶעֱקַר חָרוּב מִמְּקוֹמוֹ מֵאָה אַמָּה, וְאָמְרֵי לָהּ אַרְבַּע מֵאוֹת אַמָּה.

אָמְרוּ לוֹ, אֵין מְבִיאִין רְאָיָה מִן הֶחָרוּב.

חָזַר וְאָמַר לָהֶם, אִם הֲלָכָה כְּמוֹתִי, אַמַּת הַמַּיִם יוֹכִיחוּ. חָזְרוּ אַמַּת הַמַּיִם לַאֲחוֹרֵיהֶם.

אָמְרוּ לוֹ, אֵין מְבִיאִין רְאָיָה מֵאַמַּת הַמַּיִם.

חָזַר וְאָמַר לָהֶם, אִם הֲלָכָה כְּמוֹתִי, כּוֹתְלֵי בֵּית הַמִּדְרָשׁ
יוֹכִיחוּ. הִטּוּ כּוֹתְלֵי בֵּית הַמִּדְרָשׁ לִפֹּל.

גָּעַר בָּהֶם רַבִּי יְהוֹשֻׁעַ, אָמַר לָהֶם, אִם תַּלְמִידֵי חֲכָמִים
מְנַצְּחִים זֶה אֶת זֶה בַּהֲלָכָה, אַתֶּם מָה טִיבְכֶם?

לֹא נָפְלוּ מִפְּנֵי כְּבוֹדוֹ שֶׁל רַבִּי יְהוֹשֻׁעַ, וְלֹא זָקְפוּ מִפְּנֵי
כְּבוֹדוֹ שֶׁל רַבִּי אֱלִיעֶזֶר, וַעֲדַיִן מַטִּין וְעוֹמְדִין.

חָזַר וְאָמַר לָהֶם, אִם הֲלָכָה כְּמוֹתִי, מִן הַשָּׁמַיִם יוֹכִיחוּ.

יָצְאתָה בַּת קוֹל וְאָמְרָה, מָה לָכֶם אֵצֶל רַבִּי אֱלִיעֶזֶר, שֶׁהֲלָכָה כְּמוֹתוֹ בְּכָל מָקוֹם.

עָמַד רַבִּי יְהוֹשֻׁעַ עַל רַגְלָיו וְאָמַר, "לֹא בַשָּׁמַיִם הִיא" (דְּבָרִים ל,יב).

מַאי "לֹא בַשָּׁמַיִם הִיא"?

אָמַר רַבִּי יִרְמְיָה: שֶׁכְּבָר נִתְּנָה תּוֹרָה מֵהַר סִינַי, אֵין אָנוּ מַשְׁגִּיחִין בְּבַת קוֹל,
שֶׁכְּבָר כָּתַבְתָּ בְּהַר סִינַי בַּתּוֹרָה "אַחֲרֵי רַבִּים לְהַטֹּת" (שְׁמוֹת כג,ב).

On that day Rabbi Eliezer brought forward every imaginable argument [to prove that the *achna'i* oven is not subject to ritual defilement], but the sages did not accept his arguments.

Said Rabbi Eliezer, "If the *halachah* agrees with me, let this carob tree prove it."

Thereupon the carob tree was uprooted and moved a distance of a hundred cubits; others say, four hundred cubits.

"No proof can be brought from a carob tree," they retorted.

Again Rabbi Eliezer said to them, "If the *halachah* agrees with me, let the stream of water prove it," whereupon the stream of water began to flow backward.

"No proof can be brought from a stream of water," they rejoined.

Again he urged, "If the *halachah* agrees with me, let the walls of the academy prove it," whereupon the walls inclined to fall.

But Rabbi Yehoshua rebuked the walls, saying, "Scholars are engaged in halachic dispute; what right have you to interfere?"

The walls did not cave in completely in deference to Rabbi Yehoshua, nor did they resume their upright position in deference to Rabbi Eliezer; and they are still standing thus inclined.

Again, Rabbi Eliezer said to them, "If the *halachah* agrees with me, let heaven prove it."

Thereupon a heavenly voice proclaimed, "Why do you dispute with Rabbi Eliezer? The *halachah* follows his opinion on all matters!"

Rabbi Yehoshua rose to his feet and exclaimed, "'The Torah is not in heaven! (Deuteronomy 30:12).'"

What did he mean?

Said Rabbi Yirmiyah, "From the day the Torah was given at Sinai, we pay no regard to heavenly voices. For You have already written in the Torah, 'Follow the majority (Exodus 23:2).'"

QUESTION FOR DISCUSSION

If Rabbi Yehoshua's reasoning was correct, why did the heavenly voice intervene on behalf of Rabbi Eliezer?

Text 9

Rabbi Yosef Chaim of Baghdad, *Ben Yehoyada*, ad loc.

בְּוַדַּאי הַגָּמוּר כָּל הָאוֹתוֹת אֲשֶׁר עָשׂוּ מִן הַשָּׁמַיִם לַעֲזוֹר אֶת רַבִּי אֱלִיעֶזֶר, וְגַם יְצִיאַת בַּת קוֹל לְעֶזְרָתוֹ, הַכֹּל הָיָה בְּהַשְׁגָּחָה מֵאֵת הַשֵּׁם יִתְבָּרֵךְ, לְתִיקּוּן הָעוֹלָם מִכָּאן וּלְהַבָּא, לַעֲשׂוֹת בְּזֶה יְסוֹד חָזָק וְאַמִּיץ וְנָכוֹן וְקַיָּים לְדִבְרֵי תּוֹרָה . . .

וְהָיָה גָּלוּי וְיָדוּעַ לִפְנֵי הַקָּבָּ"ה, שֶׁהַחֲכָמִים הָהֵם תַּקִּיפִים וַאֲמִתִּיִּים, וְאַף עַל פִּי שֶׁיִּרְאוּ אוֹת וּמוֹפֵת, וְגַם יִשְׁמְעוּ דִּבְרֵי בַּת קוֹל מַכְרֶזֶת לְסַיֵּיעַ דִּבְרֵי הַיָּחִיד, הֵם לֹא יִרְצוּ לְבַטֵּל מַה שֶּׁכָּתוּב בַּתּוֹרָה "אַחֲרֵי רַבִּים לְהַטּוֹת", לְבִלְתִּי יִסְתְּרוּ דָּבָר אֶחָד מִן הַתּוֹרָה. וְלָכֵן גָּזַר הַקָּבָּ"ה לַעֲשׂוֹת כָּל הָאוֹתוֹת הַנִּסִּיִּים הָאֵלֶּה וְגַם יְצִיאַת בַּת קוֹל, וּבְכָל זֶה לֹא יַשְׁגִּיחוּ הַחֲכָמִים לְבַטֵּל דָּבָר אֶחָד מִן הַתּוֹרָה, דְּאָז בְּזֶה נַעֲשָׂה יְסוֹד גָּדוֹל מְיוּסָּד לְדוֹרוֹת הַבָּאִים, שֶׁלֹּא יוּכַל אֶחָד לְבַטֵּל אוֹת אַחַת מִן הַתּוֹרָה. כִּי בְּשָׁמְעָם שֶׁכָּל הָאוֹתוֹת הָאֵלֶּה וְגַם הַכְרָזַת בַּת קוֹל לֹא הוֹעִילוּ, מִי יוּכַל לִפְתּוֹחַ פִּיו לְבַטֵּל אוֹת אַחַת מִן הַתּוֹרָה . . .

וּבְוַדַּאי פִּרְסוּם גָּדוֹל וְנוֹרָא הַנַּעֲשָׂה בְּדָבָר זֶה, יִהְיֶה זִכְרוֹנוֹ קַיָּים עַד סוֹף כָּל הַדּוֹרוֹת.

Certainly, it was God Who caused the miracles and the heavenly voice that supported the view of Rabbi Eliezer. He did so in order to secure the future of Torah upon a steadfast foundation. . . .

God knew that the sages were resolute and truth seeking. He knew that the miracles and the heavenly voice in support of Rabbi Eliezer would not convince the sages to contravene even one command of the Torah, including the instruction to "follow the majority." God therefore caused the miracles and the heavenly voice so that the sages' disregard of it would generate an important precedent for future generations: no person would ever be able to nullify even one word of the Torah. For if even the miracles and the heavenly voice could not persuade the sages to change

Rabbi Yosef Chaim of Baghdad
(Ben Ish Chai)
1834–1909

Sefardic halachist and kabbalist. Rabbi Yosef Chaim succeeded his father as chief rabbi of Baghdad in 1859, and is best known as author of his halachic work, *Ben Ish Chai*, by which title he is also known. Also popular is his commentary on the homiletical section of the Talmud, called *Ben Yehoyadah*.

a Torah law, certainly, then, nothing would be able to persuade us to do so....

God intended that the awesomeness of this story and the publicity it engendered should result in its lesson remaining with the Jewish people for all generations.

Temporary Injunction

Text 10

Maimonides, *Mishneh Torah*, Laws of the Foundations of the Torah 9:3

אִם יֹאמַר לָנוּ הַנָּבִיא שֶׁנּוֹדַע לָנוּ שֶׁהוּא נָבִיא לַעֲבוֹר עַל אַחַת מִכָּל מִצְוֹת הָאֲמוּרוֹת בַּתּוֹרָה אוֹ עַל מִצְוֹת הַרְבֵּה, בֵּין קַלּוֹת בֵּין חֲמוּרוֹת, לְפִי שָׁעָה, מִצְוָה לִשְׁמוֹעַ לוֹ. וְכֵן לָמַדְנוּ מֵחֲכָמִים רִאשׁוֹנִים מִפִּי הַשְּׁמוּעָה: בְּכָל אִם יֹאמַר לְךָ הַנָּבִיא עֲבוֹר עַל דִּבְרֵי תּוֹרָה כְּאֵלִיָּהוּ בְּהַר הַכַּרְמֶל שְׁמַע לוֹ, חוּץ מֵעֲבוֹדַת כּוֹכָבִים, וְהוּא שֶׁיִּהְיֶה הַדָּבָר לְפִי שָׁעָה.

When people who have already established themselves as prophets instruct us to violate one of the *mitzvot* of the Torah, or many *mitzvot*, no matter their severity, but only for a limited amount of time, it is a mitzvah to listen to them. We have learned this from the earlier sages who transmitted this Received law: "Hearken to everything a prophet tells you, even to violate a precept of the Torah, like Elijah did on Mount Carmel. But only do so if this is a temporary instruction; and do not hearken, even temporarily, if he tells you to serve idols."

Text 11

Maimonides, *Mishneh Torah*, Laws of Rebels 2:4

בֵּית דִּין שֶׁרָאוּ . . . לְפִי שָׁעָה לְבַטֵּל מִצְוַת עֲשֵׂה אוֹ לַעֲבוֹר עַל מִצְוַת לֹא תַעֲשֶׂה כְּדֵי לְהַחְזִיר רַבִּים לַדָּת אוֹ לְהַצִּיל רַבִּים מִיִּשְׂרָאֵל מִלְּהִכָּשֵׁל בִּדְבָרִים אֲחֵרִים, עוֹשִׂין לְפִי מַה שֶּׁצְּרִיכָה הַשָּׁעָה. כְּשֵׁם שֶׁהָרוֹפֵא חוֹתֵךְ יָדוֹ אוֹ רַגְלוֹ שֶׁל זֶה כְּדֵי שֶׁיִּחְיֶה כּוּלוֹ, כַּךְ בֵּית דִּין מוֹרִים בִּזְמַן מִן הַזְּמַנִּים לַעֲבוֹר עַל קְצַת מִצְוֹת לְפִי שָׁעָה כְּדֵי שֶׁיִּתְקַיְּימוּ כּוּלָּם. כְּדֶרֶךְ שֶׁאָמְרוּ חֲכָמִים הָרִאשׁוֹנִים (תלמוד בבלי, יומא פה,ב), "חַלֵּל עָלָיו שַׁבָּת אַחַת כְּדֵי שֶׁיִּשְׁמוֹר שַׁבָּתוֹת הַרְבֵּה".

If a *beit din* deems it appropriate . . . to temporarily suspend a positive or negative commandment in order to bring many people back to the Jewish faith or to prevent many Jews from committing various transgressions, they may do whatever is necessary at that time. Just like a doctor amputates a person's hand or foot so that the person will live; so, too, at times, the court may rule to temporarily violate some of the *mitzvot* to preserve overall mitzvah observance. In this vein, the sages of the previous generations said (Talmud, Yoma 85b), "Desecrate one Shabbat for a person's sake so that the person will keep many a Shabbat."

Restraining Order

Text 12

Talmud, Rosh Hashanah 29b

מִדְאוֹרַיְיתָא מִישְׁרָא שָׁרֵי, וְרַבָּנָן הוּא דְגָזוּר בֵּיהּ, כִּדְרַבָּה.

דְאָמַר רַבָּה: הַכֹּל חַיָּיבִין בִּתְקִיעַת שׁוֹפָר, וְאֵין הַכֹּל בְּקִיאִין בִּתְקִיעַת שׁוֹפָר, גְּזֵירָה שֶׁמָּא יִטְּלֶנּוּ בְּיָדוֹ וְיֵלֵךְ אֵצֶל הַבָּקִי לִלְמוֹד, וְיַעֲבִירֶנּוּ אַרְבַּע אַמּוֹת בִּרְשׁוּת הָרַבִּים.

וְהַיְינוּ טַעֲמָא דְלוּלָב, וְהַיְינוּ טַעֲמָא דִמְגִילָּה.

According to biblical law, it is permissible [and obligatory to sound the *shofar* on Rosh Hashanah even when it falls on Shabbat]. However, the sages decreed that we should not do so, as was stated by Rabah.

For Rabah stated, "Everyone is obligated to hear the *shofar* [on Rosh Hashanah], but not everyone knows how to sound the *shofar*. The [sages made their] enactment [not to sound the *shofar* when Rosh Hashanah falls on Shabbat] lest someone take the *shofar* by hand and go to a knowledgeable person to learn, and thereby carry four cubits in the public domain.

The same applies to taking the *lulav* [when *Sukot* falls on Shabbat] and reading the *megilah* [on Purim, when it falls on Shabbat].

Derived and Legislated

The Judge of Those Days

Text 13

Maimonides, *Mishneh Torah*, Laws of Rebels 2:1

בֵּית דִּין גָּדוֹל שֶׁדָּרְשׁוּ בְּאַחַת מִן הַמִּדּוֹת כְּפִי מַה שֶּׁנִּרְאֶה בְּעֵינֵיהֶם שֶׁהַדִּין כָּךְ וְדָנוּ דִּין, וְעָמַד אַחֲרֵיהֶם בֵּית דִּין אַחֵר וְנִרְאֶה לוֹ טַעַם אַחֵר לִסְתּוֹר אוֹתוֹ, הֲרֵי זֶה סוֹתֵר וְדָן כְּפִי מַה שֶּׁנִּרְאֶה בְּעֵינָיו. שֶׁנֶּאֱמַר (דְּבָרִים יז,ט): "אֶל הַשּׁוֹפֵט אֲשֶׁר יִהְיֶה בַּיָּמִים הָהֵם" - אֵינְךָ חַיָּיב לָלֶכֶת אֶלָּא אַחַר בֵּית דִּין שֶׁבְּדוֹרְךָ.

If the Sanhedrin used one of the hermeneutic rules, as per their perception, to derive a law and rule accordingly, and another court arose afterward whose reasoning dictated to revoke the previous ruling, they may revoke it and rule according to their perception. As it says (Deuteronomy 17:9), "[You shall go] to the judge who will be in those days." This indicates that people are obligated to follow the court of their own generation.

Greater in Wisdom and Number

Text 14

Maimonides, *Mishneh Torah*, Laws of Rebels 2:2

בֵּית דִּין שֶׁגָּזְרוּ גְּזֵרָה אוֹ תִּקְנוּ תַּקָּנָה וְהִנְהִיגוּ מִנְהָג וּפָשַׁט הַדָּבָר בְּכָל יִשְׂרָאֵל, וְעָמַד אַחֲרֵיהֶם בֵּית דִּין אַחֵר וּבִקֵּשׁ לְבַטֵּל דְּבָרִים הָרִאשׁוֹנִים וְלַעֲקוֹר אוֹתָהּ הַתַּקָּנָה וְאוֹתָהּ הַגְּזֵרָה וְאוֹתוֹ הַמִּנְהָג, אֵינוֹ יָכוֹל עַד שֶׁיִּהְיֶה גָּדוֹל מִן הָרִאשׁוֹנִים בְּחָכְמָה וּבְמִנְיָן. הָיָה גָּדוֹל בְּחָכְמָה אֲבָל לֹא בַּמִּנְיָן, בְּמִנְיָן אֲבָל לֹא בְּחָכְמָה, אֵינוֹ יָכוֹל לְבַטֵּל אֶת דְּבָרָיו.

אֲפִילוּ בָּטֵל הַטַּעַם שֶׁבִּגְלָלוֹ גָּזְרוּ הָרִאשׁוֹנִים אוֹ הִתְקִינוּ, אֵין הָאַחֲרוֹנִים יְכוֹלִין לְבַטֵּל עַד שֶׁיִּהְוּ גְּדוֹלִים מֵהֶם.

וְהֵיאַךְ יִהְיוּ גְּדוֹלִים מֵהֶם בַּמִּנְיָן הוֹאִיל וְכָל בֵּית דִּין וּבֵית דִּין שֶׁל שִׁבְעִים וְאֶחָד הוּא, זֶה מִנְיַן חַכְמֵי הַדּוֹר שֶׁהִסְכִּימוּ וְקִבְּלוּ הַדָּבָר שֶׁאָמְרוּ בֵּית דִּין הַגָּדוֹל וְלֹא חָלְקוּ בּוֹ.

If the Sanhedrin issued a decree, instituted an edict, or established a custom and this practice spread throughout the Jewish people, but a later court arose and sought to nullify the original order and eliminate the original edict, decree, or custom—the later court does not have this authority unless it surpasses the original court in wisdom and in number. If it surpasses the original court in wisdom, but not in number, or in number, but not in wisdom, it cannot nullify its rulings.

Even if the rationale for which the original court instituted the decree or the edict is nullified, a later court does not have the authority to negate their rulings unless they are greater.

How is it possible that the later court could surpass the original court in number, considering that every Sanhedrin consists of seventy-one judges? This refers to the number of sages in the generation who endorse the Sanhedrin's ruling.

Text 15

Rabbi Yechiel Michel Halevi Epstein
1829–1908

Noted author on Jewish law. Rabbi Epstein lived in Czarist Lithuania and was chief rabbi of Novozypkov, a town near Minsk, and later, of Navahrudak, where he served until his death. A prolific writer, his primary work is *Aruch Hashulchan,* an expanded and reworked code of Jewish law.

Rabbi Yechiel Michel Epstein, *Aruch Hashulchan, Yoreh De'ah* 115:6

שֶׁכָּל גְּזֵירַת חֲכָמִים, לְבַד טַעֲמָם הַנִּגְלֶה, יֵשׁ עוֹד
הַרְבֵּה טְעָמִים כְּמוּסִים שֶׁלֹּא גִּילוּ אוֹתָם.

All laws legislated by the sages have many esoteric rationales they did not reveal, in addition to the revealed rationales.

Text 16

Rabbi Menachem Mendel of Lubavitch, *Derech Mitzvotecha* 198a

עִנְיַן יוֹם טוֹב שֵׁנִי שֶׁל גָּלֻיּוֹת, שֶׁבְּאֶרֶץ יִשְׂרָאֵל עוֹשִׂים
. . . יוֹם אֶחָד וּבְחוּץ לָאָרֶץ עוֹשִׂים שְׁנֵי יָמִים:

וְיוּבַן עַל פִּי מַה שֶּׁכָּתוּב בְּסֵפֶר אוֹר נֶעֱרַב לְהָרַב מֹשֶׁה קוֹרְדִיבוּרוֹ זִכְרוֹנוֹ לִבְרָכָה, שֶׁחוּץ לָאָרֶץ, לִהְיוֹתוֹ גַּשְׁמִי, אֵינוֹ יָכוֹל לְקַבֵּל הַהֶאָרָה בְּיוֹם אֶחָד כְּמוֹ שֶׁמְּקַבֶּלֶת אֶרֶץ יִשְׂרָאֵל, אֶלָּא מִתְחַלֶּקֶת לִשְׁנֵי יָמִים כו'.

וּפֵירוּשׁ כִּי כָּל יוֹם טוֹב הוּא הַמְשָׁכַת וְהִתְגַּלּוּת קְדוּשָּׁה עֶלְיוֹנָה מִלְמַעְלָה מֵהַזְּמַן בִּבְחִינַת זְמַן . . . וְלָכֵן עוֹשִׂים אוֹתוֹ הַיּוֹם יוֹם טוֹב.

וְהִנֵּה בְּאֶרֶץ יִשְׂרָאֵל, שֶׁהִיא אֶרֶץ אֲשֶׁר ה' דּוֹרֵשׁ אוֹתָהּ, שֶׁקְּרוֹבָה לֶאֱלֹקוּת, וּמְזוּכֶּכֶת בְּמַעֲלָה וּמַדְרֵגָה, אֲזַי יְכוֹלִים לְקַבֵּל בְּיוֹם אֶחָד אוֹתוֹ הַהֶאָרָה הַמְּאִירָה וּמִתְגַּלָּה. מַה שֶּׁאֵין כֵּן בְּחוּץ לָאָרֶץ, אֵין הֶאָרָה זוֹ מִתְיַישֶּׁבֶת בְּיוֹם אֶחָד, וְלֹא יְכוֹלִים לְהָכִילָהּ כְּלַל בְּיוֹם אֶחָד מִצַּד רִיחוּק מַעֲלַת חוּץ לָאָרֶץ מֵאֱלֹקוּת. וְלָכֵן עוֹשִׂים ב' יָמִים, שֶׁבְּמֶשֶׁךְ ב' יָמִים יְכוֹלָה הִיא שֶׁתִּתְקַבֵּל כְּמוֹ שֶׁבְּאֶרֶץ יִשְׂרָאֵל בְּיוֹם אֶחָד.

With regard to the second day of the festivals—that in Israel they celebrate . . . one day, whereas in the Diaspora they celebrate two days:

We shall understand this based on the writings of Rabbi Moshe Cordovero in his work *Or Ne'erav*. He writes that the world at large, because of its coarse nature, cannot assimilate the light and energy of the festival in one day in the way that the Land of Israel can.

Meaning, every festival consists of a revelation of supernal sanctity that transcends time. . . . This is the reason for the festival.

The Land of Israel, a land that God seeks, a land close to Godliness, a land of a lofty and pure nature, can process this illumination in one day. In the Diaspora, however, one day is not sufficient to receive this illumination, because the Diaspora's connection to God is more distant. The Diaspora requires two days to process what Israel could process in one day.

Rabbi Menachem Mendel Schneersohn of Lubavitch
(*Tsemach Tsedek*)
1789–1866

Chasidic rebbe and noted author. The *Tsemach Tsedek* was the third leader of the Chabad Chasidic movement and a noted authority on Jewish law. His numerous works include halachic responsa, Chasidic discourses, and Kabbalistic writings. Active in the plight of Russian Jewry, he worked to alleviate the plight of the Cantonists, Jewish children kidnapped to serve in the Czar's army. He passed away in Lubavitch, leaving seven sons and two daughters.

TORAH Café

Continue the JLI Learning Experience!

Visit www.TorahCafe.com/go/JD5

for a video lecture(s) related to the theme of this lesson.

Key Points

1. The Torah expresses God's wisdom and will. Just as God transcends creation and exists independently of this world, so does His wisdom and will—the Torah. The idea, then, that the *mitzvot* were responses to archaic circumstances is untenable.

2. God does not change and therefore His wisdom and will do not change either. Neither the Written Torah nor the Received Oral Torah are subject to change or modification.

3. Modifying the Torah would leave us with a new product, one that is not an expression of God's wisdom and will. This would obstruct the channels through which we experience a relationship with God.

4. The Torah instructs us to listen to the directives of legitimate prophets. We do not, however, heed their directives when they contravene the Torah, even if the prophet produces miracles.

5. In Talmudic times, a heavenly voice once declared its support for a minority opinion. The sages refused to heed the heavenly voice, sending a clear message to future generations that nothing can change a Torah law.

6. A prophet or *beit din* can issue a temporary injunction to suspend a mitzvah, but this has rarely occurred.

7. A Sanhedrin can overturn a law Derived by an earlier Sanhedrin, and we must follow the ruling of the most recent Sanhedrin.

8. To overturn a Legislated law, even if it seems that the original reason for the enactment is no longer applicable, the later Sanhedrin must be greater than the one that issued the legislation.

9. The Talmud's rulings have the same status as rulings of the Sanhedrin. Its laws are thus legally binding upon all Jews until the reestablishment of the Sanhedrin.

ADDITIONAL READINGS

MAIMONIDES' INTRODUCTION TO THE MISHNAH: PROPHECY

TRANSLATED BY FRED ROSNER, MD

Know, too, that prophecy is not helpful in the interpretation of the Torah, nor in the derivation of the details of commandments through the thirteen principles (mentioned above). Rather, that which Joshua and Pinchas wrought was (not through prophecy but) through deliberation and logical derivation, much the same as did Rabina and Rav Ashi.[1] The advantage of a prophet and his accomplishment in the matter of any commandment, if you inquire into this, is, by my life,[2] among the great principles upon which the faith is supported and founded.

I see that this is an appropriate point to explain this important subject (of prophecy). This cannot be done until we have analyzed the claim of the prophet to his prophecy, and whereby the prophecy is corroborated since this, too, is a fundamental principle. The great masses of people, as well as a number of learned individuals among them, are under a false impression in assuming[3] that prophecy cannot be attributed to one claiming it unless[4] he has performed a wondrous miracle[5], such as one of the miracles of Moses, our teacher, may his memory be blessed, or if he changes the course of nature as when Elijah, of blessed memory, brought back to life the son of the widow[6] or, as is known to all, of the miracles of Elisha,[7] may he rest in peace. This is not a correct principle, because all the miracles which Elijah, Elisha and other prophets wrought were not performed in order to substantiate their prophecy, since their prophethood had already been established previously; rather they performed these wonders for their own needs. Because of their closeness to the Holy One, Blessed Be He, he fulfilled their desires, just as He promised the righteous: *Thou shalt decree a thing and it shall be established unto thee.*[8] Prophethood becomes established in the manner we have begun to discuss. I initially state that the fundamental principle of our faith in the matter of prophecy is as follows: Those who claim to be prophets can first be divided into two categories, namely they who prophesy in the name of idolatry, and they who prophesy in the name of G'd.

The prophecy of idolaters is subdivided into two categories: THE FIRST CATEGORY is if a prophet should arise and say "that particular star set its spirit upon me and told me 'Worship me thusly' or 'Call unto me thusly and I will answer you'." Similarly, if he should call people to worship (the idol) *Ba'al* or any other image or shape saying "This (image) apprised me of such and such, and told me thusly", or "commanded me to cause it to be worshipped in such and such a way", in the manner of the prophets of *Ba'al* and of the prophets of (the idol) *Asherah.*[9] (These are false prophets.)

THE SECOND CATEGORY is if someone should say: "God's word came to me to worship a particular *Ba'al*", or "to call down such and such a heavenly power for such and such a purpose". He will teach the people matters pertaining to the worship or activi-

1 Compilers of the *Gemara* of the Babylonian Talmud.

2 Lit: let my soul live; an expression of oath common among the prophets.

3 Lit: imagining in their souls.

4 Lit: until.

5 Lit: sign.

6 First Kings 17, 21.

7 Disciple of Elijah the prophet. See Second Kings 4,1-37.

8 Job 22, 28.

9 First Kings 18, 28.

ties of that particular form of idolatry, as the Torah has described[10]. This type (of prophecy using God's name) is also considered prophecy in the name of idolatry, because this latter appellation includes both the person who states that the idol itself commanded him to worship it as well as he who states that the Holy One, Blessed Be He, commanded him to worship any of those (idols).

Should one of the two claims just described become heard from one who pretends to be a prophet, and should witnesses testify to this, then his judgment is as set down in the Torah, namely death by strangulation as the Holy One, Blessed Be He, stated: *And that prophet or that dreamer of dreams shall be put to death*[11]. We should not examine his pretention to prophesy, nor should we ask him for an (unusual) sign. Should he perform a more wondrous miracle or marvel than we have ever heard of to establish this prophecy, he should nevertheless be (punished by) strangulation. One should pay no attention to his miracles, because the reason for the occurrence of such miracles is as stated in Scriptures: *For the Lord your God is testing you.*[12] Furthermore, the intellect that belies his testimony is more reliable than the evidence of the eye which sees his miracles, because it has been made wondrously clear to intelligent people that one should not honor or worship save the One who brings forth all that exists[13] (in the world), and the One who is alone in perfection (i.e. God).

Those who prophesy in the name of God are also subdivided into two categories:

THE FIRST CATEGORY includes one who prophesies in the name of the Lord, and calls upon the populace to believe in Him. He[14] preaches regarding His worship saying that the Holy One, Blessed Be He, added a precept to His commandments, or deleted one from the sum total of those commandments that are collected in the book of the Torah. There is no difference if he[15] adds to or deletes from that which is written in the Scriptural text, or whether he adds to or deletes from the accepted interpretation thereof. The concept of adding to or deleting from a Biblical text is exemplified by his[16] saying: "The Holy One Blessed Be He told me that (the law of) *Orlah*[17] applies only for two years, and after two years it is permitted for you to eat from newly planted fruits" or if he should say "the Holy One Blessed Be He told me that *Orlah* is forbidden to be eaten until four years have passed", instead of what the Holy One Blessed Be He (really) said: *Three years shall it be as forbidden*[18] *unto you; it shall not be eaten,*[19] and the like. Another example is related to modification of anything learned through tradition, even if the apparent meaning of the text should support him, such as if he should say that the Biblical phrase *And thou shalt cut off her hand*[20] means literally to hew off her hand rather than meaning monetary compensation for the shame she caused as is the (true) traditional interpretation, and support his claim with prophecy saying: "The Holy One Blessed Be He told me that this commandment which states '*And thou shalt cut off her hand*' should be taken literally". Such a person should also be killed by strangulation, because he is a false prophet and attributes to the Holy One Blessed Be He things that He never told him. Here too one should pay no heed to the sign or miracle of such a person, because the prophet (Moses) who showed his miracles to all the people of the world and instilled in our heart to consider him righteous and to believe in him as it is written in Scriptures: *And they will also believe in Thee forever,*[21] he (Moses) related to us in the name of the Holy One Blessed Be He that no other Torah shall ever come from the Creator save this one, and this is what is meant by *It is not in Heaven.*[22] He further states: *It is in thy mouth and thy heart to*

[10] See Deut. 13,3.

[11] Deut. 13,6.

[12] Deut. 13,4.

[13] Alternate translation: all that is found.

[14] the false prophet.

[15] the false prophet.

[16] the false prophet.

[17] Lit: uncircumcised. The fruit of newly planted trees is to be rejected for the three years.

[18] Lit: uncircumcised. The fruit of newly planted trees is to be rejected for the three years.

[19] Levit. 19, 23.

[20] Deut. 25, 12.

[21] Exod. 19, 9.

[22] Deut. 30, 12.

perform it.[23] The explanation of *in thy mouth* refers to a commandment which is known by oral (tradition). *In thy heart* refers to logical derivation extracted through study which is one of the powers attributed to the heart. He (Moses) also warned us against adding to them[24] or deleting from them as it is written: *Thou shalt not add thereto nor diminish from it.*[25] For this reason the Sages of Blessed Memory stated: "No prophet may introduce any new law thereafter".[26] And since we know that his claim that he attributed to the Holy One Blessed Be He is a false one, and he attributed to Him that which He never told him, we are obligated to kill him, as written in Scripture: *And the prophet who will intentionally (speak a word in My name which I have not commanded him to speak, or who shall speak in the name of other gods), that prophet shall die.*[27]

THE SECOND CATEGORY is exemplified by a prophet calling people to worship God, commanding them (to obey) His precepts and exhorting them to observe the Torah without addition or deletion, as the last of the prophets stated: *Remember Ye the Law of Moses, my servant (which I commanded unto him in Horeb for all Israel, statutes and ordinances).*[28] He further assures rewards to those who comply, and warns all who would transgress it, of punishment, as did Isiah, Jeremiah, Ezekiel and others. He also prescribes ordinances, and decrees prohibitions on a subject which is not in the Torah, such as if he says: "Wage war with such and such a town or people now", as Samuel commanded Saul to wage war with Amalek,[29] or conversely (if he preaches) abstention from war, as Elisha did when he prevented Yehoram[30] from smiting the soldiers of Aram who had entered (the city of) Samaria, according to the well-known story[31]; or as Isaiah prevented the ringing of water inside the (city) wall[32], or as Jeremiah prevented the Jews from going into Israel,[33] and similar instances. For this reason, if a prophet claims that his statements are prophetic, and does not connect them with idolatry, nor does he add to the Torah, nor delete from it, but says different things, such as we have just described, then we are required to investigate him to ascertain the veracity of his claim,[34] for we must fulfill anything commanded by one whose prophetic claim is verified, from the smallest to the greatest task. Whosoever fails to fulfill any of his[35] commands is culpable of death by Divine agency[36], as the Holy One Blessed Be He stated regarding him who transgresses a command of a prophet: *I will require (the penalty for) it from him.*[37] However, should the prophet's claim not be substantiated, then he shall die by strangulation. The substantiation of a prophet's claim is achieved as I shall presently describe it: if a person claims prophethood, as we have explained, and he is fit for it, that is, if he is a man of learning, integrity[38], temperance, wisdom, and pleasant traits, as it is fundamental to us that prophecy cannot rest upon any other save a man who is wise, strong and rich.[39] There are many additional details regarding this subject (of prophecy), and it is impossible to collect them all together (here). Discussions thereon and proof for each one are to be found in verses of the books of the Torah and in the words of the Prophets. This whole subject would require an entire book in itself. Perhaps God will help us in compiling what is appropriate in a book on that subject.

Should now the prophet be eligible to prophesy,[40] then we tell him to provide us assurance by means of specific predictions and to tell, us things which the Holy One Blessed Be He taught him. He will then

23 Deut. 30, 14.
24 the precepts of the Torah.
25 Deut. 13, 1.
26 Tractate Megillah 2b.
27 Deut. 18, 20.
28 Malachi 3, 22.
29 First Samuel 15, 3.
30 The King of Israel.
31 Second Kings 6, 22.
32 Isaiah 22,9-10.
33 The word "Israel" here is difficult to interpret. Perhaps Jeremiah preventeel the Jews from returning to Israel before the termination of the 70 year Babylonian exile. Alternatively, the word "Israel" may be in-.correct here as it is not found in numerous manuscripts. In that case, Maimonidcs either meant that Jeremiah warned the Jews not to go to Egypt (Jeremiah 42, 15) or not to leave Jerusalem (Jeremiah 29,4).
34 lit: testimony.
35 the true prophet.
36 As distinguished from a death meted out by a human court.
37 Deut. 18,19.
38 Alternate translation: faith.
39 Tractate Shabbath 92a. Strong in character and rich in being contented with his lot.
40 If he fulfills the above criteria.

relate this to us and reassure us and, should all his predictions become fulfilled, then we will know that his entire prophecy is true. Should he falsify, though, or should one of his statements, even a minor point, be unsubstantiated,[41] then we will know he is a false prophet. This type of examination procedure is written in the Torah: *And if thou say in thine heart, how shall we know the word that God has not spoke; that which the prophet will speak in the name of the Lord and the thing will not follow nor come to pass.*[42] If he seems legitimate to us on the basis of one or two assurances, we should still not necessarily have faith in him to say that his prophecy is true; rather the matter should be suspended until there is an abundance of many true miracles whenever he speaks in God's name, time after time. For this reason it states in the story of Samuel, when it became well-known and clear that everything that he said would come about: *And all Israel from Dan even unto Beer Sheba knew that Samuel was truly a prophet of the Lord.*[43] They did not innovate anything without asking him, as a prophet, (about it). And were it not for this (want to consult prophets on all matters), Saul would not have come to Samuel (to question him) regarding the asses he had lost at the beginning of the story.[44] There is no question that this correct, because the Holy One Blessed Be He established prophets for us in place of astrologers, enchanters and diviners, to enable us to question them (i.e. the prophets) regarding generalities and specifics, and that they should tell us true things about the future, just as those diviners relate things which may or may not come true, as it is written: *For these nations which thou shalt possess hearkened unto sorcerers and unto diviners (but not so thou, the Eternal thy God has not suffered thee to do so). A prophet from thy midst from thy brethren like myself (will the Lord your God establish unto thee. Unto him shall Ye hearken).*[45] Because of these facts, a prophet was called by the name of "Seer", because he foresaw the future before it happened as it is written:

[41] Lit: fall.

[42] Deut. 18, 21.

[43] First Samuel 3, 20.

[44] *Ibid.* 9, 3-10.

[45] Deut. 18, 14-15.

For he that is today called a prophet was before time called a seer.[46]

Should anyone think to himself and say that if prophethood is established by the fulfillment of the prediction of future events by him who makes such claims, then all the enchanters, astrologers and spiritualists[47] could plead a claim of prophecy, since we often observe them, eye to eye, predicting what the future will bring. By my life[48], this is a vast topic, and it is worthy of explanation, in order to clarify the difference between the words of him who prophesies in the name of the Lord, and the words of these spiritualists. I say that the enchanters, astrologers and other people in that category do, predict common future happenings, but only some (of these predictions) will be right, and some will be wrong, of necessity. This we see constantly, and even the performers of such an art will agree to this, and they would not gainsay their own signs.[49] The advantage of each person of this type over his colleagues is that the false (predictions) of one are fewer than those of the others; but for them to be correct in all details of their predictions is impossible. Even these spiritualists do not commit themselves, nor pride themselves in being correct in all aspects of the things (they foretell); rather they say, (for example), that this year will be one of drought and that no rain will fall at all, and yet a little rain does fall; or one of them might say that tomorrow it will rain and yet rain doesn't fall until the day after tomorrow, and the like. This only happens in the case of an expert who is renowned, and of whom it is written in (astrological) books. This is the idea of the words of Isiah to Babylon: *Let now the astrologers, the stargazers and the monthly prognosticators stand up and save thee from the things that shall come upon thee*[50], and our Sages pointed out that (the verse) "from that" and not "All that" (they will predict . . .).[51]

[46] First Samuel 9,9.

[47] Lit: possessors of spiritual powers.

[48] Lit: may my soul live; an expression of oath.

[49] Derived from Job 21, 29.

[50] Isaiah 47,13.

[51] Genesis Rabbah 85, 3. The Sages deduced that the phrase "from that" meant to exclude the possibility of "all that". This is a typical hermeneutic deduction.

The timing of the prediction of (true) prophets and their promises is not so, however; rather, all of it proves to be correct to the last word. Never does even one item, small or large, of their statements ever fail, of that which they speak in the name of the Lord. Thus, if anyone of his[52] words should be unsustained,[53] then we will know his fraudulence (as a Divine prophet). This, too, is what is written (in Scriptures): *There will not fail*[54] *anything of the word of the Lord.*[55] This, also, is what Jeremiah alluded to in reference to dreamers who may have been correct in some visions, and who profess that what they see in dreams is by way of prophecy. He reproved them and demolished their claims by saying: *The prophet that hath a dream, let him tell a dream; and that hath My word, let him speak My word truthfully. What hath the chaff (straw) to do with the grain (wheat)?, saith the Lord.*[56] The Sages explained this matter (saying) that prophecy is clear and has no falsehoods mixed in, as pure grain which has been separated from the chaff. Dreams of magicians and the like are mostly false, like straw which has (a few) grains of wheat in it. They further stated: "Just as wheat cannot be without straw, so there cannot be a dream without some nonsensical parts".[57]

There is one important remaining notion which is worthy of clarification at this point. It refers to a prophet who predicts troubles or events that will befall the people of which they are deserving, such as if he warns them regarding famine, or destruction by the sword, or of an upheaval, or that hailstones will fall upon them, and the like, and afterwards none of these things come to pass. Heaven will have compassion, and all their affairs will remain in peace and contentment. One cannot, in this manner, know the untruth of such a prophet, nor can one (from this alone) say he is a false prophet and that he be guilty of the death penalty, because the Holy One Blessed Be He repented from (doing) harm. It is also possible that they[58] did penance and turned from their provocative acts, or that the Holy One blessed Be He deferred their punishment in His compassion and postponed His ire toward them until a later date,[59] as He did to Ahab in His statement through Elijah: *I will not bring the evil in his days, but in his son's days will I bring the evil.*[60] He (God) may have mercy on them[61] because of previous merits.

(The Scriptural phrase) *And the thing does not follow nor come to pass*[62] was not said for this type of example; rather it refers to the following: if he assures us that good tidings will occur at a specific time saying "In this year there will be tranquility and contentment", and then wars occurred, or if he says "This year will be one of rain and abundance," and then famine and drought occurred, and the like, then we will know that he is a false prophet, and the nullification of his claim and its untruth will be established. Concerning this does Scripture state: *The prophet has spoken presumptuously, thou shalt not be afraid of him*[63] meaning that his faith, his honesty and his wisdom should not frighten you, nor terrify you of killing him, after he dared[64] to testify to such a great (untruthful) thing, and who spoke such blasphemy about the Lord, Blessed Be He. For when the Holy One Blessed Be He promises good tidings to a people through a prophet, it is inconceivable[65] that He should not enact them to fulfill His prophecy to the people. This is what (the Sages) of Blessed Memory (meant when they) said: "Every word of blessing that issues from the mouth of the Holy One Blessed be He, even if conditional, is never withdrawn by Him".[66] We find an account of the fear of Jacob after the Holy One Blessed be He assured him of good tidings, as it is written: *And behold I am with thee*

52 A prophet's.
53 Lit: return empty.
54 Lit: fall unto the earth
55 Second Kings 10, 10.
56 Jeremiah 23, 28.
57 Tractate Berachoth 55a.

58 The people for whom ill was predicted.
59 Lit: a different time.
60 First Kings 21, 29.
61 The people for whom ill was predicted.
62 Deut. 18,22.
63 *Ibid.*
64 Lit: his heart filled him.
65 Lit: impossible.
66 Tractate Berachoth 7 a. The meaning of this phrase is that if God promises something conditionally, then if the condition is obeyed, He cannot change it although the original condition may have weakened His commitment.

and will watch over thee whithersoever thou goest[67], and he feared lest he die, as it is written: *And Jacob feared greatly and was distressed*[68]. The Sages of blessed memory say that the fear refers to the fear of sin, lest it cause him to perish, and this is what (the Sages meant when) they stated: "He thought that some sin might be the cause (of the failure) of God's promise to be fulfilled"[69]. This tells us that the Holy One Blessed Be He may promise good, and then sins prevail so that the good does not become fulfilled. One should know that this is only a matter (that occurs) between the Holy One Blessed be He and the prophet.

However, if the Holy One Blessed be He tells a prophet to assure the people of a good tiding unconditionally by an absolute statement, then for this good not to become fulfilled is impossible and cannot be. This is so because there would not exist for us any other way to establish the authenticity of the prophecy. The Holy One Blessed be He gave us in His Torah the fundamental principle that a prophet is proven when his assurances have become realized. This important theme was implied by Jeremiah in his argument with Hananiah[70], the son of Azzur, because Jeremiah prophesied evil and death saying that Nebuchadnezzar would become stronger and succeed and destroy the Holy Temple, whereas Hananiah, the son of Azzur, predicted good, and predicted the return to Jerusalem of the vessels of the Lord's House which had been taken to Babylon.[71] To this Jeremiah answered in this argumentation with him[72], applying these traditional[73]fundamental principles saying: *If my*[74] *prophecy will not be established and if Nebuchadnezzar will not be victorious and if the vessels will be returned to the House of the Lord as you*[75] *are saying, then this would not constitute a denial of my*[76] *prophecy since perhaps the Holy One Blessed be He will have mercy upon them.*[77] *However, if your*[78] *words will not become fulfilled and if the vessels will not be returned to the House of the Lord, then as a result, it will become clear that your prophecy is false. Your prophethood will not become established until the good times that you promise will become fulfilled.* This is what he[79] (meant when he also) stated: *Nevertheless hear thou now this word that I speak in thine ears and in the ears of all the people. The prophets that have been in the world before me and before thee prophesied to many countries and of great kingdoms, of war and of evil and of pestilence. The prophet that prophesieth of peace, when the word of the prophet shall come to pass, then shall the prophet be known, that the Lord hath truly sent him.*[80] By this he meant that, concerning those prophets who prophesy for good and for evil, it is not possible for us to know of all the things they prophesy for evil, whether their testimony is authentic or contrived. However, the truth of their words will become known if they promise good and it becomes fulfilled.

If the prophecy of a prophet is fulfilled in the manner we have just established, and his name becomes renowned like Samuel, Elijah and others, then that prophet has the right to do something in the Torah that no other living person can, and this is as follows. If he dictates to abolish any precept of the positive commandments[81], or if he decrees to permit any forbidden thing of the negative commandments[82], *temporarily,* due to special circumstances, then it is incumbent upon us to listen to his word and to perform his command. He who transgresses this is culpable of death by Divine decree[83106a], except (if the prophet preaches) idolatry. This is explicitly attributed to the Sages in the Talmud and is (the explanation of) what they said: "In every matter, if a prophet tells you to transgress the Commands of the Torah, obey him, with the exception of idolatry".[84] This applies

67 Genesis 28, 15.

68 *Ibid.* 32,7.

69 Tractate Berachoth 4a.

70 Jeremiah, Chapter 28.

71 Jeremiah, Chapter 28.

72 Hananiah.

73 Lit: well guarded.

74 Jeremiah.

75 Hananiah.

76 Jeremiah.

77 The Jewish people.

78 Hananiah.

79 Jeremiah.

80 Jeremiah, 28, 7-9.

81 "thou shalt . . .".

82 "thou shalt not . . .".

83 Shortening of one's natural life span.

84 Tractate Sanhedrin 90a.

only on condition that his decree should not be a permanent one and that he not say that the Holy One Blessed be He commanded to eradicate the law of the Torah forever; rather he should decree to abolish this law temporarily for a good reason. The prophet himself, when asked regarding his order to transgress one of the precepts that God commanded us through Moses, should answer that the suspension of that command will not remain (permanently) but should be obeyed at present only, temporarily, just as the Court[85] would regulate (out of necessity) for a limited time period.

This is what Elijah did on Mount Carmel when he sacrificed a burnt offering outside (the Temple)[86], while Jerusalem was intact and the Holy Temple stood in it. Anyone who performs this type of activity without prophetic command is culpable of *Kareth*[87], and the Holy One Blessed be He warned us in the Torah saying: *take heed to thyself lest thou offer thy burnt offerings in every place that thou seeth.*[88] He who acts in this manner shall be culpable of Divine Punishment[89], as it is written concerning he who offers a sacrifice outside (the sanctuary): *Blood shall be imputed unto that man, he hath shed blood; and (that man) shall be cut off from among his people.*[90] If he (Elijah), of Blessed Memory, would have been asked at the time of his offering on Mount Carmel, and had we said to him: "Can we do such as this deed for all times?", he would have answered that it is not permitted, and whosoever brings an offering outside (the sanctuary) is culpable of Divine punishment, but this action (of mine) is only for this one time to reveal the falsity of the prophets of the (idol) *Ba'al,* and to thwart their activities.[91]

This (idea) is also exemplified by what Elisha did when he commanded (the people) to wage war with Moab, and to destroy every fruit-bearing tree, as it is written: *And every good tree shall ye fell,*[92] although God restrained us from doing so when He stated: "*Thou shalt not destroy the trees thereof by forcing an axe against them*".[93] If Elisha would have been asked whether this commandment was eradicated, and whether it would be permitted for us in the future to destroy fruit-bearing trees when we besiege a city, he would have answered that it is not permissible, and the act (that he performed) was done out of momentary necessity.

I will now bring you an example to clarify this fundamental principle (which is applicable) to all commandments. If a prophet whose prophethood was clearly verified to us, (using the criteria) as we have described above, should tell us on the Sabbath that we should all rise, men and women alike, light a fire, and fashion therewith weapons of war, and that each of us should gird his weapons and wage war with the people of such and such a place on this day which is the Sabbath, plunder their spoils, and conquer their women, then it would be obligatory upon us,—we who are bound[94] by the Torah of Moses, —to immediately rise (and comply). We should not delay in that which we are commanded, and should zealously and with great love perform that which he[95] has instructed us, without any doubt, and without procrastination. We should firmly believe in all that we do on that day, even though it is the Sabbath and we are lighting a fire and doing work and killing and waging war, all of which are commands (through the prophet from God). We can hope for a goodly reward from the Holy One Blessed be He for having complied with the command of the prophet, because it is a positive commandment to observe his[96] word as it is written through the hand of Moses: *A prophet from the midst of thee, of thy brethren, like unto me, will the Lord Thy God raise unto thee; unto him shall ye hearken.*[97] This is traditionally interpreted: "In every matter if a prophet tells you to transgress the commands of the Torah, obey him, with the exception of idola-

85 Hebrew: *Beth Din.* Lit: house of judgement or law.

86 First Kings 18, 31-40.

87 Divine punishment by either sudden or premature death, or by inability to procreate.

88 Deut. 12, 13.

89 *Kareth.* see note 130 above.

90 Levit. 17, 4.

91 Lit: to put to rest that which is in their hands.

92 Second Kings 3, 19.

93 Deut. 20, 19.

94 Lit: commanded.

95 The prophet.

96 The prophet.

97 Deut. 18, 15.

try"[98] Thus, for example, if he tells us: "Worship this particular idol for this day only", or "Sacrifice[99] to this particular star at such and such a time", he should be killed and not listened to.

If a man considers in his heart that he is righteous and God-fearing, or if he should be old and advanced in years and say: "Behold, I am old and advanced in years: I have lived so and so many years and have never transgressed therein a single precept of all the commandments (of the Torah). How can I now rise on this day which is the Sabbath and transgress a prohibition, the penalty for which is death by stoning, and go to wage war? I do not have the capabilities to aid or hinder[100], and others may be found in place of me, and there are many people to accomplish this task." Such a man is rebellious and sinning against the words of God, and is culpable of death by heavenly decree[101], because he is transgressing the command of the prophet. He who commanded us to observe the Sabbath is the same One who commanded us to obey the words of the prophet and his decree. Whosoever transgresses his precept is guilty, as we have just mentioned. This is the meaning of the Scriptural verse: *And it shall be that whosoever will not hearken unto My words which he[102] shall speak in My name, I will require it of him.*[103]

In spite of all the preceding, he who ties a permanent knot[104] on that Sabbath day (and thus) performs a task which is not necessary as an aid in the fulfillment of the command which the prophet instructed, is culpable of death by stoning. Should the prophet who commanded us what he did on that Sabbath, whose order we complied with, now claim that the Sabbath limits[105] are two thousand cubits minus one cubit, or two thousand cubits plus one cubit, and if he attributes this statement as having been told to him by way of prophecy and not derived through deduction and reasoning, then we will know that he is a false prophet, and he shall die by strangulation. In this manner should you evaluate everything a prophet may command you, and all that you find in Scriptures regarding a prophet who contradicts any precept of the commandments (of the Torah). This principle is the key to this whole subject. In this alone does a prophet differ from other people in the matter of commandments. However, regarding deduction, reasoning and understanding of commandments, he is as all other Sages who have no prophethood, and they are like him. That is to say, if a prophet should argue an opinion, and similarly if a non-prophet should reason (a differing) opinion, and if the prophet should say "The Holy One Blessed be He told me that my conclusion is the correct one", one should not listen to him. Even if a thousand prophets, all of the stature of Elijah or Elisha would hold one opinion, and one thousand and one Sages would hold the opposite opinion, one must follow the majority[106], and the final ruling is in accordance with the one thousand and one Sages, and not in accordance with the one thousand honored prophets. So too did our Sages state: "By God, even if Joshua, the son of Nun, had told it to me by his own mouth, I would not have accepted it".[107] They further stated: "If Elijah should come and declare that *Halitzah*[108] may be performed with a shoe,[109] he would be obeyed; with a sandal,[110] he would not be obeyed".[111]

Thus, they mean to say that under no circumstances can one add to or delete from a precept through prophecy. So, too, if a prophet testifies that the Holy One Blessed be He told him that the final law concerning that commandment is so and so, and that the opinion of so and so is correct, such a prophet shall be

98 Tractate Sanhedrin 90a.

99 Lit: make incense.

100 Lit: to do good or evil.

101 As opposed to a human court.

102 The prophet.

103 Deut. 18, 19.

104 A prohibited principal labor on the Sabbath. See Tractate Shabbath 111b.

105 Hebrew: *Techum Shabbath*, the area around a town or place within which it is permitted to walk on the Sabbath two thousand cubits in each direction. Based on Exodus 16,29.

106 Exodus 23, 2.

107 Tractate Chullin 124a.

108 The ceremony of taking off the shoe of the brother of a husband who died childless and who does not want to or cannot fulfill the Levirate marriage. Based on Deut. 23, 5-9.

109 Made of soft leather and covering the upper part of the foot.

110 According to Rashi and other commentators this text should read: "were he to declare that *Halitzah* may not be performed with a sandal, he would not be obeyed".

111 Tractate Yebamoth 102a.

killed because he is a false prophet, as we established above. This is because no (new) Torah was given after the first prophet[112], and one may not add to nor delete from it as it is written: *It is not in heaven . . . .*[113]

The Holy One Blessed be He did not permit us to learn from prophets; rather from the Sages, people of deductive reasoning; and knowledgeable views. It is not written "And thou shalt come to the prophet that shall be in those days"; rather *And thou shalt come unto the priests, the Levites and unto the Judge that shall be in those days.*[114] The Sages dwelt at great lengths regarding this subject (of prophetic intervention in *Halachik* matters)[115], and it is correct, (as I have described it).

Maimonides' Introduction to His Commentary on the Mishnah [New Jersey: Ktav Publishers, 1995], pp. 44–63
Reprinted with permission of the publisher

112 Moses.
113 Deut. 30, 12.
114 *Ibid*, 17, 9.
115 Tractate Baba Metzia 59b.

LESSON 6

THE TRUTH OF SINAI

Is there a rational basis to accept that some 3,300 years ago, God revealed Himself to our ancestors at Sinai? Why was Maimonides—a rationalist par excellence—so convinced of the historicity of this event? And in what way is the Jewish claim of divine revelation any different from the many thousands of claims made by various other religious groups?

Evidence for Sinai

Is a Rational Basis Important?

LEARNING EXERCISE 1

Do you find it important to logically prove and establish that God revealed Himself to our ancestors at Sinai? What is your reason?

a. Very important

b. Somewhat important

c. Relatively unimportant

d. Completely unimportant

The Best Evidence

Text 1

Maimonides, Epistle to Yemen

וּדְעוּ אַחֵינוּ בַּבְּרִית הַזֹּאת וּבַסְּבָרָה הַזֹּאת, שֶׁהַדָּבָר הַגָּדוֹל הַזֶּה שֶׁנִּרְאָה בַּמְּצִיאוּת
שֶׁהֵעִיד עָלָיו מִבְחַר כָּל הָעֵדִים שֶׁלֹּא הָיָה מִקֹּדֶם כָּמוֹהוּ וְכֵן לֹא יִהְיֶה אַחֲרָיו כָּמוֹהוּ,
וְהוּא שֶׁתִּשְׁמַע אֻמָּה אַחַת בִּכְלָלָהּ דִּבּוּר הַקָּדוֹשׁ בָּרוּךְ הוּא וְשֶׁתִּרְאֶה כְבוֹדוֹ עַיִן בְּעָיִן.

Remember, my co-religionists, that this great, incomparable and unique historical event, is attested to by the best of evidence. For never before or since has a whole nation witnessed a revelation from God or beheld His splendor.

Rabbi Moshe ben Maimon
(Maimonides, Rambam)
1135–1204

Halachist, philosopher, author, and physician. Maimonides was born in Cordoba, Spain. After the conquest of Cordoba by the Almohads, he fled Spain and eventually settled in Cairo, Egypt. There, he became the leader of the Jewish community and served as court physician to the vizier of Egypt. He is most noted for authoring the *Mishneh Torah*, an encyclopedic arrangement of Jewish law, and for his philosophical work, *Guide for the Perplexed*. His rulings on Jewish law are integral to the formation of halachic consensus.

QUESTION FOR DISCUSSION

What led Maimonides (and others) to the conclusion that the event at Sinai "is attested to by the best of evidence"?

How We Evaluate Truth

LEARNING EXERCISE 2

What standard of evidence do you generally require to regard a historical report as credible?

a. Any measure of evidence

b. Evidence that proves that the event is more likely true than false

c. Evidence that meets the standard of "beyond a reasonable doubt"

d. Evidence that meets the standard of "beyond a shadow of doubt"

e. Other

The Biblical Narrative

LEARNING EXERCISE 3

Read Texts 2a, 2b, and 2c. Underline any word or phrase that indicates—according to the narrative—that God's revelation at Sinai wasn't a private matter limited to Moses or a select few people but was a public display witnessed by the Jewish masses.

Text 2a

Exodus ch. 19–20

בַּחֹדֶשׁ הַשְּׁלִישִׁי לְצֵאת בְּנֵי יִשְׂרָאֵל מֵאֶרֶץ מִצְרָיִם, בַּיּוֹם הַזֶּה בָּאוּ מִדְבַּר סִינָי.

וַיִּסְעוּ מֵרְפִידִים, וַיָּבֹאוּ מִדְבַּר סִינַי, וַיַּחֲנוּ בַּמִּדְבָּר, וַיִּחַן שָׁם יִשְׂרָאֵל נֶגֶד הָהָר . . .

וַיֹּאמֶר ה' אֶל מֹשֶׁה, הִנֵּה אָנֹכִי בָּא אֵלֶיךָ בְּעַב הֶעָנָן, בַּעֲבוּר
יִשְׁמַע הָעָם בְּדַבְּרִי עִמָּךְ, וְגַם בְּךָ יַאֲמִינוּ לְעוֹלָם . . .

וַיֹּאמֶר ה' אֶל מֹשֶׁה לֵךְ אֶל הָעָם וְקִדַּשְׁתָּם הַיּוֹם וּמָחָר, וְכִבְּסוּ שִׂמְלֹתָם.

וְהָיוּ נְכֹנִים לַיּוֹם הַשְּׁלִישִׁי, כִּי בַּיּוֹם הַשְּׁלִשִׁי יֵרֵד ה' לְעֵינֵי כָל הָעָם עַל הַר סִינָי . . .

וַיְהִי בַיּוֹם הַשְּׁלִישִׁי בִּהְיֹת הַבֹּקֶר, וַיְהִי קֹלֹת וּבְרָקִים וְעָנָן כָּבֵד עַל
הָהָר וְקֹל שֹׁפָר חָזָק מְאֹד, וַיֶּחֱרַד כָּל הָעָם אֲשֶׁר בַּמַּחֲנֶה.

וַיּוֹצֵא מֹשֶׁה אֶת הָעָם לִקְרַאת הָאֱלֹקִים מִן הַמַּחֲנֶה, וַיִּתְיַצְּבוּ בְּתַחְתִּית הָהָר . . .

וַיְדַבֵּר אֱלֹקִים אֵת כָּל הַדְּבָרִים הָאֵלֶּה לֵאמֹר.

אָנֹכִי ה' אֱלֹקֶיךָ אֲשֶׁר הוֹצֵאתִיךָ מֵאֶרֶץ מִצְרַיִם מִבֵּית עֲבָדִים . . .

וְכָל הָעָם רֹאִים אֶת הַקּוֹלֹת וְאֶת הַלַּפִּידִם וְאֵת קוֹל הַשֹּׁפָר
וְאֶת הָהָר עָשֵׁן, וַיַּרְא הָעָם וַיָּנֻעוּ, וַיַּעַמְדוּ מֵרָחֹק.

וַיֹּאמְרוּ אֶל מֹשֶׁה, דַּבֵּר אַתָּה עִמָּנוּ וְנִשְׁמָעָה, וְאַל יְדַבֵּר עִמָּנוּ אֱלֹקִים פֶּן נָמוּת . . .

וַיַּעֲמֹד הָעָם מֵרָחֹק, וּמֹשֶׁה נִגַּשׁ אֶל הָעֲרָפֶל אֲשֶׁר שָׁם הָאֱלֹקִים.

וַיֹּאמֶר ה' אֶל מֹשֶׁה כֹּה תֹאמַר אֶל בְּנֵי יִשְׂרָאֵל, אַתֶּם
רְאִיתֶם כִּי מִן הַשָּׁמַיִם דִּבַּרְתִּי עִמָּכֶם.

In the third month of the children of Israel's departure from Egypt, on this day they arrived in the desert of Sinai.

They journeyed from Refidim, and they arrived in the desert of Sinai, and they encamped in the desert, and Israel encamped there opposite the mountain. . . .

God said to Moses, "Behold, I will come to you in the thickness of the cloud, in order that the people hear when I speak to you, and they will also believe in you forever." . . .

God said to Moses, "Go to the people and prepare them today and tomorrow, and they shall wash their garments.

"They shall be prepared for the third day, for on the third day, God will descend before the eyes of all the people upon Mount Sinai."

It came to pass on the third day when it was morning, that there were thunder claps and lightning flashes, and a thick cloud was upon the mountain, and a very powerful blast of a *shofar*, and the entire nation that was in the camp shuddered.

Moses brought the people out toward God from the camp, and they stood at the bottom of the mountain. . . .

God spoke all these words, saying:

"I am the Lord, your God, Who took you out of the land of Egypt, out of the house of bondage. . . ."

All the people saw the voices and the torches, the sound of the *shofar*, and the smoking mountain, the people saw and trembled, and they stood from afar.

They said to Moses, "You speak with us, and we will hear, but let God not speak with us lest we die." . . .

The people remained far off, and Moses drew near to the opaque darkness, where God was.

God said to Moses, "So shall you say to the children of Israel, 'You have seen that from the heavens I have spoken with you. . . .'"

Text 2b

Deuteronomy 4:9–36

רַק הִשָּׁמֶר לְךָ וּשְׁמֹר נַפְשְׁךָ מְאֹד, פֶּן תִּשְׁכַּח אֶת הַדְּבָרִים אֲשֶׁר רָאוּ עֵינֶיךָ, וּפֶן יָסוּרוּ מִלְּבָבְךָ כֹּל יְמֵי חַיֶּיךָ, וְהוֹדַעְתָּם לְבָנֶיךָ וְלִבְנֵי בָנֶיךָ.

יוֹם אֲשֶׁר עָמַדְתָּ לִפְנֵי ה' אֱלֹקֶיךָ בְּחֹרֵב, בֶּאֱמֹר ה' אֵלַי, הַקְהֶל לִי אֶת הָעָם וְאַשְׁמִעֵם אֶת דְּבָרָי, אֲשֶׁר יִלְמְדוּן לְיִרְאָה אֹתִי כָּל הַיָּמִים אֲשֶׁר הֵם חַיִּים עַל הָאֲדָמָה, וְאֶת בְּנֵיהֶם יְלַמֵּדוּן.

וַתִּקְרְבוּן וַתַּעַמְדוּן תַּחַת הָהָר, וְהָהָר בֹּעֵר בָּאֵשׁ עַד לֵב הַשָּׁמַיִם חֹשֶׁךְ עָנָן וַעֲרָפֶל.

וַיְדַבֵּר ה' אֲלֵיכֶם מִתּוֹךְ הָאֵשׁ, קוֹל דְּבָרִים אַתֶּם שֹׁמְעִים וּתְמוּנָה אֵינְכֶם רֹאִים זוּלָתִי קוֹל.

וַיַּגֵּד לָכֶם אֶת בְּרִיתוֹ אֲשֶׁר צִוָּה אֶתְכֶם לַעֲשׂוֹת עֲשֶׂרֶת הַדְּבָרִים, וַיִּכְתְּבֵם עַל שְׁנֵי לֻחוֹת אֲבָנִים . . .

הֲשָׁמַע עָם קוֹל אֱלֹקִים מְדַבֵּר מִתּוֹךְ הָאֵשׁ כַּאֲשֶׁר שָׁמַעְתָּ אַתָּה וַיֶּחִי . . .

אַתָּה הָרְאֵתָ לָדַעַת כִּי ה' הוּא הָאֱלֹקִים אֵין עוֹד מִלְּבַדּוֹ.

מִן הַשָּׁמַיִם הִשְׁמִיעֲךָ אֶת קֹלוֹ לְיַסְּרֶךָּ, וְעַל הָאָרֶץ הֶרְאֲךָ אֶת אִשּׁוֹ הַגְּדוֹלָה, וּדְבָרָיו שָׁמַעְתָּ מִתּוֹךְ הָאֵשׁ.

But beware and watch yourself very well, lest you forget the things that your eyes saw and lest these things depart from your heart all the days of your life. Be sure to make them known to your children and to your children's children.

[Remember] the day you stood before the Lord your God at Horeb, when God said to me, "Assemble the people for Me, and I will let them hear My words, that they may learn to revere Me all the days that they live on the earth, and that they may teach their children."

You approached and stood at the foot of the mountain, and the mountain burned with fire up to the midst of the heavens, with darkness, a cloud, and opaque darkness.

God spoke to you out of the midst of the fire; you heard the sound of the words, but saw no image, just a voice.

He told you His covenant, which He commanded you to do, the Ten Commandments, and He inscribed them on two stone tablets. . . .

Did ever a people hear God's voice speaking out of the midst of the fire, as you have heard, and live? . . .

You have been shown, in order to know that the Lord is God; there is none else besides Him.

From the heavens, He let you hear His voice to instruct you, and upon the earth He showed you His great fire, and you heard His words out of the midst of the fire.

Text 2c

Deuteronomy 5:4–23

פָּנִים בְּפָנִים דִּבֶּר ה' עִמָּכֶם בָּהָר מִתּוֹךְ הָאֵשׁ . . .

אֶת הַדְּבָרִים הָאֵלֶּה דִּבֶּר ה' אֶל כָּל קְהַלְכֶם בָּהָר מִתּוֹךְ הָאֵשׁ הֶעָנָן וְהָעֲרָפֶל
קוֹל גָּדוֹל וְלֹא יָסָף, וַיִּכְתְּבֵם עַל שְׁנֵי לֻחֹת אֲבָנִים וַיִּתְּנֵם אֵלָי.

וַיְהִי כְּשָׁמְעֲכֶם אֶת הַקּוֹל מִתּוֹךְ הַחֹשֶׁךְ וְהָהָר בֹּעֵר בָּאֵשׁ,
וַתִּקְרְבוּן אֵלַי כָּל רָאשֵׁי שִׁבְטֵיכֶם וְזִקְנֵיכֶם.

וַתֹּאמְרוּ הֵן הֶרְאָנוּ ה' אֱלֹקֵינוּ אֶת כְּבֹדוֹ וְאֶת גָּדְלוֹ וְאֶת קֹלוֹ שָׁמַעְנוּ
מִתּוֹךְ הָאֵשׁ, הַיּוֹם הַזֶּה רָאִינוּ כִּי יְדַבֵּר אֱלֹקִים אֶת הָאָדָם וָחָי.

וְעַתָּה לָמָּה נָמוּת כִּי תֹאכְלֵנוּ הָאֵשׁ הַגְּדֹלָה הַזֹּאת אִם יֹסְפִים
אֲנַחְנוּ לִשְׁמֹעַ אֶת קוֹל ה' אֱלֹקֵינוּ עוֹד וָמָתְנוּ.

כִּי מִי כָל בָּשָׂר אֲשֶׁר שָׁמַע קוֹל אֱלֹקִים חַיִּים מְדַבֵּר מִתּוֹךְ הָאֵשׁ כָּמֹנוּ וַיֶּחִי.

Face to face, God spoke with you at the mountain out of the midst of the fire.

God spoke these words to your entire assembly at the mountain out of the midst of the fire, the cloud, and the opaque darkness, with a great voice, which did not cease. And He inscribed them on two stone tablets and gave them to me.

When you heard the voice from the midst of the darkness, and the mountain was burning with fire, you approached me, all the heads of your tribes and your elders.

You said, "Behold, God, has shown us His glory and His greatness, and we heard His voice from the midst of the fire; we saw this day that God speaks with man, yet [man] remains alive.

"So now, why should we die? For this great fire will consume us; we will die if we continue to hear the voice of God.

"For who is there of all flesh who heard the voice of the living God speaking from the midst of the fire, as we have, and lived?"

Text 3

Exodus 12:37

וַיִּסְעוּ בְנֵי יִשְׂרָאֵל מֵרַעְמְסֵס סֻכֹּתָה, כְּשֵׁשׁ מֵאוֹת אֶלֶף רַגְלִי הַגְּבָרִים לְבַד מִטָּף.

The children of Israel traveled from Ramses toward Sukot; about 600,000 adult males on foot, besides the young children.

How Did It All Start?

Present Theory and Past Theory

LEARNING EXERCISE 4

Rate the two theories, with 1 indicating "very weak" and "highly unlikely," and 5 indicating "very compelling" and "very likely."

Present Theory					Past Theory				
1	2	3	4	5	1	2	3	4	5

Shortcomings of Past Theory

Text 4

Rabbi Dovid Gottlieb, PhD, *Living Up to the Truth*, p. 32

Imagine someone making up the story and trying to sell it. He is going to come to a group of people and he is going to tell them that sometime in the past their ancestors stood at a mountain and heard G-d speak. He is not talking about people in China or Tibet. He is talking about the ancestors of his audience. He is claiming that G-d revealed Himself to all of their ancestors simultaneously and by so doing founded a new religion.

Rabbi Dovid Gottlieb, PhD

Author and lecturer. Rabbi Gottlieb received his PhD in mathematical logic at Brandeis University and went on to become professor of philosophy at Johns Hopkins University. Today he is a senior faculty member at Ohr Somayach in Jerusalem. He is the author of *The Informed Soul* and *Living Up to the Truth*.

What is the question with which the audience will confront him? The obvious question is: If this happened to our ancestors, how is it that no one knows about it but you? What happened to the memory of that event? Everybody simply forgot it? They were more interested in the soccer scores? No one told us about it? The whole religion just disappeared?

It is simply not credible to tell an entire nation that their collective ancestors witnessed such an earth-shattering event and that it was forgotten. It would be impossible to explain why the memory of the event disappeared. . . . The person inventing the story and trying to sell it will never succeed.

Text 5

Rabbi Lawrence Kelemen, in Doron Kornbluth, ed., *Jewish Matters: A Pocketbook of Knowledge and Inspiration* [Brooklyn, N.Y.: Targum/Feldheim, 1990], pp. 141–142

Rabbi Lawrence Kelemen

Educator, author, and lecturer. Rabbi Kelemen is a professor of education at Neve Yerushalayim College of Jewish Studies for Women in Jerusalem, where he teaches modern and medieval philosophy. He is the author of *Permission to Believe* and *Permission to Receive.*

A major problem with this theory is we've never heard of Fred or his heroic resurrection of Judaism. Certainly one of the most significant events in Jewish history would have been the fumble, when world Jewry forgot they were the three million prophets, and the recovery, when Fred reminded the Jews about the national prophecy at Mount Sinai. Yet in an otherwise comprehensive Jewish history we find no mention of such a claim.

Jewish texts describe myriad historical crises and the heroes who assisted during these difficult times. We know that Moses brought the Torah down from Mount Sinai,

Joshua first brought the Jews into the Land of Israel, David slew Goliath, Solomon built the Temple in Jerusalem, and Ezra brought the Jews back to the Land of Israel after the Babylonian exile. We know that Rabbi Judah the Prince compiled the Mishnah and that Ravina and Rav Ashi compiled the Talmud. We know about Maimonides, Nachmanides, and hundreds of other stars of medieval Jewry and what their respective contributions were. We possess detailed records about every great Jewish personality, except for one.

We don't have any mention of the man who reminded Jewry that they were the only people in human history ever to experience national prophecy, and we don't have any record of the amnesia Fred rescued them from.

Until two hundred years ago . . . every Jew and member of a Jewish breakaway group (like the Christians, Sadducees, and Karaites) affirmed that ancient Jewry, *their direct ancestors,* had experienced national prophecy at Mount Sinai. . . . Not a single ancient or contemporary individual or religious community has any tradition about the man who should have been the second greatest hero of Jewish history: Fred. Why?

Snowball Theory

Text 6a

Rabbi Lawrence Keleman, ibid., p. 138

The beginnings of all ancient and modern religions have a common thread: one or two people have a revelation and persuade others to follow.

Thus, for example, Buddhist writings tell us that Prince Siddhartha Gautama launched Buddhism after his solitary ascendance through the eight stages of Transic insight; Islamic texts tell us that Muhammad founded Islam following the first of many personal, prophetic experiences; Christian writings reveal that Paul first met Jesus, converted to Christianity, and spread the faith more than three decades after Jesus' death; Joseph Smith, Jr., and his partner, Oliver Cowdery, launched the Church of Jesus Christ of Latter-Day Saints (the Mormon church) after the two men were visited by angels and long-dead disciples of Jesus; and Sun Myung Moon launched the Unification Church after privately receiving direct orders to do so from Jesus himself. The beginnings of Children of God, Christian Science, Eckankar, Elan Vital, I AM, and Theosophy—in fact, the beginnings of all world religions—are equally unverifiable.

Never does a large, clearly identifiable group of people experience prophecy and live to tell others about it. Moreover, in a handful of cases wherein large groups of people supposedly witnessed miracles, rarely are these witnesses named or identified in any way that would allow for verification; and in the very exceptional cases involving clearly identified groups of witnesses, never more than one or two of the religion's current adherents claim to have met or descended directly from the named witnesses.

In all these cases, the religion's credibility rests on the credibility of its one or two founders. While it is certainly possible that the beginnings claimed by any of the thousands of sects and cults included in the world's more than three hundred major religious traditions could be true, it is easy to imagine how charismatic charlatans could have launched any of these movements.

The one known exception to this rule is Judaism.

Text 6b

Rabbi Lawrence Kelemen, *Permission to Receive: Four Rational Approaches to the Torah's Divine Origin* [Brooklyn, N.Y.: Targum/Feldheim, 1996], p. 69

Some Indian groups once possessed an oral tradition that the Hindu god Krishna addressed the millions of warriors who participated in the battle described in the *Bhagavad Gita* [a basic Hindu text]. This is not a challenge to our observations, however, since the same oral tradition also reports that all those who heard Krishna speak died in the battle. No witnesses survived to testify to the experience, and the story of this mass prophecy is only known because the god revealed it to an unnamed *individual* later in history.

Text 7

Rabbi Berel Bell, *From Sinai to Cyberspace*, [Rohr Jewish Learning Institute, Brooklyn, N.Y.: 2006], Lesson 8

Rabbi Berel Bell

Rabbinical judge and pedagogue. Rabbi Bell is the founding dean of Bais Chaya Mushka Seminary in Montreal and is a member of the Rabbinical Court of Montreal. He is a sought-after educational consultant and the author of the JLI course *From Sinai to Cyberspace: How Ancient Wisdom Guides a Modern World.*

A basic assumption of scientific method is that results are replicable. If something happens naturally once, we expect that it will happen more than once. Although history is not science, everyone knows that "history repeats itself": not in every last detail, but at least in general.

Thousands of religions have existed in the world. Nobody has documented a single one that has the same claim as Judaism. If the story evolved naturally, or was perpetrated as a hoax, why has it not happened more than once? And since it hasn't, is it irrational to believe in Sinai? Who is relying on blind faith: the one who believes in the story as written, or the one that claims—without any historical support—that it was a result of natural processes, but only happened one time, to one group, in all of recorded history?

And this simple objection will apply to any "natural" explanation that anyone will ever propose to discredit the authenticity of the Sinai revelation. If it is "natural," then why did it happen only once in recorded history?

Text 8

Deuteronomy 4:32–33

כִּי שְׁאַל נָא לְיָמִים רִאשֹׁנִים אֲשֶׁר הָיוּ לְפָנֶיךָ לְמִן הַיּוֹם אֲשֶׁר
בָּרָא אֱלֹקִים אָדָם עַל הָאָרֶץ וּלְמִקְצֵה הַשָּׁמַיִם וְעַד קְצֵה
הַשָּׁמָיִם, הֲנִהְיָה כַּדָּבָר הַגָּדוֹל הַזֶּה אוֹ הֲנִשְׁמַע כָּמֹהוּ.

הֲשָׁמַע עָם קוֹל אֱלֹקִים מְדַבֵּר מִתּוֹךְ הָאֵשׁ כַּאֲשֶׁר שָׁמַעְתָּ אַתָּה וַיֶּחִי.

For ask now regarding the early days that were before you, since the day that God created man upon the earth, and from one end of the heavens to the other end of the heavens, whether there was anything like this great thing, or was the likes of it heard?

Did ever a people hear God's voice speaking out of the midst of the fire, as you have heard, and live?

Lesson Conclusion

Text 9

The Lubavitcher Rebbe, Rabbi Menachem Mendel Schneerson, English Correspondence (1952)

Rabbi Menachem Mendel Schneerson
1902–1994

The towering Jewish leader of the 20th century, known as "the Lubavitcher Rebbe," or simply as "the Rebbe." Born in southern Ukraine, the Rebbe escaped Nazi-occupied Europe, arriving in the U.S. in June 1941. The Rebbe inspired and guided the revival of traditional Judaism after the European devastation, impacting virtually every Jewish community the world over. The Rebbe often emphasized that the performance of just one additional good deed could usher in the era of Mashiach. The Rebbe's scholarly talks and writings have been printed in more than 200 volumes.

The Divine Revelation at Mount Sinai was a fact witnessed by millions of people, all of whom reported it to its minutest detail, accurately, for the whole people of Israel stood at Mount Sinai and witnessed it.

We know that this is a fact because millions of Jews in our day accept it as such, because they received it as such from their own parents, and these millions in turn received the evidence from the previous generation, and so on, in an uninterrupted chain of transmitted evidence from millions to millions of witnesses, generation after generation, back to the original millions of witnesses who saw the event with their own eyes.

Among these original witnesses there were many who were initiated in the sciences of those days (viz. Egypt), many achievements of which are still baffling nowadays; among them were philosophers and thinkers, as well as ignorant and uneducated persons, women and children of all ages. Yet all of them reported the event and phenomena connected with it without contradiction to one another.

Such a fact is certainly indisputable. I do not believe that there is another fact which can match it for evidence and accuracy.

To deny such a fact is anything but scientific; it is the very opposite of science.

Parenthetically, it is unfortunate that this basic difference between the Jewish religion and those of others is so little known, for the Jewish religion is the only one that is not based on a single founder or a few, but is based on the Divine Revelation witnessed by all the people, numbering several millions.

This answers also . . . 's statement that "the acceptance of the Torah as being the only truth is dangerous" since "its authors were only men . . . and as men they could not have been infallible."

Jews accept the Torah precisely because it was given by G-d, not by man, and it was given in the presence of millions of people who had seen it and heard it with their own eyes and ears. That is why the Torah is the absolute truth, for G-d is absolute.

Key Points

TORAH Café™

Continue the JLI Learning Experience!

Visit www.TorahCafe.com/go/JD6

for a video lecture(s) related to the theme of this lesson.

1. For thousands of years, our people have believed that God revealed Himself to our ancestors and addressed them at Mount Sinai. Maimonides asserts that the historicity of this event is supported by "the best possible evidence."

2. The Bible repeatedly highlights that all the Jews who left Egypt, some three million strong, were present at Sinai and heard God speak.

3. It is highly implausible that someone could falsely convince an entire nation that they themselves experienced a divine revelation.

4. It is also unreasonable to assume that someone could falsely persuade an entire nation that all their ancestors experienced a divine revelation. The listeners would have refused to accept this, asserting that if it were true, they certainly would have heard of this from their parents.

5. If someone single-handedly "reminded" the Jewish people of the Sinai event, this person would be considered a Jewish super-hero and would be duly recognized in the record of Jewish history. The absence of such a figure negates the possibility of this having occurred.

6. With the singular exception of Judaism, all religions begin with a single person or a small group claiming to have experienced a vision. These claims are conveniently unfalsifiable—but also unverifiable. The fact that no other religious group lays claim to a mass revelation highlights the uniqueness of the Jewish faith.

7. It is unsound to hypothesize that the Sinai narrative began as a story of a revelation to a few that then snowballed into a story of mass revelation. If this were a possibility, it would have been replicated by others.

ADDITIONAL READINGS

DEAD SEA SCROLLS SHED NEW LIGHT

BY LAWRENCE SCHIFFMAN, PhD

The central problem facing historians of Judaism in ancient times is understanding how the Judaism we see at the end of the biblical period, circa 400 B.C.E., became the Judaism we see in the *Mishnah* (*Talmud*), edited c. 200 C.E., some six centuries later. For the early part of this period up to the Roman conquest of 63 B.C.E. and the time of Hillel and Shammai afterwards, we have few sources. Some information can be gleaned from the books of the Maccabees, Josephus, and a variety of apocryphal texts and from the small amount of material pertaining to this period preserved in rabbinic texts. Yet these sources afford us little help in our attempt to trace the historical continuity of Judaism from the Tanach, the Biblical era, to the *Mishnah*. For historians, this constitutes a central historical problem.

One of the essential beliefs of the traditional Jew is the continuity of the Jewish tradition. This continuity underlies the entire structure of rabbinic authority which provides the basis in turn for the obligation to observe not only the *Torah Shebichtav* (Written Law), but the *Torah Shebaal Peh* (Oral Law) as well. This belief does not imply that nothing has changed. We recognize, in varying degrees, that developments have taken place. These are described in the *Mishnah* and the *Talmud* at length. We believe that these developments are legitimate since they do not break the continuity of the tradition or the oral Torah, and since the Torah itself provides the basis for the authority of the Sages to sanction such developments as necessary to strengthen Torah practice in times of crisis, to make the transition from the period of prophecy to the cessation of prophecy, and later to compensate for the destruction of the Temple and the priestly establishment.

Our tradition has always felt the need to assert its own continuity. The most significant examples of this phenomenon are: The chain of tradition in the *Mishnah* (Avot 1:2–2:2), which traces the authority of the oral Torah from Moshe to the son of the *Mishnah's* redactor (collector and editor), Rabbi Yehudah HaNasi; and its parital parallel in the list of the *zugot* (pairs of leaders) who occupied the role of *nasi* (patriarch) and *av bet din* (head of the court) in the Hasmonean and early Roman periods in Jewish history, as found in the *Mishnah* (Hagigah 2:2)

In these two lists, it is fair to say that the greatest emphasis is on that part of the Greco-Roman period most problematical in regard to the claim of continuity. From the end of the Bible through the early Hellenistic period we know from archaeological and literary evidence that little changed in the ancestral way of life of the Jews. That Judaism with which the Jews had been imbued by Ezra, Nehemiah and the last of the prophets served as the basis of their lives, despite Hellenistic influence in their material culture. This changed, of course, with the Hellenistic reform of 175 B.C.E.: the attempt of a group of Hellenizing Jews to assimilate Judaism into the Hellenistic cults and Greek way of life. It is therefore to be expected that even in the aftermath of the Maccabean revolt of 168–164 B.C.E., and the establishment of the Hasmonean dynasty by Jonathan, brother of Judah the Maccabee, in 152 B.C.E., we enter into a period of profound division and sectarianism. This division and sectarianism lasts until the destruction of the

Lawrence H. Schiffman, PhD. Noted historian and authority on the Dead Sea Scrolls. Schiffman is Professor of Hebrew and Judaic Studies at New York University and director of the Global Institute for Advanced Research in Jewish Studies. He is a specialist in the Dead Sea Scrolls, Judaism in late antiquity, the history of Jewish law and Talmudic literature. He has authored many books and publications, and he is co-editor of the *Encyclopedia of the Dead Sea Scrolls*.

Temple in 70 C.E. Our Sages teach us that this disunity was among the main causes of the ultimate failure of the Maccabean revolt.

However, in the last years before the revolt (second half of the first century B.C.E.) against Rome, in the time of Hillel and Shammai and their students, we again find a trend toward communal unity as the Pharisaic-Rabbinic tradition gained the near universal acceptance of the Jewish people.

Accordingly, the years from the Maccabean revolt until the period of Hillel and Shammai, those emphasized in the chains of tradition we mentioned above, are precisely the years in which the continuity of our tradition was most under threat, and for later generations, most difficult to prove historically. Further, even the scant evidence about this period in later Rabbinic sources tell us little about the role of the Pharisees, the predecessors of the Talmudic Rabbis, and even from these sources it was possible for many modern historians to minimize this role and to consign it to the pious retrojections of later generations. Josephus helped little in this regard, partly because his information is so brief, and partly because we lacked a sufficient framework in which to evaluate his accounts.

All this was so until the discovery of the manuscripts of the Cairo Genizah at the end of the last century. Among the many texts and fragments of texts found there was one, called "Fragments of a Zadokite Work" or, alternatively, the "Damascus Covenant," which would be found later at Qumran among the Dead Sea Scrolls.

This text contained two parts: an admonition; and a series of collections of laws on specific topics, such as the Sabbath, courts and testimony, ritual purity and impurity, oaths and vows, and relations with non-Jews. These laws responded to the same issues that Mishnaic law discussed, and this fact led some scholars to see the material, falsely we now know, as proto-Pharisaic. A fierce debate ensued about the dating and provenance of this text, and a consensus emerged which dated the text to precisely our period of uncertainty, the mid-second century B.C.E. to the first century C.E.

Here, at last, was a non-Rabbinic text which cast some light on the continuity of the Rabbinic tradition. This text already indicated a few significant facts. First, this document straightforwardly argued against the Pharisaic approach, thereby illuminating it. We learned that the Pharisees (not named explicitly) were *bonei hachayitz* ("the builders of the wall" cf. Ezekiel 13:10), clearly a reference to their making "fences" around the Torah by adding prohibitions to keep us away from transgression. We also encounter the designation of the Pharisees as *dorshei chalakot* (literally, "seekers of smooth things," cf. Isaiah 30:10), clearly aimed at claiming that the laws (halachot) of the Pharisees are false. In addition, from specific laws in which the sect which authored this document argued against Pharisaic rulings, we can prove that much of the infrastructure of the Mishnaic Halachah was already in place during this period.

Yet the opportunity to gain a much more complete picture of the Judaism of the Hasmonean and early Roman periods came to the fore with the discovery of the Dead Sea Scrolls over the years 1946–56. During this period, a steady stream of texts was unearthed in the Judean desert (mostly by Bedouin and, to a much lesser extent, by archaeologists) which has revolutionized our understanding of this period. While recent controversy has highlighted the unpublished material, the documents already available and those unpublished documents for which extensive information is known, allow us to draw many conclusions regarding the Pharisaic predecessors of the Rabbis.

Indeed, with the collection now before us, we have a library of documents from the second Temple period. We now know that these documents were collected by the members of a sect which most scholars identify as the Essenes described by the Jewish philosopher Philo of Alexandria (c.20 B.C.E.–50 C.E.), the historian Josephus (c.38–100 C.E.), and some classical authors. We remain uncertain of this identification; however, choosing to postpone judgment until the entire collection has been adequately studied. In any case, this sect occupied a building complex at Qumran, on the western shore of the Dead Sea, in exactly the period we are discussing, from after c. 134 B.C.E. through 68 C.E., just after the start of the Great Revolt against Rome of 66–73 B.C.E.

In the collection of this sect were texts which represented not only its own views, but those of a variety of circles which this group regarded as its predecessors, or which it felt were sufficiently close to it to require inclusion of their books. Other manuscripts may have been accumulated for not specific reason at all. Nonetheless, from comparison of these works with the accounts of already known sources, it is safe to conclude that these documents represent a combination of the works of the Qumran sect itself, the biblical heritage of all Israel, and the wide variety of books which existed in Second temple times among various group of Jews.

It is this realization which has radically shifted the focus of Qumran research, in the hands of a new generation of scholars, in the last decade. We now seek to establish, through the study of these texts, the full history of Judaism in this period, not simply the teachings and organizational patterns of a small group of sectarians who moved to the Dead Sea.

This means that the value of the scrolls for learning about the Pharisees and the Torah is now greatly increased, despite the fact that we can expect to find no primary sources for the Pharisees, who eschewed the writing of books of Jewish law or lore, nonetheless, the anti-pharisaic polemics and historical allusions in these texts are more than enough to allow us to reconstruct the continuity of Pharisaic Rabbinic teachings in this period and to demonstrate the dominant role of the Pharisees in the affairs of the Temple and the nation for most of the period. Further, we will see that the validity of later Rabbinic traditions can be proven effectively from the Dead Sea manuscripts.

Foremost in establishing these facts is a still unpublished "halachic letter" entitled "Miktzat Maaseh HaTorah" ("Some Legal Rulings pertaining to the Torah"). This text is a foundation document of the sect that collected the manuscripts. The text purports to be a letter from the founders of the sect to the Jerusalem establishment, setting forth the reasons for the schism and enumerating some twenty-two halachot (laws) in which the authors differed with those in control of the Temple. We have determined that the laws of the authors are those of the Tzedukim (Sadducees), the priestly opponents of the Pharisees. The text makes explicit reference to the laws we recognize as Pharisaic and Rabbinic. We can demonstrate that the "letter" is to be dated to shortly after the Hasmonean takeover of the High Priesthood and the Temple. The authors were Sadducean priests unwilling to continue to serve under the Hasmoneans who were following the legal rulings of the Pharisees. Hence, we can now prove Pharisaic dominance for the years immediately after the establishment of the dynasty by Jonathan in 152 B.C.E.

Perhaps of more importance are the twenty-two laws themselves. Among them are specific cases in which the opponents of the sect take positions identified in Rabbinic sources as Pharisaic, and others in which their positions appear either anonymously in Mishnaic texts, or attributed to named authorities. Four out of five Pharisee - Sadducee disputes at the end of the *Mishnah* Yadayim (4:6–8) appear here. The upshot is that we can show from this text, and, I might add, from subtle polemics in the Temple Scroll as well, that much of the content of Mishnaic Halachah was in existence at this time, and that it—not Sadducee law—was practiced in the Temple at this time.

From the material in the Zadokite Fragments we mentioned above, of which some ten partial manuscripts were found at Qumran, we can show further evidence for the period of c.134 B.C.E. until the falling out the Hasmoneans had with the Pharisees. This dispute is documented in the well-known story of the banquet found in the *Talmud* (Kiddushin 66a) and in Josephus. Later, there was full-scale conflict between Alexander Yannai and the Pharisees. Josephus tells the story of how in 88 B.C.E. the Pharisees made common cause with the Seleucid Demetrius III against Yannai. Eventually there was a massacre of Jews by the Seleucids and the Pharisees had to change sides, siding with Yannai to rid the country of the foreign armies they had invited in. This story is fully accounted in the Qumran text "Pesher

Nachum," but actually an expression of sectarian ideology. From this document we learn also of the conflict with Yannai and his eventual reconciliation with the Pharisees. This reconciliation paved the way for the reentry of the Pharisees into a dominant role in the last days of Yannai and during the reign of his widow Shlomtzion (Salome Alexandra 76–67 B.C.E.). Again, the scrolls support the dominant role of the Pharisees.

This text goes one step further. Like the "Zadokite Fragments," it proves the existence of Pharisaic halachot and calls the Pharisee *"dorshei chalakot."* Yet, in addition, it refers to the sect's Pharisaic opponents with the words, *"asher betalmud shekaram"* ("in whose Talmud is their falsehood"). Needless to say, they are not referring to the texts we know of as the *Talmud*, edited much later in the Land of Israel and in Babylonia. Here the use of "talmud" is to refer to the way of study which the Pharisaic sages used and which the Rabbis would inherit from them, the dialectic approach to interpreting traditions. This method, the basis of the tannaitic halachic Midrashim when practiced on the Bible, and of the Gemara when practiced on the *Mishnah*, is proven by the scrolls to have existed in this period.

It is not far from the materials we have been surveying here, to the days of the teachers of Hillel and Shammai, as their teachers Shemaiah and Avtalyon played roles in the affairs of the nation in the early years of Herod when he was still only a regional governor (c. 45–40 B.C.E.). With the material in the scrolls, of which we have discussed only a small part, we have spanned the years for which we were seeking historical proof outside the Rabbinic corpus for the dominance of Pharisaic tradition in the affairs of the Jewish people and its Temple worship. We have found that much of the content of Rabbinic Judaism can be shown to exist as early as the Hasmonean and early Roman periods. It was this period which we identified as particularly problematic in this regard. We noted that to the Rabbis there was a particular need to claim such continuity, but that even they lacked extensive evidence in their corpus of oral traditions, since little survived in the academies from this period.

Out of the caves of Qumran have come materials which allow us to prove this continuity in its general outlines. As we learn more and more from the scrolls about the other forms of Judaism which existed in this period such as Sadduceeism, apocalyptic messianism, and Essenism, we will see continuing proof of the view of the Rabbis that this was period of sectarianism. Yet we will know that throughout this period the Pharisaic tradition continued to develop and play a leading role. We will have uncovered evidence for a stage in the history of our tradition and our people as a whole.

Our century has merited the opportunity of unparalleled research in Jewish history. We have recovered the Cairo Genizah, which has brought to life the previously dark ages of the geonic period and which has given us outstanding manuscript evidence for Rabbinic and medieval Jewish literature. In Israel, archaeologists continue to unearth the secrets of biblical, Second Temple and Talmudic history. We have discovered the Dead Sea Scrolls, as well as the documents from Masada and the Bar Kochba letters. Recently, the great collections of Hebrew manuscripts and Jewish archives of Eastern Europe have opened up to us. Let us take to heart the words of the Torah (Devarim 32:7): "Remember the days of old, study the years of past generations," and we will find that the more we learn about our past, the better we are able to meet the challenges of the present and future.

"From the Caves of Qumran: New Light on the History of Rabbinic Judaism from the Dead Sea Scrolls," *Jewish Action*, Spring 5752/1992, pp. 25–27

HOW DO WE KNOW THAT WE HEARD G-D AT SINAI?

BY RABBI TZVI FREEMAN

To our enlightened Master and Teacher, the Grand Rabbi of Guadalajara, may he live many years of inner peace and transcendental serenity.

Forgive our ignorance this one more time, you who know the hiding place of all hidden things! Guide us tiny mice through the maze of confusion, oh solver of all puzzles! Explain to us how we can market to the general public this Great and Awesome Event upon which the foundations of our faith are built, this idea of Mass Revelation at Sinai.

Explain to us the evidence that makes it impossible to deny that before three thousand years a heavenly voice boomed down upon the crowd, saying, "I'm the only G-d around here, so you better not have any others. And don't let me catch any one of you lying, stealing, killing, coveting or being disrespectful to your Mom and Dad!"

And then open our eyes and let us know the truth of all truths, oh truthful and authentic sage: If such evidence is so clear and absolute, then why, we beseech you, have the tenured thinkers and scribes of many academic institutions rejected it so?

Response:

Certainly, as salted surfers of the Web, you are intimately familiar with conspiracy. You have heard that no man ever landed on the moon—it was all filmed in Arizona. Continental drift was initiated in the 50's by the Pentagon to push Russia off the end of the earth. Prozac was developed by AT&T in an attempt to mold human personality to UNIX protocol. Bill Gates owns the Vatican and the Illuminati own Bill Gates. Kellogg's owns the Illuminati and you don't want to know what's in those golden flakes. Time-Warner/AOL is a front for an international association of nuns committed to directing asteroids at California. Asteroids are communist sputniks. In case you have been deluded by the propaganda that communism is dead, Bill Clinton is a communist agent and Santa Claus as well.

Conspiracies are very popular, psychologists say, because they provide simple explanations for a very complex world. But they are absurd. Because, as we all know from Poor Richard's Almanac, three people can keep a secret if two of them are dead.

The FBI, KGB, FDA, Microsoft, Vatican, Franciscan nunnery of Homeville, Tennessee—all are filled with competitive, fumbling, in-fighting human beings just like you and I (okay, maybe the nuns are a little more friendly than the guys at Microsoft. But then, so is the KGB). None of them could keep a conspiracy going longer than a week without wrangling over who is in charge, who messed up, who gets the goods, who gets the blame—and all those other fun, human games that break up rock bands, countries and corporations every day.

If the FBI would attempt a conspiracy, some branch of the CIA would get all upset because conspiracies are their department and who do those glorified police officers think they are anyway? If the commies or any other enterprising group would find a way to take over the world, Microsoft would buy them out in a snap. Everybody knows what Microsoft is up to—because everybody else invented all of it. And hey, they can't even conspire to make their OS work consistently.

The greatest conspiracy theory of all time is materialism. The idea that some 10^{80} particles of matter conspire every day to bring us the orderly form of

Rabbi Tzvi Freeman (1955–) Rabbi, computer scientist, and writer. A published expert, consultant, and lecturer in the field of educational technology, Rabbi Freeman held posts at the University of British Columbia and the Digipen School of Computer Gaming. Rabbi Freeman is the author of *Bringing Heaven Down to Earth* and *Men, Women & Kabbalah*. He is a senior editor at Chabad.org.

this world before us. Everybody knows that particles can't agree on anything.

The second greatest conspiracy theory is that the Jews invented the Torah. That millions of Jews over thousands of years could conspire to agree on a single version of a national event that never happened. If nobody else can conspire on anything for more than a week, whoever imagined that Jewish people could get a conspiracy off the ground was totally off his rocker? (Actually, we've tried it. One look at Israeli politics will tell you just how hopeless that was.)

About History

Let's examine what the study of history is. Most of us will say that history is the study of what happened. That's bunk. We barely know what's happening right now. How does anybody know what happened in the past? And what defines what really happened?

Perhaps you know the story of one great Renaissance man, Sir Francis Bacon. Sitting in his room above the tavern, he thought, "I have written on philosophy, science and mathematics. Now I will take on history." As he set his pen to the page, Sir Francis glanced out his window and observed a commotion outside. Then he went downstairs to the tavern, where he heard no less than six highly divergent versions of what had occurred. Sir Francis went back upstairs and tore up what he had written so far. He never wrote a book on history.

I think most historians will agree that history as it is practiced in academic circles can be defined as follows: The search for the most likely sequence of events to explain whatever remnants have endured till today.

Following this paradigm, let us examine our case. The evidence is as follows: Universally, there is a single account of how the Jewish people received the Torah. It states that on the sixth day of the third month of the year 2448 from Creation, an entire nation full of dissidents and skeptics gathered at the foot of a mountain in the Sinai Desert and witnessed how G-d spoke with Moses. Rather overwhelmed by the experience, they asked Moses to kindly fetch all the details of what exactly G-d would like from them and report on it. Which he did, over a period of forty years wandering in the desert. Moses also charged the people to keep multiple copies of the written record, which they did, and so we have many copies of that record to this day.

Here is the proposed most likely explanation of the existence of this record: Someone made up the whole story. Someone else later wrote it down. A third individual put it together with other manuscripts, and the entire nation conspired to agree that it had actually happened. They agreed to agree on only one version of how it had happened, eradicating any trace of dissent.

Basically, a conspiracy theory. This time, involving huge numbers of people over a very long period of time.

History is not laboratory science—you can't test it and make observations. But you can still check a theory for inconsistencies. A few bumps here and there are excusable, but with the Jewish conspiracy theory we have some blatant contradictions. For instance:

(a) According to this theory, the Jews are by far the most ingenious people ever. Out of all the peoples of the ancient world, this nation of shepherds and fig-growers came up with the classic work of all time. The work that changed all of history, brought us the concepts of creation ex-nihilo, history, purpose, monotheism, providence, human rights, gave rise to both Christianity and Islam and triggered the Reformation and modernization of western civilization when those gentiles started actually reading it. A supremacy dogma if I ever heard one!

(b) According to this theory, the Jews are by far the stupidest and most gullible people in the world. They fell for a story that restricts their diet, their domination over their slaves, their weekly work habits and their sex-life beyond what any other nation would tolerate. They bought into a lose-lose situation for everybody all 'round: The King's power is restricted, the priestly class cannot own land, and the commoners can't sell it.

They abandon their fields and towns three times a year to the mercy of the hostile nations surrounding them, let those fields lie fallow once in seven years, let their slaves go free after six years, don't charge interest—and just trust year after year that everything will be okay. After all, G-d promises that when you're planning to leave your land fallow in the seventh, He'll give you a bumper crop in the sixth. So tell me, what happens when one year this just doesn't work out? Do you leave that in the books you're writing?

Furthermore, this theory has the Jewish people making up fables about their blunders in full detail. They declare that they descend from slaves! They tell nasty stories about the forefather of their priestly class, Levi—even though the Levites were supposed to have written the book. The original high priest gets his hands dirty in the biggest scandal of their history. Who is this fable serving, anyway? Why on earth would anyone *want* to make up such a story? And what sort of crazy people would want to preserve it?

Second contradiction:

(a) According to this theory, Jews are capable of agreeing on a single version of history. Obviously, to conspire together for so many years in delivering this grand hoax to the entire world, they must be highly cooperative, submissive to authority and like-minded. They must fit well into Eric Fromm's description of the True Believer.

(b) According to this theory, Jews have purposely painted a picture of themselves as recalcitrant, argumentative, scorning of authority and primed to kvetch at the drop of a hat. Not the sort of comrades you would want involved in your classic conspiracy. A personality described by Myers-Briggs Passive-Aggressive Disorder. Of course, this purposeful self-incrimination may be part of the plot. You may decide empirically which description suits best.

The Foundations of Conspiracy

All in all, the conspiracy theory stinks. It doesn't explain anything. There's absolutely no evidence that it's true. And it's about as elegant as a walrus in a tutu.

So what does it really stand on? On the very definite assumption that Sinai could not have happened.

Think for a minute: Did those 19th century German historians who introduced us to J, E, P and D (the supposed authors of the Pentateuch) ever examine the evidence and demonstrate scientifically that Sinai could not have happened? Of course not. They didn't need to. They just knew it couldn't happen. Why? Because G-d, if there is one, doesn't speak to Man. Especially lots of men. Period. No discussion.

You know, in the 18th century, astronomers did not believe in meteorites. Museums all over Europe threw out their precious meteorite specimens as humiliating reminders of superstitious mythology. Why? Because, as Antoine Lavoisier, father of modern chemistry declared, "Stones don't fall from the sky, because there are no stones in the sky!" Period. End of discussion.

Hold it! There's one piece of evidence the biblical critics will hold up: The Pentateuch is written in third person.[2] As in "And then G-d spoke to Moses, saying..." as opposed to, "So then I had this chat with the Boss and He said..." Moses wouldn't write about himself in third person. Right? And Moses couldn't have composed the last eight verses describing his passing. So Moses couldn't have composed the Torah.

Right. We all agree on something. Moses did not compose the Torah. Nobody ever said he did. G-d composed it. Moses just wrote it down.

Rabbi Moshe ben Nachman (Ramban) writes in his introduction to his classic commentary on the Torah that this is the reason the Torah is written in third person: Because Moses is no more than a scribe

2 Actually, there are also stylistic arguments: Biblical critics find different parts of the Pentateuch to be written in differing styles with apparently different world-views. Such a method of examination, however, can hardly be called science. Don't take my word for it—try it yourself: There are articles scattered throughout the Net with the name Tzvi Freeman attached to them. Do a search, then examine the articles and determine how many Tzvi Freemans there are. Were the articles for *Game Developer Magazine* written in the same style as *Bringing Heaven Down To Earth*? How about the *Heaven Exposed Series*? There have even been wild claims that some of these were written by myself, the Guadalajara Rebbe!

copying from a primeval document. The Torah exists before creation, before time. It is G-d's wisdom, containing the original proposal, concept paper and design notes from which He created heaven and earth. Abraham knew it, Noah studied it, even Adam had the Torah. Moses was the first who was able to channel the Torah down to earth, to resolve it into ink on the page. If Moses had perceived himself as an author, as anything more than a transparent channel for G-dly wisdom, he would have been incapable of such a task.

To the point that, at the end of his transcribing, Moses attained the ultimate degree of self-abnegation: He writes about his own passing from this world. As the Talmud tells us, "G-d dictated and Moses wrote with tears."

In my humble opinion, Ramban's opinion seems much more internally consistent. It also makes fairy dust out of every other piece of evidence biblical critics will cite. And this is the traditional history stated clearly in the Torah: That an entire nation witnessed G-d speaking to Moses the Ten Commandments:

G-d said to Moses, Behold! I come to you in the thickness of the cloud, so that the people will hear as I speak to you, and they will also believe in you forever! (Exodus 19:9)

G-d spoke to you from the midst of the fire, you were hearing the sound of words, but you were not seeing a form, only a sound. He told you of His covenant, instructing you to keep the Ten Commandments, and He inscribed them on two stone tablets. (Deut.4:9-13)

Once the people had witnessed this, they believed Moses. As Maimonides writes:

Israel did not believe in Moses, our teacher, because of the miracles he performed. When you base your faith on miracles, you're still in doubt. Maybe these miracles were done through magic and witchcraft...

So why did we believe him? The revelation on Sinai which we saw with our own eyes, and heard with our own ears, not having to depend on the testimony of others... (Mishneh Torah—Foundations of Torah 8:1)

Here we have it. A simple and elegant solution to why, of all nations, this nation ended up with the most counter-intuitive set of rules and customs that have by now overthrown the hierarchy of power and world-concept of most of human society. It was a mass revelation from Above. G-d said it, they had to do it.

Problem is, this doesn't fit with our definition of history: the most *likely* sequence of events to explain whatever remnants have endured. Divine revelation, especially to a crowd, cannot be called likely. I mean, have you seen one lately? When was the last time you were in a crowd, say at the mall, and a booming voice came out of the heavens to speak to the people?

So, the historian, as we have defined him, must reject it.

Digging a little deeper: Accepting G-d speaking to us at Sinai and instructing us in our daily affairs doesn't sound right to the materialist mind—even if it believes in G-d. G-d is infinite. The world is a finite place made of finite, real things. G-d just can't fit in here. And so, even if we showed the materialist an onsite video certified by peer review, he would have to reject it. Because it just can't happen.

The human mind, when faced with a choice between the absurd and the impossible, will invariably choose the absurd. The absurd is far less frightening and easier to live with than the impossible. To accept the impossible is to undermine the very basis of the rational world we must live in. And here you are faced with just that choice: To accept an event that is totally out of the question to one who lives in a materialistic world, or simply to explain all evidence away as artifacts of an absurd conspiracy.

The world a Jew believes in was created by G-d speaking. And it is sustained in that way over and over at every moment. Every second of the day, a Jew experiences G-d speaking to him or her—through the events of life, through the mitzvahs that come our way, and especially through the Torah we learn each day. And so, what is so impossible if at one point in history the volume was turned way up and all of us heard the same thing at once? But for the materialist and his version of history, none of this is possible.

So we need another definition of history. As Thomas Kuhn would put it, a new paradigm.[3]

History, the Other Way:

In Torah Law, history is defined by the testimony of eyewitnesses. When there are no witnesses available, testimony of a court that accepted the testimony of eyewitnesses is accepted. But if something cannot be corroborated by witnesses, as far as Torah is concerned it did not happen. It is simply not part of reality.[4]

The simplest explanation for this reliance on eyewitnesses is because the Torah is not conspiracy-paranoid. Two witnesses in a decent court will have a very difficult time conspiring together if they have to describe the details of what they saw. Two people can tell the same story, but to describe the same scene precisely is next to impossible.

But if we were quantum physicists, we could philosophize about this a little. Perhaps eyewitnesses are vital because the human observer is a necessary element to all events. After all, this dichotomy of *event* and *observer* is a subjective one. Torah provides an objective view, in which event and observer are a single unit. Therefore, one does not exist without the other. In fact, this is the way most quantum physicists prefer to understand the universe. Interestingly, if you were a gentile theoretical physicist living in Germany after 1933, you were labeled a white Jew. Hey, maybe Moses was a physicist!

Furthermore, the idea of searching for the most likely path to arrive at the present smacks of causality-worship. Our white-Jew friend, Heisenberg, knocked that idol off its pedestal a long time ago. According to his way of thinking, anything could happen. In fact, as Schrodinger puts it, until an observer is there, anything *did* happen.

Having two accounts is also a good scientific approach. Any observation must be confirmed by more than one party in order to get into a textbook. Because a single observer could be reporting on no more than his own perceptual distortion, or the particular conditions of his frame of reference. Accordingly, the best testimony to any event would be that of a large and highly diverse audience.

Torah demands two witnesses. The court drills the witnesses separately to check for discrepancies in their reports. They make certain that both saw the same event at the same time from corresponding perspectives. They make sure there isn't another set of witnesses that has a conflicting eyewitness report. And then their testimony is accepted as fact. And if what the witnesses tell us is the most outrageous and preposterous event unimaginable, we must accept that as the truth.

Within this paradigm, there is no more certain event in the history of humankind than the revelation at Mount Sinai. We're not talking about a couple of broken shards, or an excavated building for archaeologists to argue over. We're not talking about the account of a single individual, or of a handful of ready-made believers. We're talking a mass eyewitness account of a wide spectrum of observers, passed down in an unbroken chain through multi-

---

3 Thomas Kuhn was a nice Jewish boy who wrote perhaps the most significant book on the history of science in the 20th century, *On the Structure of Scientific Revolution*. Significant, because it made it cool to use the term *paradigm shift*, especially on the Upper East Side of Manhattan. Basically, his work looks at science's ways of explaining things as a tool rather than a truth. When one approach to science turns out to be insufficient to explain the data, or to accommodate the world-view of the scientists, a new paradigm is sought. Neither paradigm, however, whether it be Aristotle's or Newton's or Einstein's, is necessarily closer to the underlying truth. This view has been used to dismiss apparent conflicts between theology and science.

4 Also, once a document has been ratified by two witnesses in a Jewish court, everything in that document is taken as fact. Taking this as a paradigm for defining past reality, we can understand how the classic rabbis discuss varying versions of past events, while agreeing that all versions are Torah. Why should there be only a single version of time? As long as the version is supported by the text, it has all the elements of reality. By way of analogy, this would be the same as two judges hearing the same evidence, reconstructing the scene in differing ways. Within our paradigm, neither construction is less reality than the other. It could even be proposed that once a Torah sage discovers a new way of understanding the text, as long as that interpretation is consistent with the traditional rules of exegesis, he has brought a new past reality into being.

ple paths without distortion. We have the consensus of an entire nation for over 3000 years on a single version of that event (Jewish people actually agreeing on something!).

Contrary to popular misconception, Jews don't believe the Torah is Divine because they are gullible, or because it sounds cool and resonates with their inner soul. We know the Torah is Divine because we empirically experienced that to be so. And ever since, we trust the testimony of our teachers and parents who all agree on the same, single version of that empirical event. If you can't trust them, who can you trust?

To put it in terms of Talmudic logic: If one set of witnesses says, "We speculate that it happened like this," and the other says, "We definitely saw that it happened like that," you must believe the second set. The biblical critics speculate—and they all argue with each other on those speculations. Our tradition states with certainty—in a single version.

Perhaps the story was exaggerated over the centuries? Also extremely unlikely. We have a single version in our hands. To conspire at making the same exaggerations over centuries is even more preposterous than making the whole thing up together at once and fooling the world.

So here's the paradigm score:

	Pros	Cons
Sinai Theory	Unbroken tradition from mass eye witnesses.	Sounds outrageously impossible.
Conspiracy Theory	Sounds nicer.	Explains zilch.

Myths in General

Now you're going to say, "Does this mean that if any nation tells us the legends of their people, we must accept it as truth? What if they claim that G-d gave them the truth and that their ways are the real path?"

If any people will tell you with consistency that a significant portion of their nation witnessed G-d speaking to them, believe them. We're not talking here about a legend about one hero who slew a monster. Or a wise man who heard an angel in a cave. We're talking about an account that states how a nation experienced its history.

In fact, many such legends are true. Just because anthropologists don't think they can get grants for proving native history as authentic doesn't affect history. Nineteenth century historians offhandedly assumed Homer's account of the Trojan War to be a fable, until Heinrich Schliemann went and dug up the evidence. Now the Iliad is looked to as a source of historical data. Anthropologists discounted the legends of the Hopi People of Arizona that described how some of them had travelled to a northern land of rock and ice—until very recently a lone researcher found the unmistakable traces of their journeys in the frozen north. If a people are telling you something about their origins or their history, listen up. This is important data to them, and it is generally accurately preserved.

Nevertheless, nobody ever really thought of these legends as historical fact. Until recently, most peoples never even had any concept of historical fact. Aside from the ancestral history mentioned above, they told stories to build common identity and entertain the family around a bonfire at night. Stories that happened in mythical time, long, long ago in a land far away. Back to the Hopi, for instance: They tell a story of how they originated in the bottom world of three worlds that reside below this one. When? How did they get there? That is irrelevant to the story. This part of their story reads not like history, but as a metaphor. The proof is that nobody ever asks those questions.

The Bible is unique among documents of its time in this regard. Egyptian Hieroglyphics are not history but fabulous propaganda. Even Homer was not intending to write a history, but a drama full of metaphor. From reading these things, you have no sense of real time, change and progress. The Bible, on the other hand, tells a story where there is a beginning, a middle and a result. Its narrative is within a context of definite time and space, with precision of names, quantities, dates, because *those events are of themselves vitally important.* In a fable, for example, you don't give precise measurements for a tabernacle that will never be built again, or the exact details about a one-time ceremony to inaugurate it. When telling history, you do.

But I still contend that if a nation tells you that G-d spoke to all of them at once, and they all give the same version, you should believe them. However, search the globe and you will find only one such story. Why? Isn't that a great way for the spiritual leadership to get their flock in line? I mean, there's only so far that you can go telling the masses a story about a single individual who had a dialogue with an angel. Or a small group that heard a divine voice. Wouldn't it be so much more powerful to tell them that everyone eye-witnessed the event?

Sure it would. Problem is, as we explained, nobody could ever pull that off. It couldn't even gradually evolve over the centuries. Because it's a conspiracy, and conspiracies don't work.

The very fact that no other people ever made up anything similar to the story of Sinai should be enough evidence that it must be true.

Choose Your World

In case you are planning to use the above as debate material, everything I've told you is useless. No matter what arguments you give, don't expect to convince those entrenched in a materialist reductionist view of reality. Our world is not their world. Our world is a world into which the Infinite may enter, and Sinai is a space where the Essence of that world is heard. Our Sinai cannot enter their world— you must choose between the two, but you cannot keep both.

So here is my point: To accept Sinai is to reject absolutely the concept that there is a world and there is a G-d, and that the two exist as distinct entities. But those who live in a world that is so real the infinite cannot enter, the Divine must hover beyond—they are left to accept the absurdity of conspiracy in its most implausible form.

When G-d created all things, He made two versions for you to choose from. He created, and the earth was chaos and empty—an absurd world where light cannot enter. And He created a heaven and earth of "Let there be light." A world of wonder, a place for the Infinite to dwell.

You choose in which you wish to live.

TRUE PREDICTIONS

BY RABBI DOVID GOTTLIEB, PhD

We have two conclusions from the last two chapters. (1) To act responsibly we must seek the truth and use our best estimate of the truth as our basis for action. Action on the basis of pragmatic considerations without regard to truth is irresponsible. Similarly, waiting for absolute proof before acting is irresponsible. (2) The exact weight of evidence required to mandate action cannot be stated precisely (and is even somewhat controversial). I will try to show that there is enough evidence to meet whatever standard you actually use in making your decisions. So the appeal is to consistency: If you stick to your usual standards and act responsibly, then you must live according to the Torah.

Rabbi Dovid Gottlieb, PhD. Author and lecturer. Rabbi Gottlieb received his PhD in mathematical logic at Brandeis University and went on to become professor of philosophy at Johns Hopkins University. Today he is a senior faculty member at Ohr Somayach in Jerusalem. He is the author of *The Informed Soul* and *Living Up to the Truth*.

Now we will begin a review of the evidence. I will start with two cautionary remarks. First, when I present evidence, the significance of the evidence is that it adds to the probability of the Torah being true. To respond that it is still conceivable that the Torah is false is quite correct, but irrelevant. The goal is not to remove every conceivable alternative; it is to present the Judaism as a more probable alternative.

Second, we are now gathering evidence. To gather evidence means no one piece of evidence will carry the case by itself. This is similar to a courtroom procedure. If you want to convict a murderer, just finding his fingerprints at the scene of the crime isn't enough, just finding a similar weapon to the one that caused the murder in his house is not enough, just having a motivation is not enough, just his having been seen at the place of the murder at the time of the murder is not enough. But, when you put them all together, it can be enough. So, again, it will not be relevant to respond that "This piece of evidence is not enough to justify believing that the Torah is true." Of course it isn't. No one piece of evidence is enough. It is all the evidence together which is enough. We won't begin to sum up all the evidence until the last chapter. The point, then, is for each piece of evidence to be seen as relevant, to see that the most likely interpretation of the evidence is that the Torah is true.

In Deuteronomy 28–30 there is a prediction of what will happen to the Jewish people if they don't live up to the standards of the Torah. It predicts conquest accompanied by wanton slaughter of the population: men, woman, children, old, young, and so on. It predicts an exile resulting in world-wide scatter, and that during this period of world-wide scatter, Jews will have no independent government. One result of the exile is that some Jews will be brought back by boat to Egypt to be sold as slaves, and they will not be purchased. Nevertheless, the Jewish people will survive, will never completely be destroyed, and will ultimately return to the land of Israel. It also predicts that the conqueror will speak a language that the Jewish people don't understand.

Now as we said in chapter II, what is crucial about this prediction is that it should be a unique prediction, namely, a prediction that no one else should believe. From no other perspective should such a prediction make sense. Because if it is a prediction that other people can believe in or that other people can credit, it no longer functions as a crucial experiment. It no longer distinguishes between what you are claiming and what others can claim. So, let's ask ourselves about each of the details in this prediction, whether it could have been explained by a sociological analysis of the times, or by a competing ideology—or whether it is something that someone could explain only from the Jewish point of view.

[Of course, if someone should accept our prediction from our sources, then his making that prediction cannot count for him against us! If Christians and Moslems accept Deuteronomy 28–30 and predict that the Jews will be exiled as a result of their failure to live up to the Torah, when that prediction comes true it does not give Christianity and Islam positive evidence against Judaism, since they took the prediction from us.]

I should mention that this prediction was written at least two thousand years ago. Jewish sources say it was written 3300+ years ago. Others might disagree as to when the Bible was written, as to how many authors it had, how many editors it had and so on, but no one believes that the account of the Roman conquest and exile was written after the Roman conquest.

Now, let's see which of the details of this prediction could have been explained by an observer with a point of view other than that of the Torah. The prediction of conquest was not a very daring prediction. Everybody gets conquered sooner or later.

There was a prediction of total destruction: a decimation of the population and exile. That was rare in the ancient world. It happened, but it was rare because the purpose of conquest was economic. Typically it was a question of acquiring colonies and taxing them. You can't tax people if you slaughter the population and exile them. Now, I'm not talking about theft. Of course you want to take all the gold and silver, gems, fine linen and so on. You may take the young, fine, strong men off as slaves. You may want to take the good looking, young woman for sexual purposes. But, you don't wantonly slaughter the rest of the population because there is no point in destroying your tax base! During their 300 years of rule, the Romans did this only to Carthage and the Jews. So, the prediction of the wanton slaughter of the population and exile were predictions that could not be anticipated to really occur because they were not the normal procedure in the ancient world.

Now, let's take the prediction that the conqueror will speak a language that you don't understand. Why should I think that? Couldn't you be conquered by a neighbor? Neighboring countries typically understood one another's languages. There was enough commerce and enough travel back and forth for them to be familiar with one another's languages. Couldn't we be conquered by a country that spoke an "international language?" Many Jews understood Greek. Greek was in those days similar to what English is today. Business contracts, trade and diplomacy were conducted in Greek. Had any Greek speaking nation conquered and exiled us, this prediction would have been false. It just so happens that the Romans conquered us and they spoke Latin. Latin was a language with which Jews were not familiar.

If you are going to be exiled, who says that you are going to end up all over the world? Why should that be an automatic consequence of exile? Not everyone who was exiled from their countries ended up with identifiable communities all over the world. Even when the Babylonians exiled us 500 years earlier, we didn't end up all over the world. The vast majority of the population was taken off to Babylon, a large group went to Alexandria in Egypt, but there were many places in the world where there were no identifiable groups of Jews.

If they were going to end up in exile, how could one predict with confidence that some of them will be taken back to Egypt in boats to be sold, and that there will not be anybody there to buy them? Why should one think that? It is true that there was a slave trade flourishing and that there were known slave routes, but who is to say that it would definitely happen?

If you are going to predict exile scattered all over the world, how can you be sure that at no point will any Jewish society form an independent government in some portion of the earth's surface? Don't forget, we are talking about two thousand years ago. Two thousand years ago the world wasn't organized with maps and boundary lines so that every square millimeter of the earth's surface belongs to one nation or another, and sometimes to two or three. On the contrary, there were vast areas of the earth's surface that were unclaimed, unsettled, and simply wild; for example, parts of Russia, Northern Africa, the Arabian Peninsula, and Central Africa. Who is to say that Jewish exiles would not form an independent society in one of these places?

Now that means that for each of these predictions, if I don't have a Jewish perspective, and I look at it neutrally, or I look at it as a Buddhist, a Hindu, or a Taoist, a Confucianist, or later as a Christian or Moslem, I would expect them not to occur, and I would not be able to explain them if they did occur.

If I were to assign probabilities to each of these detailed predictions from any of those non-Jewish points of view, the probabilities would be very low. Total destruction and exile, let's say that this occurred in 10% of all ancient wars. Then a non-Jewish observer would give it a probability of 1/10. That the conqueror should speak an unknown language. I don't know how often that happened, I mean neighbors often conquered one another. Let's say generously that it happened one fourth of the time giving us a probability of 1/4. Being scattered all over the world as a result of exile, as far as I know, didn't happen at all. I don't know what probability to give it, so I will be generous and give it a probability of 1/10. To take a nation that is scattered all over the world and thus be unable to organize itself into an independent society, again, I don't know what the probability of that would be, so I'll give it a probability of 1/4. To survive under these conditions and return to one's land has never happened in the history of the world—strictly speaking we should give it a probability of zero! But let's be generous and say 1/10.

Now, when you have predictions for a sequence of events, and each event has a probability, and you want to know the probability of them all coming true, you simply multiply the probabilities. So, we simply multiply 1/10 * 1/4 * 1/10 * 1/4 * 1/10 and we come out with a probability of 1/16000. This is a very small number. That is the confidence that a neutral observer would have in this prediction. What is the likelihood that a prediction like this would come true? One chance in every sixteen thousand tries. Given the evidence the observer had to go on, there is no way for him to explain why they occurred.

But, they all happened. That being the case, this is what I called earlier a unique prediction. It is a prediction that no one else would make. Had anyone seen the prediction before it happened, the response should have been that this is fantasy. No one else would be able to explain why this should happen. Therefore, when it comes true, it contributes to the truth of Judaism. It is a relevant piece of evidence.

[Three technical remarks. (1) Many details from Deuteronomy 28 have been omitted. There are two reasons: either the language in which they are expressed is poetical and cannot be precisely defined (and thus we cannot prove that the text means specifically what in fact happened), or they are predictions which are very likely to happen in the context of destruction and exile, so that they would not significantly lower the probability. (2) Some of the probabilities above are conditional—world-wide scatter given exile; no independence given world-wide scatter; survival and return given scatter. Only if they are understood this way is it appropriate to multiply them to get the probability of all the events occurring. My numbers are meant as (overly generous) estimates of these probabilities. (3) The probabilities are for the predictions coming true; they are not for the predictions having been made. We can easily think of reasons why someone would want to make a frightening prediction, but we would be very surprised if what was predicted occurred.]

Now could it have come true by accident? Yes, it could have. I freely grant that because we are not playing Descartes. We are not interested in a mere a possibility. We are interested in a possibility for which there is more evidence. Anything can happen by chance, but the likelihood of this happening by chance is one in sixteen thousand. What this indicates is that whoever wrote this had access to a source of information beyond the natural. What that source was and how to describe it we don't know so far. We are only drawing minimal inference from the events. That seems to me to be what the evidence indicates.

Finally, I will repeat again that I am not trying to prove that Judaism is true based on this one prediction. One true prediction does not prove that a theory is true. I'm merely pointing out that this is relevant evidence. The full justification will come later when we take all the evidence together. But this is certainly a piece of objective evidence which ought to interest us. It ought to show us that the quest of the realist to find a truth which can be justified is not a quest in vain.

Living Up to the Truth [Jerusalem, 1996], pp. 25–27
Reprinted with permission of the author

ACKNOWLEDGMENTS

When Moses descended from Mount Sinai and communicated G-d's words to the Jewish people, they replied with a message that still echoes today: "All that G-d commanded we will do and we will [strive to] understand" (Exodus 24:7). At that moment, the Talmud (Shabbat 88a) relates, the ministering angels placed two crowns upon each Jew: one corresponding to "we will do" and one corresponding to "we will understand." The granting of these two crowns underscores that our obedience of G-d's will should be accompanied by a vigorous desire to comprehend and appreciate it. This includes investigating the origins, nature, and development of Jewish law and tradition.

Judaism Decoded: The Origins and Evolution of Jewish Tradition fills a compelling scholastic need. This course traces the origins of the halachic system, rabbinic law, and Jewish traditions, and provides a thorough understanding of the nature and evolution of Jewish law. This course is a revised and updated version of the JLI course *From Sinai to Cyberspace: How an Ancient Wisdom Guides a Modern World. From Sinai to Cyberspace* was received with critical acclaim by JLI instructors and students alike in 2002 and 2006, and we have received numerous requests for an updated release.

We are deeply thankful to **Rabbi Berel Bell**, member of the Rabbinical Court of Montreal and founding dean of Bais Chaya Mushka Seminary in Montreal, Canada, who authored *From Sinai to Cyberspace*. This course has benefited greatly from Rabbi Bell's pedagogical mastery, his vast rabbinic scholarship, his creative thinking, and his unique ability to make learning interactive, interesting, and stimulating. We are also grateful to **Dr. Chana Silberstein,** former Dean of Curriculum at JLI, who edited and produced the second edition of *From Sinai to Cyberspace*. *Judaism Decoded* has been greatly enhanced by Dr. Silberstein's work.

Judaism Decoded has benefited from many JLI faculty members who taught *From Sinai to Cyberspace* and took the time to share their feedback and suggestions. We express our heartfelt appreciation to these devoted JLI affiliates. Special thanks to **Rabbis Benny Rapoport** and **Aaron Herman**, authors of the JLI Teens course, *OMG! The Battle between Faith and Logic*. Lesson Six of *Judaism Decoded* draws upon their work.

We extend our appreciation to **Rabbis Mordechai Dinerman** and **Naftali Silberberg,** who skillfully direct the JLI Curriculum Department and the Flagship editorial team, to **Rabbi Dr. Shmuel Klatzkin,** JLI's senior editor, and to **Rabbi Zalman Abraham,** director of marketing, who provides the strategic vision for branding JLI course offerings.

We are grateful to **Rabbis Eli Raksin** and **Shmuel Super** for their meticulous research and to **Chava Shapiro** for her careful review of the lesson drafts and her editorial and pedagogic suggestions. We thank **Rabbi Elie Estrin** for his enhancements to Lesson Three.

We acknowledge **Zeldy Nemanov** for managing the many components of course production, **Mendel Schtroks** for designing the textbooks with taste, eloquence, and patience, and **Mendel Sirota** for directing book production. **Miriam Levy-Haim, Esther Tauber, Ya'akovah Weber,** and **Rachel Witty** enhanced the quality and professionalism of the course with their copyediting and proofing.

Mrs. Nechama Rivkah Shagalow and **Yisrael Silman** head the production team charged with producing the videos for this course. They are assisted by **Neria Ben-Avi, Moshe Raskin,** and **Getzy Raskin. Mushka Lisker** and **Rivka Rapoport** designed the course's PowerPoints.

We acknowledge the hard work and efforts of JLI's support staff and administration, whose contributions to this course were critical, but whose names are too many to enumerate.

We are immensely grateful for the encouragement of JLI's visionary chairman and vice-chairman of Merkos L'Inyonei Chinuch—Lubavitch World Headquarters, **Rabbi Moshe Kotlarsky.** Rabbi Kotlarsky has been highly instrumental in building the infrastructure for the expansion of Chabad's international network and is the architect of scores of initiatives and services to help Chabad representatives across the globe succeed in their mission. We are blessed to have the unwavering support of JLI's principal benefactor, **Mr. George Rohr,** who is fully invested in our work and continues to be instrumental in JLI's monumental expansion.

The commitment and sage direction of JLI's dedicated executive board—**Rabbis Chaim Block, Hesh Epstein, Ronnie Fine, Yosef Gansburg, Shmuel Kaplan, Yisrael Rice,** and **Avrohom Sternberg**—and the countless hours they devote to the development of JLI is what drives the vision, growth, and flourishing of the organization.

Finally, JLI represents an incredible partnership of more than 350 *shluchim* and *shluchos,* who give of their time and talent to further Jewish adult education. We thank them for generously sharing feedback and making suggestions that steer JLI's development and growth. They are our most valuable critics and our most cherished contributors.

Inspired by the call of the **Lubavitcher Rebbe,** of righteous memory, it is the mandate of the Rohr JLI to encourage all Jews throughout the world to experience and participate in their precious heritage of Torah learning. May this course succeed in fulfilling this sacred charge.

On behalf of the Rohr Jewish Learning Institute,

Rabbi Efraim Mintz, Executive Director
Rabbi Yisrael Rice, Chairman, Editorial Board

11 Nissan, 5775

The Rohr Jewish Learning Institute

An affiliate of
Merkos L'Inyonei Chinuch
The Educational Arm of
The Chabad Lubavitch Movement
822 Eastern Parkway, Brooklyn, NY 11213

Rabbi Shraga Sherman
Merion Station, PA

Rabbi Avraham Steinmetz
S. Paulo, BR

Rabbi Avrohom Sternberg
New London, CT

Rabbi Aryeh Weinstein
Newtown, PA

Rabbi Motti Wilhelm
Portland, OR

Multimedia Development

Mrs. Rivkah Shagalow
Director

Rabbi Yisroel Silman
Creative Director

Mrs. Neria Ben Avi
Mrs. Mushka Lisker
Mrs. Rivkah Rapoport
Mrs. Chava Shapiro
Rabbi Chesky Edelman
Getzy Raskin
Moshe Raskin

Administration

Mrs. Chana Dechter

Affiliate Support

Rabbi Mendel Sirota
Mrs. Fraydee Kessler
Mrs. Mindy Wallach

Online Division

Rabbi Mendy Elishevitz
Director

Rabbi Elchonon Korenblit
Ram Rabins
Mrs. Rochie Rivkin
Avi J. Levy

Marketing and Branding

Rabbi Zalman Abraham
Director

Mrs. Shevi Rivkin
Graphic Design

Rabbi Yossi Klein
Marketing for Results

Rabbi Shmuel Loebenstein
Writer

Marketing Committee

Rabbi Simcha Backman
Glendale, CA

Rabbi Ronnie Fine
Montreal, QC

Rabbi Ovadia Goldman
Oklahoma City, OK

Rabbi Mendy Halberstam
Miami Beach, FL

Rabbi Reuven New
Boca Raton, FL

Rabbi Yehuda Shemtov
Yardley, PA

Marketing Consultants

JJ Gross
New York, NY

Warren Modlin
MednetPro, Inc.
Alpharetta, GA

Alan Rosenspan
Alan Rosenspan & Associates
Sharon, MA

Gary Wexler
Passion Marketing
Los Angeles, CA

Publication Design

Rabbi Zalman Abraham
Mendel Schtroks

Printing

Shimon Leib Jacobs
Point One Communications
Montreal, QC

Distribution

Mary Stevens
Nixa, MO

Accounting

Musie Karp
Mrs. Shaina B. Mintz
Mrs. Shulamis Nadler

JLI Departments

Rabbi Levi Kaplan
Director of Operations

Rabbi Dubi Rabinowitz
Administrator

JLI Flagship

Rabbi Yisrael Rice
Chairman
S. Rafael, CA

Rabbi Mordechai Dinerman
Rabbi Naftali Silberberg
Editors-in-Chief

Rabbi Yanky Tauber
Course Editor

Rabbi Dr. Shmuel Klatzkin
Senior Editor
Dayton, OH

Rabbi Eli Raksin
Rabbi Yanky Raskin
Associate Editors

Zeldy Nemanow
Administrative Assistant

Rabbi Mendel Sirota
Production Manager

Miriam Levy-Haim
Mrs. Naomi Saul
Mrs. Rachel Witty
Proofreaders

Department of Continuing Education

Mrs. Mindy Wallach
Director

Musie Karp
Registrar

Mrs. Shulamis Nadler
Service and Support

JLI International Desk

Rabbi Avrohom Sternberg
Chairman
New London, CT

Rabbi Dubi Rabinowitz
Director
Brooklyn, NY

Chava Farkash
Administrative Assistant

Mendel Schtroks
Content Manager

Rabbi Yosef Yitzchok Noiman
Administrator, JLI Israel
In Partnership with
Tzeirei Agudat Chabad

Rabbi Eli Wolf
Administrator, JLI in the CIS
In Parternship with the Federation of Jewish Communities of the CIS

Rabbi Avraham Golovacheov
Regional Respresentative
German Division

Rabbi Nochum Schapiro
Regional Respresentative
Australia

Beis Medrosh L'Shluchim

in partnership with
Shluchim Exchange

Rabbi Mendy Yusewitz
Director

Rabbi Mendel Margolin
Producer

Steering Committee

Rabbi Simcha Backman
Rabbi Mendy Kotlarsky
Rabbi Efraim Mintz

JLI Academy

Rabbi Hesh Epstein
Chairman

Rabbi Yossi Klein
Director

JLI Teens

in partnership with
CTeeN: Chabad Teen Network

Rabbi Chaim Block
Chairman
San Antonio, TX

Rabbi Elya Silfen
Director

Rabbi Michoel Shapiro
Editor in Chief

Mrs. Nechi Gudelsky
Program Administrators

Advisory Board

Rabbi Mendy Cohen
Merion Station, PA

Rabbi Yitzi Hein
Pittsford, NY

Rabbi Zalman Marcus
Mission Viejo, CA

Land and Spririt
Israel Experience

Shmuly Karp
Director

Steering Committee

Rabbi Yechiel Baitelman
Rabbi Dovid Flinkenstein
Rabbi Chanoch Kaplan
Rabbi Levi Klein
Rabbi Mendy Mangel
Rabbi Sholom Raichik
Rabbi Avi Richler

Machon Shmuel
The Sami Rohr Research Institute

Rabbi Avrohom Bergstein
Dean

Rabbinic Advisory Board

Rabbi Chaim Rapoport
Rabbi Gedalya Oberlander
Rabbi Chaim Schapiro
Rabbi Levi Yitzchak Raskin
Rabbi Mordechai Farkash
Rabbi Moshe Miller
Rabbi Yossi Yaffe

Research Fellows

Rabbi Menachem Aizenman
Rabbi Yehudah Altein
Rabbi Binyomin Bitton
Rabbi Moshe Chanunu
Rabbi Yaakov Gershon
Rabbi Levi Kessler
Rabbi Nesanel Loeb
Rabbi Mendel Mellul
Rabbi Zushe Wilmowsky
Rabbi Eliezer Raksin
Rabbi Menachem Rifkind
Rabbi Mendel Zirkind
Rabbi Yehudah Dovber Zirkind

Mishnah Project

Rabbi Elya Silfen
Director

myShiur:
Advanced Learning Initiative

Rabbi Shmuel Kaplan
Chairman
Potomac, MD

Rabbi Levi Kaplan
Director

National Jewish Retreat

Rabbi Hesh Epstein
Chairman
Columbia, SC

Mrs. Shaina B. Mintz
Administrator

Bruce Backman
Coordinator

Rabbi Mendy Weg
Founding Director

Rochelle Katzman
Program Coordinator

Shmuly Karp
Shluchim Liaison

Rosh Chodesh Society

Rabbi Shmuel Kaplan
Chairman
Baltimore, MD

Mrs. Shaindy Jacobson
Director

Mrs. Chava Shapiro
Associate Director

Mrs. Fraydee Kessler
Administrator

Gitty Hanokah
Administrative Assistant

Steering Committee

Mrs. Malka Bitton
Mrs. Shula Bryski
Mrs. Rochel Holzkenner
Mrs. Devorah Kornfeld
Mrs. Chana Lipskar
Mrs. Ahuva New
Mrs. Binie Tenenbaum

Sinai Scholars Society
in partnership with Chabad on Campus

Rabbi Menachem Schmidt
Chairman
Philadelphia, PA

Rabbi Dubi Rabinowitz
Director

Devorah Leah Notik
Associate Director

Mrs. Devorah Zlatopolsky
Administrator

Executive Committee

Rabbi Moshe Chaim Dubrowski
Rabbi Yossy Gordon
Rabbi Efraim Mintz
Rabbi Menachem Schmidt
Rabbi Nechemia Vogel
Rabbi Eitan Webb
Rabbi Avi Weinstein
Dr. Chana Silberstein

Curriculum Committee

Rabbi Zalman Bluming
Rabbi Shlomie Chein
Rabbi Shlomo Rothstien

Steering Committee

Rabbi Shlomie Chein
Rabbi Moshe Laib Gray
Rabbi Dovid Gurevitch
Rabbi Mendel Matusof
Rabbi Yisroel Wilhelm

TorahCafe.com
Online Learning

Rabbi Levi Kaplan
Director

Rabbi Yisroel Silman
Creative Director

Rabbi Simcha Backman
Dr. Michael Kigel
Consultants

Rabbi Mendy Elishevitz
Rabbi Elchonon Korenblit
Website Development

Gitty Hanoka
Administrator

Mendel Serebryanski
Content Manager

Avrohom Shimon Ezagui
Rafi Roston
Filming Crew

Moshe Levin
Elya Silfen
Video Editing

Torah Studies

Rabbi Yosef Gansburg
Chairman
Toronto, ON

Rabbi Meir Hecht
Founding Director

Rabbi Zalman Margolin
Director

Rabbi Ahrele Loschak
Managing Editor

Steering Committee

Rabbi Levi Fogelman
Rabbi Yaacov Halperin
Rabbi Nechemia Schusterman
Rabbi Ari Sollish

JLI Central
Founding Department Heads

Rabbi Mendel Bell
Brooklyn, NY

Rabbi Zalman Charytan
Acworth, GA

Rabbi Mendel Druk
Cancun, Mexico

Rabbi Menachem Gansburg
Toronto, ON

Rabbi Yoni Katz
Brooklyn, NY

Rabbi Chaim Zalman Levy
New Rochelle, NY

Rabbi Benny Rapoport
Clarks Summit, PA

Dr. Chana Silberstein
Ithaca, NY

Rabbi Elchonon Tenenbaum
Napa Valley, CA

Rohr JLI Faculty

ALABAMA

BIRMINGHAM
Rabbi Yossi Friedman
205.970.0100

ARIZONA

CHANDLER
Rabbi Mendel Deitsch
480.855.4333

FLAGSTAFF
Rabbi Dovie Shapiro
928.255.5756

PHOENIX
Rabbi Zalman Levertov
Rabbi Yossi Friedman
602.944.2753

SCOTTSDALE
Rabbi Yossi Levertov
480.998.1410

ARKANSAS

LITTLE ROCK
Rabbi Pinchus Ciment
501.217.0053

CALIFORNIA

AGOURA HILLS
Rabbi Moshe Bryski
Rabbi Shlomo Bistritsky
818.991.0991

BEL AIR
Rabbi Chaim Mentz
310.475.5311

BEVERLY HILLS
Rabbi Chaim I. Sperlin
310.734.9079

BRENTWOOD
Rabbi Boruch Hecht
Rabbi Mordechai Zaetz
310.826.4453

BURBANK
Rabbi Shmuly Kornfeld
818.954.0070

CARLSBAD
Rabbi Yeruchem Eilfort
Mrs. Nechama Eilfort
760.943.8891

CENTURY CITY
Rabbi Tzemach Cunin
310.860.1260

CHATSWORTH
Rabbi Yossi Spritzer
818.718.0777

CONTRA COSTA
Rabbi Dovber Berkowitz
925.937.4101

CORONADO
Rabbi Eli Fradkin
619.365.4728

ENCINO
Rabbi Joshua Gordon
Rabbi Aryeh Herzog
818.784.9986

FOLSOM
Rabbi Yossi Grossbaum
916.608.9811

GLENDALE
Rabbi Simcha Backman
818.240.2750

HUNTINGTON BEACH
Rabbi Aron Berkowitz
714.846.2285

IRVINE
Rabbi Alter Tenenbaum
Rabbi Elly Andrusier
949.786.5000

LA JOLLA
Rabbi Baruch Shalom Ezagui
858.455.5433

LAGUNA BEACH
Rabbi Elimelech Gurevitch
949.499.0770

LOMITA
Rabbi Eli Hecht
Rabbi Sholom Pinson
310.326.8234

LONG BEACH
Rabbi Abba Perelmuter
562.621.9828

LOS ANGELES
Rabbi Leibel Korf
323.660.5177

MARINA DEL REY
Rabbi Danny Yiftach-Hashem
Rabbi Dovid Yiftach
310.859.0770

NORTH HOLLYWOOD
Rabbi Nachman Abend
818.989.9539

NORTHRIDGE
Rabbi Eli Rivkin
818.368.3937

PACIFIC PALISADES
Rabbi Zushe Cunin
310.454.7783

PALO ALTO
Rabbi Yosef Levin
Rabbi Ber Rosenblatt
650.424.9800

Rabbi Menachem Landa
CLASSES IN HEBREW
650.322.1708

PASADENA
Rabbi Chaim Hanoka
626.564.8820

RANCHO MIRAGE
Rabbi Shimon H. Posner
760.770.7785

RANCHO PALOS VERDES
Rabbi Yitzchok Magalnic
310.544.5544

RANCHO S. FE
Rabbi Levi Raskin
858.756.7571

REDONDO BEACH
Rabbi Yossi Mintz
Rabbi Zalman Gordon
310.214.4999

SACRAMENTO
Rabbi Mendy Cohen
916.455.1400

S. BARBARA
Rabbi Zalman Kudan
CHAPTER FOUNDED BY RABBI YOSEF LOSCHAK, OBM
805.683.1544

S. CLEMENTE
Rabbi Menachem M. Slavin
949.489.0723

S. DIEGO
Rabbi Motte Fradkin
858.547.0076

S. DIEGO-UNIVERSITY CITY
Rabbi Yudell Reiz
619.723.2439

S. FRANCISCO
Rabbi Shlomo Zarchi
415.752.2866

Rabbi Peretz Mochkin
415.571.8770

S. LUIS OBISPO
Rabbi Chaim Leib Hilel
805.706.0256

S. MATEO
Rabbi Yossi Marcus
Rabbi Moishe Weinbaum
650.341.4510

S. MONICA
Rabbi Boruch Rabinowitz
310.394.5699

S. RAFAEL
Rabbi Yisrael Rice
415.492.1666

SOUTH LAKE TAHOE
Rabbi Mordechai Richler
530.314.7677

STOCKTON
Rabbi Avremel Brod
209.952.2081

STUDIO CITY
Rabbi Yossi Baitelman
818.508.6633

THOUSAND OAKS
Rabbi Chaim Bryski
805.493.7776

TUSTIN
Rabbi Yehoshua Eliezrie
714.508.2150

VENTURA
Rabbi Yakov Latowicz
Mrs. Sarah Latowicz
805.658.7441

YORBA LINDA
Rabbi Dovid Eliezrie
714.693.0770

COLORADO

ASPEN
Rabbi Mendel Mintz
970.544.3770

DENVER
Rabbi Mendel Popack
720.515.4337

Rabbi Yossi Serebryanski
303.744.9699

FORT COLLINS
Rabbi Yerachmiel Gorelik
970.407.1613

HIGHLANDS RANCH
Rabbi Avraham Mintz
303.694.9119

LONGMONT
Rabbi Yakov Dovid Borenstein
303.678.7595

VAIL
Rabbi Dovid Mintz
970.476.7887

WESTMINSTER
Rabbi Benjy Brackman
303.429.5177

CONNECTICUT

GREENWICH
Rabbi Yossi Deren
Rabbi Menachem Feldman
203.629.9059

NEW HAVEN
Rabbi Yosef Y. Hodakov
203.795.5261

NEW LONDON
Rabbi Avrohom Sternberg
860.437.8000

STAMFORD
Rabbi Yisrael Deren
Rabbi Levi Mendelow
203.3.CHABAD

WEST HARTFORD
Rabbi Yosef Gopin
Rabbi Shaya Gopin
860.659.2422

WESTPORT
Rabbi Yehuda L. Kantor
Mrs. Dina Kantor
203.226.8584

DELAWARE

WILMINGTON
Rabbi Chuni Vogel
302.529.9900

FLORIDA

BAL HARBOUR
Rabbi Dov Schochet
305.868.1411

BOCA RATON
Rabbi Zalman Bukiet
Rabbi Moishe Denburg
Rabbi Arele Gopin
561.417.7797

BOYNTON BEACH
Rabbi Yosef Yitzchok Raichik
561.732.4633

BRADENTON
Rabbi Menachem Bukiet
941.388.9656

CAPE CORAL
Rabbi Yossi Labkowski
239.541.1777

CORAL SPRINGS
Rabbi Yankie Denburg
954.471.8646

DELRAY BEACH
Rabbi Sholom Ber Korf
561.496.6228

EAST BOCA RATON
Rabbi Ruvi New
561.417.7797

FORT LAUDERDALE
Rabbi Yitzchok Naparstek
954.568.1190

FORT MYERS
Rabbi Yitzchok Minkowicz
Mrs. Nechama Minkowicz
239.433.7708

HOLLYWOOD
Rabbi Leizer Barash
954.965.9933

KENDALL
Rabbi Yossi Harlig
305.234.5654

LAKELAND
Rabbi Moshe Lazaros
863.510.5968

LAKE MARY
Rabbi Yanky Majesky
407.878.3011

MIAMI BEACH
Rabbi Mendy Levy
305.342.6665

OCALA
Rabbi Yossi Hecht
352.291.2218

ORLANDO
Rabbi Yosef Konikov
407.354.3660

PALM BEACH GARDENS
Rabbi Dovid Vigler
561.624.2223

PALMETTO BAY
Rabbi Zalman Gansburg
786.282.0413

PLANTATION
Rabbi Pinchas Taylor
954.644.9177

PONTE VEDRA BEACH
Rabbi Nochum Kurinsky
904.543.9301

SARASOTA
Rabbi Chaim Shaul Steinmetz
941.925.0770

SATELLITE BEACH
Rabbi Zvi Konikov
321.777.2770

SOUTH PALM BEACH
Rabbi Leibel Stolik
561.889.3499

SOUTH TAMPA
Rabbi Mendy Dubrowski
813.287.1795

SUNNY ISLES BEACH
Rabbi Alexander Kaller
305.803.5315

Weston
Rabbi Yisroel Spalter
954.349.6565

West Palm Beach
Rabbi Yoel Gancz
561.659.7770

Venice
Rabbi Sholom Ber Schmerling
941.493.2770

GEORGIA

Alpharetta
Rabbi Hirshy Minkowicz
770.410.9000

Atlanta
Rabbi Yossi New
Rabbi Isser New
404.843.2464

Atlanta: Intown
Rabbi Eliyahu Schusterman
Rabbi Ari Sollish
404.898.0434

Gwinnett
Rabbi Yossi Lerman
678.595.0196

Marietta
Rabbi Ephraim Silverman
770.565.4412

IDAHO

Boise
Rabbi Mendel Lifshitz
208.853.9200

ILLINOIS

Champaign
Rabbi Dovid Tiechtel
217.355.8672

Chicago
Rabbi Meir Hecht
312.714.4655

Rabbi Yosef Moscowitz
773.772.3770

Rabbi Levi Notik
773.274.5123

Chicago-Hyde Park
Rabbi Yossi Brackman
773.955.8672

Glenview
Rabbi Yishaya Benjaminson
847.998.9896

Highland Park
Mrs. Michla Schanowitz
847.266.0770

Naperville
Rabbi Mendy Goldstein
630.778.9770

Northbrook
Rabbi Meir Moscowitz
847.564.8770

Rabbi Menachem Slavaticki
Classes in Hebrew
847.350.9770

Oak Park
Rabbi Yitzchok Bergstein
708.524.1530

Peoria
Rabbi Eli Langsam
309.692.2250

Rockford
Rabbi Yecheskel Rothman
815.596.0032

Skokie
Rabbi Yochanan Posner
847.677.1770

Wilmette
Rabbi Dovid Flinkenstein
847.251.7707

INDIANA

Indianapolis
Rabbi Mendel Schusterman
317.251.5573

KANSAS

Overland Park
Rabbi Mendy Wineberg
913.649.4852

KENTUCKY

Louisville
Rabbi Avrohom Litvin
502.459.1770

LOUISIANA

Metairie
Rabbi Yossie Nemes
Rabbi Mendel Ceitlin
504.454.2910

MARYLAND

Baltimore
Rabbi Elchonon Lisbon
410.358.4787

Rabbi Velvel Belinsky
Classes in Russian
410.764.5000

Bel Air
Rabbi Yekusiel Schusterman
443.353.9718

Bethesda
Rabbi Bentzion Geisinsky
Rabbi Sender Geisinsky
301.913.9777

Columbia
Rabbi Hillel Baron
Rabbi Yosef Chaim Sufrin
410.740.2424

Frederick
Rabbi Boruch Labkowski
301.996.3659

Gaithersburg
Rabbi Sholom Raichik
301.926.3632

Olney
Rabbi Bentzy Stolik
301.660.6770

Owings Mills
Rabbi Nochum H. Katsenelenbogen
410.356.5156

Potomac
Rabbi Mendel Bluming
301.983.4200

Rabbi Mendel Kaplan
301.983.1485

Rockville
Rabbi Moishe Kavka
301.836.1242

MASSACHUSETTS

Andover
Rabbi Asher Bronstein
Rabbi Zalman Borenstein
978.470.2288

Cape Cod
Rabbi Yekusiel Alperowitz
508.775.2324

Chestnut Hill
Rabbi Mendy Uminer
617.738.9770

Longmeadow
Rabbi Yakov Wolff
413.567.8665

Newton
Rabbi Shalom Ber Prus
617.244.1200

Milford
Rabbi Mendy Kievman
508.473.1299

Sudbury
Rabbi Yisroel Freeman
978.443.3691

Swampscott
Mrs. Layah Lipsker
781.581.3833

MICHIGAN

Ann Arbor
Rabbi Aharon Goldstein
734.995.3276

Grand Rapids
Rabbi Mordechai Haller
616.957.0770

West Bloomfield
Rabbi Elimelech Silberberg
248.855.6170

MINNESOTA

Minnetonka
Rabbi Mordechai Grossbaum
952.929.9922

S. Paul
Rabbi Shneur Zalman Bendet
651.278.8401

MISSOURI

S. Louis
Rabbi Yosef Landa
314.725.0400

MONTANA

Bozeman
Rabbi Chaim Shaul Bruk
406.585.8770

NEVADA

Summerlin
Rabbi Yisroel Schanowitz
Rabbi Tzvi Bronchtain
702.855.0770

NEW JERSEY

Basking Ridge
Rabbi Mendy Herson
908.604.8844

Cherry Hill
Rabbi Mendy Mangel
856.874.1500

Clinton
Rabbi Eli Kornfeld
908.623.7000

Fair Lawn
Rabbi Avrohom Bergstein
718.839.5296

Fanwood
Rabbi Avrohom Blesofsky
908.790.0008

Fort Lee
Rabbi Meir Konikov
201.886.1238

Franklin Lakes
Rabbi Chanoch Kaplan
201.848.0449

Haskell
Rabbi Mendy Gurkov
201.696.7609

Hillsborough
Rabbi Shmaya Krinsky
908.874.0444

Holmdel
Rabbi Shmaya Galperin
732.772.1998

Madison
Rabbi Shalom Lubin
973.377.0707

Manalapan
Rabbi Boruch Chazanow
Rabbi Levi Wolosow
732.972.3687

Medford
Rabbi Yitzchok Kahan
609.953.3150

Mountain Lakes
Rabbi Levi Dubinsky
973.551.1898

Mullica Hill
Rabbi Avrohom Richler
856.733.0770

North Brunswick
Rabbi Levi Azimov
732.398.9492

Old Tappan
Rabbi Mendy Lewis
201.767.4008

Rockaway
Rabbi Asher Herson
Rabbi Mordechai Baumgarten
973.625.1525

Teaneck
Rabbi Ephraim Simon
201.907.0686

Tenafly
Rabbi Mordechai Shain
Rabbi Yitzchak Gershovitz
201.871.1152

Toms River
Rabbi Moshe Gourarie
732.349.4199

West Orange
Rabbi Mendy Kasowitz
973.486.2362

Woodcliff Lake
Rabbi Dov Drizin
201.476.0157

NEW YORK

Bedford
Rabbi Arik Wolf
914.666.6065

Binghamton
Mrs. Rivkah Slonim
607.797.0015

Brighton Beach
Rabbi Zushe Winner
Rabbi Moshe Winner
718.946.9833

Bronxville
Rabbi Sruli Deitsch
917.755.0078

Brooklyn Heights
Rabbi Mendy Hecht
Rabbi Ari Raskin
347.378.2641

Cedarhurst
Rabbi Zalman Wolowik
516.295.2478

Chestnut Ridge
Rabbi Chaim Tzvi Ehrenreich
845.356.6686

Commack
Rabbi Mendel Teldon
631.543.3343

Dix Hills
Rabbi Yaakov Saacks
631.351.8672

Dobbs Ferry
Rabbi Benjy Silverman
914.693.6100

East Hampton
Rabbi Leibel Baumgarten
Rabbi Mendy Goldberg
631.329.5800

Forest Hills
Rabbi Yossi Mendelson
917.861.9726

Great Neck
Rabbi Yoseph Geisinsky
516.487.4554

Ithaca
Rabbi Eli Silberstein
607.257.7379

Kingston
Rabbi Yitzchok Hecht
845.334.9044

Larchmont
Rabbi Mendel Silberstein
914.834.4321

Long Beach
Rabbi Eli Goodman
516.897.2473

NYC Kehilath Jeshurun
Rabbi Elie Weinstock
212.774.5636

NYC Tribeca
Rabbi S. Zalman Paris
646.510.3109

NYC Midtown
Mrs. Raizy Metzger
212.758.3770

Ossining
Rabbi Dovid Labkowski
914.923.2522

Port Washington
Rabbi Shalom Paltiel
516.767.8672

Riverdale
Rabbi Levi Shemtov
718.549.1100

Rochester
Rabbi Nechemia Vogel
585.271.0330

Roslyn
Rabbi Yaakov Reiter
516.484.8185

Sea Gate
Rabbi Chaim Brikman
718.266.1736

Rabbi Nachman Segal
Classes in Hebrew
718.761.4483

Stony Brook
Rabbi Shalom Ber Cohen
631.585.0521

Suffern
Rabbi Shmuel Gancz
845.368.1889

Westbury
Rabbi Mendy Brownstein
516.850.4486

NORTH CAROLINA

Asheville
Rabbi Shaya Susskind
828.505.0746

Caryy
Rabbi Yisroel Cotlar
919.651.9710

Chapel Hill
Rabbi Zalman Bluming
919.630.5129

Charlotte
Rabbi Yossi Groner
Rabbi Shlomo Cohen
704.366.3984

Greensboro
Rabbi Yosef Plotkin
336.617.8120

Raleigh
Rabbi Pinchas Herman
Rabbi Lev Cotlar
919.637.6950

Wilmington
Rabbi Moshe Lieblich
910.763.4770

NORTH DAKOTA

Fargo
Rabbi Yonah Grossman
701.212.4164

OHIO

Beachwood
Rabbi Shmuli Friedman
Rabbi Moshe Gancz
216.370.2887

Blue Ash
Rabbi Yisroel Mangel
513.793.5200

Columbus
Rabbi Areyah Kaltmann
Rabbi Levi Andrusier
614.294.3296

OKLAHOMA

Oklahoma City
Rabbi Ovadia Goldman
405.524.4800

Tulsa
Rabbi Yehuda Weg
918.492.4499

OREGON

Portland
Rabbi Moshe Wilhelm
Rabbi Mordechai Wilhelm
503.977.9947

Salem
Rabbi Avrohom Yitzchok Perlstein
503.383.9569

PENNSYLVANIA

Ambler
Rabbi Shaya Deitsch
215.591.9310

Bala Cynwyd
Rabbi Shraga Sherman
610.660.9192

Lafayette Hill
Rabbi Yisroel Kotlarsky
347.526.1430

Lancaster
Rabbi Elazar Green
717.368.6565

Newtown
Rabbi Aryeh Weinstein
215.497.9925

Philadelphia: Center City
Rabbi Yochonon Goldman
215.238.2100

Pittsburgh
Rabbi Yisroel Altein
412.422.7300 ext. 269

Pittsburgh: South Hills
Rabbi Mendy Rosenblum
412.278.3693

Rydal
Rabbi Zushe Gurevitz
215.572.1511

Wynnewood
Rabbi Moishe Brennan
610.529.9011

RHODE ISLAND

Warwick
Rabbi Yossi Laufer
401.884.7888

SOUTH CAROLINA

Columbia
Rabbi Hesh Epstein
Rabbi Levi Marrus
803.782.1831

TENNESSEE

Chattanooga
Rabbi Shaul Perlstein
423.490.1106

Knoxville
Rabbi Yossi Wilhelm
865.588.8584

Memphis
Rabbi Levi Klein
901.766.1800

TEXAS

Arlington
Rabbi Levi Gurevitch
817.451.1171

Dallas
Rabbi Peretz Shapiro
Rabbi Moshe Naparstek
972.818.0770

Fort Worth
Rabbi Dov Mandel
817.263.7701

Houston
Rabbi Moishe Traxler
713.774.0300

Houston: Rice University Area
Rabbi Eliezer Lazaroff
713.522.2004

League City
Rabbi Yitzchok Schmukler
713.398.2460

Plano
Rabbi Mendel Block
Rabbi Yehudah Horowitz
972.596.8270

S. Antonio
Rabbi Chaim Block
Rabbi Levi Teldon
210.492.1085

The Woodlands
Rabbi Mendel Blecher
281.719.5213

UTAH

Salt Lake City
Rabbi Benny Zippel
801.467.7777

VERMONT

BURLINGTON
Rabbi Yitzchok Raskin
802.658.5770

VIRGINIA

ALEXANDRIA/ARLINGTON
Rabbi Mordechai Newman
703.370.2774

FAIRFAX
Rabbi Leibel Fajnland
703.426.1980

NORFOLK
Rabbi Aaron Margolin
Rabbi Levi Brashevitzky
757.616.0770

RICHMOND
Rabbi Shlomo Pereira
804.740.2000

TYSONS CORNER
Rabbi Chezzy Deitsch
CHAPTER FOUNDED BY RABBI LEVI DEITSCH, OBM
703.829.5770

WASHINGTON

MERCER ISLAND
Rabbi Elazar Bogomilsky
206.527.1411

OLYMPIA
Rabbi Cheski Edelman
360.584.4306

SEATTLE
Rabbi Avrohom Kavka
206-730-2775

SPOKANE COUNTY
Rabbi Yisroel Hahn
509.443.0770

WISCONSIN

MADISON
Rabbi Avremel Matusof
608.231.3450

MILWAUKEE
Rabbi Mendel Shmotkin
414.961.6100

WAUKESHA
Rabbi Levi Brook
925.708.4203

PUERTO RICO

CAROLINA
Rabbi Mendel Zarchi
787.253.0894

ARGENTINA

BUENOS AIRES
Rabbi Mendel Levy
Rabbi Shlomo Levy
54.11.4807.2223

CAPITAL FEDERAL
Rabbi Mendy Gurevitch
54.11.4545.7771

PALERMO NUEVO
Rabbi Mendy Grunblatt
54.11.4772.1024

RECOLETA
Rabbi Hirshel Hendel
54.11.4807.7073

AUSTRALIA

AUSTRALIAN CAPITAL TERRITORY
CANBERRA
Rabbi Shmuel Feldman
614.3167.7805

NEW SOUTH WALES
BONDI BEACH
Rabbi Aron Moss
612.8005.6613

DOUBLE BAY
Rabbi Yanky Berger
Rabbi Yisroel Dolnikov
612.9327.1644

DOVER HEIGHTS
Rabbi Motti Feldman
612.9387.3822

NORTH SHORE
Rabbi Nochum Schapiro
Mrs. Fruma Schapiro
612.9488.9548

SOUTH HEAD
Rabbi Benzion Milecki
612.9337.6775

QUEENSLAND
BRISBANE
Rabbi Levi Jaffe
617.3843.6770

SOUTH AUSTRALIA
GLENSIDE
Rabbi Yossi Engel
618.8338.2922

VICTORIA
BENTLEIGH EAST
Rabbi Mendel Raskin
613.9570.6707

CAULFIELD SOUTH
Rabbi Peretz Schapiro
613.9532.9180

ELSTERNWICK
Rabbi Chaim Cowen
614.3330.8584

Rabbi Motty Liberow
613.9533.0090

MALVERN
Rabbi Zev Slavin
614.0476.6759

Rabbi Shimshon Yurkowicz
613.9822.3600

MELBOURNE
Rabbi Mendel Groner
613.9532.7299

Rabbi Dovid Gutnick
614.3038.4948

MOORABBIN
Rabbi Elisha Greenbaum
614.0349.0434

WESTERN AUSTRALIA
PERTH
Rabbi Shalom White
618.9275.2106

BELARUS

GRODNO
Rabbi Yitzchak Kofman
375.29.644.3690

BRAZIL

RIO DE JANEIRO
Rabbi Yehoshua Binyomin Goldman
Rabbi Avrohom Tsvi Beuthner
55.21.2294.3138

S. PAULO
Rabbi Avraham Steinmetz
55.11.3081.3081

CANADA

ALBERTA
CALGARY
Rabbi Mordechai Groner
403.238.4880

EDMONTON
Rabbi Ari Drelich
Rabbi Mendy Blachman
780.851.1515

BRITISH COLUMBIA
RICHMOND
Rabbi Yechiel Baitelman
604.277.6427

VANCOUVER
Rabbi Yitzchok Wineberg
604.266.1313

VICTORIA
Rabbi Meir Kaplan
250.595.7656

MANITOBA
WINNIPEG
Rabbi Avrohom Altein
Rabbi Shmuel Altein
204.339.8737

NOVA SCOTIA
HALIFAX
Rabbi Mendel Feldman
902.422.4222

ONTARIO
HAMILTON
Rabbi Chanoch Rosenfeld
905.529.7458

LAWRENCE/EGLINTON
Rabbi Menachem Gansburg
416.546.8770

LONDON
Rabbi Eliezer Gurkow
519.434.3962

MISSISSAUGA
Rabbi Yitzchok Slavin
905.820.4432

NIAGARA FALLS
Rabbi Zalman Zaltzman
905.356.7200

OTTAWA
Rabbi Menachem M. Blum
613.823.0866

RICHMOND HILL
Rabbi Mendel Bernstein
905.770.7700

Rabbi Yossi Hecht
905.773.6477

TORONTO AREA BJL
Rabbi Leib Chaiken
416.916.7202

GREATER TORONTO
REGIONAL OFFICE & THORNHILL
Rabbi Yossi Gansburg
905.731.7000

YORK MILLS
Rabbi Levi Gansburg
647.345.3800

WATERLOO
Rabbi Moshe Goldman
226.338.7770

WHITBY
Rabbi Tzali Borenstein
905.493.9007

QUEBEC
MONTREAL
Rabbi Ronnie Fine
Pesach Nussbaum
514.342.3.JLI

Rabbi Levi Y New
514.739.0770

TOWN OF MOUNT ROYAL
Rabbi Moshe Krasnanski
Rabbi Shneur Zalman Rader
514.739.0770

VILLE S. LAURENT
Rabbi Schneur Zalmen Silberstein
514.808.1418

WESTMOUNT
Rabbi Yossi Shanowitz
Mrs. Devorah Leah Shanowitz
514.937.4772

SASKATCHEWAN
SASKATOON
Rabbi Raphael Kats
306.384.4370

CAYMAN ISLAND
GRAND CAYMAN
Rabbi Berel Pewzner
717.798.1040

COLOMBIA
BOGOTA
Rabbi Yehoshua B. Rosenfeld
Rabbi Chanoch Piekarski
571.635.8251

DENMARK
COPENHAGEN
Rabbi Yitzchok Lowenthal
45.3316.1850

ESTONIA
TALLINN
Rabbi Shmuel Kot
372.662.30.50

GEORGIA
TBILISI
Rabbi Meir Kozlovsky
995.593.23.91.15

GERMANY
BERLIN
Rabbi Yehuda Tiechtel
49.30.2128.0830

COLOGNE
Rabbi Mendel Schtroks
49.22.1240.3902

DUSSELDORF
Rabbi Chaim Barkahn
49.21.1420.9693

HAMBURG
Rabbi Shlomo Bistriztsky
49.40.4142.4190

MUNICH
Rabbi Yochonon Gordon
49.89.4190.2812

GREECE
ATHENS
Rabbi Mendel Hendel
30.210.520.2880

GUATEMALA
GUATEMALA CITY
Rabbi Shalom Pelman
502.2485.0770

ISRAEL
ASHKELON
Rabbi Shneor Lieberman
054.977.0512

BALFURYA
Rabbi Noam Bar-Tov
054.580.4770

CAESAREA
Rabbi Chaim Meir Lieberman
054.621.2586

EVEN YEHUDA
Rabbi Menachem Noyman
054.777.0707

GANEI TIKVA
Rabbi Gershon Shnur
054.524.2358

GIV'ATAYIM
Rabbi Pinchus Bitton
052.643.8770

HAIFA
Rabbi Yehuda Dunin
054.426.3763

KARMIEL
Rabbi Mendy Elishevitz
054.521.3073

KFAR SABBA
Rabbi Yossi Baitch
054.445.5020

KIRYAT BIALIK
Rabbi Pinny Marton
050.661.1768

KIRYAT MOTZKIN
Rabbi Shimon Eizenbach
050.902.0770

KOCHAV YAIR
Rabbi Dovi Greenberg
054.332.6244

MACCABIM RE'UT
Rabbi Yosef Yitzchak Noiman
054.977.0549

MODIIN
Rabbi Boruch Slonim
054.300.1770

NES ZIYONA
Rabbi Menachem Feldman
054.497.7092

NETANYA
Rabbi Schneur Brod
054.579.7572

RAMAT GAN-KRINITZI
Rabbi Yisroel Gurevitz
052.743.2814

RAMAT GAN-MAROM NAVE
Rabbi Binyamin Meir Kali
050.476.0770

RAMAT YISHAI
Rabbi Shneor Zalman Wolosow
052.324.5475

Rishon Lezion
Rabbi Uri Keshet
050.722.4593

Rosh Pina
Rabbi Sholom Ber Hertzel
052.458.7600

Yehud
Rabbi Shmuel Wolf
053.536.1479

ITALY
Firenze
Rabbi Levi Wolvovsky
39.389.595.2034

KAZAKHSTAN
Almaty
Rabbi Shevach Zlatopolsky
7.7272.77.59.77

LATVIA
Riga
Rabbi Shneur Zalman Kot
371.6733.1520

NETHERLANDS
Den Haag
Rabbi Shmuel Katzman
31.70.347.0222

Noord-Holland
Amsterdam
Rabbi Yanki Jacobs
31.6.4498.8627

PANAMA
Panama City
Rabbi Ari Laine
Rabbi Gabriel Benayon
507.223.3383

RUSSIA
Astrakhan
Rabbi Yisroel Melamed
7.851.239.28.24

Bryansk
Rabbi Menachem Mendel Zaklas
7.483.264.55.15

Chelyabinsk
Rabbi Meir Kirsh
7.351.263.24.68

Moscow-Marina Rosha
Rabbi Mordechai Weisberg
7.495.645.50.00

Moscow-Sokolniki
Rabbi Avraham Bekerman
7.495.660.07.70

Nizhny Novgorod
Rabbi Shimon Bergman
7.920.253.47.70

Omsk
Rabbi Osher Krichevsky
7.381.231.33.07

Perm
Rabbi Zalman Deutch
7.342.212.47.32

Samara
Rabbi Shlomo Deutch
7.846.333.40.64

Saratov
Rabbi Yaakov Kubitshek
7.8452.21.58.00

S. Petersburg
Rabbi Zvi Pinsky
7.812.713.62.09

Rostov
Rabbi Chaim Danzinger
7.8632.99.02.68

Togliatti
Rabbi Meier Fischer
7.848.273.02.84

Ufa
Rabbi Dan Krichevsky
7.347.244.55.33

Voronezh
Rabbi Levi Stiefel
7.473.252.96.99

SINGAPORE
Singapore
Rabbi Mordechai Abergel
656.337.2189

Rabbi Netanel Rivni
Classes in Hebrew
656.336.2127

SOUTH AFRICA
Johannesburg
Rabbi Dovid Hazdan
Rabbi Shmuel Simpson
27.11.728.8152

Rabbi Dovid Masinter
Rabbi Ari Kievman
27.11.440.6600

SWEDEN
Stockholm
Rabbi Chaim Greisman
468.679.7067

SWITZERLAND
Basel
Rabbi Zalman Wishedski
41.76.559.9236

Lugano
Rabbi Yaakov Tzvi Kantor
41.91.921.3720

Luzern
Rabbi Chaim Drukman
41.41.361.1770

UKRAINE
Cherkassy
Rabbi Dov Axelrod
380.472.45.7080

Dnepropetrovsk
Rabbi Dan Makagon
380.504.51.13.18

Nikolayev
Rabbi Sholom Gotlieb
380.512.37.37.71

Zhitomir
Rabbi Shlomo Wilhelm
380.504.63.01.32

Odessa
Rabbi Avraham Wolf
Rabbi Yaakov Neiman
38.048.728.0770 ext. 280

UNITED KINGDOM
Edgeware
Rabbi Leivi Sudak
Rabbi Yaron Jacobs
44.208.905.4141

Leeds
Rabbi Eli Pink
44.113.266.3311

London
Rabbi Gershon Overlander
Rabbi Dovid Katz
44.208.202.1600

Rabbi Nissan D. Dubov
44.20.8944.1581

Manchester
Rabbi Akiva Cohen
Rabbi Levi Cohen
44.161.740.4243

VENEZUELA
Caracas
Rabbi Yehoshua Rosenblum
58.212.264.7011

JLI

JEWISH LEARNING INSTITUTE

THE JEWISH LEARNING MULTIPLEX

Brought to you by the Rohr Jewish Learning Institute

In fulfillment of the mandate of the Lubavitcher Rebbe, of blessed memory, whose leadership guides every step of our work, the mission of the Rohr Jewish Learning Institute is to transform Jewish life and the greater community through the study of Torah, connecting each Jew to our shared heritage of Jewish learning.

While our flagship program remains the cornerstone of our organization, JLI is proud to feature additional divisions catering to specific populations, in order to meet a wide array of educational needs.

THE ROHR JEWISH LEARNING INSTITUTE,
a subsidiary of *Merkos L'Inyonei Chinuch*,
is the adult education arm of the Chabad-Lubavitch Movement.

TORAH STUDIES

Torah Studies provides a rich and nuanced encounter with the weekly Torah reading.

MYSHIUR
TALMUD LEARNING INITIATIVE

MyShiur courses are designed to assist students in developing the skills needed to study Talmud independently.

SINAI SCHOLARS SOCIETY
IN PARTNERSHIP WITH CHABAD ON CAMPUS

This rigorous fellowship program invites select college students to explore the fundamentals of Judaism.

JLI TEENS
YOUNG SMART JEWISH
IN PARTNERSHIP WITH CTEEN: CHABAD TEEN NETWORK

Jewish teens forge their identity as they engage in Torah study, social interaction, and serious fun.

ROSHCHODESH society

The Rosh Chodesh Society gathers Jewish women together once a month for intensive textual study.

TORAHCafé™

TorahCafe.com provides an exclusive selection of top-rated Jewish educational videos.

BRILLIANT LEARNING, NATURALLY
National JEWISH RETREAT

This yearly event rejuvenates mind, body, and spirit with a powerful synthesis of Jewish learning and community.

the LAND the SPIRIT
ISRAEL EXPERIENCE

Participants delve into our nation's rich past while exploring the Holy Land's relevance and meaning today.

PEDAGOGY • CURRICULUM • MARKETING
JLI ACADEMY

Select affiliates are invited to partner with peers and noted professionals, as leaders of innovation and excellence.

מכון שמואל
THE SAMI ROHR RESEARCH INSTITUTE

Machon Shmuel is an institute providing Torah research in the service of educators worldwide.

לזכרון ולעילוי נשמת
העלמה היקרה

חנה מרים ע"ה בת יבלחט"א הרה"ח הרה"ת **דובער** הכהן שליט"א **בעל**

נפטרה י"ט שבט, ה'תשס"ו

Dedicated in memory of

Chana Miriam Bell ז"ל

Made in the USA
Las Vegas, NV
28 October 2025

33260721R00138